THE PRINCIPLES OF
NATURAL AND POLITIC LAW

NATURAL LAW AND
ENLIGHTENMENT CLASSICS

Knud Haakonssen
General Editor

Jean-Jacques Burlamaqui

The Principles of Natural and Politic Law

Jean-Jacques Burlamaqui

Translated by Thomas Nugent

Edited and with an Introduction by
Petter Korkman

LIBERTY FUND

Indianapolis

This book is published by Liberty Fund, Inc., a foundation established to encourage study of the ideal of a society of free and responsible individuals.

The cuneiform inscription that serves as our logo and as the design motif for our endpapers is the earliest-known written appearance of the word "freedom" (*amagi*), or "liberty." It is taken from a clay document written about 2300 B.C. in the Sumerian city-state of Lagash.

10 09 08 07 06 C 5 4 3 2 1
10 09 08 07 06 P 5 4 3 2 1

Frontispiece and cover: Portrait of Jean-Jacques Burlamaqui by Robert Gardelle. Courtesy of Genève, Bibliothèque publique et universitaire.

Library of Congress Cataloging-in-Publication Data
Burlamaqui, J. J. (Jean Jacques), 1649–1748.
[Principes du droit natural et politique. English]
The principles of natural and politic law/Jean-Jacques Burlamaqui; translated by Thomas Nugent; edited and with an introduction by Petter Korkman.
p. cm.—(Natural law and enlightenment classics)
Includes bibliographical references and index.
ISBN-13: 978-0-86597-496-8 (alk. paper)   ISBN-10: 0-86597-496-9 (alk. paper)
ISBN-13: 978-0-86597-497-5 (pbk.: alk. paper)   ISBN-10: 0-86597-497-7 (pbk.: alk. paper)
I. Natural law—Early works to 1800.   I. Nugent, Thomas, 1700?–1772.
II. Korkman, Petter.   III. Title.   IV. Series.
K457.B85P7513   2006
340′.112—dc22   2005029195

LIBERTY FUND, INC.
8335 Allison Pointe Trail, Suite 300
Indianapolis, Indiana 46250-1684

CONTENTS

INTRODUCTION

Jean-Jacques Burlamaqui (1694–1748) was a natural law professor at the Academy of Geneva. He was brought up in a family with long traditions both of wealth and of political influence. Not only was Jean-Jacques's father a member of the ruling Genevan small council (*petit conseil*), but his grandfather had held a position in the council of two hundred (*grand conseil*) and his forefathers had been prominent in the politics of Lucca in Italy, the area from which his family originally came. In 1709 Jean-Jacques began studying philosophy and law at the Academy of Geneva, where he acquainted himself with Pufendorf's newly translated natural law treatises. (Jean Barbeyrac's famous French translations of Pufendorf's two main natural law treatises were published in 1706 and 1707.) In 1716 Burlamaqui became a lawyer, but instead of working as such he started giving private lectures on natural law and in 1720 applied to the small council for the title of honorary professor. In 1720 and 1721 Burlamaqui traveled in Europe, visiting London, Oxford, Amsterdam, and Groningen, where he met Barbeyrac. Burlamaqui was made a member of the council of two hundred while away, and he remained active in Genevan politics for the rest of his life.

In Burlamaqui's time, Geneva was ruled mainly by the twenty-five members of the small council, though important decisions were also taken by the council of two hundred. The so-called general council (*conseil général*), comprehending all citizens (in itself a rather restricted category), had lost much of its influence. The Burlamaquis were a well-represented family in the two select councils. When Burlamaqui married the daughter of Jacob de Chapeaurouge, one of Geneva's most influential men, in 1717, he became even better connected. When the small council created two professorships in jurisprudence, Burlamaqui complained that the planned posts involved more teaching duties than he could manage, given his ill health and popular private lessons. The small council, convoked without the Burlamaquis and Chapeaurouges, concluded that they'd have to leave one post unfilled for the time being. In this situation, the Burlamaquis and the Chapeaurouges took action: after a few maneuvers, the Burlamaquis and the Chapeaurouges succeeded in securing one of the posts for Jean-Jacques with only half the teaching originally planned for the post.

Ill health, which Burlamaqui had already complained of in 1720, and his numerous private lessons made Burlamaqui desire a redefinition of his tasks, and in 1740 he was relieved of his teaching duties altogether. Failing health, including impaired eyesight, may also have influenced his published work, which he composed from lecture notes between 1740 and his death in 1748. By that time he had become a much respected and influential member of Geneva's de facto aristocracy, a member of the small council (in 1742), and a defender of its authority against the demands of the bourgeoisie that power should be wielded by the general council. Respected as a teacher and a friend of the arts, Burlamaqui was involved in the public library and in the creation of a drawing school in Geneva.

Burlamaqui's lectures drew foreign students to Geneva, and his natural law treatise was translated into English, Latin, Dutch, Danish, Italian, and Spanish and republished in more than sixty different editions. The English translation became a standard textbook both at Cambridge and at the foremost American colleges. The first scholarly work on Burlamaqui was written by an American, Ray Forrest Harvey, who argued that the Genevan was well known by the Founding Fathers and that his writings exerted considerable influence on the American constitutional system.[1] Furthermore, Burlamaqui's work was important to *philosophes* such as Jean-Jacques Rousseau and Denis Diderot. However, whether the ideas thus disseminated were Burlamaqui's own has been a debated

---

1. Ray Forrest Harvey, *Jean-Jacques Burlamaqui: A Liberal Tradition in American Constitutionalism* (Chapel Hill: University of North Carolina Press, 1937). See also Morton White, *The Philosophy of the American Revolution* (Oxford: Oxford University Press, 1978).

issue. It can be shown that Burlamaqui's published work borrows extensively from Jean Barbeyrac's French translations of the main natural law treatises of his time, especially Pufendorf's *Les devoirs de l'homme et du citoyen* (DHC) and *Le droit de la nature et des gens* (DNG) and from Grotius's *Le droit de la guerre et de la paix* (DGP).[2] Often Burlamaqui omits mention of his sources, as most of his commentators have noted. The typical reaction has been to declare Burlamaqui an unoriginal plagiarist.[3]

The heavy reliance of the *Principles of Natural and Politic Law*, especially its second part, on Barbeyrac's editions requires an explanation. Burlamaqui published only one book in his lifetime, *Principes du droit naturel* (Geneva, 1747). Burlamaqui himself thought of the book as an introduction to a complete system of the law of nature and nations for students and beginners. He never published the whole system himself, but he laid out the main lines of one in lectures, which were preserved in students' notes. These lecture notes had already attracted attention before Burlamaqui's death, and his main reason for publishing the work was, as he states in his introduction, that he "began to apprehend, lest this work should be published against my will, in a very imperfect and mangled condition."

After Burlamaqui died in 1748, many felt that more of the master's system should be published. Theology professor Jacob Vernet, who had been present at Burlamaqui's death "as a friend and vicar," wrote in a letter on the day of the interment that the notes on civil government were among Burlamaqui's most original. Burlamaqui, Vernet wrote, had been editing his notes on "droit politique" but had not finished, so Vernet, possibly with other friends and colleagues, took the task upon him-

---

2. References to DHC and DGP are to the facsimile editions published by Centre de Philosophie Politique et Juridique in Caen, which are also available as downloadable files from the Internet server of the *Bibliothèque Nationale de France*, www.bnf.fr. For references to DNG, I have used the 1740 London edition. In a few cases I have referred to the earlier edition published in the above-mentioned Centre series. This edition I refer to as DNG 1732. The abbreviations indicated in the text will be used throughout.

3. See Robert Derathé, *Jean-Jacques Rousseau et la science politique de son temps* (Paris: Presses Universitaires de France, 1950), p. 86, and Giorgio del Vecchio, "Burlamaqui and Rousseau," *Journal of the History of Ideas* (vol. 3, no. 3, 1962): 420–23.

self. The result of these endeavors, *Principes du droit politique* (Geneva, 1751), remained unfinished in some central respects. It contained a great number of unidentified quotations and extracts, especially from the natural law treatises translated by Barbeyrac, and large portions of the book added little to Grotius, Pufendorf, and Barbeyrac. In the *Principes du droit naturel,* which Burlamaqui had reworked for publication, unidentified quotations are less common, and Burlamaqui's own position is more fully worked out.

It is not difficult to imagine how lecture notes might differ from a finalized publication. Burlamaqui's systematic lectures drew on and provided a summary of the most up-to-date political science available in his day. Apparently Burlamaqui felt that his students did not need to know which claims were directly from Grotius, Pufendorf, or Barbeyrac and which claims were his own. In a published book, by contrast, the reader would have expected the sources to be indicated.[4] However, as Bernard Gagnebin notes in what is thus far the best monograph on Burlamaqui, "the editors of the *Principes du droit politique* published all these quotations, without indicating the sources."[5]

Burlamaqui had entrusted the manuscript containing his reworked chapters on civil government to his sister and daughter, expressly demanding that it not be published. When the *Principes du droit politique* was announced, Burlamaqui's sister and daughter protested. They pointed out that the original manuscript with Burlamaqui's emendations had never left their hands, and they refused to recognize the publication as being by their father and brother. After an official investigation, it was decided that the *Principes du droit politique* could not be sold with a title indicating that it was written by Burlamaqui. Officially, then, only half of the present work is by Burlamaqui. Few contemporaries outside Geneva would have realized this, however. The publishers com-

---

4. The Danish natural law theorist Martin Hübner commented on the prevalence of unidentified quotations from Barbeyrac (*Essai sur l'histoire du droit naturel,* 2 vols., London, 1757–58, vol. 2, p. 381), although not with the vehemence that Giorgio del Vecchio ascribes to him; see del Vecchio, "Burlamaqui and Rousseau," p. 421.

5. Bernard Gagnebin, *Burlamaqui et le droit naturel* (Geneva: La Frégate, 1944), p. 86; see also pp. 81, 85.

plied with the demands and published the *Principes du droit politique* anonymously. This simply made the book look all the more like a second volume of the large natural law treatise that Burlamaqui had been planning. There is little doubt that it was the unpolished *Principes du droit politique* that earned Burlamaqui the reputation of being unoriginal. Large portions provide pedagogical summaries of contemporary political science (natural law) without either references or the kind of independent reflection one would expect in a published work. Burlamaqui's efforts to hinder his work from being published "in a very imperfect and mangled condition" had failed.

At the time of Burlamaqui's death, the first reviews of the *Principes du droit naturel* had just been published. Rumors that there would be an English translation had also reached Geneva. That translation, by Thomas Nugent, was published in London in 1748. Nugent's fame was to be based on travel books, such as *The Grand Tour; or, A Journey through the Netherlands, Germany, Italy, and France* (1749), and on translations of thinkers better remembered than he, such as Montesquieu, Rousseau, and Condillac. He also translated the *Principes du droit politique* as *Principles of Politic Law,* adding "being a sequel to the Principles of natural law." This was published in 1752, one year after the original French text was published in Geneva. The same London publisher, J. Nourse, also produced the first combined two-volume *Principles of Natural and Politic Law* in 1763; a comparable French edition appeared in 1764. The English 1763 edition was essentially nothing more than the *Principles of Natural Law* and the *Principles of Politic Law* sold with one title. Some minor changes were introduced at the beginning of the second volume (the *Principles of Politic Law*), apparently with a view to merging the two books into a seamless whole. Nugent, who died in 1772, was probably involved in making those changes; they are noted in the present edition.

The Burlamaqui that reached British and American universities and was read for generations was *Principles of Natural and Politic Law.* Much of Burlamaqui's audience took the latter half of this work to be just as much his as the former, reading his painstaking extracts from Pufendorf, Grotius, and Barbeyrac as the original insights of the Genevan natural law professor. Others who had read their Pufendorf with care may have recognized many borrowed passages but would have had a hard time identifying exactly the places where Burlamaqui parts company from his predecessors. The present edition helps the reader by identifying the sources from which Burlamaqui borrowed his observations. This is, however, a complicated task, and no doubt there remain paragraphs built on passages in the above works or elsewhere that have not been identified.

Even after the publication of the *Principes du droit politique,* many of Burlamaqui's lecture notes remained in circulation. Some were published in 1766–68 by Fortuné-Barthélemy de Félice, an Italian professor of philosophy and mathematics who moved to Yverdon, converted to Protestantism, and became director of a printing press. Having secured a set of Burlamaqui's own lecture notes, de Félice reworked the material, adding new chapters to the published books, fusing some chapters, deleting passages and inserting new ones as he saw fit, and adding a commentary of his own. Finally, in 1775, Burlamaqui's lecture notes were published in Lausanne by the publisher Grasset as *Éléments du droit naturel.* These editions provide information on themes that Burlamaqui discussed in his lectures but that fall outside the scope of the present book. De Félice's edition contains eight volumes: the first two constitute the *Principes du droit naturel,* the last three the *Principes du droit politique.* Between these de Félice inserted three volumes of material from Burlamaqui's lecture notes on man's primitive state, on his duties to God and to himself, and on the main laws of sociability. Under duties to God, Burlamaqui discusses natural religion in more detail and makes more use of Barbeyrac's defense of religious toleration and freedom of conscience than he does in the present work.

Burlamaqui's lectures took the usual form of a commentary on Pufendorf's DHC, interspersed with more elaborate discussions from DNG and Grotius's DGP, all in Barbeyrac's French translations.[6] The first half of the present work often presents Burlamaqui's understanding of Pufendorf, Grotius, and Barbeyrac, usually with some indication of

6. See note 2 above.

his sources, followed by Burlamaqui taking sides on controversial points or arguing that all three are in need of rectification. Despite the standard view of Burlamaqui, his standpoints are not unoriginal. On controversial issues he is often far from the standard positions; I discuss a few cases below. The second half of the present work is less original since, as explained, it was not prepared for publication by Burlamaqui, excepting a few long chapters. It clearly and systematically presents the main issues of contemporary natural law theory, but it was not common practice for a lecturer in all cases to point out his modern sources.

Yet even in the latter half of the work, Burlamaqui is often at variance with his predecessors. One clue for understanding these differences is Burlamaqui's status as a member of the upper strata of the Genevan aristocracy. His long discussion of the best form of government—one of the few chapters that had clearly been prepared for publication— engages in Genevan politics. As a council member and as an expert on natural law, Burlamaqui participated in formulating the ruling elite's intellectual response to the bourgeoisie's claim that the small council was usurping power that constitutionally and traditionally belonged to the general council.[7] Burlamaqui's chapter on forms of government is very critical of democratic regimes and argues (against Pufendorf) for the advantages of a "mixed" government like the Genevan "aristo-democracy," to use an expression from the Genevan elite's reply to the bourgeoisie's demands.[8] The best political regime, Burlamaqui argues, is the one that most safely helps men achieve the happiness they naturally aspire to, and such a regime is government by the ablest, the elite. Burlamaqui's defense of aristo-democracy supports the authority of Geneva's small council, which explains why Rousseau, who defended the rights of the general council and upheld the political rights of the bourgeoisie, adopted such

7. For a fuller treatment of the role of natural law and of Burlamaqui as an individual in Genevan politics, see Helena Rosenblatt, *Rousseau and Geneva: From the First Discourse to the Social Contract, 1749–1762* (Cambridge: Cambridge University Press, 1997), especially pp. 101–2, 128–29, 133–35, and 154–55. See also Gagnebin, *Burlamaqui et le droit naturel,* especially pp. 51–61.

8. See Gagnebin, *Burlamaqui et le droit naturel,* p. 56.

a hostile attitude to Burlamaqui's writings and even to natural law theory in general.[9]

Burlamaqui's natural law theory also differs from Pufendorf's in its foundational principles. The context was the more optimistic trends in Genevan Calvinism at this time. For Burlamaqui, man is first and foremost a being that strives for happiness or felicity; this is the *primum mobile* behind all human action. When Burlamaqui insists that self-love is not "the fruit of human depravation" (I.1.5 §7), he is quite in line with the happy egoism of many theologians of his day.[10] His views are very different from those defended by Pufendorf, who stressed men's inclinations to evil and who saw natural laws not as rules to make men happy but as rules needed for them to survive each other's company. Burlamaqui by contrast claims that the natural laws do not exist merely to hinder men from harming each other but to guide their natural striving for happiness, a concept that Burlamaqui offers in the first paragraph of his book. The same approach is applied by Burlamaqui to civil laws. The most central task of the civil state is to help men become happier than they could on their own. Civil laws can thus be used to force men to become happy. This also implies that persons involved in legislation should have a more solid understanding of what makes the subjects virtuous and happy than the uneducated citizens generally have themselves. For Burlamaqui, the science of natural law is in effect a science of happiness. In all of these views, Burlamaqui defends a different understanding of politics and law than most Pufendorfians.[11]

Burlamaqui's distinct approach to natural law is also obvious in his opposition to Pufendorf's and Hobbes's claim that all obligation derives

---

9. This argument is one of the building blocks of Rosenblatt's analysis of Rousseau's main political writings in Rosenblatt, *Rousseau and Geneva*.

10. See Rosenblatt, *Rousseau and Geneva*, pp. 12ff.

11. For indications of how Burlamaqui's approach to the tasks of the state differs from Barbeyrac's, see my "Civil Sovereigns and the King of Kings: Barbeyrac and the Creator's Right to Rule," in *Natural Law and Civil Sovereignty: Moral Right and State Authority in Early Modern Political Thought,* ed. Ian Hunter and David Saunders (New York: Palgrave, 2002), pp. 109–22.

from the commands of a superior.[12] Burlamaqui argues that reason provides a simple rule for man by pointing out to him the shortest route to his happiness. This rule brings with it what Burlamaqui sometimes terms "primitive obligation" (I.i.5 §9). As the term indicates, all other sorts of obligation are ultimately derived from the primitive rule. The reason why men ought to obey the natural laws, then, is not that God has commanded such obedience. It is rather that God is more competent at providing a legislation conducive to human happiness than we are ourselves. This makes reason as the judge of the means to happiness the real source of obligation, not (divine) will. Although the commands of a legitimate superior add an external component to obligation, they do so only by adding stronger motives for obeying, that is, by providing sanctions for the laws (I.ii.7 §13).

Burlamaqui's approach to obligation, which he articulates, for example, in his chapter "Of the Foundation of Sovereignty, or the Right of Commanding" (I.i.9), implies that the obligation to obey a law or a sovereign must be explained in terms of the motives that make a person desire to obey. Pufendorf by contrast drew a sharp distinction between the motives working on the human will on the one hand and moral obligation or duty on the other. This distinction was further emphasized by Barbeyrac in his replies to Leibniz's famous critique of Pufendorf's principles: the natural laws impose absolute duties, telling us what we must do, not what we desire to do.[13] Burlamaqui rejects Pufendorf's and Barbeyrac's approach to moral obligation. Rather than restraints by a

---

12. For a careful discussion of Pufendorf's account of the foundations of sovereignty, see Kari Saastamoinen, *The Morality of the Fallen Man: Samuel Pufendorf on Natural Law* (Helsinki: Societas Historica Finlandiae, 1995), pp. 95ff.

13. Barbeyrac's replies are in his translation of Leibniz's critique; see "The Judgment of an Anonymous Writer," in Samuel Pufendorf, *The Whole Duty of Man, According to the Law of Nature*, ed. Ian Hunter and David Saunders (Indianapolis: Liberty Fund, 2003), pp. 267–305. For the different ways in which Pufendorf's theory of obligation was interpreted by Barbeyrac and Burlamaqui, see my article "Voluntarism and Moral Obligation: Barbeyrac's Defence of Pufendorf Revisited," in *Early Modern Natural Law Theories: Contexts and Strategies in the Early Enlightenment*, ed. T. J. Hochstrasser and Peter Schröder (International Archives of the History of Ideas 186; Dordrecht: Kluwer Academic Publishers, 2003), pp. 195–226, especially pp. 209–10.

superior, the laws of nature are the rational egoist's principles for finding the shortest road to felicity. In many respects, Burlamaqui's understanding of the natural laws is closer to Leibniz, or to medieval natural law theory, than it is to the Pufendorfian tradition.

In his political theory Burlamaqui stands out, together with Barbeyrac, as one of the early modern natural law theorists with something resembling a theory of human rights. According to Harvey, "Burlamaqui was the first modern philosopher to enumerate happiness as a natural right—a right which forms the basis of the state."[14] Burlamaqui in fact holds that all men have a "right of endeavoring to provide for their safety and happiness, and of employing force and arms against those who declare themselves their enemies" (II.iv.1 §5). Yet, as we have seen, the obvious way to pursue happiness is to submit to the rule of the ablest. The Genevan citizen has an inalienable right to pursue his own felicity by submitting to the small council's expert decisions.[15] The sovereign, conversely, not only has a duty to hinder men from harming each other but must through legislation and education also ensure that the citizens become happy and virtuous.[16] This gives the state a role as moral tutor of the individual that Pufendorf had consistently denied it.[17] In spite of his copious use of Pufendorf's and Barbeyrac's words, Burlamaqui

14. Harvey also argues that it is Burlamaqui rather than James Wilson or Lord Kames that was Jefferson's central source in his declaration of inalienable human rights; see Harvey, *Jean-Jacques Burlamaqui: A Liberal Tradition in American Constitutionalism,* pp. 119–24.

15. Knud Haakonssen is thus right to emphasize how rights theories in the early modern natural law tradition generally, and Burlamaqui's in particular, often have had considerably more muted consequences than scholars would sometimes attribute to them; see Haakonssen, "The Moral Conservatism of Natural Rights," in *Natural Law and Civil Sovereignty: Moral Right and State Authority in Early Modern Political Thought,* ed. Ian Hunter and David Saunders (New York: Palgrave, 2002), pp. 27–42, at pp. 27–28 and 38–39.

16. Barbeyrac, "Discourse on What Is Permitted by the Laws," in Samuel Pufendorf, *The Whole Duty of Man, According to the Law of Nature,* ed. Ian Hunter and David Saunders (Indianapolis: Liberty Fund, 2003), pp. 316–20.

17. An important analysis of how Pufendorf "desacralized" natural law theory into a theory of the conditions of worldly peace alone is Ian Hunter's *Rival Enlightenments: Civil and Metaphysical Philosophy in Early Modern Germany* (Cambridge: Cambridge University Press, 2001).

in fact rejects or alters the legacy of his predecessors in fundamental respects.

Petter Korkman

Note on the Text

The present edition is based on the text of the 1763 London edition. The original spelling of the translation has been retained, but typographical errors have been silently removed. Footnotes have been added to point out passages where the translation differs from the original. In addition, the editor has added footnotes to help the reader perceive when Burlamaqui's paragraphs are taken verbatim from, or reproduce, the central content of passages in the DHC, DNG, and DGP. Page breaks in the 1763 edition are indicated by the use of angle brackets. For example, page 112 begins after <112>.

ACKNOWLEDGMENTS

This work has been completed in the supportive and friendly atmosphere of the Helsinki Collegium for Advanced Studies. I am grateful to colleagues at the Collegium and elsewhere for helpful discussions both within the framework of our conference on the history of rights discourse and in numerous private conversations. Special thanks go to Timo Kaitaro for important observations on a number of topics and to Juha Himanka for an unfailing ability to apply surprising perspectives. I am also grateful to Klaus Karttunen for expert assistance with Greek quotations and to Sari Kivistö for answering my questions concerning some of the Latin quotations. I owe a particular debt of gratitude to Knud Haakonssen, friend and editor of this series, for his patience, his friendly encouragement, and his untiring professionalism. Thanks also go to Åsa Söderman, to Liberty Fund's indexer, and to production editor Diana Francoeur.

I am grateful to members of the international Pufendorf circles with whom I have discussed my views on Burlamaqui and Barbeyrac, in particular Kari Saastamoinen, Knud Haakonssen, Ian Hunter, Hans Blom, and Tim Hochstrasser.

I was supported in one manner by the Helsinki Collegium for Advanced Studies, the Academy of Finland, and the Ella and Georg Ehrnrooth Foundation, and in another by Leena, Elsa, Lisa, and Kaius. Thank you.

VOLUME I
THE PRINCIPLES OF NATURAL LAW

THE
PRINCIPLES

OF

NATURAL and POLITIC

LAW,

IN TWO VOLUMES,

By *J. J. BURLAMAQUI,*

Counsellor of State, and late Professor of NATURAL
and CIVIL LAW at GENEVA.

Translated into ENGLISH by Mr. NUGENT.

The SECOND EDITION, revised and corrected.

VOL. I.

LONDON,
printed for J. NOURSE, Bookseller in Ordinary to his
MAJESTY.

To Dr. MEAD.

Sir,

To intrude in this manner upon your time, so usefully employed in the duties of your profession, would expose me in some measure to blame, were it upon a less important occasion than that of recommending the following work to your generous protection. The dignity of the subject, which, handled by other pens, has been thought worthy of being inscribed to the most illustrious personages of the last and present age, will plead, I hope, some excuse for an address, which is designed not so much to interrupt your occupations, as to avail itself of the sanction of your name in introducing this work to the public. And indeed a nobler subject I could not select for the favour of your acceptance, than that which so nearly relates to the moral duties of life, and the foundation of human contentment and happiness; a subject moreover illustrated by one of the ablest masters of the present age, whose extraordinary ability and skill in curing the disorders of the mind, may be compared very aptly to yours in removing those of the body.[1] One of the principal encouragements I had to this address, is the near relation between the following work, and those elevated sentiments with which you have been always inspired. Such an admirable system of moral precepts, such noble maxims of true Christian policy, and such excellent rules for the government of our lives, cannot but be acceptable to a gentleman, who, in the whole tenor of his conduct, has been an illustrious example of those rules and maxims which are here most judiciously established. A very good opportunity this of entering upon the encomium of those virtues which have so eminently distinguished you at the head of your profession; but the little value any commendations of mine would have, the apprehension I should be under of being suspected of adulation, and the danger I should incur of offending your modesty, obliges me to wave any attempt

1. Richard Mead (1673–1754) was one of the foremost physicians of his day and a member of the Royal Society. His collection of books exceeded ten thousand volumes, and he had a considerable collection of fine art.

of this nature. However, I cannot help taking notice of that true magnificence with which you have at all times contributed to the advancement of learning, and whereby you have justly acquired the title of patron and protector of letters. In fact, the extensive blessings that fortune has bestowed upon you, have been employed not as instruments of private luxury, but as means of promoting those arts, which have received an additional lustre, since they have shone so conspicuously in your person. Your friendship and correspondence have been courted by the greatest men of the present age; and your house, like that of Atticus, has been open to the learned of all orders and ranks, who unanimously respect you, not only as a supreme judge of learning and wit, but, moreover, as an *arbiter elegantiarum,* and master of finished urbanity. Your collection of valuable curiosities and books, wherein you have rivalled the magnificence of sovereigns, is the admiration and talk of all Europe, and will be a lasting monument of your love of literature. The polite reception you have always given to the learned of foreign nations has rendered your name so respectable abroad, that you are never mentioned but with expressions denoting the high idea they entertain of your singular munificence. These, Sir, are not particular sentiments of mine; they are the sentiments of the public, whose voice I utter; they are the sentiments of your learned friends abroad, which I have been desired to repeat to you upon a late occasion, together with their compliments of thanks for the marks they have received of your great and disinterested civility.[2] It is with pleasure I embrace this opportunity of executing my commission, and of declaring in this public manner the profound respect and esteem with which I have the honour of subscribing myself,

SIR,

Your most humble and

Gray's Inn,   Obedient Servant,

June 4, 1748.   Thomas Nugent.

---

2. Thomas Nugent earned his fame as a translator but also as a traveler and the author of books on travels in Europe. He translated mainly from French to English, and produced English translations of such works as Montesquieu's *L'esprit des loix,* Rousseau's *Émile,* and Condillac's *Essai sur l'origine des connaissances humaines.* See the introduction.

THE
TRANSLATOR
TO THE
READER.

The author of the following work, M. J. J. Burlamaqui, was descended from one of those noble families of Lucca, which, upon their embracing the Protestant religion, were obliged about two centuries ago to take shelter in Geneva. His father was counsellor and secretary of state; honours which are frequently conferred in that city upon such as acquit themselves worthily of a professorship in the academy, particularly that of law, the fittest without doubt to form able judges, magistrates, and statesmen. The son, upon his return from his travels, was immediately nominated professor of this science, in which post he continued a considerable number of years, till the republic thought proper to remunerate his long and eminent services, by raising him to the same dignity as his father. The great reputation he acquired in his professorship, was less owing to his immense erudition, in which he equalled if not excelled all his predecessors, than to the quickness of his understanding, the clearness of his ideas, his sound and judicious views in the study of jurisprudence, and especially to the solidity of his principles on natural law and civil government. With regard to the occasion of his publishing these *principles,* he observes himself in his preface, that it was in some measure to comply with the importunity of his friends, but chiefly to prevent his reputation from being injured by a precipitate impression from any of those imperfect and surreptitious copies which had been handed about by his pupils. The public indeed had flattered themselves a long time with the hopes of seeing a complete course of the law of nature and nations from this eminent hand; but his occupations and infirmity obliged him to frustrate their expectations. However, as a good introduction to this science was extremely wanted, he thought proper, till he could publish his larger work, to favour us with the following principles, being convinced that in this, as in every other branch of learning, the most essential part is the laying of a proper and solid foundation. In fact, we daily observe that most errors in life proceed rather from wrong principles, than from ill-drawn consequences.

M. Burlamaqui is so modest as to consider these principles, as calculated only for young people, who are desirous of being initiated into the study of natural law; and yet we may venture to affirm it is a performance of general utility, but especially to such as have had the misfortune of neglecting this science in their younger days. It is a performance that must certainly be allowed to have the merit of an original undertaking, by our author's ascending always to the first principles, by his illustrating and extending them, by his connecting them with each other, and by exhibiting them frequently in a new light. But his singular beauty consists in the alliance he so carefully points out between ethics and jurisprudence, religion and politics, after the example of Plato and Tully, and the other illustrious masters of antiquity. In effect, these sciences have the same basis, and tend to the same end; their business is to unravel the system of humanity, or the plan of providence with regard to man; and since the unity of this system is an unquestionable point, so soon as writers ascend to the principles, in order to view and contemplate the whole, it is impossible but they all should meet.

Our author's method has nothing of the scholastic turn. Instead of starting new difficulties, he prevents them by the manner of laying his thesis; instead of disputing, he reconciles. Far from pursuing any idle or too subtle ideas, he follows nature step by step, and derives his arguments from sense and experience. His thoughts he unfolds with the greatest perspicuity and order; and his style is pure, clear, and agreeable, such as properly becomes a didactic work. In fine, he has the honour of preserving the character of a Christian philosopher, by inculcating the value we ought to set upon the light of revelation, a light which so advantageously assists the feeble glimmerings of reason in the high and important concerns of our civil and religious duties.

Author's Advertisement.

This treatise on the *Principles of Natural Law,* is an introduction to a larger work, or to a complete system of the law of nature and nations, which some time or other I proposed to publish. But having met with several obstructions in my attempt, through a variety of occupations, and principally from my indifferent state of health, I had almost lost sight of my original design. Being informed however that some manuscript copies of the papers I had drawn up for my own private use, when I gave lectures of jurisprudence, were multiplied and got into a number of hands, I began to apprehend lest this work should be published against my will, in a very imperfect and mangled condition. This induced me at length to yield to the sollicitations of several of my friends, by communicating the following essay to the public. Dubious whether I shall ever be able to finish the larger work, I have endeavoured to give such an extent to these *Principles,* as may render them in some measure serviceable to such as are desirous of being initiated into the knowledge of the law of nature. As for those who are masters of this subject, the present work is not designed for them: my view will be sufficiently fulfilled, if it should prove of any utility to young beginners in the study of this important science.

CONTENTS[1]

1. The page numbers in the Contents are those of the 1763 edition.
2. Read: "deduce."

CHAPTER II

Continuation of the principles relative to the nature of man. Of will and liberty.   13

CHAPTER III

That man thus constituted, is a creature capable of moral direction, and accountable for his actions.

CHAPTER IV

Further inquiry into what relates to human nature, by considering the different states of man.

CHAPTER VII

Of right considered as a faculty, and of the obligation thereto corresponding.

CHAPTER X

CHAPTER XI

PART II

Of the Law of Nature.

CHAPTER I

In what the law of nature consists, and that there is such a thing.
First considerations drawn from the existence of God and his
authority over us.   125

CHAPTER IV

Of the principles from whence reason may deduce the law
of nature.

CHAPTER VII

Whether there is any morality of actions, any obligation or duty,
antecedent to the law of nature, and independent of the idea of a
legislator.

CHAPTER VIII

CHAPTER IX

CHAPTER X

CHAPTER XII

CHAPTER XIV

That the proofs we have alledged have such a probability and fitness, as renders them sufficient to fix our belief, and to determine our conduct.   297

THE
PRINCIPLES
OF
NATURAL LAW

General Principles of Right.

CHAPTER I

Of the Nature of Man considered with Regard to Right: Of the Understanding, and whatever is relative to this Faculty.

I. My design is to enquire into those rules which nature[1] alone prescribes to man, in order to conduct him safely to the end, which every one has, and indeed ought to have, in view, namely, true and solid happiness. The system or assemblage of these rules, considered as so many laws imposed by God on man, is generally distinguished by the name of *Natural Law.* This science includes the most <2> important principles of morality, jurisprudence, and politics, that is, whatever is most interesting in respect as well to man as to society. There can be nothing therefore more deserving of the application of a rational being, of a being that has its perfection and felicity seriously at heart. A just knowledge of the maxims we ought to follow in the course of life, is the principal object of wisdom;

Design of this work: What is meant by Natural Law.

---

1. "La seule raison," that is, "reason unaided."

and virtue consists in putting them constantly in practice, without being ever diverted from so noble a pursuit.

We must deduce the principles of this science from the nature and state of man.

II. The idea of *Right,* and much more that of *Natural Right,* are undoubtedly relative to the nature of man. It is from this nature therefore, from the constitution and state of man, that we are to deduce the principles of this science.

The word *Right* (*Droit**) in its original signification, comes from the verb *dirigo,* which implies, to conduct a person to some certain end by the shortest road. Right, therefore, in its proper and most general sense, and that to which all the others must be reduced, is whatever directs, or is properly directed. This being premised, the first thing we have to examine is, whether man is susceptible of direction and rule in respect to his actions. That we may attempt this with a greater probability of success, we are to trace matters to their very origin, and ascending as high as the nature and constitution of man, we must there unravel the principle of his actions, and the several states that properly belong to him, in order to demonstrate afterwards in what manner, and how <3> far, he is susceptible of direction in his conduct. This is the only method of knowing what is *right,* and what is not.

Definition of man; what his nature is.

III. Man is an animal endowed with understanding, and reason; a being composed of an organized body, and a rational soul.

With regard to his body, he is pretty similar to other animals, having the same organs, properties, and wants. This is a living body, organized and composed of several parts; a body that moves of itself, and feeble in the commencement, increases gradually in its progress by the help of nourishment, till it arrives to a certain period, in which it appears in its flower and vigor, from whence it insensibly declines to old age, which conducts it at length to dissolution. This is the ordinary course of human life, unless it happens to be abridged by some malady or accident.

But man, besides the marvelous disposition of his body, has likewise

* The etymology given here by the Author was intended only for the French word *Droit.*

a rational soul, which eminently discriminates him from brutes. It is by this noble part of himself that he thinks, and is capable of forming just ideas of the different objects that occur to him; of comparing them together; of inferring from known principles unknown truths; of passing a solid judgment on the mutual fitness or agreement of things, as well as on the relations they bear to us; of deliberating on what is proper or improper to be done; and of determining consequently to act one way or other. The mind recollects what is past, joins it with the present, and extends its views to futurity. It is capable of penetrating into the causes, progress, and consequence of things, and of disco-<4>vering, as it were at one glance, the intire course of life, which enables it to lay in a store of such things as are necessary for making a happy career. Besides, in all this, it is not subject to a constant series of uniform and invariable operations, but finds itself at liberty to act or not to act, to suspend its actions and motions, to direct and manage them as it thinks proper.[2]

IV. Such is the general idea we are to form of the nature of man. What results from hence is, that there are several sorts of human actions: Some are purely spiritual, as to think, to reflect, to doubt, &c. others are merely corporeal, as to breathe, to grow, &c. and some there are that may be called mixt, in which the soul and body have both a share, being produced by their joint concurrence, in consequence of the union which God has established between these two constituent parts of man; such as to speak, to work, &c.

Different actions of man: Which are those that are the object of Right?

Those actions, which either in their origin or direction depend on the soul, are called human or voluntary; all the rest are termed merely physical. The soul is therefore the principle of human actions; and these actions cannot be the object of rule, but inasmuch as they are produced and directed by those noble faculties with which man has been inriched by his Creator. Hence it is necessary to enter into a particular inquiry concerning this subject, and to examine closely into the faculties and operations of the soul, in order to discover in what manner they concur

2. This paragraph and the next are based on DNG I.1 §2 and DHC I.1 §§2–3, together with Barbeyrac's notes.

to the production of human actions. This will help us, at the same time, to unfold the nature of <5> these actions, to assure ourselves whether they are really susceptible of rule, and how far they are subject to human command.

Principal faculties of the soul.

V. Let man reflect but ever so little on himself, sense and experience will soon inform him, that his soul is an agent, whose activity displays itself by a series of different operations; which having been distinguished by separate names, are likewise attributed to different faculties. The chief of these faculties are the understanding, will, and liberty. The soul is, indeed, a simple being; but this does not hinder us, when we attend to its different ways of operating, from considering it as a subject in which different powers of acting reside, and from giving different denominations to these powers. If we consider the thing in this manner, we shall find it will give a greater exactness and perspicuity to our ideas. Let us remember therefore, that these faculties are nothing else but the different powers of acting inherent in the mind, by means of which it performs all its operations.

The understanding; truth.

VI. The principal faculty of the soul, that which constitutes the fundamental part of its being, and serves, as it were, for its intrinsic light, is the understanding. We may define it that faculty or power, by which the mind perceives, and forms ideas of things, in order to come at the knowledge of truth. Truth may be taken here in two significations; either for the nature, state, and mutual relations of things; or for the ideas agreeable to this nature, state, and relations. To have a knowledge therefore of truth, <6> is to perceive things such as they are in themselves, and to form ideas concerning them conformable to their nature.

Principle. The understanding is naturally right.

VII. We must therefore set out with acknowledging as a fixt and uncontestable principle, that the human understanding is naturally right, and has within itself a strength sufficient to arrive at the knowledge of truth, and to distinguish it from error; especially in things wherein our respective duties are concerned, and which are requisite to form man for a virtuous, honourable, and quiet life; provided, however, he employs all the care and attention that lies in his power.

Sense[3] and experience concur to convince us of the truth of this principle; which is the hinge, as it were, whereon the whole system of humanity turns. It cannot be called in question, without sapping the foundation, and intirely subverting the whole structure of society; because this would be annulling all manner of distinction between truth and error, and between good and evil; and by a natural consequence of this subversion, we should find ourselves reduced to the necessity of doubting of every thing; which is the highest pitch of human extravagance.

Those who pretend that reason and its faculties are depraved in such a manner, as to be no longer capable of serving as a sure and faithful guide to man, either in respect to his duties, or particularly with regard to religion; do not reflect that they have adopted for the basis of their system, a principle destructive of all truth, and consequently of religion. Thus we see that the sacred scripture, far from <7> establishing any such maxim, assures us,* that *when the Gentiles which have not the law, do by nature the things contained in the law; these having not the law, are a law to themselves. Which shew the work of the law written in their hearts, their conscience also bearing witness.*

True it is, that a bad education, vicious habits, and irregular passions, may offuscate the mind; and that neglect, levity, and prejudices, precipitate men frequently into the grossest errors in point of religion and morals. But this proves only that men may make a bad use of their reason, and not that the natural rectitude of the faculties is subverted. What we have still to say, concerning this point, will help to set it in a clearer light.[4]

---

* Rom. ii. 14, 15.

3. "Le sentiment intérieur," that is, the "internal sentiment" or "internal sense," in the original.

4. This paragraph is based on DHC I.1 §4 together with Barbeyrac's comments in footnote 2 to that paragraph.

In what manner perception, attention, and examen, are formed.

VIII. Let us proceed now to a closer inquiry into the operations of the understanding.[5] The perception, or view and knowledge of things, is commonly formed by the concurrence of two actions; one from the object, and is the impression which this object makes on us; the other from the mind, and is properly a glance, or simple view of the soul, on the object it is desirous of knowing. But as a first view is not always sufficient, it is necessary that the mind should apply itself for some time to a serious consideration of the object, to the end it may acquire a just knowledge of things, and form thereof exact ideas. This application, with which the soul continues to view the object in order to know it well, is called attention; and if it turns itself different ways, to consider the object on all sides, this is <8> termed examen or inquiry. We may therefore affirm, that the perception or knowledge of things depends intirely, in respect to the mind, on its natural vigor and attention.

Evidence; Probability.

IX. It is by these helps, drawn from his own fund, that man attains at length a clear and distinct knowledge of things, and their relations; as also of ideas, and the conformity of those ideas to their originals; in short, that he acquires the knowledge of truth. We give the name of evidence, to this clear and distinct view of things, and of their mutual relations; a point to which we should be particularly attentive. For this evidence being the essential characteristic of truth, or the sure mark whereby one cannot help distinguishing it, the consequence is, that it necessarily produces such an internal conviction, as forms the highest degree of certainty. It is true that all objects do not present themselves with so strong a light, and that notwithstanding the great care and application a man may use, all that he is frequently able to attain, is only a glimmering light, which, according to its strength or weakness, produces different degrees of probability and seeming truth. But this must be absolutely the case of every being, whose faculties are limited: It is

5. Burlamaqui's discussion of how the will, through its dual functions of steering the attention and participating in the formation of assent, is a Cartesian legacy. Barbeyrac refers to the matter in, for example, DNG I.3 §2 note 1, where he indicates LeClerc and Malebranche as central sources.

sufficient that man, in respect to his destination and state, is capable of knowing with certainty those things which concern his perfection and happiness; and moreover, that he is able to distinguish between probability and evidence, as also between the different degrees of probability, in order to proportion his assent to those differences. Now a person need but enter never so little into him-<9>self, and reflect on the operations of his mind, to be convinced, beyond any possibility of doubt, that man is really possessed of this discernment.

X. The senses, taken for the sensitive faculty, the imagination also, and the memory, must be all reduced to the understanding. In fact, the senses, considered in this manner, are nothing else but the understanding itself, as it makes use of the senses and organs of the body, to perceive corporeal objects. The imagination likewise is nothing but the understanding, as it perceives absent objects, not in themselves, but by their images formed in the brain. The memory, in fine, is no more than the understanding, considered as possessed of the faculty of retaining the ideas it forms of things, and capable of representing them to itself whenever there is occasion; advantages that principally depend on the care we take in repeating frequently those ideas.

Of the senses, the imagination, and memory.

XI. From what has been hitherto said with regard to the understanding, it follows, that the object of this faculty of the soul is truth, with all the acts and means that lead us to it. Upon this supposition, the perfection of the understanding consists in the knowledge of truth, this being the end for which it is designed.

There are two things, among others, opposite to this perfection, ignorance and error, which are two maladies, as it were, of the mind. Ignorance is no more than a privation of ideas or knowledge; but error is a nonconformity or opposition of our ideas to the nature and state of things. Error being therefore <10> the subversion of truth, is much more opposite to it than ignorance, which is a kind of medium between truth and error.

It is to be observed here, that we do not speak of the understanding, truth, ignorance, and error, purely to know what these things are in

The perfection of the understanding consists in the knowledge of truth. Two obstacles to this perfection, ignorance and error.

themselves; our main design is to consider them as principles of our actions. In this light, ignorance and error, though naturally distinct from one another, are generally mixt, as it were, and confounded; insomuch, that whatsoever is said of one, ought equally to be applied to the other. Ignorance is frequently the cause of error; but whether joined or separate, they follow the same rules, and produce the same effect by the influence they have over our actions or omissions. Perhaps, were we to examine into things exactly, error only, properly speaking, can be looked upon as a principle of action, and not simple ignorance, which being nothing more of itself than a privation of ideas, cannot be productive of any thing.

Different sorts of errors. 1. Error of the law, and of the fact. 2. Voluntary and involuntary. 3. Essential and accidental.

XII. There are several sorts of ignorance and error, whose different divisions it is proper for us to observe. 1. Error considered in respect to its object, is either of the law or of the fact. 2. With regard to its origin, ignorance is voluntary or involuntary, error is vincible or invincible. 3. In relation to the influence of the error on a particular affair or action, it is esteemed essential or accidental.

Error is of the law or fact according as people are mistaken either in respect to the disposition of the law, or in regard to a fact that is not sufficiently known.[6] For instance, it would be an error of the <11> law, were a prince to suppose himself intitled to declare war against a neighbouring state, only because it insensibly increases in strength and power. Such was likewise the error so common formerly among the Greeks and Romans, that it was allowable for parents to expose their children.* On the contrary, the idea Abimelech had of Sarah the wife of Abraham, by taking her for an unmarried person, was an error of the fact.

The ignorance a person lies under through his own fault, or an error contracted by neglect, and which might have been avoided by using all possible care and attention, is a voluntary ignorance, or a vincible and

---

* See another example in St. Matthew, chap. xv. 4, 5.

6. The discussion of error of the law and error of fact (including the examples) is borrowed from Barbeyrac, DHC I.1 §7 note 1.

surmountable error. Thus the polytheism of the Pagans was a vincible error; for they had only to make a right use of their reason, in order to be convinced that there was no necessity for supposing a plurality of gods.[7] The same may be said of an opinion established among most of the ancients, that piracy was lawful against those with whom there was no treaty subsisting, and that it was allowable to consider them as enemies. Ignorance is involuntary, and error invincible, when they are such as could neither have been prevented nor removed, even by all the care and endeavours that are morally possible; that is, judging of them according to the constitution of human things, and of common life. Thus the ignorance of the christian religion, under which the people of America laboured, before they had any communication with the Europeans, was an involuntary and invincible ignorance. <12>

In fine, we understand by an essential error,[8] that whose object is some necessary circumstance in the affair, and which for this very reason has a direct influence on the action done in consequence thereof; insomuch, that were it not for this error, the action would never have been done. Hence this is denominated likewise an efficacious error. By necessary circumstances, we are to understand those which are necessarily required, either by the very nature of the thing, or by the intention of the agent, formed at the proper time, and made known by suitable indications. It was thus, for instance, an essential error in the Trojans, at the taking of their town, to shoot their darts against their own people, mistaking them for enemies, because of their being armed after the Greek manner. Again; a person marries another man's wife, supposing her to be a maid, or not knowing that her husband is still living: this regards the very nature of the thing, and is of course an essential error.

On the contrary, accidental error is that which has no necessary connexion of itself with the affair, and consequently cannot be considered as the real cause of the action. A person abuses or insults another, taking

7. See Barbeyrac's note 1 in DHC I.1 §7, and DHC I.1 §9 note 1.
8. Barbeyrac recommends the essential/accidental distinction as preferable in DHC I.1 §8 note 2; see also DNG I.3 §10 note 2.

him for somebody else, or because he supposes the prince is dead, as it had been groundlessly reported, &c. These are errors merely accidental, which subsist indeed in the mind of the agent, and have accompanied him in the action, but cannot be considered as its real cause.

It is likewise observable, that these different qualities of ignorance or error may concur, and be found united in the same case. It is thus an error of the fact may <13> be either essential or accidental; and both the one and the other may be either voluntary or involuntary, vincible or invincible.

So much may suffice for what regards the understanding. Let us proceed now to examine into the other faculties of the soul, which concur also to the production of human actions.

CHAPTER II

Continuation of the Principles relative to the nature of man. Of will and liberty.

The Will. What happiness and good consist in.

I. It was not sufficient, pursuant to the views of the Creator, that the human mind should be possessed of the faculty of knowing things, and of forming thereof ideas; it was likewise requisite it should be endowed with an active principle to set it in motion, and with a power whereby man, after knowing the objects that occur to him, should be capable of determining to act or not to act, according as he judges proper. This faculty is what we call the will.

The will is therefore nothing else but that power of the soul, by which it is determined of itself, and by virtue of an active principle inherent in its nature, to seek for what is agreeable to it, to act after a certain manner, and to do or to omit an action, with a view of happiness.

By *Happiness* we are to understand the internal satisfaction of the mind, arising from the possession <14> of good; and by good whatever is suitable or agreeable to man for his preservation, perfection, conveniency, or pleasure. The idea of good determines that of evil, which, in its most general signification, implies whatever is opposite to the preservation, perfection, conveniency, or pleasure of man.

II. Instincts, inclinations, and passions, are reducible to the will.[1] In- stincts are sentiments excited in the soul by the wants of the body, which determine it to provide immediately against them. Such are hunger, thirst, the aversion for whatever is hurtful, &c. The inclinations are a propensity of the will, which leads it rather towards some sorts of objects than others, but in an even tranquil manner, a manner so proportioned to all its operations, that instead of obstructing or interrupting, it generally facilitates them. As for the passions, they are, indeed, in the same manner as the inclinations, motions of the will towards certain objects, but motions of a more impetuous and turbulent kind, motions that dispossess the soul of its natural tranquillity, and hinder it from directing properly its operations. Then it is that the passions become most dangerous distempers. The cause of the passions is, generally, the allurement of some sensible good, which solicits the soul, and impels it with too violent an impression.

It is easy to conceive, by what has been here said, that the inclinations, passions, and instincts, have a very great affinity with one another. They are all alike propensies or motions, which have frequently the same objects; but there is this difference between <15> these three species of motions, that instincts are necessarily the same in all men, by a natural consequence of their constitution, and of the union between the body and the soul; whereas the inclinations and passions, particularly considered, have nothing necessary in their nature, and are surprisingly different in different men.

Let us make an observation here, which falls in very naturally: it is that we often give the name of *Heart* to the will, considered as susceptible of the forementioned motions; and the reason of this in all probability is, because these motions were supposed to have their seat in the heart.

III. Such is the nature of the soul, that the will not only acts always spontaneously, that is, of its own proper motion, of its own accord, and by an internal principle; but likewise, that its determinations are generally accompanied with liberty.

---

1. The original's "se rapportent" could also be translated "are related to."

We give the name of liberty to that force or power of the soul, whereby it modifies and regulates its operations as it pleases, so as to be able to suspend, continue, or alter its deliberations and actions; in a word, so as to be capable to determine and act with choice, according as it thinks proper. It is by this excellent faculty, that man has a kind of command over himself and his actions: and as he is hereby rendered also capable of conforming to rule, and answerable for his conduct, it is therefore necessary to give a further explication of the nature of this faculty.

Will and liberty being faculties of the soul, they cannot be blind or destitute of knowledge; but <16> necessarily suppose the operation of the understanding. How is it possible in fact to determine, suspend, or alter our resolutions, unless we know what is proper for us to chuse? It is contrary to the nature of an intelligent and rational being to act without intellection and reason. This reason may be either superficial or bad; yet it has some appearance at least, some glimmering, that makes us give it a momentary approbation. Wherever there is election or choice, there must be a comparison; and a comparison implies at least a confused reflection, a kind of deliberation, though of a quick and almost imperceptible nature, on the subject before us.

The end of[2] our deliberations is to procure us some advantage. For the will tends generally towards good, that is, to whatsoever is really or apparently proper for rendering us happy; insomuch, that all actions depending on man, and that are any way relative to his end, are for this very reason subject to the will. And as truth, or the knowledge of things, is agreeable to man; and in this signification truth is also a good, it follows therefore that truth forms one of the principal objects of the will.

Liberty, like the will, has goodness and truth for its object; but it has less extent with regard to actions; for it does not exercise itself in all the

---

2. The translation omits a significant "all," by which Burlamaqui stresses that no single deliberation is free from this essential orientation toward happiness. The classical work on the significance of happiness as a key term in the systems of moral and social philosophy in French-language eighteenth-century literature is Robert Mauzi's *L'idée du bonheur dans la littérature et la pensée françaises au XVIIIe siècle* (Paris: Armand Colin, 1960; Genève: Slatkine Reprints, 1979).

acts of the will, but only in those which the soul has a power of suspending or altering as she pleases.[3]

IV. But if any one should inquire which are those acts wherein liberty displays itself? We answer, that they are easily known, by attending to what passes within us, and to the manner in which the mind <17> conducts itself in the several cases that daily occur: as, in the first place, in our judgments concerning true and false; secondly, in our determinations in relation to good and evil; and finally, in indifferent matters. These particulars are necessary, in order to be acquainted with the nature, use, and extent of liberty.

Use of liberty in our judgments in respect to truth.

With regard to truth, we are formed in such a manner, that so soon as evidence strikes the mind, we are no longer at liberty to suspend our judgment. Vain would be the attempt to resist this sparkling light; it absolutely forces our assent. Who, for example, could pretend to deny that the whole is greater than its part, or that harmony and peace are preferable, either in a family or state, to discord, tumults, and war?

The same cannot be affirmed in regard to things that have less perspicuity and evidence; for in these the use of liberty displays itself in its full extent. It is true our mind inclines naturally to that side which seems the most probable; but this does not debar it from suspending its assent, in order to seek for new proofs, or to refer the whole inquiry to another opportunity. The obscurer things are, the more we are at liberty to hesitate, to suspend, or defer our determination. This is a point sufficiently evinced by experience. Every day, and at every step, as it were, disputes arise, in which the arguments on both sides leave us, by reason of our limited capacity, in a kind of doubt and equilibrium, which permits us to suspend our judgment, to examine the thing anew, and to incline the balance at length to one side more than the other. We find, for example,

3. Burlamaqui's explanation, in this and the following paragraphs, of how liberty "displays itself" in our judgments concerning true and false, follows closely the Cartesian doctrine as presented in the fourth part of the *Mediatationes de prima philosophia*. Burlamaqui's Cartesian discussion goes further in this respect than those of Pufendorf and Barbeyrac; see DNG I.3 §§1–2, especially §2 note 1; see also DHC I.1 §9, especially note 1.

<18> that the mind can hesitate a long time, and forbear determining itself, even after a mature inquiry, in respect to the following questions: Whether an oath extorted by violence is obligatory? Whether the murder of Caesar was lawful? Whether the Roman senate could with justice refuse to confirm the promise made by the Consuls to the Samnites, in order to extricate themselves from the *Caudine Forks;* or whether they ought to have ratified and given it the force of a public treaty? &c.[4]

Liberty has its exercise, even in regard to things that are evident.

V. Though there is no exercise of liberty in our judgment, when things present themselves to us in a clear and distinct manner; still we must not imagine that the intire use of this faculty ceases in respect to things that are evident. For in the first place, it is always in our power to apply our minds to the consideration of those things, or else to divert them from thence, by transferring somewhere else our attention. This first determination of the will, by which it is led to consider or not to consider the objects that occur to us, merits particular notice, because of the natural influence it must have on the very determination, by which we conclude to act or not to act, in consequence of our reflexion and judgment. Secondly, we have it likewise in our power to create, as it were, evidence in some cases, by dint of attention and inquiry; whereas at first setting out, we had only some glimmerings, insufficient to give us an adequate knowledge of the state of things. In fine, when we have attained this evidence, we are still at liberty to dwell more or less on the consideration thereof; which is also of great consequence, because on this depends its greater or lesser degree of impression. <19>

Objection.

These remarks lead us to an important reflexion, which may serve for answer to an objection raised against liberty. "It is not in our power (say they) to perceive things otherwise than as they offer themselves to our mind; now our judgments are formed on this perception of things; and

---

4. The Romans suffered a humiliating defeat against the Samnites in the Caudine Forks in 321 B.C. The Roman Senate extricated itself from the peace treaty signed by its consuls by regarding it as expressing the commitment not of Rome but of those individual senators.

it is by these judgments that the will is determined: The whole is therefore necessary and independent of liberty."

But this difficulty carries little more with it than an empty appearance. Let people say what they will, we are always at liberty to open or to shut our eyes to the light; to exert, or relax our attention. Experience shews, that when we view an object in different lights, and determine to search into the bottom of matters, we descry several things that escaped us at first sight. This is sufficient to prove that there is an exercise of liberty in the operations of the understanding, as well as in the several actions thereon depending.

VI. The second question we have to examine, is whether we are equally free in our determinations, in regard to good and evil.

To decide this point, we need not stir out of our selves; for here also by facts, and even by our internal experience,[5] the question may be determined. Certain it is, that in respect to good and evil considered in general, and as such, we cannot, properly speaking, exercise our liberty, by reason that we feel ourselves drawn towards the one by an invincible propensity, and estranged from the other by a natural and insuperable aversion. Thus it has been ordered <20> by the author of our being, whilst man has no power in this respect to change his nature. We are formed in such a manner, that good of necessity allures us; whereas evil, by an opposite effect, repels us, as it were, and deters us from attempting to pursue it.

But this strong tendency to good, and natural aversion to evil in general, does not debar us from being perfectly free in respect to good and evil particularly considered; and though we cannot help being sensible of the first impressions which the objects make on us, yet this does not invincibly determine us to pursue or shun those objects. Let the most beautiful and most fragrant fruit, replenished with exquisite and delicious juice, be unexpectedly set before a person oppressed with thirst

Marginal notes:

Answer.

Use of liberty with regard to good and evil.

---

5. The translator's "internal experience" stands for the less technical and more open-ended "ce que nous éprouvons au-dédans de nous-mêmes," that is, "what we feel within ourselves."

and heat; he will find himself instantly inclined to seize on the blessing offered to him, and to ease his inquietude by a salutary refreshment. But he can also stop, and suspend his action, in order to examine whether the good he proposes to himself, by eating this fruit, will not be attended with evil; in short, he is at liberty to weigh and deliberate,[6] in order to embrace the safest side of the question. Besides, we are not only capable, with the assistance of reason, to deprive ourselves of a thing, whose flattering idea invites us; but moreover we are able to expose ourselves to a chagrin or pain, which we dread and would willingly avoid, were we not induced by superior considerations to support it. Can any one desire a stronger proof of liberty?

With regard to indifferent things.

VII. True it is notwithstanding, that the exercise of this faculty never displays itself more than in in-<21>different things. I find, for instance, that it depends intirely on myself to stretch out or draw back my hand; to sit down or to walk; to direct my steps to the right or left, &c. On these occasions, where the soul is left intirely to itself, either for want of external motives, or by reason of the opposition and, as it were, the equilibrium of these motives, if it determines on one side, this may be said to be the pure effect of its pleasure and good will, and of the command it has over its own actions.

Why the exercise of liberty is restrained to non-evident truths, and particular goods.

VIII. Let us stop here a while to inquire, how comes it that the exercise of this power is limited to particular goods and non-evident truths, without extending itself to good in general, or to such truths as are perfectly clear. Should we happen to discover the reason thereof, it will furnish us with a new subject to admire the wisdom of the Creator in the constitution of man, and with a means at the same time of being better acquainted with the end and true use of liberty.

And first we hope there is no body but will admit, that the end of God in creating man was to render him happy. Upon this supposition, it will be soon agreed, that man cannot attain to happiness any other way than by the knowledge of truth, and by the possession of real good.

6. The original is more mathematical: "délibérer et calculer."

This is evidently the result of the notions above given of good and happiness. Let us therefore direct our reflexions towards this prospect. When things, that are the object of our researches, present themselves to our minds with a feeble light, and are not accompanied with that splendor and clearness, which enables us to know them <22> perfectly, and to judge of them with full certainty; it is proper and even necessary for us to be invested with a power of suspending our judgment; to the end that, not being necessarily determined to acquiesce in the first impression, we should be still at liberty to carry on our inquiry, till we arrive to a higher degree of certainty, and if possible, as far as evidence itself. Were not this the case, we should be exposed every moment to error, without any possibility of being undeceived. It was therefore extremely useful and necessary to man, that under such circumstances he should have the use and exercise of his liberty.

But when we happen to have a clear and distinct view of things and their relations, that is, when evidence strikes us, it would be of no manner of signification to have the use of liberty, in order to suspend our judgment. For certainty being then in its very highest degree, what benefit should we reap by a new examen or inquiry, were it in our power? We have no longer occasion to consult a guide, when we see distinctly the end we are tending to, and the road we are to take. It is therefore an advantage to man to be unable to refuse his assent to evidence.

IX. Let us reason pretty near in the same manner on the use of liberty with respect to good and evil. Man designed for happiness, should certainly have been formed in such a manner, as to find himself under an absolute necessity of desiring and pursuing good, and of shunning on the contrary evil in general. Were the nature of these faculties such, as to <23> leave him in a state of indifference, so as to be at liberty in this respect to suspend or alter his desires, plain it is, that this would be esteemed a very great imperfection in him; an imperfection that would imply a want of wisdom in the author of his being, as a thing directly opposite to the end he proposed in giving him life.

No less an inconveniency would it be on the other hand, were the necessity which man is under of pursuing good and avoiding evil to be such as would insuperably determine him to act or not to act, in consequence of the impressions made on him by each object. Such is the state of human things, that we are frequently deceived by appearances; it is very rare that good or evil presents itself to us pure and without mixture; but there is almost always a favourable and adverse side, an inconveniency mixt with utility. In order to act therefore with safety, and not to be mistaken in our account, it is generally incumbent upon us to suspend our first motions, to examine more closely into things, to make distinctions, calculations, and compensations; all which require the use of liberty. Liberty is therefore, as it were, a subsidiary faculty, which supplies the deficiencies of the other powers, and whose office ceaseth as soon as it has redressed them.

Hence let us conclude, that man is provided with all the necessary means for attaining to the end for which he is designed; and that in this, as in every other respect, the Creator has acted with wonderful wisdom.

The proof of liberty drawn from our inward sense, is superior to any other.

X. After what has been said concerning the nature, operations, and use of liberty, it may seem perhaps <24> unnecessary to attempt here to prove that man is indeed a free agent, and that we are as really invested with this as with any other faculty.

Nevertheless, as it is an essential principle, and one of the fundamental supports of our edifice, it is proper to make the reader sensible of the indubitable proof with which we are furnished by daily experience. Let us therefore consult only ourselves. Every one finds that he is master, for instance, to walk or sit, to speak or hold his tongue. Do not we also experience continually, that it depends intirely on ourselves to suspend our judgment, in order to proceed to a new inquiry? Can any one seriously deny, that in the choice of good and evil our resolutions are unconstrained; that, notwithstanding the first impression, we have it in our power to stop of a sudden, to weigh the arguments on both sides, and to do, in short, whatever can be expected from the freest agent? Were I invincibly drawn towards one particular good rather than another, I should feel then the same impression as that which inclines me to good in general, that is, an impression that would necessarily drag me along, an impression which there would be no possibility of resisting. Now experience makes me feel no such violence with respect to any par-

ticular good. I find I can abstain from it; I can defer using it; I can prefer
something else to it; I can hesitate in my choice; in short, I am my own
master to chuse, or, which is the same thing, I am *free*.

Should we be asked, how comes it, that not being free in respect to
good in general, yet we are at liberty with regard to particular goods? My
answer is, that the natural desire of happiness does not in-<25>superably
draw us towards any particular good, because no particular good includes that happiness for which we have a necessary inclination.

Sensible proofs, like these, are superior to all objection, and productive of the most inward conviction, by reason it is impossible, that when
the soul is modified after a certain manner, it should not feel this modification, and the state which consequently attends it. What other certainty have we of our existence? And how is it we know that we think,
we act, but by our inward sense?[7]

This sense of liberty is so much the less equivocal, as it is not momentary or transient: It is a sense that never leaves us, and of which we
have a daily and continual experience.

Thus we see there is nothing better established in life, than the strong
persuasion which all mankind have of liberty. Let us consider the system
of humanity, either in general or particular, we shall find that the whole
is built upon this principle. Reflexions, deliberations, researches, actions,
judgments; all suppose the use of liberty. Hence the ideas of good and
evil, of vice and virtue: hence, as a natural consequence, arises praise or
blame, the censure or approbation of our own, or other people's conduct. The same may be said of the affections and natural sentiments of
men towards one another, as friendship, benevolence, gratitude, hatred,
anger, complaints, and reproaches: none of these sentiments could take
place, unless we were to admit of liberty. In fine, as this prerogative is
in some measure the key of the human system, he that does not allow
it to man, subverts all order, and introduces a general confusion. <26>

7. This is a reference to the Cartesian "cogito" argument: I know that I exist because when I think this thought, "I exist," I can feel my existence in this act of the
internal sense.

How comes it
that liberty
has been
contested.

XI. It is natural here to inquire, how it was ever possible for any body seriously to doubt, whether man is master of his actions, whether he is free? I should be less surprized at this doubt, were it concerning a strange or remote fact, a fact that was not transacted within ourselves. But the question is in regard to a thing, of which we have an internal immediate feeling, a constant and daily experience. Strange, that any one should call in question a faculty of the soul! May not we as well doubt of the understanding and will, as of the liberty of man? For if we are content to abide by our inward sense,[8] there is no more room to dispute of one than of the other. But some too subtle philosophers, by considering this subject in a metaphysical light, have stript it, as it were, of its nature; and finding themselves at a loss to solve a few difficulties, they have given a greater attention to these difficulties than to the positive proofs of the thing; which insensibly led them to imagine that the notion of liberty was all an illusion. I own it is necessary, in the research of truth, to consider an object on every side, and to balance equally the arguments for and against; nevertheless we must take care we do not give to those objections more than their real weight. We are informed by experience, that in several things which in respect to us are invested with the highest degree of certainty, there are many difficulties notwithstanding, which we are incapable of resolving to our satisfaction: and this is a natural consequence of the limits of the mind. Let us conclude therefore from hence, that when a truth is sufficiently evinced by solid reasons, whatever can be objected against it, ought not to <27> stagger or weaken our conviction, as long as they are such difficulties only as embarrass or puzzle the mind, without invalidating the proofs themselves. This rule is so

8. Burlamaqui sometimes uses the expression "internal sense" ("sentiment intérieur"), but not as systematically as the translator; the original in this instance reads "le sentiment que nous avons de l'un et de l'autre," that is, "the sentiment we have of the one [understanding and will] and of the other [liberty]." Nevertheless, later chapters will confirm an influence from Francis Hutcheson, whose language Burlamaqui's discussion of internal sentiment often reflects.

very useful in the study of the sciences, that one should keep it always in sight.* Let us resume now the thread of our reflexions.

XII. The denomination of voluntary or human actions in general is given to all those that depend on the will; and that of free, to such as come within the jurisdiction of liberty, which the soul can suspend or turn as it pleases. The opposite of voluntary is involuntary; and the contrary of free is necessary, or whatever is done by force or constraint. All human actions are voluntary, inasmuch as there are none but what proceed from ourselves, and of which we are the authors. But if violence, used by an external force, which we are incapable to resist, hinders us from acting, or makes us act without the consent of our will; as when a person stronger than ourselves lays hold of our arm to strike or wound another person, the action resulting from thence being involuntary, is not, properly speaking, our deed or action, but that of the agent from whom we suffer this violence. <28>

Actions are voluntary, and involuntary; free, necessary, and constrained.

The same cannot be said of actions that are forced and constrained, only as we are determined to commit them, through fear of a great and imminent evil with which we are menaced: As for instance, were an unjust and cruel prince to oblige a judge to condemn an innocent person, by menacing to put him to death if he did not obey his orders. Actions of this sort, though forced in some sense, because we commit them with reluctancy, and would never consent to them were it not for a very pressing necessity; such actions, I say, are ranked nevertheless among the

---

* *There is a wide difference between seeing that a thing is absurd, and not knowing all that regards it; between an unanswerable question in relation to a truth, and an unanswerable objection against it; though a great many confound these two sorts of difficulties. Those only of the latter order are able to prove, that what was taken for a known truth cannot be true, because otherwise some absurdity must ensue. But the others prove nothing but the ignorance we are under in relation to several things that regard a known truth.* Biblioth. Raison. Tom. 7. p. 346. [These words are drawn from the anonymous review article of *A Philosophical Inquiry Concerning the Connexion Betwixt the Doctrines and Miracles of Jesus Christ* (London: R. Willock, 1731). Barbeyrac's words, for he was the author of the review article, are extricated from his argument that while resurrection might (at least for now) be impossible for us to understand, this does not mean that we should regard it as impossible.]

number of voluntary actions, because, after all, they are produced by a deliberation of the will, which chuses between two inevitable evils, and determines to prefer the least to the greatest. This will become more intelligible by a few examples.

A person gives alms to a poor man, who exposes his wants and misery to him; this action is at the same time both voluntary and free. But suppose a man that travels alone and unarmed, falls into the hands of robbers, and that these miscreants menace him with instant death, unless he gives them all he has; the surrender which this traveller makes of his money in order to save his life, is indeed a voluntary action, but constrained at the same time, and void of liberty. For which reason there are some that distinguish these actions by the name of mixt,* as partaking of the voluntary and involuntary. They are voluntary, by reason the principle that produces them is in the agent itself, and the will determines to commit them as the least of two evils: but they <29> partake of the involuntary, because the will executes them contrary to its inclination, which it would never do, could it find any other expedient to clear itself of the dilemma.

Another necessary elucidation is, that we are to suppose that the evil with which we are menaced is considerable enough to make a reasonable impression upon a prudent or wise man, so far as to intimidate him; and besides that, the person who compels us has no right to restrain our liberty; insomuch that we do not lie under an obligation of bearing with any hardship or inconveniency, rather than displease him. Under these circumstances, reason would have us determine to suffer the lesser evil, supposing at least that they are both inevitable. This kind of constraint lays us under what is called a moral necessity; whereas, when we are absolutely compelled to act, without being able, in any shape whatsoever, to avoid it, this is termed a physical necessity.

It is therefore a necessary point of philosophical exactness to distinguish between voluntary and free. In fact, it is easy to comprehend, by what has been now said, that all free actions are indeed voluntary, but all voluntary actions are not free. Nevertheless, the common and vulgar

* See Puffendorf on the law of nature and nations, book i. chap. iv. § 9.

way of speaking frequently confounds those two terms, of which we ought to take particular notice, in order to avoid all ambiguity.

We give likewise the name of manners sometimes to free actions, inasmuch as the mind considers them as susceptible of rule. Hence we call morality the art which teaches the rules of conduct, and the method of conforming our actions to those rules. <30>

XIII. We shall finish what relates to the faculties of the soul by some remarks, which will help us to understand better their nature and use.

Our faculties help one another reciprocally.

1. Our faculties assist one another in their operations, and when[9] they are all united in the same subject, they act always jointly. We have already observed that the will supposes the understanding, and that the light of reason serves for a guide to liberty. Thus the understanding, the will, and liberty; the senses, the imagination, and memory; the instincts, inclinations, and passions; are like so many different springs, which concur all to produce a particular effect; and it is by this united concurrence we attain at length to the knowledge of truth, and the possession of solid good, on which our perfection and happiness depends.

XIV. 2. But in order to procure to ourselves those advantages, it is not only necessary that our faculties be well constituted in themselves, but moreover we ought to make a good use of them, and maintain the natural subordination there is between them, and the different motions which lead us towards, or divert us from, certain objects. It is not therefore sufficient to know the common and natural state of our faculties, we should likewise be acquainted with their state of perfection, and know in what their real use consists. Now truth being, as we have seen, the proper object of the understanding, the perfection of this faculty is to have a distinct knowledge of truth; at least of those important truths, which concern our duty and happi-<31>ness. For such a purpose, this faculty should be formed to a close attention, a just discernment, and solid reasoning. The understanding thus perfected, and considered as having actually the principles which enable us to know and to distinguish

Of reason and virtue.

9. "Because" is closer to the original and makes more sense.

the true and the useful, is what is properly called reason; and hence it is that we are apt to speak of reason as of a light of the mind, and as of a rule by which we ought always to be directed in our judgments and actions.

If we consider in like manner the will in its state of perfection, we shall find it consists in the force and habit of determining always right, that is, not to desire any thing but what reason dictates, and not to make use of our liberty but in order to chuse the best. This sage direction of the will is properly called Virtue, and sometimes goes by the name of Reason. And as the perfection of the soul depends on the mutual succours which the faculties, considered in their most perfect state, lend to one another; we understand likewise sometimes by reason, taken in a more vague, and more extensive sense, the soul itself, considered with all its faculties, and as making actually a good use of them. Thus the term *reason* carries with it always an idea of perfection, which is sometimes applied to the soul in general, and at other times to some of the faculties in particular.

Causes of the diversity we observe in the conduct of men.

XV. 3. The faculties, of which we are treating, are common to all mankind; but they are not found always in the same degree, neither are they determined after the same manner. Besides, they have their periods in every man; that is, their in-<32>crease, perfection, infeebling, and decay, in the same manner almost as the organs of the body. They vary likewise exceedingly in different men: one has a brighter understanding; another a quicker sensation; this man has a strong imagination; while another is swayed by violent passions. And all this is combined and diversified an infinite number of ways, according to the difference of temperaments, education, examples, and occasions that furnish an opportunity for exercising certain faculties or inclinations rather than others: for it is the exercise that strengthens them more or less. Such is the source of that prodigious variety of geniuses, tastes, and habits, which constitutes what we call the characters and manners of men; a variety which, considered in general, very far from being unserviceable, is of great use in the views of providence.

XVI. But whatever strength may be attributed to the inclinations, passions, and habits, still it is necessary to observe, that they have never enough to impel man invincibly to act contrary to reason. Reason has it always in her power to preserve her superiority and rights. She is able, with care and application, to correct vicious dispositions, to prevent and even to extirpate bad habits; to bridle the most unruly passions by sage precautions, to weaken them by degrees, and finally to destroy them intirely, or to reduce them within their proper bounds. This is sufficiently proved by the inward feeling, that every man has of the liberty with which he determines to follow this sort of impressions; proved by the secret reproaches we make to ourselves, when <33> we have been too much swayed by them; proved, in fine, by an infinite variety of examples. True it is, that there is some difficulty in surmounting these obstacles; but this is richly compensated by the glory attending so noble a victory, and by the solid advantages from thence arising.

Reason has it always in her power to remain mistress.

CHAPTER III

That man thus constituted, is a creature capable of moral direction, and accountable for his actions.

I. After having seen the nature of man, considered in respect to right, the result is, that he is a creature really susceptible of choice and direction in his conduct. For since he is capable, by means of his faculties, of knowing the nature and state of things, and of judging from this knowledge; since he is invested with the power of determining between two or several offers made to him; in fine, since, with the assistance of liberty, he is able, in certain cases, to suspend or continue his actions, as he judges proper; it evidently follows, that he is master of his own actions, and that he exercises a kind of authority and command over them, by virtue of which he can direct and turn them which way he pleases. Hence it appears how necessary it was for us to set out, as we have done, with inquiring previously into the nature and faculties of man. For how could we have <34> discovered the rules by which he is to square his conduct,

Man is capable of direction in regard to his conduct.

unless we antecedently know in what manner he acts, and what are the springs, as it were, that put him in motion?

He is accountable for his actions: they can be imputed to him.

II. Another remark, which is a consequence of the foregoing, is, that since man is the immediate author of his actions, he is accountable for them; and in justice and reason they can be imputed to him. This is a point of which we think it necessary to give here a short explication.

The term of *imputing* is borrowed of arithmetic, and signifies properly, to set a sum down to somebody's account. To impute an action therefore to a person, is to attribute it to him as to its real author, to set it down, as it were, to his account, and to make him answerable for it. Now it is evidently an essential quality of human actions, as produced and directed by the understanding and will, to be susceptible of imputation; that is, it is plain that man can be justly considered as the author and productive cause of those actions, and that for this very reason it is right to make him accountable for them, and to lay to his charge the effects that arise from thence as natural consequences. In fact, the true reason why a person cannot complain of being made answerable for an action, is that he has produced it himself knowingly and willingly. Every thing almost that is said and done in human society, supposes this principle generally received, and every body acquiesces in it from an inward conviction. <35>

Principle of imputability. We must not confound it with imputation.

III. We must therefore lay down, as an incontestable and fundamental principle of the imputability of human actions, that every voluntary action is susceptible of imputation; or, to express the same thing in other terms, that every action or omission subject to the direction of man, can be charged to the account of the person in whose power it was to do it or let it alone; and on the contrary, every action, whose existence or non-existence does not depend on our will, cannot be imputed to us. Observe here, that omissions are ranked by civilians and moralists among the number of actions; because they apprehend them as the effect of a voluntary suspension of the exercise of our faculties.

Such is the foundation of imputability, and the true reason why an action or omission is of an imputable nature. But we must take particular notice, that though an action is imputable, it does not ensue from thence only, that it merits actually to be imputed. Imputability and imputation are two things, which we should carefully distinguish. The latter supposes, besides the imputability, some moral necessity of acting or not, after a certain manner; or, which amounts to the same, some obligation that requires a thing to be done or omitted that can be really done or omitted.

Puffendorf * does not seem to have sufficiently distinguished between these two ideas. It is enough for our present purpose to point out the distinction, <36> deferring to treat of actual imputation, and to establish the principles thereof, till we have explained the nature of obligation, and shewn that man is actually obliged to conform his actions to rule.

What has been hitherto advanced, properly regards the nature of the human mind; or the internal faculties of man, as they render him capable of moral direction. But in order to complete our knowledge of human nature, we should view it likewise in its extrinsic condition, in its wants and dependancies, and in the various relations wherein it is placed; in fine,[1] in what we may call the different states of man. For it is our situation in life that decides the use we ought to make of our faculties.

CHAPTER IV

Further inquiry into what relates to human nature,
by considering the different states of man.

I. The different states of man are nothing more than the situation wherein he finds himself in regard to the beings that surround him, with the relations from thence resulting.

We shall be satisfied with taking here a cursory view of some of the principal states, and to render them distinguishable by their essential

Definition.
Division.

* See the Law of nature and nations, book i. chap. v. § 5. and the Duties of man and a citizen, book i. chap. i. § 17. [Burlamaqui's critical comments on Pufendorf are from Barbeyrac's note 1 to the paragraph in DHC I.1 §17.]

1. The original has "in a word" ("en un mot").

characteristics, without entering into an exact inquiry, which should naturally take place, when treating in particular of each state.[1] <37>

All these different states may be ranged under two general classes: some are primitive and original; others adventitious.

Primitive and original states.

II. Primitive and original states are those in which man finds himself placed by the very hand of God, independent of any human action.

1. State of man with regard to God.

Such is, in the first place, the state of man with regard to God; which is a state of absolute dependance. For let us make but never so small a use of our faculties, and enter into the study of ourselves, it will evidently appear, that it is from this first Being we hold our life, reason, and all other concomitant advantages; and that in this and every other respect we experiance daily, in the most sensible manner, the effects of the power and goodness of the Creator.

2. State of society.

III. Another primitive and original state, is that wherein men find themselves in respect to one another. They are all inhabitants of the same globe,[2] placed in a kind of vicinity to each other; have all one common nature, the same faculties, same inclinations, wants and desires. They cannot do without one another; and it is only by mutual assistance they are capable of attaining to a state of ease and tranquillity. Hence we observe a natural inclination in mankind that draws them towards each other, and establishes a commerce of services and benevolence between them, from whence results the common good of the whole, and the particular advantage of individuals. The natural state therefore of men among themselves, is a state of union and society; society being nothing more than the union <38> of several persons for their common advantage. Besides, it is evident that this must be a primitive state, because it is not the work of man, but established by divine institution. Natural society is a state of equality and liberty; a state in which all men enjoy the same prerogatives, and an intire independance on any other power

1. The two first paragraphs rephrase DHC II.1 §§1–2.
2. The original has "Terre" (earth) rather than globe. Burlamaqui returns to this theme in paragraph 5.

but God. For every man is naturally master of himself, and equally to his fellow-creatures, so long as he does not subject himself to another person's authority by a particular convention.

IV. The opposite state to that of society, is solitude; that is, the condition in which we imagine man would find himself, were he to live absolutely alone, abandoned to his own thoughts, and destitute of all commerce with those of his own species. Let us suppose a man arrived to the age of maturity, without having had the advantage of education or any correspondence at all with the rest of mankind, and consequently without any other knowledge but that which he has of himself acquired; such a man would be undoubtedly the most miserable of all animals. We should discover nothing in him but weakness, savageness, and ignorance; scarce would he be able to satisfy the wants of his body, exposed, poor wretch, to perish with hunger or cold, or by the ravenous teeth of wild beasts. What a vast difference between such a state and that of society, which by the mutual succours that men receive from one another, procures them all the knowledge, conveniency, and ease, that form the security, pleasure, and happiness of life? True it is, that all these advantages suppose that men, far from prejudicing one <39> another, live in harmony and concord, and entertain this union by mutual good offices. This is what we call a state of *peace,* whereas those who endeavour to do harm, and those also who find themselves obliged to guard against it, are in a state of war; a state of violence, diametrically opposite to that of society.[3]

3. State of solitude.
4. Peace: War.

V. Let us observe, in the next place, that man finds himself naturally attached to the earth, from whose bosom he draws whatever is necessary for the preservation and conveniences of life. This situation produces another primitive state of man, which is likewise deserving of our attention.

State of man with regard to the goods of the earth.

3. This paragraph follows Pufendorf in DHC II.1 §9. Note that Burlamaqui does not voice any of the objections that Barbeyrac raised against this Hobbesian analysis of the state of nature in DNG II.2 §2, notes 7–17.

Such in effect is the natural constitution of the human body, that it cannot subsist intirely of itself, and by the sole force of its temperament. Man, at all ages, stands in need of several external succours for his nourishment, as well as for repairing his strength, and keeping his faculties in proper order. For this reason our Creator has sown plentifully around us such things as are necessary for our wants, and has implanted in us at the same time the instincts and qualifications proper for applying these things to our advantage. The natural state therefore of man considered in this light, and in respect to the goods of the earth, is a state of indigence and incessant wants, against which he would be incapable to provide in a suitable manner, were he not to exercise his industry by constant labour. Such are the principal of those states that are called primitive and original. <40>

Adventitious states.
1. Family.
2. Marriage.

VI. But man being naturally a free agent, he is capable of making great modifications in his primitive state, and of giving by a variety of establishments a new face to human life. Hence those adventitious states are formed, which are properly the work of man, wherein he finds himself placed by his own act, and in consequence of establishments, whereof he himself is the author. Let us take a cursory view of the principal of these states.

The first that presents itself to us, is the state of families. This is the most natural and most ancient of all societies, and the very foundation of that which is called national; for a people or nation is only an assemblage or composition of several families.

Families begin by marriage; and it is nature itself that invites men to this union. Hence children arise, who by perpetuating the several families, prevent the extinction of human societies, and repair the breaches made every day by death.[4]

The family state is productive of various relations; as those of hus-

4. This paragraph is a brief summary of DHC II.2 §§1–2. Burlamaqui had explained his views on marriage more extensively in a letter to Thomas Needham. The letter was published in 1761 in Jacob Vernet's *Choix littéraire* and was later added as a *supplément* to the 1784 Lausanne edition of the *Principes du droit naturel et politique*.

band, wife, father, mother, children, brothers, sisters, and all the other degrees of kindred, which are the first tie of human society.

VII. Man considered in his birth is weakness and impotency itself, in regard as well to the body, as to the soul. It is even remarkable, that the state of weakness and infancy lasts longer in man than in any other animal. He is beset and pressed on all sides by a thousand wants, and destitute of knowledge, as well as strength, finds himself in an absolute incapacity of relieving them: he is therefore under a par-<41>ticular necessity of recurring to external assistance. Providence for this reason has inspired parents with that instinct or natural tenderness, which prompts them so eagerly to delight in the most troublesome cares, for the preservation and good of those whom they have brought into the world. It is likewise in consequence of this state of weakness and ignorance in which children are born, that they are naturally subject to their parents; whom nature has invested with all the authority and power necessary for governing those, whose advantage they are to study and procure.[5]

> 3. Weakness of man at his birth.
> 4. Natural dependance of children on their parents.

VIII. The property of goods is another very important establishment, which produces a new adventitious state. It modifies the right which all men had originally to earthly goods; and distinguishing carefully what belongs to individuals, ensures the quiet and peaceable enjoyment of what they possess; by which means it contributes to the maintenance of peace and harmony among mankind. But since all men had originally a right to a common use of whatever the earth produces for their several wants; it is evident therefore, that if this natural power is actually restrained and limited in divers respects, this must necessarily arise from some human act; and consequently the state of property, which is the cause of those limitations, ought to be ranked among the adventitious states.

> The state of property.

5. While Pufendorf had insisted on tacit consent on the part of the infant, Burlamaqui follows Barbeyrac's view as expressed in DHC II.3 §2 note 1 and DNG VI.2 §4 notes 1–2.

Civil state and government.

IX. But among all the states established by the act of man, there is none more considerable than the civil state, or that of civil society and government. The <42> essential character of this society, which distinguishes it from the forementioned society of *nature,* is the subordination to a supreme authority, exclusive of equality and independance. Mankind were originally divided into families only, and not into nations. Those families lived under the paternal government of the person who was their chief, as their father or grandfather. But when they came afterwards to increase and unite for their common defence, they composed a national body, governed by the will of him, or of those on whom they had conferred the authority. This is the origin of what we call civil government, and of the distinction of sovereign and subjects.

The civil state and property of goods give rise to several other adventitious states.

X. The civil state and property of goods produced several other establishments, which form the beauty and ornament of society, and from whence so many adventitious states arise: such as the different posts or offices of those who have any share in the government; as magistrates, judges, state-officers, ministers of religion, physicians, &c. To which may be added the polite arts, trades, agriculture, navigation, commerce, with their several dependancies, whereby human life is so agreeably and advantageously diversified.

True idea of the natural state of man.

XI. Such are the principal states produced by human consent. And yet, as these different modifications of the primitive state of man are the effect of his natural liberty, the new relations and different states from thence arising, may be very well considered as so many natural states; provided however that the use which men make of their liberty, in this re-<43>spect, has nothing in it unconformable to their natural constitution, that is, to reason and the state of society.

It is therefore proper to observe, in relation to this subject, that when we speak of the natural state of man, we are to understand not only that natural and primitive state, in which he is placed, as it were, by the hands of nature herself; but moreover all those into which man enters by his own act and agreement, and that are conformable in the main to his nature, and contain nothing but what is agreeable to his constitution and the end for which he was formed. For since man himself, as a free and intelligent being, is able to see and know his situation, as also to discover his ultimate end, and in consequence thereof to take the right measures to attain it; it is properly in this light we should consider his natural state, to form thereof a just idea. That is, the natural state of man is, generally speaking, that which is conformable to his nature, constitution, and reason, as well as to the good use of his faculties, considered in their full maturity and perfection. We shall be particularly attentive to this remark, the importance of which will appear more sensibly by the application and use that may be made thereof on several occasions.

XII. Let us not forget to observe likewise, that there is this difference between the primitive and adventitious states, that the former being annexed, as it were, to the nature and constitution of man, such as he has received them from God, are, for this very reason, common to all mankind. The same cannot be said of the adventitious states; which, supposing an hu-<44>man act or agreement, cannot of themselves be indifferently suitable to all men, but to those only that contrived and procured them.

Difference between original and adventitious states.

Let us add, in fine, that several of those states may be found combined and united in the same person, provided they have nothing incompatible in their nature. Thus the same person may be father of a family, judge, minister of state, &c. all at the same time.

Such are the ideas we are to form of the nature and different states of man; and it is of all these parts united and compacted together, that the intire system of humanity is formed. These are like so many wheels of the same machine, which combined and managed by a dexterous hand, conspire all to the same end; and, on the contrary, unskilfully directed, embarrass and destroy each other. But how man, in fine, is enabled to conduct himself in this prudent manner, and what rule he is to observe in order to attain this happy end, is what we have still to inquire, and forms the subject of the following chapters.

CHAPTER V

That man ought to square his conduct by rule;
the method of finding out this rule;
and the foundations of right in general.

Definition
of a rule.

I. Let us begin with an explication of the terms. A rule, in its proper signification, is an instrument, by means of which we draw the shortest <45> line from one point to another, which for this very reason is called a straight line.[1]

In a figurative and moral sense, a rule imports nothing else, but a principle, or maxim, which furnishes man with a sure and concise method of attaining to the end he proposes.

It is not con-
venient, that
man should
live without
a rule.

II. The first thing we are to inquire in regard to this subject* is, whether it is really agreeable to the nature of man to submit his actions to a fixt and invariable rule; or whether, on the contrary, he is allowed to abandon himself indifferently to all the motions of his will, and thus to enjoy, without either limit or impediment, the extreme facility with which this faculty turns itself on all sides, in consequence of its natural flexibility.

The reflexions we have given in the preceding chapters, are of themselves, and independent of any other argument, a sufficient and convincing proof, that the nature and constitution of man requires the establishment of some rule. Every thing in nature has its destination and end; and consequently, each creature is conducted to its end by a proper principle of direction. Man, who holds a considerable rank among the beings that surround him, participates undoubtedly of this fixt and universal order. And whether we consider him in himself as an intelligent and rational being; or view him as a member of society; or whether, in fine, we regard him as the handy-work of God, and deriving from this first being his faculties, state, and existence; all these circumstances <46>

---

* See Puffendorf, Law of nature and nations, book ii. chap. i.

1. Burlamaqui exploits the ambiguity of the word "droit," which can mean either upright or right.

evidently indicate an end, a destination, and consequently imply the necessity of a rule. Had man been created to live at random without any fixt and determinate view, without knowing whither he is to direct his course, or what road he ought to take; it is evident that his noblest faculties would be of no manner of use to him. Wherefore waving all disquisitions concerning the necessity of a rule, let us endeavour rather to discover what this rule is, which alone, by enlightening the understanding, and directing our actions to an end worthy of him, is capable of forming the order and beauty of human life.

III. When we speak of a rule in relation to human actions, two things are manifestly supposed: the first, that human conduct is susceptible of direction, as we have already proved; the second, that man in all his steps and actions proposes to himself a scope or end which he is desirous to attain. *A rule supposes an end, an aim.*

IV. Now let man reflect but never so little on himself, he will soon perceive that every thing he does is with a view of happiness, and that this is the ultimate end he proposes in all his actions, or the last term to which he reduces them. This is a first truth, of which we have a continual conviction from our own internal sense. Such, in effect, is the nature of man, that he necessarily loves himself, that he seeks in every thing and every where his own advantage, and can never be diverted from this pursuit. We naturally desire, and necessarily wish for good. This desire anticipates all our reflexions, and is not in our own election; it predominates in us, and becomes <47> the primum mobile of all our determinations; our hearts being never inclined towards any particular good, but by the natural impression which determines us to good in general. It is not in our power to change this bent of the will, which the Creator himself has implanted in us.[2] *The ultimate end of man is happiness.*

2. Burlamaqui's account differs from those of Pufendorf and Barbeyrac through its insistence on how all moral obligation stems from the human being's ineradicable orientation toward felicity or happiness. See the next two footnotes.

It is the system of providence.

V. This system of providence extends to all beings endowed with sense and knowledge. Even animals themselves have a like instinct; for they all love themselves, endeavouring at self-preservation by all sorts of means, eagerly pursuing whatever seems good or useful to them, and turning, on the contrary, from whatever appears prejudicial or bad. The same propensity shews itself in man, not only as an instinct, but more-over as a rational inclination approved and strengthened by reflexion. Hence whatsoever presents itself to us as an object proper to promote our happiness, must of necessity please us; and every thing that appears opposite to our felicity, becomes of course the object of our aversion. The more we study man, the more we are convinced that here, in reality, lies the source of all our tastes; here the grand spring which sets us in motion.

The desire of happiness is essential to man, and inseparable from reason.

VI. And indeed, if it be natural to every intelligent and rational being, to act always with a fixt view and determinate end; it is no less evident, that this view or end must be ultimately reduced to himself, and con-sequently to his own advantage and happiness. The desire therefore of happiness is as essential to a man, and as inseparable from his nature, <48> as reason itself; for reason, as the very etymology of the word im-plies, is nothing more than a calculation and account. To reason, is to calculate, and to draw up an account, after balancing every thing, in order to see on which side the advantage lies. It would therefore imply a contradiction, to suppose a rational being, that could absolutely forego its interest, or be indifferent with regard to its own felicity.[3]

Self-love is a principle that has nothing vicious in itself.

VII. We must therefore take care not to consider self-love, and that sense or inclination which fixes us so strongly to our happiness, as a principle naturally vicious, and the fruit of human depravation. This would be accusing the author of our existence, and converting his noblest gifts

---

3. Burlamaqui's insistence that a rational being could not be supposed to disregard his own happiness is directed against Barbeyrac's account of moral obligation. See, for example, "The Judgment of an Anonymous Writer," in Pufendorf, *The Whole Duty of Man, According to the Law of Nature* (Indianapolis: Liberty Fund, 2003), p. 293. Burlamaqui mentions this passage in paragraph 12 of the next chapter.

into poison. Whatever comes from a being supremely perfect, is in itself good; and were we to condemn the sense or inclination of self-love as bad in itself, under a pretence that by a misconstruction and wrong use thereof it is the source of an infinite number of disorders, we should for the very same motives be obliged to condemn reason; because it is from the abuse of this faculty that the grossest errors and most extravagant irregularities of men proceed.[4]

It may appear surprizing to some that we should have stopt here, to investigate and explain the truth of a principle, which one would imagine is obvious to every body, to the learned as well as the vulgar. And yet it was absolutely necessary; because this is a truth of the very last importance, which gives us the key, as it were, of the human system. It is true, that all ethic writers agree that man is made for happiness, and naturally desires it (for how is it <49> possible not to hear the voice of nature,[5] which rises from the very bottom of the heart?). But a great many, after acknowledging this principle, seem to lose sight of it, and not attending to the consequences that flow from thence, they erect their systems on different, and sometimes quite opposite foundations.

VIII. But if it be true that man does nothing but with a view of happiness, it is no less certain that reason is the only way he has to attain it.

In order to establish this second proposition or truth, we have only to attend to the very idea of happiness, and to the notion we have of good and evil. Happiness is that internal satisfaction of the soul which arises from the possession of good; good is whatever is agreeable to man for his preservation, perfection, entertainment, and pleasure. Evil is the opposite of good.

Man incessantly experiences, that there are some things convenient, and others inconvenient to him; that the former are not all equally con-

Man cannot attain to happiness but by the help of reason.

---

4. A more optimistic approach to self-love was a central theme in eighteenth-century Genevan Calvinism; see, for example, Helena Rosenblatt, *Rousseau and Geneva: From the First Discourse to the Social Contract, 1749–1762* (Cambridge: Cambridge University Press, 1997), pp. 11–17, 66–67.

5. "Ce cri de la nature" in the original.

venient, but some more than others; in fine, that this conveniency depends, for the most part, on the use he knows how to make of things, and that the same thing which may suit him, using it after a certain manner and measure, becomes unsuitable when this use exceeds its limits. It is only therefore by investigating the nature of things, as also the relations they have between themselves and with us, that we are capable of discovering their fitness or disagreement with our felicity, of discerning good from evil, of ranging every thing in its proper order, of setting a right <50> value upon each, and of regulating consequently our researches and desires.

But is there any other method of acquiring this discernment, but by forming just ideas of things and their relations, and by deducing from these first ideas the consequences that flow from thence by exact and close argumentations? Now it is reason alone that directs all these operations. Yet this is not all: for as in order to arrive at happiness, it is not sufficient to form just ideas of the nature and state of things, but it is also necessary that the will should be directed by those ideas and judgments in the series of our conduct; so it is certain, that nothing but reason can communicate and support in man the necessary strength for making a right use of liberty, and for determining in all cases according to the light of his understanding, in spite of all the impressions and motions that may lead him to a contrary pursuit.

Reason is therefore the primitive rule of man.

IX. Reason is therefore the only means, in every respect, that man has left to attain to happiness, and the principal end for which he has received it. All the faculties of the soul, its instincts, inclinations, and even the passions, are relative to this end; and consequently it is this same reason that is capable of pointing out the true rule of human actions, or, if you will, she herself is this primitive rule. In fact, were it not for this faithful guide, man would lead a random life, ignorant even of what regards himself, unacquainted with his own origin and destination, and with the use he ought to make of whatever surrounds him; stumbling, like a blind man, at every <51> step; lost, in fine, and bewildered in an inextricable labyrinth.

X. Thus we are conducted naturally to the first idea of the word *Right*,   What is Right
which in its most general sense, and that to which all the particular sig-   in general?
nifications bear some relation, is nothing else but whatever reason certainly acknowledges as a sure and concise means of attaining happiness,
and approves as such.

This definition is the result of the principles hitherto established. In
order to be convinced of its exactness, we have only to draw these principles together, and unite them under one prospect. In fact, since right
(*droit*) in its primary notion signifies whatever directs, or is well directed;
since direction supposes a scope and an end, to which we are desirous
of attaining; since the ultimate end of man is happiness; and, in fine,
since he cannot attain to happiness but by the help of reason; does it
not evidently follow, that Right in general is whatever reason approves
as a sure and concise means of acquiring happiness? It is likewise in consequence of these principles, that reason giving its approbation to itself,
when it happens to be properly cultivated, and arrived to that state of
perfection in which it knows how to use all its discernment, bears, by
way of preference or excellence, the appellation of right reason, as being
the first and surest means of direction, whereby man is enabled to acquire felicity.

That we may not forget any thing in the analysis of these first ideas,
it is proper to observe here, that the Latins express what we call *Right* by
the <52> word *jus,* which properly signifies an order or precept.* These
different denominations undoubtedly proceed from this, that reason
seems to command with authority whatever it avows to be a right and
sure means of promoting our felicity. And as we have only to seek for
what is right, in order to know what reason commands us, hence the
natural connexion of these two ideas arose in respect to the rules of right
reason. In a word, of two ideas naturally connected, the Latins have
followed one, and we the other.

---

* *Jus a jubendo: Jura* enim veteres *Jusa* vel *Jussa* vocabant. Festus: *Jusa, Jura.*

CHAPTER VI

General rules of conduct prescribed by reason.
Of the nature and first foundations of obligation.

Reason gives
us several rules
of conduct.

I. It is already a great point gained, to have discovered the primitive rule of human actions, and to know this faithful guide, which is to direct the steps of man, and whose directions and counsels he may follow with an intire confidence. But let us not stop here; and since experience informs us that we are frequently mistaken in our judgments concerning good and evil, and that these erroneous judgments throw us into most dangerous irregularities, let us consult therefore our <53> guide, and learn which are the characters of real good and evil, in order to know in what true felicity consists, and what road we are to take in order to attain it.

First rule.
To make a
right distinc-
tion of good
and evil.

II. Though the general notion of good and evil be fixed in itself, and invariable, still there are various sorts of particular goods and evils, or of things that pass for such in the minds of men.

1. The first counsel therefore that reason gives us, is to examine well into the nature of good and evil, and to observe carefully their several differences, in order to set upon each thing its proper value.[1]

This distinction is easily made. A very slight attention to what we continually experience, informs us, that man being composed of body and soul, there are consequently two sorts of goods and evils, spiritual and corporeal. The first are those that proceed only from our thoughts; the second arise from the impressions of external objects on our senses. Thus, the sensible pleasure resulting from the discovery of an important truth; or the self-approbation arising from a consciousness of having discharged our duty, &c. are goods purely spiritual: as the chagrin of a geometrician for being unable to find out a demonstration; or the remorse a person feels for having committed a bad action, &c. are mere spiritual pains. With regard to corporeal goods and evils, they are sufficiently known; on one side, they are health, strength, beauty; on the

---

1. The original has a "prix" or "price."

other, sickness, weakness, pain, &c. These two sorts of goods and evils are interesting to man, and cannot be reckoned indifferent, by reason that man being com-<54>posed of body and soul, it is plain his perfection and happiness depend on the good state of these two parts.

2. We likewise observe, that appearances frequently deceive us, and what at first sight carries with it the face of good, proves to be a real evil, whilst an apparent evil oftentimes conceals an extraordinary good. We should therefore make a distinction between real goods and evils, and those that are false and apparent. Or, which amounts to pretty near the same thing, there is sometimes a pure good and a pure evil, and sometimes there is a mixture of both, which does not obstruct our discerning what part it is that prevails, and whether the good or evil be predominant.

3. A third difference regards their duration. In this respect goods and evils have not all the same nature; some are solid and durable, others transitory and inconstant. Whereto we may add, that there are goods and evils of which we are masters, as it were, and which depend in such a manner on ourselves, that we are able to fix the one, in order to have a constant enjoyment of them, and to shun or get rid of the others. But they are not all of this kind; some goods there are that escape our most eager pursuits, whilst some evils overtake us, notwithstanding our most sollicitous efforts to avoid them.

4. There are at present goods and evils, which we actually feel; and future goods and evils, which are the objects of our hopes or fears.

5. There are particular goods and evils, which affect only some individuals; and others that are <55> common and universal, of which all the members of the society partake. The good of the whole is the real good; that of one of the parts, opposite to the good of the whole, is only an apparent good, and consequently a real evil.

6. From all these remarks we may in fine conclude, that goods and evils not being all of the same species, there are consequently some differences amongst them, and that compared together, we find there are some goods more excellent than others, and evils more or less incommodious. It happens likewise, that a good compared with an evil, may be either equal or greater, or lesser; from whence several differences or gradations arise, that are worthy of special notice.

These particulars are sufficient to shew the utility of the principal rule we have given, and how essential it is to our happiness to make a just distinction of goods and evils. But this is not the only counsel that reason gives us, we are going to point out some others that are not of less importance.

Second rule. True happiness cannot consist in things that are inconsistent with the nature and state of man. III. 2. True happiness cannot consist in things that are inconsistent with the nature and state of man. This is another principle, which naturally flows from the very notion of good and evil. For whatsoever is inconsistent with the nature of a being, tends for this very reason to degrade or destroy it, to corrupt or alter its constitution; which being directly opposite to the preservation, perfection, and good of this being, subverts the foundation of its felicity. Wherefore reason being the noblest part of man, and constituting his prin-<56>cipal essence, whatever is inconsistent with reason, cannot form his happiness. To which I add, that whatever is incompatible with the state of man, cannot contribute to his felicity; and this is a point as clear as evidence can make it. Every being, that by its constitution has essential relations to other beings, which it cannot shake off, ought not to be considered merely as to itself, but as constituting a part of the whole to which it is related. And it is sufficiently manifest, that it is on its situation in regard to the beings that surround it, and on the relations of agreement or opposition it has with them, that its good or bad state, its happiness or misery, must in great measure depend.

Third rule. To compare the present and the future together. IV. 3. In order to procure for ourselves a solid happiness, it is not sufficient to be attentive to the present good and evil, we must likewise examine their natural consequences; to the end, that comparing the present with the future, and balancing one with the other, we must know beforehand what may be the natural result.

Fourth rule. 4. It is therefore contrary to reason, to pursue a good that must certainly be attended with a more considerable evil.*

* See the third note of Mons. Barbeyrac on the duties of man and a citizen, book i. chap. i. § 11.

5. But on the contrary, nothing is more reasonable than to resolve to bear with an evil, from whence a greater good must certainly arise.

The truth and importance of these maxims are self-obvious. Good and evil being two opposites, <57> the effect of one destroys that of the other; that is to say, the possession of a good, attended with a greater evil, renders us really unhappy; and on the contrary, a slight evil, which procures us a more considerable good, does not hinder us from being happy. Wherefore, every thing well considered, the first ought to be avoided as a real evil, and the second should be courted as a real good.

The nature of human things requires us to be attentive to these principles. Were each of our actions restrained in such a manner, and limited within itself, as not to be attended with any consequence, we should not be so often mistaken in our choice, but should be almost sure of grasping the good. But informed as we are by experience, that things have frequently very different effects from what they seemed to promise, insomuch that the most pleasing objects are attended with bitter consequences, and on the contrary a real and solid good is purchased with labour and pains, prudence does not allow us to fix our whole attention on the present. We should extend our views to futurity, and equally weigh and consider the one and the other, in order to pass a solid judgment on them, a judgment sufficient to fix properly our resolutions.

V. 6. For the same reason, we ought to prefer a greater to a lesser good; we ought always to aspire to the noblest goods that suit us, and proportion our desires and pursuits to the nature and merit of each good. This rule is so evident, that it would be losing time to pretend to prove it. <58>

VI. 7. It is not necessary to have an intire certainty in regard to considerable goods and evils: Mere possibility, and much more so, probability, are sufficient to induce a reasonable person to deprive himself of some trifling good, and even to suffer some slight evil, with a design of acquiring a far greater good, and avoiding a more troublesome evil.

This rule is a consequence of the foregoing ones; and we may affirm, that the ordinary conduct of men shews they are sensibly convinced of the prudence and necessity thereof. In effect, what is the aim of all this tumult of business into which they hurry themselves? To what end and purpose are all the labours they undertake, all the pains and fatigues they endure, all the perils to which they constantly expose themselves? Their intent is to acquire some advantages which they imagine they do not purchase too dear; though these advantages are neither present, nor so certain, as the sacrifices they must make in order to obtain them.

This is a very rational manner of acting. Reason requires, that in default of certainty we should take up with probability as the rule of our judgment and determination; for probability in that case is the only light and guide we have. And unless it is more eligible to wander in uncertainty, than to follow a guide; unless we are of opinion that our lamp ought to be extinguished when we are deprived of the light of the sun; it is reasonable to be directed by probability, when we are incapable to come at evidence. It is easier to attain our aim by the help <59> of a faint or glimmering light, than by continuing in darkness.*

* In the ordinary course of life, we are generally obliged to be determined by probability, for it is not always in our power to attain to a complete evidence. Seneca the philosopher has beautifully established and explained this maxim: *"Huic respondebimus, nunquam expectare nos certissimam rerum comprehensionem: quoniam in arduo est veri exploratio: sed eâ ire, qua ducit veri similitudo.* OMNE HAC VIA PROCEDIT OFFICIUM. *Sic serimus, sic navigamus, sic militamus, sic uxores ducimus, sic liberos tollimus; quum omnium horum incertus sit eventus. Ad ea accedimus, de quibus bene sperandum esse credimus. Quis enim polliceatur serenti proventum, naviganti portum, militanti victoriam, marito pudicam uxorem, patri pios liberos? Sequimur quâ ratio, non qua veritas trahit. Exspecta, ut nisi bene cessura non facias, & nisi comperta veritate nihil moveris: relicto omni actu, vita consistit. Dum verisimilia me in hoc aut illud impellant, non verebor beneficium dare ei, quem verisimile erit gratum esse."* De Benefic. lib. 4. c. 33. ["To this objector we shall answer, that we never should wait for absolute knowledge of the whole case, since the discovery of truth is an arduous task, but should proceed in the direction in which truth appeared to direct us. All our actions proceed in this direction: it is thus that we sow seed, that we sail upon the sea, that we serve in the army, marry, and bring up children. The result of all these actions is uncertain, so we take that course from which we believe that good results may be hoped for. Who can guarantee a harvest to the sower, a harbour to the sailor, victory to the soldier, a modest wife to the husband, dutiful children to the father? We proceed in the way in which reason, not absolute truth, directs us. Wait, do nothing that will not turn out well, form no opinion until you have searched out the truth, and your life will pass in absolute inaction. Since it is only the appearance of truth, not truth

VII. 8. We should be sollicitous to acquire a taste for true goods, inso- much that goods of an excellent nature, and acknowledged as such, should excite our desires, and induce us to make all the efforts necessary for getting them into our possession.

Eighth rule. To have a relish for true goods.

This last rule is a natural consequence of the others, ascertaining their execution and effects. It is not sufficient to have enlightened the mind in respect to the nature of these goods and evils that are capable of ren- dering us really happy or unhappy; we should likewise give activity and efficacy to these principles, by forming the will so as to determine itself by taste and habit, pursuant to the counsels of enlightened reason. And let no one think it impossible to change <60> our inclinations, or to reform our tastes. It is with the taste of the mind, as with that of the palate. Experience shews, that we may alter both, so as to find pleasure at length in things that before were disagreeable to us. We begin to do a thing with pain, and by an effort of reason; afterwards we familiarise ourselves to it by degrees; then a frequency of acts renders it easier to us, the repugnance ceases, we view the thing in a different light from what we did before; and use at length makes us love a thing that before was the object of our aversion. Such is the power of habit: it makes us in- sensibly feel so much ease and satisfaction in what we are acustomed to, that we find it difficult afterwards to abstain from it.

VIII. These are the principal counsels we receive from reason. They are in some measure[2] a system of maxims, which drawn from the nature of things, and particularly from the nature and state of man, acquaint us with what is essentially suitable to him, and include the most necessary rules for his perfection and happiness.

Our mind acquiesces naturally in these maxims; and they ought to influence our conduct.

These general principles are of such a nature, as to force, as it were, our assent; insomuch that a clear and cool understanding, disengaged

---

itself, which leads me hither or thither, I shall confer benefits upon the man who apparently will be grateful." Seneca, *On Benefits,* trans. Aubrey Stewart, Project Gu- tenberg etext no. 3794 (Oxford, Miss.: Project Gutenberg Literary Archive Foun- dation, 2003), http://www.gutenberg.org/etext/3794.

2. The original has an unqualified "tout autant."

from the prejudice and tumult of passions, cannot help acknowledging their truth and prudence. Every one sees how useful it would be to man to have these principles present always in his mind, that by the application and use of them in particular cases, they may insensibly become the uniform and constant rule of his inclinations and conduct. <61>

Maxims, in fact, like these are not mere speculations: they should naturally influence our morals, and be of service to us in practical life. For to what purpose would it be to listen to the advice of reason, unless we intended to follow it? Of what signification are those rules of conduct, which manifestly appear to us good and useful, if we refuse to conform to them? We ourselves are sensible that this light was given us to regulate our steps and motions. If we deviate from these maxims, we inwardly disapprove and condemn ourselves, as we are apt to condemn any other person in a similar case. But if we happen to conform to these maxims, it is a subject of internal satisfaction, and we commend ourselves, as we commend others who have acted after this manner. These sentiments are so very natural, that it is not in our power to think otherwise. We are forced to respect these principles, as a rule agreeable to our nature, and on which our felicity depends.

Of obligation generally considered. IX. This agreeableness sufficiently known implies a necessity of squaring our conduct by it. When we mention necessity, it is plain we do not mean a physical but moral necessity, consisting in the impression made on us by some particular motives, which determine us to act after a certain manner, and do not permit us to act rationally the opposite way.

Finding ourselves in these circumstances, we say we are under an obligation of doing or omitting a certain thing; that is, we are determined to it by solid reasons, and engaged by cogent motives, which, like so many ties, draw our will to that side. It is in this sense a person says he is obliged. For whether <62> we are determined by popular opinion, or whether we are directed by civilians and ethic writers, we find that the one and the other make obligation properly consist in a reason, which being well understood and approved, determines us absolutely to act after a certain manner preferable to another. From whence it follows, that the whole force of this obligation depends on the judgment, by which we approve or condemn a particular manner of acting. For to approve, is acknowledging we ought to do a thing; and to condemn, is owning we ought not to do it. Now *ought* and to *be obliged* are synonymous terms.

We have already hinted at the natural analogy between the proper and literal sense of the word *obliged,* and the figurative signification of this same term. Obligation properly denotes a tie;* a man *obliged,* is therefore a person who is *tied.* And as a man bound with cords or chains, cannot move or act with liberty, so it is very near the same case with a person who is *obliged;* with this difference, that in the first case, it is an external and physical impediment which prevents the effect of one's natural strength; but in the second it is only a moral tie, that is, the subjection of liberty is produced by reason, which being the primitive rule of man and his faculties, directs and necessarily modifies his operations in a manner suitable to the end it proposed.

We may therefore define obligation, considered in general and in its first origin, a restriction of natural liberty, produced by reason; inasmuch as the counsels which reason gives us, are so many motives, that determine man to act after a certain manner preferable to another. <63>

X. Such is the nature of primitive and original obligation. From thence it follows, that this obligation may be more or less strong, more or less rigorous; according as the reasons that establish it have more or less weight, and consequently as the motives from thence resulting have more or less impression on the will. For manifest it is, that the more these motives are cogent and efficacious, the more the necessity of conforming our actions to them becomes strong and indispensable.

Obligation may be more or less strong.

XI. I am not ignorant, that this explication of the nature and origin of obligation is far from being adopted by all civilians and ethic writers. Some pretend, †*that the natural fitness or unfitness which we acknowledge in certain actions, is the true and original foundation of all obligation; that*

Dr. Clark's opinion on the nature and origin of obligation.

---

* *Obligatio* a *ligando.*
† See Dr. Clark on the evidence of natural and revealed religion.

*virtue has an intrinsic beauty which renders it amiable of itself, and that
vice on the contrary is attended with an intrinsic deformity, which ought to
make us detest it, and this antecedent to and independent of the good and
evil, of the rewards and punishments which may arise from the practice of
either.*

But this opinion, methinks, can be supported no farther than as it is
reduced to that which we have just now explained. For to say that virtue
has of itself a natural beauty, which renders it worthy of our love, and
that vice, on the contrary, merits our aversion; is not this acknowledging,
in fact, that we have *reason* to prefer one to the other? Now whatever
this reason be, it certainly can never become <64> a motive capable of
determining the will, but inasmuch as it presents to us some good to
acquire, or tends to make us avoid some evil; in short, only as it is able
to contribute to our satisfaction, and to place us in a state of tranquillity
and happiness. Thus it is ordained by the very constitution of man, and
the nature of human will. For as good, in general, is the object of the
will; the only motive capable of setting it in motion, or of determining
it to one side preferable to another, is the hope of obtaining this good.
To abstract therefore from all interest in respect to man, is depriving him
of all motive of acting, that is, reducing him to a state of inaction and
indifference. Besides, what idea should we be able to form of the agreeableness or disagreeableness of human actions, of their beauty or turpitude, of their proportion or irregularity, were not all this referred to
man himself, and to what his destination, his perfection, his welfare, and,
in short, his true felicity requires?

**Monsieur
Barbeyrac's
opinion
concerning
this subject.** XII. Most civilians are of a different opinion from that of Dr. Clark.
"*They establish as a principle of obligation, properly so called, the will
of a superior being, on whom dependance is acknowledged. They pretend there is nothing but this will, or the orders of a being of this kind,
that can bridle our liberty, or prescribe particular rules to our actions.

---

* See the judgment of an anonymous writer, &c. § 15. This is a small work of Mr.
Leibnitz, on which Mr. Barbeyrac has made some remarks, and which is inserted in
the fifth edition of his translation of the duties of man and a citizen.

They add, that neither the relations of proportion nor disagreement which we acknow-<65>ledge in the things themselves, nor the approbation they receive from reason, lay us under an indispensable necessity of following those ideas, as the rules of our conduct. That our reason being in reality nothing else but ourselves, no body, properly speaking, can lay himself under an obligation. From whence they conclude, that the maxims of reason, considered in themselves, and independent of the will of a superior, have nothing obligatory in their nature."

This manner of explaining the nature, and laying the foundation of obligation, appears to me insufficient, because it does not ascend to the original source, and real principles. True it is, that the will of a superior obliges those who are his dependants; yet this will cannot have such an effect, but inasmuch as it meets with the approbation of our reason. For this purpose, it is not only necessary that the superior's will should contain nothing in itself opposite to the nature of man; but moreover it ought to be proportioned in such a manner to his constitution and ultimate end, that we cannot help acknowledging it as the rule of our actions; insomuch that there is no neglecting it without falling into a dangerous error; and, on the contrary, the only means of attaining our end is to be directed by it. Otherwise, it is inconceivable how man can voluntarily submit to the orders of a superior, or determine willingly to obey him. Own indeed I must, that, according to the language of civilians, the idea of a superior who commands, must intervene to establish an obligation, such as is commonly considered. But unless we trace things higher, by grounding even the authority of this <66> superior on the approbation he receives from reason, it will produce only an external constraint, very different from obligation, which hath of itself a power of penetrating the will, and moving it by an inward sense; insomuch that man is of his own accord, and without any restraint or violence, inclined to obey.[3]

3. Compare with DNG I.6 §5 and with DHC I.2 §5 note 2.

Two sorts of obligations; internal and external.

XIII. From all these remarks we may conclude, that the differences between the principal systems concerning the nature and origin of obligation, are not so great as they appear at first sight. Were we to make a closer inquiry into these opinions, by ascending to their primitive sources, we should find that these different ideas, reduced to their exact value, far from being opposite, agree very well together, and ought even to concur, in order to form a system connected properly with all its essential parts, in relation to the nature and state of man. This is what we intend more particularly to perform hereafter.* It is proper at present to observe, that there are two sorts of obligations, one internal, and the other external. By internal obligation, I understand that which is produced only by our own reason, considered as the primitive rule of conduct, and in consequence of the good or evil the action in itself contains. By external obligation, we mean that which arises from the will of a being, on whom we allow ourselves dependent, and who commands or prohibits some particular things, under a commination of punishment. Whereto we must add, that these two obligations, far from being opposite to each other, have, on the contrary, a perfect agreement. For as the external obligation <67> is capable of giving a new force to the internal, so the whole force of the external obligation ultimately depends on the internal; and it is from the agreement and concurrence of these two obligations that the highest degree of moral necessity arises, as also[4] the strongest tie, or the properest motive to make impression on man, in order to determine him to pursue steadily and never to deviate from some fixt rules of conduct; in a word, by this it is that the most perfect obligation is formed.

* See the second part, chap. vii.

4. The translator adds this "as also," which obscures Burlamaqui's meaning, that full moral obligation is the strongest tie, or "the properest motive to make an impression on man."

CHAPTER VII

Of right considered as a faculty, and of the obligation thereto corresponding.

I. Besides the general idea of right, such as has been now explained, considering it as the primitive rule of human actions; this term is taken in several particular significations, which we must here point out.

But, previous to every thing else, we should not forget the primitive and general notion we have given of right. For since it is from this notion, as from its principle, that the subject of this and the following chapters is deduced; if our reasonings are exact in themselves, and have a necessary connexion with the principle, this will furnish us with a new argument in its favour. But if, unexpectedly, it should turn out otherwise, we shall have at least the advantage of detecting the error in its very source, and of being better able to correct it. Such is the effect of a just method: we are convinced that a general idea is exact, <68> when the particular ideas are reducible to it as different branches to their trunk.

II. In the first place, Right is frequently taken for a personal quality, for a power of acting or faculty. It is thus we say, that every man has a right to attend to his own preservation; that a parent has a right to bring up his children; that a sovereign has a right to levy troops for the defence of the state, &c.

In this sense we must define Right, a power that man hath to make use of his liberty and natural strength in a particular manner, either in regard to himself, or in respect to other men, so far as this exercise of his strength and liberty is approved by reason.

Thus, when we say that a father has a right to bring up his children, all that is meant hereby is, that reason allows a father to make use of his liberty and natural force in a manner suitable to the preservation of his children, and proper to cultivate their understandings, and to train them up in the principles of virtue. In like manner, as reason gives its approbation to the sovereign in whatever is necessary for the preservation and welfare of the state, it particularly authorises him to raise troops and

The word right is taken in several particular senses, which are all derived from the general notion.

Definition of right, considered as a faculty.

bring armies into the field, in order to oppose an enemy; and in consequence hereof we say he has a right to do it. But, on the contrary, we affirm, that a prince has no right, without a particular necessity, to drag the peasant from the plough, or to force poor tradesmen from their families; that a father has no right to expose his children, or to put them to death, &c. because these things, far from being approved, are expresly condemned by reason. <69>

We must take care to distinguish between simple power and right.

III. We must not therefore confound a simple power with right. A simple power is a physical quality; it is a power of acting in the full extent of our natural strength and liberty: but the idea of right is more confined. This includes a relation of agreeableness to a rule which modifies the physical power, and directs its operations in a manner proper to conduct man to a certain end. It is for this reason we say, that right is a moral quality. It is true there are some that rank power as well as right among the number of moral qualities:* but there is nothing in this essentially opposite to our distinction. Those who rank these two ideas among moral entities, understand by power, pretty near the same thing as we understand by right; and custom seems to authorise this confusion; for we equally use, for instance, *paternal power,* and *paternal right,* &c. Be this as it will, we are not to dispute about words. The main point is to distinguish here between *physical* and *moral;* and it seems that the word *right,* as Puffendorf himself insinuates,† is fitter of itself than *power,* to express the moral idea. In short, the use of our faculties becomes a right, only so far as it is approved by reason, and is found agreeable to this primitive rule of human actions. And whatever a man can <70> *reasonably* perform, becomes in regard to him a right, because reason is the only means that can conduct him in a short and sure manner to the end he proposes. There is nothing therefore arbitrary in these ideas; they are

---

* See Puffendorf on the law of nature and nations, book i. chap. i. § 19.

† *There seems to be this difference between the terms of* power *and* right; *that the first does more expresly import the presence of the said quality, and does but obscurely denote the manner how any one acquired it. Whereas the word* right *does properly and clearly shew, that the quality was fairly got, and is now fairly possessed.* Puffendorf on the law of nature and nations, book i. chap. i. § 20.

borrowed from the very nature of things, and if we compare them to the foregoing principles, we shall find they flow from thence as necessary consequences.

IV. If any one should afterwards inquire, on what foundation it is that reason approves a particular exercise of our strength and liberty, in preference to another; the answer is obvious. The difference of those judgments arises from the very nature of things and their effects. Every exercise of our faculties, that tends of itself to the perfection and happiness of man, meets with the approbation of reason, which condemns whatever leads to a contrary end.

General foundation of the rights of man.

V. Obligation answers to right, taken in the manner above explained, and considered in its effects with regard to another person.

Right produces obligation.

What we have already said, in the preceding chapter, concerning obligation, is sufficient to convey a general notion of the nature of this moral quality. But in order to form a just idea of that which comes under our present examination, we are to observe, that when reason allows a man to make a particular use of his strength and liberty, or, which is the same thing, when it acknowledges he has a particular right; it is requisite, by a very natural consequence, that in order to ensure this right to man, he[1] should acknowledge at the same time, that other people ought <71> not to employ their strength and liberty in resisting him in this point; but on the contrary, that they should respect his right, and assist him in the exercise of it, rather than do him any prejudice. From thence the idea of obligation naturally arises; which is nothing more[2] than a restriction of natural liberty produced by reason; inasmuch as reason does not permit an opposition to be made to those who use their right, but on the contrary it obliges every body to favour and abet such as do noth-

1. The original states that "reason" (rather than "man," as the translation has it) "should acknowledge at the same time," etc.

2. The original says "which is nothing more here than a restriction," but the translation omits the "here." Burlamaqui does, however, recognize other types of obligation as well, although based on this type of internal or primitive obligation.

ing but what it authorises, rather than oppose or traverse them in the execution of their lawful designs.

Right and obligation are two relative terms.

VI. Right therefore and obligation are, as the logicians express it, two *correlative* terms: one of these ideas necessarily supposes the other; and we cannot conceive a right without a corresponding obligation. How, for example, could we attribute to a father the right of forming his children to wisdom and virtue by a perfect education, without acknowledging at the same time that children ought to submit to paternal direction, and that they are not only obliged not to make any resistance in this respect, but moreover they ought to concur, by their docility and obedience, to the execution of their parents views? Were it otherwise, reason would be no longer the rule of human actions: it would contradict itself, and all the rights it grants to man would become useless and of no effect; which is taking from him with one hand what it gives him with the other.

At what time man is susceptible of right and obligation.

VII. Such is the nature of right taken for a faculty, and of the obligation thereto corresponding. <72> It may be generally affirmed, that man is susceptible of these two qualities, as soon as he begins to enjoy life and sense. Yet we must make some difference here, between right and obligation, in respect to the time in which these qualities begin to unfold themselves in man.[3] The obligations a person contracts as man, do not actually display their virtue till he is arrived to the age of reason and discretion. For, in order to discharge an obligation, we must be first acquainted with it, we must know what we do, and be able to square our actions by a certain rule. But as for those rights that are capable of procuring the advantage of a person without his knowing any thing of the matter, they date their origin, and are in full force from the very first moment of his existence, and lay the rest of mankind under an obligation of respecting them. For example, the right which requires that no body should injure or offend us, belongs as well to children, and even

3. This discussion is drawn from DNG I.1 §7 and Barbeyrac's notes 4 and 5 to the same.

to infants that are still in their mothers wombs, as to adult persons. This is the foundation of that equitable rule of the Roman law, which declares, *That infants who are as yet in their mothers wombs, are considered as already brought into the world, whenever the question relates to any thing that may turn to their advantage. But we cannot with any exactness affirm, that an infant, whether already come or coming into the world, is actu-<73>ally subject to any obligation with respect to other men. This state does not properly commence with respect to man, till he has attained the age of knowledge and discretion.

VIII. Various are the distinctions of rights and obligations; but it will be sufficient for us to point out those only, that are most worthy of notice.†

Several sorts of rights and obligations.

In the first place, rights are natural, or acquired. The former are such as appertain originally and essentially to man, such as are inherent in his nature, and which he enjoys as man, independent of any particular act on his side. Acquired rights, on the contrary, are those which he does not naturally enjoy, but are owing to his own procurement. Thus the right of providing for our preservation, is a right natural to man; but sovereignty, or the right of commanding a society of men, is a right acquired.

Secondly, rights are perfect, or imperfect. Perfect rights are those which may be asserted in rigour, even by employing force to obtain the execution, or to secure the exercise thereof in opposition to all those who should attempt to resist or disturb us. Thus reason would impower us to use force against any one that would make an unjust attack upon our

---

* *Qui in utero est, perinde ac si in rebus humanis esset custoditur, quotiens de commodo ipsius partus, quaeritur.* L. 7. de statu homin. lib. 1. tit. 3. Another civilian establishes this rule: *Itaque pati quis injuriam, etiamsi non sentiat, potest: facere nemo, nisi qui scit se injuriam facere, etiamsi nesciat cui faciat.* L. 3. § 2. D. de injuriis. lib. 47. tit. 10. ["Thus, someone can suffer an insult, even though unaware, but no one can perpetrate one without knowing what he is doing, even though he does not know to whom he is doing it." Alan Watson, ed., *The Digest of Justinian,* rev. English language ed. (Philadelphia: University of Pennsylvania Press, 1998), D 47. 10. 3. 2.]

† See Puffendorf on the law of nature and nations, book i. chap. i. § 19. and Grotius on the rights of war and peace, book i. chap. i. § 4, 5, 6, 7. with Barbeyrac's notes.

lives, our goods, or our liberty. But when reason does not allow us to use forcible methods, in order to secure the enjoyment of the rights it grants us, then these rights are called imperfect. Thus, notwithstanding <74> reason authorises those, who of themselves are destitute of means of living, to apply for succour to other men; yet they cannot, in case of refusal, insist upon it by force, or procure it by open violence. It is obvious, without our having any occasion to mention it here, that obligation answers exactly to right, and is more or less strong, perfect, or imperfect, according as right itself is perfect or imperfect.

Thirdly, another distinction worthy of our attention, is, that there are rights which may be lawfully renounced, and others that cannot.[4] A creditor, for example, may forgive a sum due to him, if he pleases, either in the whole or part; but a father cannot renounce the right he has over his children, nor leave them in an intire independence. The reason of this difference is, that there are rights which of themselves have a natural connexion with our duties, and are given to man only as means to perform them. To renounce this sort of rights, would be therefore renouncing our duty, which is never allowed. But with respect to rights that no way concern our duties, the renunciation of them is licit, and only a matter of prudence. Let us illustrate this with another example. Man cannot absolutely, and without any manner of reserve, renounce his liberty; for this would be manifestly throwing himself into a necessity of doing wrong, were he so commanded by the person to whom he has made this subjection. But it is lawful for us to renounce a part of our liberty, if we find ourselves better enabled thereby to discharge our duties, and to acquire some certain and reasonable advantage. It is with these modifications <75> we must understand the common maxim, *That it is allowable for every one to renounce his right.*

Fourthly; Right, in fine, considered in respect to its different objects, may be reduced to four principal species. 1. The right we have over our

---

4. The original has "à l'égard desquels cela n'est pas permis," that is, "with respect to that which is not permitted": Burlamaqui is not here interested in rights that a person is (physically or psychologically) incapable of renouncing. The discussion is based on DNG I.7 §17 note 2.

own persons and actions, which is called *Liberty.* 2. The right we have over things or goods that belong to us, which is called *Property.* 3. The right we have over the persons and actions of other men, which is distinguished by the name of *Empire* or *Authority.* 4. And, in fine, the right one may have over other men's things, of which there are several sorts. It suffices, at present, to have given a general notion of these different species of right. Their nature and effects will be explained, when we come to a particular inquiry into these matters.

Such are the ideas we ought to have of right, considered as a faculty. But there is likewise another particular signification of this word, by which it is taken for *law;* as when we say, that natural right is the foundation of morality and politics;[5] that it forbids us to break our word; that it commands the reparation of damage, &c. In all these cases, right is taken for *law.* And as this kind of right agrees in a particular manner with man, it is therefore a matter of importance to clear and explain it well, which we shall endeavour to perform in the following chapters.
<76>

CHAPTER VIII[*]

Of Law in general.

I. In the researches hitherto made concerning the rule of human actions, we have consulted only the nature of man, his essence, and what belongs to his internal part. This inquiry has shewn us, that man finds within himself, and in his own *Reason,* the rule he ought to follow; and since the counsels which reason gives him, point out the shortest and safest road to his perfection and happiness, from thence arises a principle of obligation, or a cogent motive to square his actions by this primitive rule. But in order to have an exact knowledge of the human system, we must

---

* See Puffendorf on the law of nature and nations, book i. chap. vi.

5. The original states that "le droit naturel," which refers to the system of natural laws, is the foundation of morality and politics. The ambiguities of the relevant terms do not work quite alike in English and in French.

not stop at these first considerations; we should likewise, pursuant to the method already pointed out in this work,* transfer our attention to the different states of man, and to the relations from thence arising, which must absolutely produce some particular modifications in the rules he is to follow. For, as we have already observed, these rules ought not only to be conformable to the nature of man, but they should be proportionable moreover to his state and situation.

As man by nature is a dependent being, the law ought to be the rule of his actions.

II. Now among the primitive states of man, dependance is one of those which merits the most attention, and ought to have the greatest influence on <77> the rule he is to observe. In fact, a being independent of every body else, has no other rule to pursue but the counsels of his own reason; and in consequence of this independance he is freed from all subjection to another's will; in short, he is absolute master of himself and his actions. But the case is not the same with a being who is supposed to be dependent on another, as on his superior and master. The sense of this dependance ought naturally to engage the inferior to take the will of him on whom he depends for the rule of his conduct; since the subjection in which he finds himself, does not permit him to entertain the least reasonable hopes of acquiring any solid happiness, independent of the will of his superior, and of the views he may propose in relation to him.†
Besides, this has more or less extent and effect, in proportion as the superiority of the one, and the dependance of the other, is greater or less, absolute or limited. It is obvious that all these remarks are in a particular manner applicable to man; so that as soon as he acknowledges a superior, to whose power and authority he is naturally subject; in consequence of this state, he must acknowledge likewise the will of this superior to be the rule of his actions. This is the *Right* we call *Law*.

It is to be understood however, that this will of the superior has nothing in it contrary to reason, the primitive rule of man. For were this the case, it would be impossible for us to obey him. In order to render a law the rule of human actions, it should be absolutely agreeable to the nature

* See chap. iii. of this part, § 3.
† See chap. vi. § 3.

and constitution <78> of man, and be ultimately designed for his happiness, which reason makes him necessarily pursue. These remarks, though clear enough of themselves, will receive a greater light, when we have more particularly explained the nature of law.

III. Law I define, a rule prescribed by the sovereign of a society to his subjects, either in order to lay an obligation upon them of doing or omitting certain things, under the commination of punishment; or to leave them at liberty to act or not in other things just as they think proper, and to secure to them, in this respect, the full enjoyment of their rights.[1]

> Definition of law.

By thus defining law, we deviate a little from the definitions given by Grotius and Puffendorf. But the definitions of these authors are, methinks, somewhat too vague, and besides do not seem to agree with law considered in its full extent. This opinion of mine will be justified by the particular explication I am going to enter upon, provided it be compared with the passages here referred to.*

IV. I say that *law is a rule,* to signify, in the first place, what law has in common with counsel; which is, that they are both rules of conduct; and secondly, to distinguish law from the transient orders which may be given by a superior, and not being permanent rules of the subject's conduct, are not properly laws. The idea of *rule* includes prin-<79>cipally these two things, *universality* and *perpetuity;* and both these characters being essential to rule, generally considered, help to discriminate law from any other particular will of the sovereign.

> Why law is defined *a rule prescribed.*

I add, that *law is a rule prescribed;* because a simple resolution confined within the sovereign's mind, without manifesting itself by some external sign, can never be a law. It is requisite that this will be notified in a proper manner to the subjects; so that they be acquainted with what the sov-

---

* See Grotius on the rights of war and peace, book i. chap. i. § 9. And Puffendorf on the law of nature and nations, book i. chap. vi. § 4. To which we may add Mons. Barbeyrac's notes.

1. Burlamaqui's definition of law differs from Pufendorf's to the extent that it makes place for permission as a positive act of the law, a point on which Barbeyrac insisted vigorously in his footnotes. See, for example, DNG I.6 §15 note 2.

ereign requires of them, and with the necessity of squaring thereby their conduct. But in what manner this notification is to be made, whether *viva voce,* by writing, or otherwise, is a matter of mere indifference. Sufficient it is, that the subjects be properly instructed concerning the will of the legislator.

What is understood by a sovereign, sovereignty, and the right of commanding.

V. Let us finish the explication of the principal ideas that enter into the definition of law. Law is prescribed by the *sovereign;* this is what distinguishes it from *counsel,* which comes from a friend or equal; who, as such, has no power over us, and whose advices, consequently, neither have the same force, nor produce the same obligation as law, which coming from a sovereign, has for its support the command and authority of a superior.* Counsels are followed for reasons drawn from the nature of the thing; laws are obeyed, not only on account of the reasons on which they are established, but likewise because of the authority of the sovereign <80> that prescribes them. The obligation arising from counsel is merely internal; that of law is both internal and external.†

Society, as we have already observed, is the union of several persons for a particular end, from whence some common advantage arises. The end, is the effect or advantage which intelligent beings propose to themselves, and are willing to procure. The union of several persons, is the concurrence of their will to procure the end they aim at in common. But though we make the idea of society enter into the definition of law, it must not be inferred from thence, that society is a condition absolutely essential and necessary to the enacting of laws. Considering the thing exactly, we may very well form a conception of law, when the sovereign has only a single person subject to his authority; and it is only in order to enter into the actual state of things, that we suppose a sovereign commanding a society of men. We must nevertheless observe, that the relation there is between the sovereign and the subjects, forms a society between them, but of a particular kind, which we may call *society of inequality,* where the sovereign commands, and the subjects obey.

---

* See the Law of nature and nations, book i. chap. vi. § 1.
† See above, chap. vi. § 13.

The sovereign is therefore he who has a right to command in the last resort. To command, is directing the actions of those who are subject to us, according to our own will, and with authority or the power of constraint. I say that *the sovereign commands in the last resort,* to shew that as he has the first rank in society, his will is superior to any other, and holds all the members of the society in subjec-<81>tion. In fine, the right of commanding is nothing more than the power of directing the actions of others with authority. And as the power of exercising one's force and liberty is no farther a right, than as it is approved and authorized by reason, it is on this approbation of reason, as the last resort, that the right of commanding is established.

VI. This leads us to inquire more particularly into the natural foundation of empire or sovereignty; or, which amounts to the same thing, what is it that confers or constitutes a right of laying an obligation on another person, and of requiring his submission and obedience. This is a very important question in itself; important also in its effects. For the more we are convinced of the reasons, which establish on the one hand authority, and dependance on the other, the more we are inclined to make a real and voluntary submission to those on whom we depend. Besides, the diversity of sentiments, in relation to the manner of laying the foundation of sovereignty, is a sufficient proof that this subject requires to be treated with care and attention.[2]

---

2. Burlamaqui's reference to the "diversity of sentiments" regarding the foundation of sovereign power alludes to the controversy around Pufendorf's definition of a superior in DHC I.2 §5. Leibniz presented a severe criticism of Pufendorf's position, which he understood as making God's right to rule over men into something unexplainable. Burlamaqui read the criticism in the "Judgment of an Anonymous Writer" that Barbeyrac published together with the DHC, and which contained Barbeyrac's replies to Leibniz's critique (see especially paragraphs 15 and 19 in Samuel Pufendorf, *The Whole Duty of Man, According to the Law of Nature,* ed. Ian Hunter and David Saunders [Indianapolis: Liberty Fund, 2003], pp. 267–305). The next chapter provides Burlamaqui's own account of the various arguments presented by Hobbes (whom both Pufendorf and Leibniz had criticized), Pufendorf, Leibniz, and Barbeyrac.

CHAPTER IX

Of the foundation of sovereignty, or the right of commanding.

First remark.
The question
is, in regard to
a necessary
sovereignty.

I. Inquiring here into the foundation of the right of command, we consider the thing only in a general and metaphysical manner. The <82> question is to know the foundation of a necessary sovereignty and dependance; that is, such as is founded on the very nature of things, and is a natural consequence of the constitution of those beings to whom it is attributed. Let us therefore wave whatever relates to a particular species of sovereignty, in order to ascend to the general ideas from whence the first principles are derived. But as general principles, when just and well founded, are easily applied to particular cases; it follows therefore, that the first foundation of sovereignty, or the reasons on which it is established, ought to be laid in such a manner, as to be easily applicable to the several species that fall within our knowledge. By this means, as we observed before, we can be fully satisfied with regard to the justness of the principles, or distinguish whether they are defective.

Second
remark.
There is
neither sover-
eignty nor
necessary
dependance be-
tween beings
perfectly equal.

II. Another general and preliminary remark is, that there can be neither sovereignty nor natural and necessary dependance between beings, which by their nature, faculties, and state, have so perfect an equality, that nothing can be attributed to one which is not alike applicable to the other. In fact, in such a supposition, there could be no reason, why one should arrogate an authority over the rest, and subject them to a state of dependance, of which the latter could not equally avail themselves against the former. But as this reduces the thing to an absurdity, it follows, that such an equality between several beings excludes all subordination, all empire and necessary dependance of one on the other; just as the equality of two weights keeps these in a perfect equilibrium. There must <83> be therefore in the very nature of those beings, who are supposed to be subordinate one to the other, an essential difference of qualities, on which the relation of superior and inferior may be founded. But the sentiments of writers are divided in the determination of those qualities.

III. 1. Some pretend that the sole superiority of strength, or, as they express it, an irresistible power, is the true and first foundation of the right of imposing an obligation, and prescribing laws. "This superiority of power gives, according to them, a right of reigning, by the impossibility in which it places others, of resisting him who has so great an advantage over them."*

2. Others there are, who derive the origin and foundation of sovereignty, from the eminency or superior excellence of nature; "which not only renders a being independent of all those who are of an inferior nature; but moreover causes the latter to be regarded as made for the former. And of this, say they, we have a proof in the very constitution of man, where the soul governs, as being the noblest part; and it is likewise on this foundation, that the empire of man over brutes is grounded."†

3. A third opinion, which deserves also our notice, is that of Barbeyrac.‡ According to this ju-<84>dicious author, "there is, properly speaking, only one general foundation of obligation, to which all others may be reduced, and that is, our natural dependance on God, inasmuch as he has given us being, and has consequently a right to require we should apply our faculties to the use for which he has manifestly designed them. An artist," he continues, "as such, is master of his own work, and can dispose of it as he pleases. Were a sculptor capable of making animated statues, this alone would intitle him to insist, that the marble shaped by his own hands, and endowed by him with understanding, shall be subject to his will.———But God is the author of the matter and form of the parts of which our being is composed, and he has given them all the faculties, with which they are invested. To these faculties, therefore, he has a right to prescribe what limits he pleases, and to require that men should use them in such or such a manner, &c."

* See Hobbes de Cive, cap. 15. § 5.
† See Puffendorf on the law of nature and nations, book i. chap. vi. § 11. [This is a view that Pufendorf reports in passing and disapproves of, not one he would himself defend.]
‡ It is found in the second note on section 12. of Puffendorf on the law of nature and nations, book 1. chap. 6. and in the third note on § 5. of the duties of man and a citizen, book 1. chap. 2.

Examen of
those opinions.
1. The sole
superiority
of power is
insufficient
to found a
right of
commanding.

IV. Such are the principal systems on the origin and foundation of sovereignty and dependance. Let us examine them thoroughly, and in order to pass a right judgment, let us take care not to forget the distinction of physical and moral necessity, nor the primitive notions of right and obligation, such as have been above explained.*

1. This being premised, I affirm, that those who found the right of prescribing laws on the sole superiority of strength, or on an irresistible power, establish an insufficient principle, and which, rigorously <85> considered, is absolutely false. In fact, it does not follow, that because I am incapable to resist a person, he has therefore a right to command me, that is, that I am bound to submit to him by virtue of a principle of obligation, and to acknowledge his will as the universal rule of my conduct. Right being nothing else but that which reason approves, it is this approbation only which reason gives to him who commands, that is capable of founding his right, and, by a necessary consequence, produces that inward sense,[1] which we distinguish by the name of Obligation, and inclines us to a spontaneous submission. Every obligation therefore supposes some particular reasons that influence the conscience and bend the will, insomuch that, pursuant to the light of our own reason, we should think it criminal to resist, were it even in our power, and should conclude that we have therefore no right to do it. Now a person that alledges no other reason, but a superiority of force, does not propose a motive sufficient to oblige the will. For instance, the power which may chance to reside in a malignant being, neither invests him with any right to command, nor imposes any obligation on us to obey; because this is evidently repugnant even to the very idea of right and obligation. On the contrary, the first counsel which reason gives us in regard to a malignant power, is to resist, and, if possible, to destroy him.[2] Now, if we have a right to resist, this right is inconsistent with the obligation of obeying, which is evidently thereby excluded. True it is, that if we clearly

* Chap. vi. and vii.
1. The "inward sense" is a translation for a more prosaic "ce sentiment," that is, "this sentiment."
2. Burlamaqui here repeats Pufendorf's criticism of Hobbes in DNG I.6 §10.

see that all our efforts will be useless, and that our resistance must only subject us to a greater evil; we should chuse to sub-<86>mit, though with reluctance for a while, rather than expose ourselves to the attacks and violence of a malignant power. But in this case we should be constrained, though not under an obligation. We endure, in spite of us, the effects of a superior force, and whilst we make an external submission, we inwardly feel our nature rise and protest against it. This leaves us always a full right to attempt all sorts of ways to shake off the unjust and oppressive yoke. There is therefore properly speaking, no obligation in that case; now the default of obligation implies the default of right.* We have omitted making mention here of the dangerous consequences of this system, it is sufficient at present to have refuted it by principles; and perhaps we shall have occasion to take notice of these consequences another time.

V. The other two opinions have something in them that is plausible and even true; yet they do not seem to me to be intirely sufficient. The principles they establish are too vague, and have need to be reduced to a more determinate point.

2. Nor the sole excellence or superiority of nature.

2. And, indeed, I do not see, that the sole excellency of nature is sufficient to found a right of sovereignty.[3] I will acknowledge, if you please, this excellency, and agree to it as a truth that I am well convinced of: This is the whole effect that must naturally arise from this hypothesis. But here I make a halt; and the knowledge I have of the excellency of a superior being does not alone afford me a motive sufficient to subject myself to him, and to induce me to abandon my own will, in order to <87> take his for my rule. So long as I am confined to these general heads, and am informed of nothing more, I do not feel myself inclined by an internal motion to submit; and without any reproach of conscience, I may sincerely judge, that the intelligent principle within me, is sufficient to direct my conduct. So far we confine ourselves to mere speculation.

* See chap. viii. § 6.
3. The refutation of the superiority of nature argument is from DNG I.6 §11.

But if you should attempt to require any thing more of me, the question would then be reduced to this point: How and in what manner does this being, whom you suppose to surpass me in excellence, intend to conduct himself with regard to me; and by what effects will this superiority or excellence be displayed? Is he willing to do me good or harm, or is he, in respect to me, in a state of indifference? To these interrogations there must be absolutely some answer given; and according to the side that is chosen, I shall agree perhaps, that this being has a right to command me, and that I am under an obligation of obeying. But these reflections are, if I am not mistaken, a demonstrative proof, that it is not sufficient to alledge merely and simply the excellence of a superior being, in order to establish the foundation of sovereignty.

3. Nor the sole quality of Creator.

VI. Perhaps there is something more exact in the third hypothesis. "God," say they, "is the Creator of man; it is from him he has received and holds his life, his reason, and all his faculties, he is therefore master of his work, and can of course prescribe what rules he pleases. Hence our dependance, hence the absolute empire of God over us naturally arises; and this is the very origin or first foundation of all authority." <88>

The sum of what is here alledged to found the empire of God over man, is reduced to his supreme power. But does it follow from thence only, and by an immediate and necessary consequence, that he has a right to prescribe laws to us? That is the question. The sovereign power of God enables him to dispose of man as he has a mind, to require of him whatever he pleases, and to lay him under an absolute necessity of complying: For the creature cannot resist the Creator, and by its nature and state it finds itself in so absolute a dependance, that the Creator may, if so is his pleasure, even annihilate and destroy it. This we own, is certain; and yet it does not seem sufficient to establish the right of the Creator. There is something more than this requisite to form a moral quality of a simple power, and to convert it into right.* In a word, it is necessary,

* See chap. vii. § 3.

as we have more than once observed, that the power be such as ought to be approved by reason; to the end that man may submit to it willingly, and by that inward sense which produces obligation.

Here I beg leave to make a supposition that will set the thing in a much clearer light. Had the Creator given existence to the creature only to render it unhappy, the relation of Creator and creature would still subsist, and yet we could not possibly conceive, in this supposition, either right or obligation. The irresistible power of the Creator might indeed constrain the creature; but this constraint would never form a reasonable obligation, a moral tie; because an obligation of this nature always supposes the concurrence of the will, and an approbation or an acquiescence on the part <89> of man, from whence a voluntary submission arises. Now this aquiescence could never be given to a being, that would exert his supreme power only to oppress his creature, and render it unhappy.

The quality therefore of Creator is not alone and of itself sufficient to establish the right of command, and the obligation of obeying.

VII. But if to the idea of Creator we join (which Barbeyrac probably supposed, though he has not distinctly expressed it) the idea of a being perfectly wise and sovereignly good, who has no desire of exercising his power but for the good and advantage of his creatures; then we have every thing necessary to found a legitimate authority.

True foundation of sovereignty: Power, wisdom, and goodness joined together.

Let us only consult ourselves, and suppose, that we not only derive our existence, life, and all our faculties, from a being infinitely superior to us in power; but moreover, that we are perfectly convinced that this being, no less wise than powerful, had no other aim in creating us, but to render us happy, and that with this view he is willing to subject us to laws: certain it is, that under these circumstances, we could not avoid approving of such a power, and the exercise thereof in respect to us. Now this approbation is acknowledging the right of the superior; and consequently the first counsel that reason gives us, is to resign ourselves to the direction of such a master, to subject ourselves to him, and to conform all our actions to what we know in relation to his will. And why so? because it is evident to us, from the very nature of things, that this is the surest and shortest way to arrive at hap-<90>piness, the end to which all mankind aspire. And from the manner we are formed, this knowledge will be necessarily attended with the concurrence of our will, with our acquiescence, and submission; insomuch that if we should act contrary to those principles, and any misfortune should afterwards befall us, we could not avoid condemning ourselves, and acknowledging, that we have justly drawn upon ourselves the evil we suffer. Now this is what constitutes the true character of obligation, properly so called.

Explication of our opinion. VIII. If we have therefore a mind to embrace and take in the whole, in order to form a complete definition, we must say, that the right of sovereignty arises from a superiority of power, accompanied with wisdom and goodness.

I say, in the first place, *a superiority of power,* because an equality of power, as we have observed in the very beginning, excludes all empire, all natural and necessary subordination; and besides, sovereignty and command would become useless and of no manner of effect, were they not supported by a sufficient power. What would it avail a person to be a sovereign, unless he were possessed of effectual methods to enforce his orders and make himself obeyed?

But this is not yet sufficient; wherefore I say, in the second place, that this power ought to be *wise and benevolent: wise,* to know and to chuse the properest means to make us happy; and *benevolent,* to be generally inclinable to use those means that tend to promote our felicity. <91>

In order to be convinced of this, it will be sufficient to remark three cases, which are the only ones that can be here supposed. Either he is, with respect to us, an indifferent power, that is, a power willing to do us neither good nor harm, as no ways interesting himself in what concerns us; or he is a malignant power; or, in fine, he is a propitious and benevolent power.

In the first case, our question cannot take place. How superior soever a being is in regard to me, so long as he does not concern himself about me, but leaves me intirely to myself; I remain in as complete a liberty, in respect to him, as if he were not known to me, or as if he did not at all exist.* Wherefore there is no authority on his side, nor obligation on mine.

But if we suppose a malignant power; reason, far from approving, revolts against him, as against an enemy, so much the more dangerous, as he is invested with greater power. Man cannot acknowledge such a power has a right; on the contrary, he finds himself authorized to leave no measure untried to get rid of so formidable a master, in order to be sheltered from the evils with which he might otherwise be unjustly afflicted. <92>

But let us suppose a being equally wise and beneficent. Man, instead of being able to refuse him his approbation, will feel himself inwardly and naturally inclined to submit and acquiesce intirely in the will of such a being, who is possessed of all the qualities necessary to conduct him to his ultimate end. By his *power,* he is perfectly able to procure the good of those who are subject to him, and to remove whatever may possibly injure them. By his *wisdom,* he is thoroughly acquainted with the nature and constitution of those on whom he imposes laws, and knows their faculties and strength, and in what their real interests consist. He cannot therefore be mistaken, either in the designs he proposes for their benefit, or in the means he employs in order to attain them. In fine, *goodness* inclines such a sovereign to be really willing to render his subjects happy, and constantly to direct to this end the operations of his wisdom and power. Thus the assemblage of these qualities, by uniting in the very highest degree all that is capable of deserving the approbation of reason, comprizes whatsoever can determine man, and lay him under an internal as well as external obligation of submission and obedience. Here therefore lies the true foundation of the right of sovereignty.

---

* *And therefore though that notion of the Epicureans was most senseless and impious, in which they described the Gods, as enjoying their own happiness with the highest peace and tranquillity, far removed from the troublesome care of human business, and neither smiling at the good, nor frowning at the wicked deeds of men; yet they rightly enough inferred, that upon this supposition, all religion, and all fear of divine powers, was vain and useless.* Puffendorf, Law of nature and nations, book i. chap. vi. § 11. See Cicero de Nat. Deor. lib. 1. cap. 2.

We must not
separate the
qualities which
form the right
of sovereignty.
IX. In order to bind and subject free and rational creatures, there is no necessity, properly speaking, for more than an empire or authority, whose wisdom and lenity would forcibly engage the approbation of reason, independent of the motives excited by the apprehension of power. But as it easily happens, <93> from the manner that men are formed, that either through levity and neglect, or passion and malice, they are not so much struck as they ought, with the wisdom of the legislator, and with the excellency of his laws; it was therefore proper there should be an efficacious motive, such as the apprehension of punishment, in order to have a stronger influence over the will. For which reason it is necessary that the sovereign should be armed with power and force, to be better able to maintain his authority. Let us not separate therefore these different qualities, which form, by their concurrence, the right of the sovereign. As power alone, unaccompanied with benevolence, cannot constitute any right; so benevolence, destitute of power and wisdom, is likewise insufficient for this effect. For from this only, that a person wishes another well, it does not follow, that he is his master: neither are a few particular acts of benevolence sufficient for that purpose. A benefit requires no more than gratitude and acknowledgment; for in order to testify our gratitude, it is not necessary we should subject ourselves to the power of our benefactor. But let us join these ideas, and suppose, at one and the same time, a sovereign power, on which every one actually and really depends; a sovereign wisdom, that directs this power; and a supreme goodness, by which it is animated. What can we desire more, to establish, on the one side, the most eminent authority, and, on the other, the greatest subordination? We are compelled then, as it were, by our own reason, which will not so much as suffer us to deny, that such a superior is invested with <94> a true right to command, and that we are under a real obligation to obey.*

* It may indeed be said, that the foundation of external obligation is the will of a superior (see above, chap. vi. § xiii.) provided this general proposition be afterwards explained by the particulars into which we have entered. But when some add, that force has nothing to do with the foundation of this obligation, and that it only serves to enable the superior to exert his right (see Barbeyrac's 1st note on the 9th section of Puffendorf's large work, book 1. chap. 6.) this notion does not appear to me to

X. The notions of sovereign and sovereignty being once settled, it is easy to fix those of subjection and dependance.[4]

Subjects therefore are persons, that are under an obligation of obeying. And as it is power, wisdom, and benevolence, that constitute sovereignty; we must suppose, on the contrary, in subjects the weakness and wants, from whence dependance arises.

It is therefore right in Puffendorf to remark,* that what renders man susceptible of an obligation produced by an external principle, is that he naturally depends on a superior, and that moreover as a free and intelligent being, he is capable of knowing the rules given him, and of chusing to conform his actions to them. But these are rather condi-<95>tions necessarily supposed, and of themselves understood, than the exact and immediate causes of subjection. More important it is to observe, that as the power of obliging a rational creature is founded on the ability and will of making him happy, if he obeys; unhappy, if he disobeys; this supposes that this creature is capable of good and evil, sensible of pleasure and pain, and besides that his state of happiness or misery may be either increased or diminished. Otherwise, he might be forced indeed, by a superior power, to act after a certain manner, but he could not be properly obliged.

Definition of subjection. Foundation of dependance.

XI. Such is the true foundation of sovereignty and dependance; a foundation that might be still better established, by applying these general principles to the particular species of known sovereignty or empire, such as that of God over man, that of a prince over his subjects, and the power of fathers over their children. We should be convinced thereby, that all these species of authority are originally founded on the principles above

The obligation produced by law, is the most perfect that can be imagined.

---

be exact; and methinks that this abstract manner of considering the thing, subverts the very foundation of the obligation here in question. There can be no external obligation without a superior, nor a superior without force, or, which is the same thing, without power: force therefore or power is a necessary part of the foundation of obligation.

* See the Duties of man and a citizen, book 1. chap. 2. § 4. And the Law of nature and nations, book 1. chap. 6. § 6, 8.

4. According to the original, to fix the notions of sovereign and sovereignty is at the same time to fix those of subjection and dependence.

established; which would serve for a new proof of the truth of those principles.* But it is sufficient to have hinted here in general at this remark; the particulars we reserve for another place.

An authority established on such a foundation, and which comprizes whatever can be imagined most efficacious and capable to bind man, and to incline him to be steadily directed by certain rules of conduct, undoubtedly forms the completest and strongest obligation. For there is no obligation more perfect than <96> that which is produced by the strongest motives to determine the will, and the most capable, by their preponderancy, to prevail over all other contrary reasons.† Now every thing concurs here to this effect: the nature of the rules prescribed by the sovereign, which of themselves are the fittest to promote our perfection and felicity; the power and authority with which he is invested, whereby he is enabled to decide our happiness or misery; and, in fine, the intire confidence we have in him, because of his power, wisdom, and goodness. What can we imagine more to captivate the will, to gain the heart, to oblige man, and to produce within him the highest degree of moral necessity, which constitutes the most perfect obligation? I say, *moral necessity;* for we are not to destroy the nature of man; he remains always what he is, a free and intelligent being; and as such, the sovereign undertakes to direct him by his laws. Hence it is that even the strictest obligations never force the will; but, rigorously speaking, man is always at liberty to comply or not, though, as we commonly say, at his risk and peril. But if he consults reason, and is willing to follow its dictates, he will take particular care to avoid exercising this metaphysical power, in opposition to the views of his sovereign; an opposition that must terminate in his own misery and ruin.

Obligation is internal and external at the same time.

XII. We have already observed, that there are two sorts of obligation;‡ the one internal, which is the work of reason only, and founded on the good or evil we perceive in the very nature of things: <97> the other

* See section i.
† See chap. vi. § 10.
‡ See chap. vi. § 13.

external, which is produced by the will of him whom we acknowledge our superior and master. Now the obligation produced by law, unites these two sorts of ties, which by their concurrence strengthen each other, and thus form the completest obligation that can possibly be imagined. It is probably for this reason, that most civilians acknowledge no other obligation properly so called, but that which is the effect of law, and imposed by a superior. This is true, if we mean only an external obligation, which indeed is the strongest tie of man. But it must not be inferred from thence, that we ought to admit no other sort of obligation. The principles we established, when inquiring into the first origin and the nature of obligation generally considered, and the particular remarks we have just now made on the obligation arising from law, are sufficient, if I am not mistaken, to evince, that there is a primitive, original, and internal obligation, which is inseparable from reason, and ought necessarily to concur with the external obligation, in order to communicate to the latter all the necessary force for determining and bending the will, and for influencing effectually the human heart.

By distinguishing rightly these ideas, we shall find, perhaps, that this is one way of reconciling opinions, which seem to be wide from each other, only because they are misunderstood.* Sure it is at least, that the manner in which we have explained the foundation of sovereignty and dependance, coincides, in the main, with Puffendorf's system, as will easily <98> appear by comparing it with what this author says, whether in his large work, or in his abridgment.†

---

* See the second part, chap. vii.

† See the law of nature and nations, book i. chap. vi. § 5, 6, 8, and 9. And the duties of man and a citizen, book i. chap. ii. § 3, 4, 5. [This is a contentious statement: Barbeyrac, as Burlamaqui well knew, presented a quite opposite interpretation of Pufendorf's theory of sovereignty and obligation.]

CHAPTER X

Of the end of laws; of their characters, differences, &c.

Of the end of
laws, either in
regard to the
subjects, or in
respect to the
sovereign.
I. Some perhaps will complain, that we have dwelt too long on the nature and foundation of sovereignty. But the importance of the subject required us to treat it with care, and to unravel properly its principles. Besides, we apprehend, that nothing could contribute better to a right knowledge of the nature of law; and we shall presently see, that whatever in fact remains for us still to say concerning this subject, is deduced from the principles just now established.

In the first place, it may be asked, what is the end and design of laws?

This question presents itself in two different lights; namely, with respect to the subject, and with regard to the sovereign: a distinction that must be carefully observed.

The relation of the sovereign to his subjects forms a kind of society between them, which the sovereign directs by the laws he establishes.* But as society <99> naturally requires there should be some provision made for the good of all those who are the constituent parts thereof, it is by this principle we must judge of the end of laws: and this end, considered with respect to the sovereign, ought to include nothing in it opposite to the end of these very laws considered with regard to the subject.

II. The end of the law in regard to the subject is, that he should conform his actions to it, and by this means acquire happiness. As for what concerns the sovereign, the end he aims at for himself, by giving laws to his subjects, is the satisfaction and glory arising from the execution of the wise designs he proposes, for the preservation[1] of those who are subject to his authority. These two ends of the law should never be separated, one being naturally connected with the other; for it is the happiness of the subject that forms the satisfaction and glory of the sovereign.

* See chap. viii. § 3.
1. The translation omits "and happiness" from this sentence.

III. We should therefore take care not to imagine that laws are properly made in order to bring men under a yoke. So idle an end would be quite unworthy of a sovereign, whose goodness ought to be equal to his power and wisdom, and who should always act up to these perfections. Let us say rather, that laws are made to oblige the subject to pursue his real interest, and to chuse the surest and best way to attain the end he is designed for, which is happiness.[2] With this view the sovereign is willing to direct his people better than they could themselves, and gives a check to their liberty, lest they should <100> make a bad use of it contrary to their own and the public good. In short, the sovereign commands rational beings; it is on this footing he treats with them; all his ordinances have the stamp of reason; he is willing to reign over our hearts; and if at any time he employs force, it is in order to bring back to reason those who have unhappily strayed from it, contrary to their own good and that of society.

The end of laws is not to lay a restraint upon liberty, but to direct it in a proper manner.

IV. Wherefore Puffendorf, methinks, speaks somewhat loosely in the comparison he draws between law and counsel, where he says, "That counsel tends to the ends proposed by those to whom it is given, and that they themselves can judge of those ends, in order to approve or disapprove them.———Whereas law aims only at the end of the person that establishes it, and if sometimes it has views in regard to those for whom it is made, it is not their business to examine them—this depends intirely on the determination of the legislator."* It would be a much juster way, methinks, of expressing the thing, to say, that laws have a double end, relative to the sovereign and the subject; that the intent of the sovereign in establishing them, is to consult his own satisfaction and glory, by rendering his subjects happy; that these two things are inseparable; and that it would be doing injustice to the sovereign to imagine he thinks only of himself, without any regard to the good of those who

Examen of what Puffendorf says concerning this subject.

---

* See the Law of nature and nations, book i. chap. vi. § 1.

2. For a discussion of Burlamaqui's emphasis on man's desire for felicity as the foundation of both natural law and civil legislation, see the introduction.

are his dependants. Puffendorf seems here, as well as in some other places, to give a little too much into Hobbes's principles. <101>

Of the distinc-
tion of law
into obliga-
tory, and that
of simple
permission.
V. We defined law, a rule which lays an obligation on subjects of doing or omitting certain things, and leaves them at liberty to act or not to act in other matters, according as they judge proper, &c. This is what we must explain here in a more particular manner.

A sovereign has undoubtedly a right to direct the actions of those who are subject to him, according to the ends he has in view. In consequence of this right, he imposes a necessity on them of acting or not acting after a particular manner in certain cases; and this obligation is the first effect of the law. From thence it follows, that all actions, not positively commanded or forbidden, are left within the sphere of our natural liberty; and that the sovereign is hereby supposed to grant every body a permission to act in this respect as they think proper; and this permission is a second effect of the law. We may therefore distinguish the law, taken in its full extent, into an obligatory law, and a law of simple permission.

The opinion of
Grotius and
Puffendorf
upon this
subject.
[VI.] It is true, Grotius,* and after him Puffendorf, are of opinion, that permission is not properly, and of itself, an effect or consequence of the law, but a mere inaction of the legislator. †*Whatever things,* says Puffendorf, *the law permits, those it neither commands nor forbids, and therefore it really doth nothing at all concerning them.* <102>

But though this different manner of considering the thing be not perhaps of any great consequence, yet Barbeyrac's opinion, such as he has explained it in his notes on the forecited passages, appears to be much more exact. A permission arising from the legislator's silence cannot be considered as a simple inaction. The legislator does nothing but with deliberation and wisdom. If he is satisfied with imposing, only in some cases, an indispensable necessity of acting after a certain manner, and does not extend this necessity further, it is because he thinks it agreeable to the end he proposes, to leave his subjects at liberty in some cases to

* See the Rights of war and peace, book i. chap. i. § 9.
† See the Law of nature and nations, book i. chap. vi. § 15.

do as they please. Wherefore, the silence of the legislator imports a positive though tacit permission of whatsoever he has not forbidden or commanded, though he might have done it, and would certainly have done it, had he thought proper. Insomuch that as the forbidden or commanded actions are positively regulated by the law, actions permitted are likewise positively determined by the same law, though after their manner and according to the nature of the thing. In fine, whoever determines certain limits, which he declares we ought not to exceed, does hereby point out how far he permits and consents we should go. Permission therefore is as positive an effect of the law as obligation.

VII. This will appear still more evident, if we consider, that having once supposed that we all depend on a superior, whose will ought to be the universal rule of our conduct, the rights attributed to man in this state, by virtue of which he may act safely and with impunity, are founded on the express <103> or tacit permission received from the sovereign or the law. Besides, every body agrees that the permission granted by the law, and the right from thence resulting, lay other men under an obligation not to resist the person that uses his right, but rather to assist him in this respect, than do him any prejudice. Obligation, therefore, and permission are naturally connected with each other; and this is the effect of the law, which likewise authorizes those, who are disturbed in the exercise of their rights, to employ force, or to have recourse to the sovereign, in order to remove these impediments. Hence it is, that after having mentioned in the definition of law, that it leaves us in certain cases at liberty to act or not to act, we added, that it secures the subjects in the full enjoyment of their rights.*

The rights which men enjoy in society, as founded on this permission.

VIII. The nature and end of laws shew us their matter or object. The matter of laws in general are all human actions, internal and external; thoughts, and words, as well as deeds; those which relate to another, and those which terminate in the person itself; so far, at least, as the direction

The matter of laws.

* See chap. viii. § 3.

of those actions may essentially contribute to the particular good of each person, to that of society in general, and to the glory of the sovereign.

Internal conditions of a law; that it be possible, useful, and just.

IX. This supposes naturally the three following conditions. 1. That the things ordained by the law be possible to fulfil; for it would be folly, and even cruelty, to require of any person, under the least commination of punishment, whatever is and always has <104> been above his strength. 2. The law must be of some utility; for reason will never allow any restraint to be laid on the liberty of the subject, merely for the sake of the restraint, and without any benefit or advantage arising to him. 3. In fine, the law must be in itself just; that is, conformable to the order and nature of things, as well as to the constitution of man: this is what the very idea of rule requires, which, as we have already observed, is the same as that of law.[3]

External conditions of law; that it may be made known; and accompanied with a sanction.

X. To these three conditions, which we may call the internal characteristics of law, namely, that it be possible, just, and useful, we may add two other conditions, which in some measure are external; one, that the law be made sufficiently known; the other, that it be attended with a proper sanction.

1. It is necessary that the laws be sufficiently notified to the subject;* for how could he regulate his actions and motions by those laws, if he had never any knowledge of them? The sovereign ought therefore to publish his laws in a solemn, clear, and distinct manner. But, after that, it is the subject's business to be acquainted with the will of the sovereign; and the ignorance or error he may lie under in this respect, cannot, generally speaking, be a legitimate excuse in his favour. This is what the civilians mean, when they lay down as a maxim, † *That ignorance or error in regard to the law is blameable and hurtful.* Were it not so, the laws would <105> be of no effect, but might always, under a pretext of ignorance, be eluded with impunity.[4]

---

* See chap. viii. § 4.

† *Regula est, juris quidem ignorantiam cuique nocere.* Digest. lib. 22. tit. 6. leg. 9. pr.

3. The two first conditions are taken from DHC I.2 §8, the third from footnote 1 to the same.

4. Based on DHC I.2 §6.

XI. 2. The next thing requisite is, that the law be attended with a proper sanction.

Sanction is that part of the law, which includes the penalty enacted against those who transgress it. With regard to the penalty, it is an evil with which the sovereign menaces those subjects who should presume to violate his laws, and which he actually inflicts, whenever they violate them: and this with a design of procuring some good; such as to correct the culpable, and to admonish the rest; but ultimately, that his laws being respected and observed, society should enjoy a state of security, quiet, and happiness.

All laws have therefore two essential parts: the first is the disposition of the law, which expresseth the command or prohibition; the second is the sanction, which pronounces the penalty; and it is the sanction that gives it the proper and particular force of law. For were the sovereign contented with merely ordaining or forbidding certain things, without adding any kind of menace; this would be no longer a law prescribed by authority, but merely a prudent counsel.[5]

It is not however absolutely necessary that the nature or quality of the punishment be formally specified in the law; it is sufficient that the sovereign declares he will punish, reserving to himself the species and degree of chastisement according to his prudence.* <106>

We must also observe, that the evil, which constitutes the punishment properly so called, ought not to be a natural production, or a necessary consequence of the action intended to be punished. It should be, as it

---

* *Ex quo etiam intelligitur omni legi civili annexam esse poenam, vel explicitè, vel implicitè; nam ubi poena neque scripta, neque exemplo alienjus qui poenas legis jam transgressae dedit, definitur, ibi subintelligitur poenam arbitrariam esse, nimirum ex arbitrio pendere legislatoris.* Hobbes de Cive, cap. 14. § 8. ["From hence also we may understand, that every civill Law hath a penalty annexed to it, either explicitly, or implicitly; For where the penalty is not defined, neither by any writing, nor by example of any one who hath suffered the punishment of the transgressed Law there the penalty is understood to be arbitrary, namely, to depend on the will of the Legislator, that is to say, of the supreme Commander." Thomas Hobbes, *De Cive, a Critical Edition,* ed. Howard Warrender (Oxford: Clarendon Press, 1987), chap. 14, §8, pp. 172–73.]

5. Thus far based on DHC I.2 §7 or on DNG I.6 §14. The following remark on unspecified punishment is based on Barbeyrac's footnote 1 to the first-mentioned paragraph.

were, an occasional evil, and inflicted by the will of the sovereign. For whatever the action may have bad of itself and dangerous in its effects and inevitable consequences, cannot be reckoned as proceeding from the law, since it would equally happen without it. The menaces therefore of the sovereign must, in order to have some weight, be inflictive of such punishments as differ from the evil that necessarily arises from the nature of the thing.*

Whether the promise of recompence is equally capable, as the commination of punishment, to constitute the sanction of law.

XII. It may be asked, in fine, whether the sanction of laws may not as well consist in the promise of a recompence, as in the commination of punishment? I answer, that this depends, in general, on the will of the sovereign, who may use either of these ways; or even employ them both, according as his prudence directs. But since the question is to know, which is the most effectual method the sovereign can use, in order to enforce the observance of his laws; and since it is certain that man is naturally more sensibly affected by evil than good,[6] it seems more proper to establish the sanction of law <107> in the commination of punishment, than in the promise of recompence. People are seldom induced to violate the law, unless it be with the hope of procuring at least some apparent good. The best way therefore to prevent this deception, is to remove the bait that allures them, and to annex, on the contrary, a real and inevitable evil to disobedience. Suppose, for instance, two legislators, willing to establish the same law, proposed, one of them great rewards, and the other severe punishments, the latter would undoubtedly dispose men more effectually to compliance than the former. The most specious promises do not always determine the will; but the view of a rigorous punishment staggers and intimidates it.† But if the sovereign, by a particular effect of his bounty and wisdom, is willing to join these two means, and to enforce the law by a double motive of observance;

* See Locke's Essay on human understanding, book 2. chap. 28. § 6.

† See Puffendorf, Law of nature and nations, book i. chap. vi. § 14. with Barbeyrac's notes.

6. A short overview of this debate on the relative merits of punishments and rewards (or on whether man is more sensitive to pleasure or to pain) is provided by Barbeyrac in DNG I.6 §14 note 4.

there is then nothing wanting to complete its force, since in every respect it is a perfect sanction.

XIII. The obligation which the laws impose,[7] have as great an extent as the right of the sovereign; and consequently it may be said in general, that all those who are dependent on the legislator, are subject to this obligation. But each law in particular obliges those subjects only, to whom the subject matter may be applied; and this is easily known from the very nature of each law, by which the intention of the legislator is sufficiently expressed. <108>

Who those are whom the law obliges. Of dispensation.

Nevertheless it sometimes happens, that particular persons are exempted from the obligation of observing the law; and this is what we call dispensation, on which we have a few remarks to make.

1. If the legislator can intirely abrogate a law, by a much stronger reason he can suspend the effect thereof, with regard to any particular person.

2. But we must likewise acknowledge, that none but the legislator himself is invested with this power.

3. He never ought to use it without very good reasons, and then he should act with moderation, and according to the rules of equity and prudence. For were he, without discretion or choice, to favour too great a number of people with dispensations, he would enervate the authority of the law; or were he to refuse it in cases perfectly alike, so unreasonable a partiality would certainly be attended with jealousy and discontent.

XIV. As for what concerns the duration of laws, and the manner in which they are abolished, we are to observe the following principles.[8]

Of the duration of laws, and how they are abolished.

1. In general the duration of a law, as well as its first establishment, depends on the free will and pleasure of the sovereign, who cannot reasonably tie up his own hands in this respect.

7. Read "has." This and the next paragraph are based on DNG I.6 §17 or DHC I.2 §9.
8. Burlamaqui's discussion is based on DHC I.2 §10 note 2, where Barbeyrac criticizes Pufendorf for omitting to discuss the duration of the laws.

2. And yet every law, of itself and by its nature, is supposed perpetual, when it contains nothing in its disposition, or in the circumstances attending it, that evidently denotes a contrary intention of the legislator, or that may induce us reasonably to presume that it was only a temporary ordinance. The law is a rule; now every rule is <109> of itself perpetual; and, generally speaking, when the sovereign establishes a law, it is not with a design to repeal it.

3. But as the state of things may happen to alter in such a manner, that the law, grown useless or hurtful, can no longer be put in execution; the sovereign can, and ought, in that case, to repeal and abolish it. It would be absurd and pernicious to society, to pretend that laws once enacted ought to subsist for ever, let what inconveniency soever arise.

4. This repeal may be made in two different manners, either expresly or tacitly. For when the sovereign, well acquainted with the state of things, neglects for a long time to enforce the observance of the laws, or formally permits, that affairs relating thereto be regulated in a manner contrary to his disposition; from thence a strong presumption arises of the abrogation of this law, which falls thus of itself, though the legislator has not expresly abolished it.

It is plain we have only glanced here upon the general principles. As for the application that ought to be made of them to each species of laws, it requires some modification, pursuant to their different nature. But it is not our business to enter here into those particulars.

How many sorts of laws. XV. Law may be divided, 1. into divine or human, according as it has God or man for its author.[9]

2. Divine law may be subdivided into two sorts, namely, natural and positive or revealed. <110>

Natural law is that which so necessarily agrees with the nature and state of man, that without observing its maxims, the peace and happiness of society can never be preserved. As this law has an essential agreeableness with the constitution of human nature, the knowledge thereof may be attained merely by the light of reason; and hence it is called natural.

9. The paragraph is based on DNG I.6 §18 or on DHC I.2 §16.

Positive or revealed law is that which is not founded on the general constitution of human nature, but only on the will of God; though in other respects this law is established on very good reasons, and procures the advantage of those who receive it.

We meet with examples of these two sorts of laws in the ordinances which God gave formerly to the Jews. It is easy to distinguish such as were natural, from those that, being merely ceremonial or political, had no other foundation than the particular will of God, accommodated to the actual state of that people.

With regard to human laws, considered strictly as such, viz. as originally proceeding from a sovereign who presides over society, they are all positive. For though some natural laws are made the subject of human laws, they do not derive their obligatory force from the human legislator; since they would oblige all the same without any intervention on his part, because they come from God.

Before we leave these definitions, we must not forget to observe, that the science or art of making and explaining laws, and of applying them to human actions, goes by the general name of *Jurisprudence.* <111>

CHAPTER XI

Of the morality of human actions. *

I. Law being the rule of human actions, in a comparative view, we observe that the latter are either conformable or opposite to the former; and this sort of qualification of our actions in respect to the law, is called *morality.*

The term of *morality* comes from *mores* or manners. Manners, as we have already observed, are the free actions of man, considered as susceptible of direction and rule. Thus we call morality the relation of human actions to the law, by which they are directed; and we give the name

In what the morality of actions consists.

---

* See the law of nature and nations, book i. chap. vii. and the duties of man and a citizen, book i. chap. ii. § 11. &c.

of moral philosophy[1] to the collection of those rules by which we are to square our actions.

Actions are, 1. either commanded, or forbidden, or permitted. II. The morality of actions may be considered in two different lights: 1. in regard to the manner in which the law disposes of them; and 2. in relation to the conformity or opposition of those same actions to the law.

In the first consideration, human actions are either commanded, or forbidden, or permitted.

As we are indispensably obliged to do what is commanded, and to abstain from what is forbidden by a lawful superior, civilians consider commanded actions as necessary, and forbidden actions as im-<112> possible. Not that man is deprived of a physical power of acting contrary to law, and incapable, if he has a mind, of exercising this power. But since his acting after this manner would be opposite to right reason, and inconsistent with his actual state of dependance; it is to be presumed that a reasonable and virtuous man, continuing and acting as such, could not make so bad a use of his liberty; and this presumption is in itself too reasonable and honourable for humanity, not to meet with approbation. *Whatever* (say the Roman lawyers)* *is injurious to piety, reputation, or modesty, and in general to good manners, ought to be presumed impossible.*

Remarks on permitted actions. III. With regard to permitted actions, they are such as the law leaves us at liberty to do, if we think proper.† Upon which we must make two or three remarks.

1. We may distinguish two sorts of permission; one full and absolute, which not only gives us a right to do certain things with impunity, but moreover is attended with a positive approbation of the legislator: The

---

* *Nam quae facta laedunt pietatem, existimationem, verecundiam nostram, & (ut generaliter dixerim) contra bonos mores fiunt, nec facere nos posse credendum est.* L. 15. D. de condit. Institut.

† See chap. x. § 5.

1. The original distinguishes between the morality (moralité) of actions and morals (morale) as the collection of moral rules, not between morality and moral philosophy.

other is an imperfect permission, or a kind of toleration, which implies no approbation but a simple impunity.

2. The permission of natural laws always denotes a positive approbation of the legislator; and whatever happens in consequence thereof, is innocently <113> done, and without any violation of our duty. For it is evident, that God could not positively permit the least thing that is bad in its nature.

3. It is otherwise in respect to the permission of human laws. We may, indeed, justly and with certainty infer, that a sovereign has not thought proper to forbid or punish some particular things; but it does not always from thence follow, that he really approves those things, and much less that they may be innocently done, and without any breach of duty.

IV. The other manner in which we may view the morality of human actions, is with regard to their conformity or opposition to the law. In this respect, actions are divided into good or just, bad or unjust, and indifferent.

2. Actions are good or just, bad or unjust, and indifferent.

An action morally good or just, is that which in itself is exactly conformable to some obligatory law, and moreover is attended with the circumstances and conditions required by the legislator.

I said, 1. A *good or just action;* for there is properly no difference between the goodness and justice of actions; and there is no necessity to deviate here from the common language, which confounds these two ideas.[2] The distinction which Puffendorf makes between these two qualities is quite arbitrary, and even he himself afterwards confounds them.* <114>

2. I said, an action *morally good;* because we do not consider here the intrinsic and natural goodness of actions, by virtue of which they redound to the physical good of man; but only the relation of agreeableness they have to the law, which constitutes their moral goodness. And though these two sorts of goodness are always found inseparably united

---

* Compare what he says in the Law of nature and nations, book i. chap. vii. § 7. in the beginning, with § 4. of the same chapter.

2. Burlamaqui's comment comes from Barbeyrac's note 1 in DNG I.7 §7.

in things ordained by natural law, yet we must not confound these two different relations.

Conditions requisite to render an action morally good. V. In fine, to distinguish the general conditions, whose concurrence is necessary in order to render an action morally good, with respect to the agent; I have added, *that this action ought to be in itself exactly conformable to the law, and accompanied moreover with the circumstances and conditions required by the legislator.* And firstly, it is necessary that this action should comply exactly, and through all its parts, with the tenor of what the law ordains. For as a right line is that whose points correspond to the rule without the least deviation; in like manner an action, rigorously speaking, cannot be just, good, or right, unless it agrees exactly, and in every respect with the law. But even this is not sufficient; the action must be performed also pursuant to the manner required and intended by the legislator. And in the first place, it is necessary it be done with a competent knowledge, that is, we must know that what we do is conformable to the law: otherwise the legislator would have no regard for the action, and our labour would be intirely lost. In the next place, we must act with an upright intention and for a good end, namely, to fulfill the views of the legislator, and to <115> pay a due obedience to the law: For if the agent's intention be bad, the action, instead of being deemed good, may be imputed to him as vicious. In fine, we should act through a good motive, I mean a principle of respect for the sovereign, of submission to the law, and from a love of our duty; for plain it is, that all these conditions are required by the legislator.[3]

Of the nature of bad or unjust actions. VI. What has been above affirmed concerning good actions, sufficiently shews us the nature of those which are bad or unjust. These are, in general, such as of themselves, or by their concomitant circumstances, are contrary to the disposition of an obligatory law, or to the intention of the legislator.

There are, therefore, two general springs of injustice in human actions; one proceeds from the action considered in itself, and from its

3. This paragraph is based on DNG I.8 §§1–3 and on DHC I.2 §11 note 3.

manifest opposition to what is commanded or prohibited by the law. Such as, for example, the murder of an innocent person. And all these kinds of actions intrinsically bad can never become good, whatever may be in other respects the intention or motive of the agent. We cannot employ a criminal action as a lawful means to attain an end in itself good; and thus we are to understand the common maxim, *evil must not be done, that good may come of it.* But an action intrinsically and as to its substance good, may become bad, if it be accompanied with circumstances directly contrary to the legislator's intention; as for instance, if it be done with a bad view, and through a vicious motive. To be liberal and generous towards our fellow-citizens, <116> is a good and commendable thing in itself; but if this generosity is practised merely with ambitious views, in order to become insensibly master of the commonwealth, and to oppress the public liberty; the perversity of the motive, and the injustice of the design, render this action criminal.[4]

VII. All just actions are, properly speaking, equally just; by reason that they have all an exact conformity to the law. It is not the same with unjust or bad actions; which, according as they are more or less opposite to the law, are more or less vicious; similar in this respect to curve lines, which are more or less so, in proportion as they deviate from the rule. We may therefore be several ways wanting in our duty. Sometimes people violate the law deliberately, and *with malice prepense;* which is undoubtedly the very highest degree of iniquity, because this kind of conduct manifestly indicates a formal and reflective contempt of the legislator and his orders; but sometimes we are apt to sin through neglect and inadvertency, which is rather a fault than a crime. Besides, it is plain that this neglect has its degrees, and may be greater or lesser, and deserving of more or less censure. And as in every thing unsusceptible of an exact and mathematical measure, we may always distinguish at least three degrees, namely, two extremes and a middle: Hence the civilians distinguish three degrees of fault or negligence; a gross fault, a slight one, and a very slight one. It is sufficient to have mentioned these principles, the explication

All just actions are equally just; but unjust actions are more or less unjust.

4. This paragraph is based on DNG I.8 §4.

and distinct account whereof will naturally take place, <117> when we come to the particular questions relating to them.

Essential character of unjust actions. VIII. But we must carefully observe, that what essentially constitutes the nature of an unjust action, is its direct opposition or contrariety to the disposition of the law, or to the intention of the legislator; which produces an intrinsic defect in the matter or form of that action. For though in order to render an action morally good, it is necessary, as we have already observed, that it be intirely conformable to the law, with respect as well to the substance, as to the manner and circumstances; yet we must not from thence conclude, that the defect of some of those conditions always renders an action positively bad or criminal. To produce this effect, there must be a direct opposition, or formal contrariety between the action and the law; a simple defect of conformity being insufficient for that purpose. This defect is, indeed, sufficient to render an action not positively good or just; however, it does not become therefore bad, but only indifferent. For example, if we perform an action good in itself, without knowing for what reason, or even that it is commanded by the law; or if we act through a different motive from that prescribed by the law, but in itself innocent and not vicious; the action is reputed neither good nor bad, but merely indifferent.

Of indifferent actions. IX. There is therefore such a thing as indifferent actions, which hold a middle rank, as it were, between just and unjust. These are such as are neither <118> commanded nor prohibited, but which the law leaves us at liberty to do or to omit, according as we think proper. That is, those actions are referred to a law of simple permission, and not to an obligatory law.

Now that such actions there are, is what no one can reasonably question. For what a number of things are there, which being neither commanded nor forbidden by any law, whether divine or human, have consequently nothing obligatory in their nature, but are left to our liberty, to do or to omit, just as we think proper? It is therefore an idle subtlety in schoolmen to pretend that an action cannot be indifferent, unless it be in an abstract consideration, as stript of all the particular circumstances of person, time, place, intention, and manner. An action divested of all these circumstances, is a mere *Ens rationis;* and if there be really any indifferent actions, as undoubtedly there are, they must be relative to particular circumstances of person, time, and place, &c.[5]

X. Good or bad actions may be ranged under different classes, according to the object to which they relate. Good actions referred to God, are comprised under the name of *Piety.* Those which relate to ourselves, are distinguished by the words, *Wisdom, Temperance, Moderation.* Those which concern other men, are included under the terms of *Justice* and *Benevolence.* We only anticipate here the mentioning of this distinction, because we must return to it again when we come to treat of natural law. The same distinction is applicable to bad ac-<119>tions, which belong either to *Impiety, Intemperance,* or *Injustice.*[6]

Division of good and bad actions.

XI. It is common to propose several divisions of justice. That we may not be silent on this article, we shall observe,

Of justice, and its different kinds.

1. That justice may, in general, be divided into perfect or rigorous, and imperfect or not rigorous. The former is that by which we perform towards our neighbour whatever is due to him in virtue of a perfect or rigorous right, that is, the execution of which he may demand by forcible means, unless we satisfy him freely and with a good will; and it is in this strict sense that the word *Justice* is generally understood. The second is that by which we perform towards another the duties owing to him only in virtue of an imperfect and non-rigorous obligation, which cannot be insisted upon by violent methods; but the fulfilling of them is left to each person's honour and conscience.* These kinds of duties are generally comprehended under the appellations of humanity, charity, or benevolence, in opposition to rigorous justice, or justice properly so called.

* See chap. vii. § 8.
5. This paragraph is based on DNG I.7 §5 note 5.
6. This paragraph is based on DHC I.2 §13 note 1 and DNG I.7 §7 note 1.

This division of justice coincides with that of Grotius, into *expletive* and *attributive*.[7]

2. We might subdivide rigorous justice into that which is exercised between equals, and that which takes place between superior and inferior.* The former contains as many different species as there are <120> duties, which one man may in rigour require of every other man, considered as such, and one citizen of every fellow-citizen. The latter includes as many species as there are different societies, where some command, and others obey.†

3. There are other divisions of justice, but such as seem useless, and far from being exact. For example, that of universal and particular justice, taken in the manner as Puffendorf explains it, appears incorrect, inasmuch as one of the members of the division is included in the other.‡ The subdivision of particular justice into distributive and commutative, is incomplete; because it includes only what is due to another, by virtue of some pact or engagement, notwithstanding there are many things which our neighbour may require of us in rigour, without any regard to pact or convention. And we may observe in general, by reading what Grotius and Puffendorf have wrote concerning this subject, that they are at a loss themselves, to give a clear and exact idea of these different kinds of justice. Hence it is manifest, that we had better wave all these scholastic divisions, contrived in imitation of those of Aristotle, and abide by our first division. And indeed, it is only out of respect to the common opinion, that we have taken any notice thereof.§ <121>

---

* This amounts to the same thing very near, as the *Jus rectorium* and *aequatorium* of Grotius. Book i. chap. 1. § 3. num. 3.

† See Buddaeus, Elementa philos. pract. part ii. cap. ii. § 46.

‡ Law of nature and nations, book i. chap. vii. § 8. And the Duties of man and a citizen, book i. chap. ii. § 14. with Barbeyrac's notes.

§ See Grotius, Rights of war and peace, book i. chap. i. § 8. and Puffendorf, Law of nature and nations, book i. chap. vii. § 9, 10, 11, 12. with Barbeyrac's notes.

7. Grotius makes the distinction in DGP I.1 §8.

XII. Besides what we may call the quality of moral actions, they have likewise a kind of quantity, which, by comparing the good actions to one another, as also the bad in the same manner, leads us to a sort of relative estimation, in order to mark the greater or lesser degree of evil to be found in each.[8] We shall give here the principles necessary for this estimation.

Of the relative estimations of moral actions.

1. These actions may be considered with regard to their object. The nobler the object, the higher the excellence of the good action done towards this object; and a bad action, on the contrary, becomes more criminal.

2. In respect to the quality and state of the agent. Thus a favour or benefit received of an enemy, excels that which is conferred upon us by a friend. And, on the contrary, an injury done us by a friend, is more sensible, and more attrocious, than that which is committed by an enemy.

3. In reference to the very nature of the action, according as there is more or less trouble to perform. The more a good action is difficult, supposing every thing else equal, the more worthy it is of praise and admiration. But the easier it is to abstain from a bad action, the more it is blameable and enormous in comparison to another of the same species.

4. In relation to the effects and consequences of the action. An action is so much the better or worse, in proportion as we foresee that its consequences must be more or less advantageous or hurtful. <122>

5. We may add the circumstances of time, place, &c. which are also capable of making the good or bad actions surpass one another in excellence or badness. We have borrowed these remarks from one of Barbeyrac's notes on Puffendorf.*

XIII. Let us observe, in fine, that morality is attributed to persons as well as actions; and as actions are good or bad, just or unjust, we say likewise of men, that they are good or bad, virtuous or vicious.

Morality is applicable to persons as well as actions.

A virtuous man is he that has a habit of acting conformably to the laws and his duty. A vicious man is one that has the opposite habit.

---

* See the Law of nature and nations, book i. chap. viii. § 5. note 1.
8. Based on DHC I.2 §13 note 1.

Virtue therefore consists in a habit of acting according to the laws; and vice in the contrary habit.

I said that virtue and vice are habits. Hence to judge properly of these two characters, we should not stop at some particular action; we ought to consider the whole series of the life and ordinary conduct of man. We should not therefore rank among the number of vicious men, those who through weakness, or otherwise, have been sometimes induced to commit a bad action; as on the other hand, those who have done a few acts of virtue, do not merit the title of honest men. There is no such thing to be found in this world as virtue in every respect complete; and the weakness inseparable from man, requires we should not judge him <123> with full rigour. Since it is allowed that a virtuous man may, through weakness and surprize, commit some unjust action; so it is but right we should likewise allow, that a man who has contracted several vicious habits, may notwithstanding, in particular cases, do some good actions, acknowledged and performed as such. Let us not suppose men worse than they really are, but take care to distinguish the several degrees of iniquity and vice, as well as those of probity and virtue.

The End of the First Part. <124> <125>

∞ PART II ∞

Of the Law of Nature.

CHAPTER I

In what the law of nature consists, and that there is such a thing. First considerations drawn from the existence of God and his authority over us.

I. After having settled the general principles of law, our business is now to apply them to natural law in particular. The questions we have to examine in this second part are of no less importance than to know, whether man, by his nature and constitution, is really subject to laws properly so called? What are these <126> laws? Who is the superior that imposes them? By what method or means is it possible to know them? From whence results the obligation of observing them? What consequence may follow from our negligence in this respect? And, in fine, what advantage on the contrary may arise from the observance of these laws? Subject of this second part.

II. Let us begin with a proper definition of the terms. By natural law we understand, a law that God imposes on all men, and which they are able to discover and know by the sole light of reason, and by attentively considering their state and nature.

Natural law is likewise taken for the system, assemblage, or body of the laws of nature.

Natural jurisprudence is the art of attaining to the knowledge of the laws of nature, of explaining and applying them to human actions.

Whether there are any natural laws.

III. But whether there be really any natural laws, is the first question that presents itself here to our inquiry. In order to make a proper answer, we must ascend to the principles of natural theology, as being the first and true foundation of the law of nature. For when we are asked, whether there are any natural laws, this question cannot be resolved, but by examining the three following articles. 1. Whether there is a God? 2. If there is a God, whether he has a right to impose laws on man? 3. Whether God actually exercises his right in this respect, by really giving us laws, and requiring we should square thereby our actions? These three points will furnish the subject of this and the following chapters.[1] <127>

Of the existence of God.

IV. The existence of God, that is, of a first, intelligent, and self-existent being, on whom all things depend as on their first cause, and who depends himself on no one; the existence, I say, of such a being, is one of those truths that shew themselves to us at the first glance. We have only to attend to the evident and sensible proofs, that present themselves to us, as it were, from all parts.

The chain and subordination of causes among themselves, which necessarily requires we should fix on a first cause; the necessity of acknowledging a first mover; the admirable structure and order of the universe; are all so many demonstrations of the existence of God, within the reach of every capacity. Let us unfold them in a few words.

---

1. Pufendorf had indeed stressed that the natural laws are divine commands and that their character as law is dependent on their expressing the divine will (see, e.g., DNG I.1 §4, DNG I.2 §6, and DNG II.3 §20). Pufendorf also emphasized (see, e.g., DHC I.3 §11) that man has "natural" knowledge of God and of God's intentions to a sufficient extent for the natural laws to be perceived by all as divinely imposed. Yet Pufendorf did not use the term "natural theology," nor did he or Barbeyrac stop to prove God's existence as Burlamaqui does in this chapter; Pufendorf simply made a few offhand remarks in DHC I.4 §2. Barbeyrac does, however, refer his readers to Locke's *Essay Concerning Human Understanding* IV.10 for a more extensive discussion. He does so in footnote 1 to DNG II.3 §20.

V. 1. We behold an infinite number of objects, which form all together the assemblage we call the universe. Something therefore must have always existed. For were we to suppose a time in which there was absolutely nothing, it is evident that nothing could have ever existed; because whatsoever has a beginning, must have a cause of its existence; since nothing can produce nothing.[2] It must be therefore acknowledged that there is some eternal being, who exists necessarily and of himself; for he can be indebted to no one else for his origin; and it implies a contradiction that such a being does not exist.

Moreover, this eternal being, who necessarily and of himself subsists, is endued with reason and understanding. For to pursue the same manner of arguing, were we to suppose a time in which there was nothing but inanimate beings, it would have been <128> impossible for intelligent beings, such as we now behold, ever to exist. Intellection can no more proceed from a blind and unintelligent cause, than a being, of any kind whatsoever, can come from nothing. There must therefore have always existed a father of spiritual beings, an eternal mind, the source from whence all others derive their existence. Let what system soever be adopted concerning the nature and origin of the soul, our proof subsists still in its full force. Were it even to be supposed that the cogitative part of man is no more than the effect of a certain motion or modification of matter; yet we should still want to know how matter acquired this activity, which is not essential to it, and this particular and so much admired organization, which it cannot impart to itself. We should inquire, who is it that has modified the body in a manner proper to produce such wonderful operations as those of intellection, which reflects, which acts on the very body itself with command, which surveys the earth, and measures the heavens, recollects past transactions, and extends its views to futurity. Such a master-piece must come from the hands of an intel-

First proof. The necessity of a self-existent and intelligent being.

2. The word Burlamaqui uses is "néant" or "nothingness," a term he may have taken from Coste's translation of Locke's *Essay Concerning Human Understanding* IV.10 §§2–3. Locke's discussions in those and the following paragraphs of the *Essay* seem to constitute the main source for Burlamaqui's arguments in this paragraph and in this chapter as a whole.

ligent cause; wherefore it is absolutely necessary to acknowledge a first, eternal, and intelligent being.

We must not seek for this being in this universe.

VI. An eternal spirit, who has within himself the principle of his own existence, and of all his faculties, can be neither changed nor destroyed; neither dependent nor limited; he should even be invested with infinite perfection, sufficient to render him the sole and first cause of all, so that we may have no occasion to seek for any other. <129>

But does not (some will ask) this quality of an eternal and intelligent being, belong to matter itself, to the visible world, or to some of the parts thereof?

I answer, that this supposition is absolutely contrary to all our ideas. Matter is not essentially and of itself intelligent; nor can it be supposed to acquire intellection but by a particular modification received from a cause supremely intelligent.[3] Now this first cause cannot have such a modification from any other being; for he thinks essentially and of himself; wherefore he cannot be a material being. Besides, as all the parts of the universe are variable and dependent, how is it possible to reconcile this with the idea of an infinite and all perfect being?

As for what relates to man, his dependance and weakness are much more sensible than those of other creatures. Since he has no life of himself, he cannot be the efficient cause of the existence of others. He is unacquainted with the structure of his own body, and with the principle of life; incapable of discovering in what manner motions are connected with ideas, and which is the proper spring of the empire of the will. We must therefore look out for an efficient, primitive, and original cause of mankind, beyond the human chain, be it supposed ever so long; we must trace the cause of each part of the world beyond this material and visible world.

Second proof. The necessity of a first mover.

VII. 2. After this first proof drawn from the necessity of a first, eternal, and intelligent being, distinct from matter; we proceed to a second, which shews us the Deity in a more sensible manner, and more within

3. Burlamaqui repeats Locke, *Essay Concerning Human Understanding* IV.10 §§10–11 and §§13–17.

the reach of common capacities. The <130> proof I mean, is the contemplation of this visible world, wherein we perceive a motion and order, which matter has not of itself, and must therefore receive from some other being.

Motion or active force is not an essential quality of body: extension is of itself rather a passive being; it is easily conceived at rest, and if it has any motion, we may well conceive it may lose it without being stript of its existence; it is a quality or state that passes, and is accidentally communicated from one body to another. The first impression must therefore proceed from an extrinsic cause; and as Aristotle has well expressed it, *The first mover of bodies must not be moveable himself, must not be a body.* This has been also agreed to by Hobbes. †*But the acknowledging,* says he, *of one God eternal, infinite, and omnipotent, may more easily be derived, from the desire men have to know the causes of natural bodies, and their several virtues and operations, than from the fear of what was to befall them in time to come. For he that from any effect he seeth come to pass, should reason to the next and immediate cause thereof, and from thence to the cause of that cause, and plunge himself profoundly in the pursuit of causes; shall at last come to this, that there must be (as even the heathen philosophers confessed) one first mover; that is, a first and eternal cause of all things; which is that which men mean by the name of God.*

VIII. 3. But if matter has not been able to move of itself, much less was it capable to move to the <131> exact degree, and with all the determinations, necessary to form such a world as we behold, rather than a confused chaos.

Third proof. The structure, order, and beauty of the universe.

In fact, let us only cast our eyes on this universe, and we shall every where discover, even at the first glance, an admirable beauty, regularity, and order; and this admiration will increase in proportion, as in searching more closely into nature, we enter into the particulars of the structure, proportion, and use of each part. For then we shall clearly see, that every thing is relative to a certain end, and that these particular ends,

* Aristot. Metaphys.
† Leviathan, chap. xii. p. 53. edit. 1651.

though infinitely varied among themselves, are so dextrously managed and combined, as to conspire all to a general design. Notwithstanding this amazing diversity of creatures, there is no confusion; we behold several thousand different species, which preserve their distinct form and qualities. The parts of the universe are proportioned and balanced, in order to preserve a general harmony; and each of those parts has exactly its proper figure, proportions, situation, and motion, either to produce its particular effect, or to form a beautiful whole.

It is evident therefore, that there is a design, a choice, a visible reason in all the works of nature; and consequently there are marks of wisdom and understanding, obvious, as it were, even to our very senses.

The world is not the effect of chance. IX. Though there have been some philosophers who have attributed all these phaenomena to chance, yet this is so ridiculous a thought, that I question whether a more extravagant chimera ever entered into the mind of man. Is it possible for any one <132> to persuade himself seriously, that the different parts of matter having been set in some unaccountable manner in motion, produced of themselves the heavens, the stars, the earth, the plants, and even animals and men, and whatever is most regular in the organization? A man that would pass the like judgment on the least edifice, on a book or picture, would be looked upon as a mad extravagant person. How much more shocking is it to common sense, to attribute to chance so vast a work, and so wonderful a composition as this universe?

It is not eternal. X. It would be equally frivolous to alledge the eternity of the world, in order to exclude a first intelligent cause. For besides the marks of novelty we meet with in the history of mankind, as the origin of nations and empires, and the invention of arts and sciences, &c. besides the assurance we have from the most general and most ancient tradition that the world has had a beginning (a tradition which is of great weight in regard to a matter of fact, like this) besides, I say, all this, the very nature of the thing does not allow us to admit of this hypothesis no more than that of chance. For the question is still to explain whence comes this beautiful order, this regular structure and design, in a word, whence proceed those marks of reason and wisdom that are so visibly displayed in all parts of the universe. To say that it has been always so, without the intervention of an intelligent cause, does not explain the thing, but leaves us in the same embarrassment, and advances the same absurdity as those <133> who a while ago were speaking to us of chance. For this is in reality telling us that whatever we behold throughout the universe, is blindly ranged, without design, choice, cause, reason, or understanding. Hence the principal absurdity of the hypothesis of chance, occurs likewise in this system; with this difference only, that by establishing the eternity of the world, they suppose a chance that from all eternity hit upon order; whereas those who attribute the formation of the world to the fortuitous junction of its parts, suppose that chance did not succeed till a certain time, when it fell in at length with order after an infinite number of trials and fruitless combinations. Both acknowledge therefore no other cause but chance, or properly speaking they acknowledge none at all; for chance is no real cause, it is a word that cannot account for a real effect, such as the arrangement of the universe.

It would not be a difficult matter to carry these proofs to a much greater length, and even to increase them with an additional number. But this may suffice for a work of this kind; and the little we have said, intitles us, methinks, to establish the existence of a *First Cause,* or of a *Creator,* as an incontestable truth, that may serve henceforward for the basis of all our reasonings.

XI. As soon as we have acknowledged a Creator, it is evident, that he has a supreme right to lay his commands on man, to prescribe rules of conduct to him, and to subject him to laws; and it is no less evident, that man on his side finds himself, by his natural constitution, under an ob-<134>ligation of subjecting his actions to the will of this supreme Being.

God has a right to prescribe laws to man.

We have already shewn,* that the true foundation of sovereignty in the person of the sovereign, is power united with wisdom and goodness; and that, on the other hand, weakness and wants in the subjects, are the natural cause of dependance. We have only therefore to see, whether all these qualities of the sovereign are to be found in God; and whether

---

* See part i. chap. ix.

men, on their side, are in a state of infirmity and wants, so as to depend necessarily on him for their happiness.

This is a
consequence of
his power,
wisdom, and
goodness. XII. It is beyond doubt, that he who exists necessarily and of himself, and has created the universe, must be invested with an infinite power. As he has given existence to all things by his own will, he may likewise preserve, annihilate, or change them as he pleases.

But his wisdom is equal to his power. Having made every thing, he must know every thing, as well the causes as the effects from thence resulting. We see besides in all his works the most excellent ends, and a choice of the most proper means to attain them; in short, they all bear, as it were, the stamp of wisdom.

XIII. Reason informs us, that God is a being essentially good; a perfection which seems to flow naturally from his wisdom and power. For how is it possible for a being, who of his nature is infinitely wise and powerful, to have any inclination to hurt? Surely no sort of reason can ever determine him to it. Malice, cruelty, and injustice, are always a con-<135> sequence of ignorance or weakness.[4] Let man therefore consider but never so little the things which surround him, and reflect on his own constitution, he will discover both within and without himself the benevolent hand of his Creator, who treats him like a father. It is from God we hold our life and reason; it is he that supplies most abundantly our wants, adding the useful to the necessary, and the agreeable to the useful. Philosophers observe, that whatever contributes to our preservation, has been arrayed with some agreeable quality.* Nourishment, repose, action,

---

* See an excellent treatise lately published, (at Geneva, for Barillot and son, in 12mo, 1747.) intitled, *The Theory of agreeable Sensations;* where, after pointing out the rules that nature follows in the distribution of pleasure, the principles of natural theology and ethics are established. [When Burlamaqui wrote this, the small book by Louis de Pouilly had recently been published in a new edition (Geneva, 1747) with a foreword by Jacob Vernet. The book glorifies God's wisdom in creating man, who naturally desires felicity and finds his way toward that goal through reasoning as well as instinct and sentiment.]

4. This argument is familiar from DHC I.4 §5 and from DNG II.1 §3, including note 4, as well as from DNG II.3 §§5–6.

heat, cold, in short, whatever is useful to us, pleases us in its turn, and so long as it is useful. Should it cease to be so, because things are carried to a dangerous excess, we have notice therefore by an opposite sensation. The allurement of pleasure invites us to use them when they are necessary for our wants; disrelish and lassitude induce us to abstain from them, when they are likely to hurt us. Such is the happy and sweet oeconomy of nature, which annexes a pleasure to the moderate exercise of our senses and faculties, insomuch that whatever surrounds us becomes a source of satisfaction, when we know how to use it with discretion. What can be more magnificent, for example, than this great theatre of the world in which we live, and this glittering decoration of heaven and earth, exhibiting a thousand agreeable objects to our view? What <136> satisfaction does not the mind receive from the sciences, by which it is exercised, inlarged, and improved? What conveniences do not we draw from human industry? What advantages do not we derive from an intercourse with our equals! What charms in their conversation! What sweetness in friendship, and the other connexions of the heart! When we avoid the excess and abuse of things, the greatest part of human life abounds with agreeable sensations. And if to this we add, that the laws which God gives us, tend, as hereafter we shall see, to perfect our nature, to prevent all kind of abuse, and to confine us to a moderate use of the good things of life, on which the preservation, excellence, and happiness, as well public as private, of man depends; what more is there wanting to convince us, that the goodness of God is not inferior either to his wisdom or power?

We have therefore a superior undoubtedly invested with all the qualities necessary to found the most legitimate and most extensive authority: And since on our side experience shews us, that we are weak and subject to divers wants; and since every thing we have, we have from him, and he is able either to augment or diminish our enjoyments; it is evident, that nothing is wanting here to establish on the one side the absolute sovereignty of God, and on the other our unlimited dependance. <137>

CHAPTER II

That God, in consequence of his authority over us,
has actually thought proper to prescribe to us laws
or rules of conduct.

God exercises
his authority
over us, by
prescribing
laws to us.

I. To prove the existence of God, and our dependance in respect to him, is establishing the right he has of prescribing laws to man. But this is not sufficient; the question is, whether he has actually thought proper to exercise this right. He can undoubtedly impose laws on us; but has he really done it? and though we depend on him for our life, and for our physical faculties, has he not left us in a state of independance in respect to the moral use to which we are to apply them? This is the third and capital point we have still left to examine.

First proof,
drawn from
the very rela-
tions of which
we have been
speaking.

II. 1. We have made some progress already in this research, by discovering all the circumstances necessary to establish an actual legislature. On the one side we find a superior, who by his nature is possessed in the very highest degree of all the conditions requisite to establish a legitimate authority; and on the other we behold man, who is God's creature, endowed with understanding and liberty, capable of acting with knowledge and choice, sensible of pleasure and pain, susceptible of good and evil, of rewards and punishments. Such an aptitude of giving and receiving laws cannot be useless. This concurrence of relations and circumstances undoubtedly denotes an end, and must have <138> some effect; just as the particular organization of the eye shews we are destined to see the light. Why should God have made us exactly fit to receive laws, if he intended none for us? This would be creating so many idle and useless faculties. It is therefore not only possible, but very probable, that our destination in general is such, unless the contrary should appear from much stronger reasons. Now instead of there being any reason to destroy this first presumption, we shall see that every thing tends to confirm it.[1]

---

1. The question whether God deems it fit that man should live without law frames

III. 2. When we consider the beautiful order which the supreme wisdom has established in the physical world, it is impossible to persuade ourselves, that he has abandoned the spiritual or moral world to chance and disorder. Reason, on the contrary, tells us, that a wise being proposes to himself a reasonable end in every thing he does, and that he uses all the necessary means to attain it. The end which God had in view with regard to his creatures, and particularly with respect to man, cannot be any other, on the one side, than his glory; and on the other, the perfection and happiness of his creatures, so far as their nature or constitution will admit. These two views, so worthy of the Creator, are perfectly combined. For the glory of God consists in manifesting his perfections, his power, his goodness, wisdom, and justice; and these virtues are nothing else but the love of order and of the good of the whole. Thus a being absolutely perfect and supremely happy, willing to conduct man to that state of order and happiness which suits his nature, cannot but be willing at the same time to employ whatever is necessary for <139> such an end; and consequently he must approve of those means that are proper, and disapprove of such as are improper for attaining it. Had the constitution of man been merely physical or mechanical, God himself would have done whatever is expedient for his work: But man being a free and intelligent creature, capable of discernment and choice; the means which the Deity uses to conduct him to his end, ought to be proportioned to his nature, that is, such as man may engage in, and concur with, by his own actions.

Now as all means are not equally fit to conduct us to a certain end, all human actions cannot therefore be indifferent. Plain it is, that every action, contrary to the ends which God has proposed, is not agreeable to the divine Majesty; and that he approves, on the contrary, those which of themselves are proper to promote his ends. Since there is a choice to be made, who can question but our Creator is willing we should take the right road; and that, instead of acting fortuitously and rashly, we should behave like rational creatures, by exercising our liberty, and the

Second proof, drawn from the end which God proposed to himself with respect to man, and from the necessity of moral laws, to accomplish this end.

---

the beginning of DNG book 2. Burlamaqui's first argument that this is not the case is drawn from DNG II.1 §5.

other faculties he has given us, in the manner most agreeable to our state and destination, in order to promote his views, and to advance our own happiness, together with that of our fellow-creatures?[2]

Confirmation
of the
preceding
proofs.
IV. These considerations assume a new force, when we attend to the natural consequences of the opposite system. What would become of man and society, were every one to be so far master of his actions, as to do every thing he listed, without having any <140> other principle of conduct than caprice or passion? Let us suppose, that God abandoning us to ourselves, had not actually prescribed any rules of life, or subjected us to laws; most of our talents and faculties would be of no manner of use to us. To what purpose would it be for man to have the light of reason, were he to follow only the impulse of instinct, without watching over his conduct? What would it avail him to have the power of suspending his judgment, were he to yield stupidly to the first impressions? And of what service would reflexion be, were he neither to chuse nor deliberate; and were he, instead of listening to the counsels of prudence, to be hurried away by blind inclinations? These faculties, which form the excellence and dignity of our nature, would not only be rendered hereby entirely frivolous, but, moreover, would become prejudicial even by their excellence; for the higher and nobler the faculty is, the more the abuse of it proves dangerous.

This would be not only a great misfortune for man considered alone, and in respect to himself; but would still prove a greater evil to him when viewed in the state of society. For this more than any other state requires laws, to the end that each person may set limits to his pretensions, without invading another man's right. Were it otherwise, licentiousness must be the consequence of independance. To leave men abandoned to themselves, is leaving an open field to the passions, and paving the way for

2. For Burlamaqui, happiness is both the goal that every man sets before himself as a matter of fact and a goal that God imposes on man as a matter of duty. Given that Burlamaqui tends to deduce man's duty to obey God from God's ability to help man secure the end he in fact proposes to himself, that is, happiness, the resulting theory is somewhat ambiguous.

injustice, violence, perfidy and cruelty. Take away natural laws, and that moral tie which supports justice and honesty in a whole nation, and establishes <141> also particular duties either in families, or in the other relations of life; man would be then the most savage and ferocious of all animals. The more dexterous and artful he is, the more dangerous he would prove to his equals; his dexterity would degenerate into craft, and his art into malice. Then we should be divested of all the advantages and sweets of society; and thrown into a state of war and libertinism.[3]

V. 3. Were any one to say, that man himself would not fail to remedy these disorders, by establishing laws in society; (beside that human laws would have very little force were they not founded on the principles of conscience); this remark shews there is a necessity for laws in general, whereby we gain our cause. For if it be agreeable to the order of reason that men should establish a rule of life among themselves, in order to be screened from the evils they might apprehend from one another, and to procure those advantages that are capable of forming their private and public happiness; this alone ought to convince us, that the Creator, infinitely wiser and better than ourselves, must have undoubtedly pursued the same method. A good parent that takes care to direct his children by his authority and counsels, is able to preserve peace and order in his family; is it then to be imagined, that the common father of mankind should neglect to give us the like assistance? and if a wise sovereign has nothing so much at heart as to prevent licentiousness by salutary regulations; how can any one believe that God, who is a much greater friend to man than man is to his equals, has left all mankind without direction and <142> guide, even on the most important matters, on which our whole happiness depends? Such a system would be no less contrary to the goodness than to the wisdom of God. We must therefore have recourse to other ideas, and conclude that the Creator having, through a pure effect of his bounty, created man for happiness, and having im-

Third proof, drawn from the goodness of God.

---

3. Libertinism does not here refer to freethinking: the original's "brigandage" denotes robbery and other specifically lawless actions. Burlamaqui's discussion draws on DNG II.1 §§6–8.

planted in him an insuperable inclination to felicity, subjecting him at the same time to live in society, he must have given him also such principles as are capable of inspiring him with a love of order, and rules to point out the means of procuring and attaining it.

Fourth proof, drawn from the principles of conduct which we actually find within ourselves.

VI. 4. But let us enter into ourselves, and we shall actually find, that what we ought to expect in this respect from the divine wisdom and goodness, is dictated by right reason,[4] and by the principles engraved in our hearts.

If there be any speculative truths that are evident, or if there be any certain axioms that serve as a basis to sciences; there is no less certainty in some principles that are laid down in order to direct our conduct, and to serve as the foundation of morality. For example; *That the all-wise and all bountiful Creator merits the respects of the creature: That man ought to seek his own happiness: That we should prefer the lesser to the greater evil: That a benefit deserves a grateful acknowledgment: That the state of order excels that of disorder, &c.* Those maxims, and others of the same sort, differ very little in evidence from these, *The whole is greater than its part; or the cause precedes the effect, &c.* Both are dictated by pure reason; and hence we feel ourselves <143> forced, as it were, to give our assent to them. These general principles are seldom contested; if there be any dispute, it relates only to their application and consequences. But so soon as the truth of those principles is discovered, their consequences, whether immediate or remote, are entirely as certain, provided they be well connected; the whole business being to deduce them by a train of close and conclusive argumentations.

These principles are obligatory of themselves.

VII. In order to be sensible of the influence which such principles, with their legitimate consequences, ought to have over our conduct, we have only to recollect what has been already said in the first part of this work,* concerning the obligation we are under of following the dictates of reason. As it would be absurd in speculative matters, to speak and judge

* Chap. vi.
4. The translator avoids Burlamaqui's formulation "the right reason that he [God] gave us."

otherwise than according to that light which makes us discern truth from falshood; so it would be no less preposterous to deviate in our conduct from those certain maxims which enable us to discern good from evil. When once it is manifest, that a particular manner of acting is suitable to our nature, and to the great end we have in view; and that another, on the contrary, does not suit our constitution or happiness; it follows, that man, as a free and rational creature, ought to be very attentive to this difference, and to take his resolutions accordingly. He is obliged to it by the very nature of the thing; because it is absolutely necessary when a person is desirous of the end, to be desirous also of the means; and he is obliged to it moreover, because he cannot mistake the intention and will of his superior in this respect. <144>

VIII. In effect God being the author of the nature of things, and of our constitution, if, in consequence of this nature and constitution, we are reasonably determined to judge after a certain manner, and to act according to our judgment, the Creator sufficiently manifests his intention, so that we can no longer be ignorant of his will. The language therefore of reason is that of God himself. When our reason tells us so clearly, *that we must not return evil for good,* it is God himself, who by this internal oracle gives us to understand what is good and just, what is agreeable to him and suitable to ourselves. We said that it is not at all probable, that the good and wise Creator should have abandoned man to himself, without a guide and direction for his conduct. We have here a direction that comes from him; and since he is invested in the very highest degree, as we have already observed, with the perfections on which a legitimate superiority is founded, who can pretend to question that the will of such a superior is a law to us? The reader, I suppose, has not forgot the conditions requisite to constitute a law; conditions that are all to be met with in the present case. 1. There is a rule. 2. This rule is just and useful. 3. It comes from a superior on whom we entirely depend. 4. In fine, it is sufficiently made known to us, by principles engraved in our hearts, and even by our own reason. It is therefore a law properly so called, which we are really obliged to observe. But let us inquire a little further, by what means this natural law is discovered, or,

They are obligatory by the divine will, and thus become real laws.

which amounts to the same thing, from what <145> source we must derive it. What we have hitherto proved only in a general manner, will be further illustrated and confirmed by the particulars on which we are now going to inlarge. For nothing can be a stronger proof of our having hit upon the true principles, than when unfolding and considering them in their different branches, we find they are always conformable to the nature of things.

CHAPTER III

*Of the means by which we discern what is just
and unjust, or what is dictated by natural law;
namely, 1. moral instinct, and 2. reason.*

First means of discerning moral good and evil, namely, instinct or inward sense.

I. What has been said in the preceding chapter already shews, that God has invested us with two means of perceiving or discerning moral good and evil; the first is only a kind of instinct; the second is reason or judgment.

Moral instinct I call that natural bent or inclination which prompts us to approve of certain things as good and commendable, and to condemn others as bad and blameable, independent of reflexion. Or if any one has a mind to distinguish this instinct by the name of moral sense, as Mr. Hutchinson has done, I shall then say, that it is a faculty of the mind, which instantly discerns, in certain cases, moral good and evil, by a kind of sensation and taste, independent of reason and reflexion.[1] <146>

Examples.

II. Thus at the sight of a man in misery or pain, we feel immediately a sense of compassion, which prompts us to relieve him. The first emotion that strikes us, after receiving a benefit, is to acknowledge the favour, and to thank our benefactor. The first disposition of one man towards an-

---

1. The author is Francis Hutcheson, who developed Shaftesbury's notion of a "moral sense" into a central element in his theory.

other, abstracting from any particular reason he may have of hatred or fear, is a sense of benevolence, as towards his fellow-creature, with whom he finds himself connected by a conformity of nature and wants. We likewise observe, that without any great thought or reasoning, a child, or untutored peasant, is sensible that ingratitude is a vice, and exclaims against perfidy, as a black and unjust action, which highly shocks him, and is absolutely repugnant to his nature. On the contrary, to keep one's word, to be grateful for a benefit, to pay every body their due, to honour our parents, to comfort those who are in distress or misery, are all so many actions which we cannot but approve and esteem as just, good, honest, beneficent, and useful to mankind. Hence the mind is pleased to see or hear such acts of equity, sincerity, humanity, and beneficence; the heart is touched and moved; and reading them in history we are seized with admiration, and extol the happiness of the age, nation, or family, distinguished by such noble examples. As for criminal instances, we cannot see or hear them mentioned, without contempt or indignation.

III. If any one should ask, from whence comes this emotion of the heart, which prompts us, almost <147> without any reasoning or inquiry, to love some actions and to detest others; the only answer I am able to give, is, that it proceeds from the author of our being, who has formed us after this manner, and whom it has pleased that our nature or constitution should be such, that the difference of moral good and evil should, in some cases, affect us exactly in the same manner as physical good and evil. It is therefore a kind of instinct, like several others which nature has given us, in order to determine us with more expedition and vigour, where reflexion would be too slow. It is thus we are informed of our corporeal wants by our inward sense; while our outward senses acquaint us with the quality of the objects that may be useful or prejudicial to us, in order to lead us, as it were, mechanically to whatever is requisite for our preservation. Such is also the instinct that attaches us to life, and the desire of happiness, the primum mobile of all our actions. Such is likewise the almost blind, but necessary tenderness of parents towards their

Whence these sensations proceed.

children. The pressing and indispensable wants of man required he should be directed by the way of sense, which is always quicker and readier than that of reason.

IV. God has therefore thought proper to use this method in respect to the moral conduct of man, by imprinting within us a sense or taste of virtue and justice, which anticipates, in some measure, our reason, decides our first motions, and happily supplies, in most men, the want of attention or reflexion. For what numbers of people would never <148> trouble their heads with reflecting? What multitudes are there of stupid wretches, that lead a mere animal life, and are scarce able to distinguish three or four ideas, in order to form what is called a ratiocination? It was therefore our particular advantage, that the Creator should give us a discernment of good and evil, with a love for the one, and an aversion for the other, by means of a quick and lively kind of faculty, which has no necessity to wait for the speculations of the mind.

V. If any one should dispute the reality of these sensations, by saying they are not to be found in all men, because there are savage people who seem to have none at all; and even among civilized nations we meet with such perverse and stubborn minds, as do not appear to have any notion or sense of virtue: I answer, 1. that the most savage people have nevertheless the first ideas above mentioned; and if there are some who seem to give no outward signs or demonstrations thereof, this is owing to our not being sufficiently acquainted with their manners; or because they are intirely stupified, and have stifled almost all sentiments of humanity; or, in fine, by reason that in some respects they fall into an abuse contrary to these principles, not by rejecting them positively, but through some prejudice that has prevailed over their good sense and natural rectitude, and inclines them to make a bad application of these principles. For example, we see savages who devour their enemies whom they have made prisoners, imagining it to be the right of war, and that since they have liberty to kill them, nothing ought to hin-<149>der them from benefiting by their flesh, as their proper spoils. But those very savages would not treat in that manner their friends or countrymen: They have laws and rules among themselves; sincerity and plain dealing are esteemed there as in other places, and a grateful heart meets with as much commendation among them as with us.

VI. 2. With regard to those who in the most enlightened and civilized countries seem to be void of all shame, humanity, or justice, we must take care to distinguish between the natural state of man, and the depravation into which he may fall by abuse, and in consequence of irregularity and debauch. For example, what can be more natural than paternal tenderness? And yet we have seen men who seemed to have stifled it, through violence of passion, or by force of a present temptation, which suspended for a while this natural affection. What can be stronger than the love of ourselves and of our own preservation? It happens, nevertheless, that whether through anger, or some other motion which throws the soul out of its natural position, a man tears his own limbs, squanders his substance, or does himself some great prejudice, as if he were bent on his own misery and destruction.

2. We must distinguish between the natural state of man, and that of his depravation.

VII. 3. In fine, if there are people, who cooly, and without any agitation of mind, seem to have divested themselves of all affection and esteem for virtue; (besides, that monsters like these are as rare, I hope, in the moral as in the physical world); we only see thereby the effects of an exquisite and inveterate de-<150>pravation. For man is not born thus corrupted; but the interest he has in excusing and palliating his vices, the habit he has contracted, and the sophistical arguments to which he has recourse, may stifle, in fine, or corrupt the moral sense of which we have been speaking; as we see that every other faculty of the soul or body may by long abuse be altered or corrupted. Happily nevertheless we observe, that our spiritual senses are less subject than our corporeal ones to depravity and corruption. The principle is almost always preserved; it is a fire, that when it seems even to be extinct, may kindle again and throw out some glimmerings of light, as we have seen examples in very profligate men, under particular conjunctures.

3. If there be any monsters in the moral order, they are very rare, and no consequence can be drawn from them.

Second means
of discerning
moral good
and evil; which
is reason.

VIII. But notwithstanding God has implanted in us this instinct or sense, as the first means of discerning moral good and evil, yet he has not stopt here; he has also thought proper that the same light which serves to direct us in every thing else, that is, reason, should come to our assistance, in order to enable us the better to discern and comprehend the true rules of conduct.

Reason I call the faculty of comparing ideas, of investigating the mutual relations of things, and from thence inferring just consequences. This noble faculty, which is the directress of the mind, serves to illustrate, to prove, to extend, and apply what our natural sense already gave us to understand, in relation to justice and injustice. As reflexion, instead of diminishing paternal tenderness, tends to strengthen it, by making us observe how agreeable it is to the relation of father and son, to the advantage <151> not only of a family, but of the whole species; in like manner the natural sense we have of the beauty and excellence of virtue, is considerably improved by the reflexions we are taught by reason, in regard to the foundations, motives, relations, and the general as well as particular uses of this same virtue, which seemed so beautiful to us at first sight.

First advantage
of reason in
respect to
instinct; it
serves to
verify it.

IX. We may even affirm, that the light of reason has three advantages here in respect to this instinct or sense.

1. It contributes to prove its truth and exactness; in the same manner as we observe in other things that study and rules serve to verify the exactness of taste, by shewing us it is neither blind nor arbitrary, but founded on reason, and directed by principles: or as those who are quick-sighted, judge with greater certainty of the distance or figure of an object, after having compared, examined, and measured it quite at their leisure, than if they had depended intirely on the first sight. We find likewise that there are opinions and customs, which make so strong and so general an impression on our minds, that to judge of them only by the sentiment they excite, we should be in danger of mistaking prejudice for truth. It is reason's province to rectify this erroneous judgment, and to counterbalance this effect of education, by setting before us the true principles on which we ought to judge of things.

X. 2. A second advantage which reason has in respect to simple instinct, is, that it unfolds the ideas better, by considering them in all their relations <152> and consequences. For we frequently see that those, who have had only the first notion, find themselves embarrassed and mistaken, when they are to apply it to a case of the least delicate or complicated nature. They are sensible indeed of the general principles, but they do not know how to follow them through their different branches, to make the necessary distinctions or exceptions, or to modify them according to time and place. This is the business of reason, which it discharges so much the better, in proportion as there is care taken to exercise and improve it.

Second advantage: it unfolds the principles, and from thence infers proper consequences.

XI. 3. Reason not only carries its views farther than instinct, with respect to the unfolding and application of principles; but has also a more extensive sphere, in regard to the very principles it discovers, and the objects it embraces. For instinct has been given us only for a small number of simple cases, relative to our natural state, and which require a quick determination. But besides those simple cases, where it is proper that man should be drawn and determined by a first motion; there are cases of a more composite nature, which arise from the different states of man, from the combination of certain circumstances, and from the particular situation of each person; on all which it is impossible to form any rules but by reflexion, and by an attentive observation of the relations and agreements of each thing.

Third advantage: reason is an universal means, and applicable to all cases.

Such are the two faculties with which God has invested us, in order to enable us to discern between good and evil. These faculties happily joined, and subordinate one to the other, concur to the same effect. One gives the first notice, the other verifies <153> and proves it; one acquaints us with the principles, the other applies and unfolds them; one serves for a guide in the most pressing and necessary cases, the other distinguishes all sorts of affinity or relation, and lays down rules for the most particular cases.

It is thus we are enabled to discern what is good and just, or, which amounts to the same thing, to know what is the divine will, in respect to the moral conduct we are to observe. Let us unite at present these two means, in order to find the principles of the law of nature.

CHAPTER IV

Of the principles from whence reason may deduce the law of nature.*

From whence are we to deduce the principles of the law of nature?

I. If we should be afterwards asked, what principles ought reason to make use of, in order to judge of what relates to the law of nature,[1] and to deduce or unfold it? our answer is in general, that we have only to attend to the nature of man, and to his states or relations; and as these relations are different, there may be likewise different principles, that lead us to the knowledge of our duties.

But before we enter upon this point, it will be proper to make some preliminary remarks on what we call *principles of natural law;* in order to prevent the ambiguity or equivocation, that has often entangled this subject. <154>

Preliminary remarks. What we understand by principles of natural law.

II. 1. When we inquire here, which are the first principles of natural law, the question is, which are those truths or primitive rules, whereby we may effectually know the divine will in regard to man; and thus arrive, by just consequences, to the knowledge of the particular laws and duties which God imposes on us by right reason?

2. We must not therefore confound the principles here in question, with the efficient and productive cause of natural laws, or with their obligatory principle.[2] It is unquestionable, that the will of the supreme

---

* See on this, and the following chapter, Puffendorf's Law of nature and nations, book ii. chap. iii.

1. Here as elsewhere, the translator gives the singular "law of nature" for Burlamaqui's plural "les lois naturelles."

2. In his critique of Pufendorf, Leibniz had stated that it is surprising and contradictory to argue that God's will constitutes the "efficient cause" of natural law. See "The Judgment of an Anonymous Writer" §13, in Samuel Pufendorf, *The Whole Duty of Man, According to the Law of Nature,* ed. Ian Hunter and David Saunders (Indianapolis: Liberty Fund, 2003), pp. 267–305. See the introduction.

Being is the efficient cause of the law of nature, and the source of the obligation from thence arising. But this being taken for granted, we have still to inquire how man may attain to the knowledge of this will, and to the discovery of those principles, which acquainting us with the divine intention, enable us to reduce from thence all our particular duties, so far as they are discoverable by reason only. A person asks, for example, whether the law of nature requires us to repair injuries, or to be faithful to our engagements? If we are satisfied with answering him, that the thing is incontestable, because so it is ordered by the divine will; it is plain that this is not a sufficient answer to his question; and that he may reasonably insist to have a principle pointed out, which should really convince him that such in effect is the will of the Deity; for this is the point he is in search of.

III. Let us afterwards observe, that the first principles of natural laws, ought to be not only true, <155> but likewise simple, clear, sufficient, and proper for those laws.

Character of those principles.

They ought to be true; that is, they should be taken from the very nature and state of the thing. False or hypothetic principles must produce consequences of the same nature; for a solid edifice can never be raised on a rotten foundation. They ought to be simple and clear of their own nature, or at least easy to apprehend and unfold. For the laws of nature being obligatory for all mankind, their first principles should be within every body's reach, so that whosoever has common sense may be easily acquainted with them. It would be very reasonable therefore to mistrust principles that are far-fetched, or of too subtle and metaphysical a nature.

I add, that these principles ought to be sufficient and universal. They should be such as one may deduce from thence, by immediate and natural consequences, all the laws of nature, and the several duties from thence resulting; insomuch that the exposition of particulars be properly only an explication of the principles; in the same manner, pretty near, as the production or increase of a plant is only an unfolding of the seed.

And as most natural laws are subject to divers exceptions, it is likewise necessary that the principles be such as include the reasons of the very exceptions; and that we may not only draw from thence all the common rules of morality, but that they also serve to restrain these rules, according as place, time, and occasion require.

In fine, those first principles ought to be established in such a manner, as to be really the proper and <156> direct foundation of all the duties of natural law; insomuch that whether we descend from the principle to deduce the consequences, or whether we ascend from the consequences to the principle, our reasonings ought always to be immediately connected, and their thread, as it were, never interrupted.

Whether we ought to reduce the whole to one single principle.

IV. But, generally speaking, it is a matter of mere indifference, whether we reduce the whole to one single principle, or establish a variety of them. We must consult and follow in this respect a judicious and exact method. All that can be said on this head, is, that it is not at all necessary to the solidity or perfection of the system, that all natural laws be deduced from one single and fundamental maxim: nay, perhaps the thing is impossible. Be that as it may, it is idle to endeavour to reduce the whole to this unity.[3]

Such are the general remarks we had to propose. If they prove just, we should reap this double advantage from them, that they will instruct us in the method we are to follow, in order to establish the true principles of natural law; and at the same time they will enable us to pass a solid judgment on the different systems concerning this subject. But it is time now to come to the point.

Man cannot attain to the knowledge of natural laws, but by examining his nature, constitution, and state.

V. The only way to attain to the knowledge of natural law, is to consider attentively the nature and constitution of man, the relations he has to the beings that surround him, and the states from thence resulting. In fact, the very term of *natural law,* and the notion we have given of it, shew that the <157> principles of this science must be taken from the very nature and constitution of man. We shall therefore lay down two

---

3. Burlamaqui sides with Pufendorf's critics, many of whom agreed that it was a mistake for Pufendorf to deduce all natural law duties (including, e.g., man's religious duties) from the needs of society and of social life. Burlamaqui follows Barbeyrac in deducing the natural law duties from three separate sources: see DHC I.3 §13 note 1; see also DNG II.3 §15 note 5.

general propositions, as the foundation of the whole system of the law
of nature.

First Proposition.

Whatever is in the nature and original constitution of man, and appears
a necessary consequence of this nature and constitution, certainly indicates the intention or will of God with respect to man, and consequently acquaints us with the law of nature.

Second Proposition.

But in order to have a complete system of the law of nature, we must
not only consider the nature of man, such as it is in itself; it is also necessary to attend to the relations he has to other beings, and to the different states from thence arising: otherwise it is evident we should have
only an imperfect and defective system.

We may therefore affirm, that the general foundation of the system
of natural law, is the nature of man considered under the several circumstances that attend it, and in which God himself has placed him for
particular ends; inasmuch as by this means we may be acquainted with
the will of God. In short, since man holds from the hand of God himself
whatever he possesses, as well with regard to his existence, as to his manner of existing; it is the study of human nature only, that can fully instruct us concerning the views which God proposed to himself in giving
<158> us our being, and consequently with the rules we ought to follow,
in order to accomplish the designs of the Creator.

VI. For this purpose we must recollect what has been already said, of
the manner in which man may be considered under three different respects or states, which embrace all his particular relations. In the first
place we may consider him as God's creature, from whom he has received
his life, his reason, and all the advantages he enjoys. Secondly, man may
be considered in himself as a being, composed of body and soul, and
endowed with many different faculties; as a being that naturally loves

Three states of man.

himself, and necessarily desires his own felicity. In fine, we may consider him as forming a part of the species, as placed on the earth near several other beings of a similar nature, and with whom he is inclined, nay, by his natural condition, obliged to live in society.[4] Such, in fact, is the system of humanity, from whence results the most common and natural distinction of our duties, taken from the three different states here mentioned; duties towards God, towards ourselves, and towards the rest of mankind.*

Religion: principle of the natural laws, that have God for their object.

VII. In the first place, since reason brings us acquainted with God as a self-existent being, and so-<159>vereign Lord of all things, and in particular as our creator, preserver, and benefactor; it follows therefore that we ought necessarily to acknowledge the sovereign perfection of this supreme Being, and our absolute dependance on him: which by a natural consequence inspires us with sentiments of respect, love, and fear, and with an intire submission to his will. For why should God have thus manifested himself to mankind, were it not that their reason should teach them to entertain sentiments proportioned to the excellence of his nature, that is, they should honour, love, adore, and obey him?[5]

Consequences of this principle.

VIII. Infinite respect is the natural consequence of the impression we receive from a prospect of all the divine perfections. We cannot refuse love and gratitude to a being supremely beneficent. The fear of displeasing or offending him, is a natural effect of the idea we entertain of his justice and power, and obedience cannot but follow from the knowledge

* We meet with this division in Cicero: Philosophy, says he, teaches us in the first place the worship of the deity; secondly, the mutual duties of men, founded on human society; and, in fine, moderation and greatness of soul. "*Haec* (*philosophia*) *nos primum ad illorum* (*deorum*) *cultum, deinde ad jus hominum, quod situm est in generis humani societate, tum ad modestiam magnitudinemque animi erudivit.*" Cic. Tusc. quaest. lib. 1. cap. 26.

4. This threefold division is in DHC I.3 §13.

5. Burlamaqui's discussion of man's duties toward God is mainly based on Pufendorf in DHC I.4, but without Pufendorf's insistence on the social dangers of atheism and his discussion of religion as "the strongest bond of human society," DHC I.4 §9.

of his legitimate authority over us, of his bounty, and supreme wisdom, which are sure to conduct us by the road most agreeable to our nature and happiness. The assemblage of these sentiments, deeply engraved in the heart, is called *Piety.*

Piety, if it be real, will shew itself externally two different ways, by our morals, and by outward worship. I say, 1. by *our morals,* because a pious man, sincerely penetrated with the abovementioned sentiments, will find himself naturally inclined to speak and act after the manner he knows to be most conformable to the divine will and perfections: this is his rule and model; from whence the practice of the most excellent virtues arises. <160>

2. But besides this manner of honouring God, which is undoubtedly the most necessary and most real, a religious man will consider it as a pleasure and duty to strengthen himself in these sentiments of piety, and to excite them in others. Hence external worship, as well public as private, is derived. For whether we consider this worship as the first and almost only means of exciting, entertaining, and improving religious and pious sentiments in the mind; or whether we look upon it as a homage, which men, united by particular or private societies, pay in common to the Deity; or whether, in fine, both these views are joined, reason represents it to us as a duty of indispensable necessity.[6]

This worship may vary indeed in regard to its form; yet there is a natural principle which determines its essence, and preserves it from all frivolous and superstitious practices; viz. that it consists in instructing mankind, in rendering them pious and virtuous, and in giving them just ideas of the nature of God, as also of what he requires from his creatures.

The different duties here pointed out, constitute what we distinguish by the name of *Religion.* We may define it, a connexion which attaches man to God, and to the observance of his laws, by those sentiments of respect, love, submission, and fear, which the perfections of a supreme Being, and our intire dependance on him, as an all-wise, and all-bountiful Creator, are apt to excite in the human mind.

Thus by studying our nature and state, we find, in the relation we

---

6. Observations on the need for external worship based on DNG II.4 §3 note 2.

have to the Deity, the proper principle from whence those duties of natural law, that have God for their object, are immediately derived. <161>

Self-love: the principle of those natural laws which concern ourselves.

IX. If we search afterwards for the principle of those duties that regard ourselves, it will be easy to discover them, by examining the internal constitution of man, and inquiring into the Creator's views in regard to him, in order to know for what end he has endowed him with those faculties of mind and body that constitute his nature.

Now it is evident, that God, by creating us, proposed our preservation, perfection, and happiness. This is what manifestly appears, as well by the faculties with which man is invested, which all tend to the same end; as by the strong inclination that prompts us to pursue good, and shun evil. God is therefore willing, that every one should labour for his own preservation and perfection, in order to acquire all the happiness of which he is capable according to his nature and state.

This being premised, we may affirm that self-love (I mean an enlightened and rational love of ourselves) may serve for the first principle with regard to the duties which concern man himself; inasmuch as this sensation being inseparable from human nature, and having God for its author, gives us clearly to understand in this respect the will of the supreme Being.[7]

Yet we should take particular notice, that the love of ourselves cannot serve us as a principle and rule, but inasmuch as it is directed by right reason, according to the exigencies or necessities of our nature and state.

For thus only it becomes an interpreter of the Creator's will in respect to us; that is, it ought to be managed in such a manner, as not to offend the laws of religion or society. Otherwise this self-love <162> would become the source of a thousand iniquities; and so far from being of any service, would prove a snare to us, by the prejudice we should certainly receive from those very iniquities.

---

7. Pufendorf treats man's duties to himself in, for example, DHC I.5; Burlamaqui summarizes Pufendorf's long chapter, but he also follows Barbeyrac in making self-love the source of these duties; see DHC I.5 §1 note 1.

X. From this principle, thus established, it is easy to deduce the natural laws and duties that directly concern us. The desire of happiness is attended, in the first place, with the care of our preservation. It requires next, that (every thing else being equal) the care of the soul should be preferred to that of the body. We ought not to neglect to improve our reason, by learning to discern truth from falshood, the useful from the hurtful, in order to acquire a just knowledge of things that concern us, and to form a right judgment of them. It is in this that the perfection of the understanding, or wisdom, consists. We should afterwards be determined, and act constantly according to this light, in spite of all contrary suggestion and passion. For it is properly this vigour or perseverance of the soul, in following the counsels of wisdom, that constitutes virtue, and forms the perfection of the will, without which the light of the understanding would be of no manner of use.

Natural laws derived from this principle.

From this principle all the particular rules arise. You ask, for example, whether the moderation of the passions be a duty imposed upon us by the law of nature? In order to give you an answer, I inquire, in my turn, whether it is necessary to our preservation, perfection, and happiness? If it be, as undoubtedly it is, the question is decided. You have a mind to know whether the love of occupation, the discerning between permitted and forbidden <163> pleasures, and moderation in the use of such as are permitted, whether, in fine, patience, constancy, resolution, &c. are natural duties; I shall always answer, by making use of the same principle; and, provided I apply it well, my answer cannot but be right and exact; because the principle conducts me certainly to the end, by acquainting me with the will of God.

XI. There remains still another point to investigate, namely, the principle from whence we are to deduce those natural laws that regard our mutual duties, and have society for their object. Let us see whether we cannot discover this principle, by pursuing the same method. We ought always to consult the actual state of things, in order to take their result.

Man is made for society.

I am not the only person upon earth; I find myself in the middle of an infinite number of other men, who resemble me in every respect; and I am subject to this state, even from my nativity, by the very act of providence. This induces me naturally to think, it was not the intention of God that each man should live single and separate from the rest; but that, on the contrary, it was his will they should live together, and be joined in society. The Creator might certainly have formed all men at the same time, though separated from one another, by investing each of them with the proper and sufficient qualities for this kind of solitary life. If he has not followed this plan, it is probably because it was his will that the ties of consanguinity and birth should begin to form a more extensive union, which he was pleased to establish amongst men. <164>

The more I examine, the more I am confirmed in this thought. Most of the faculties of man, his natural inclinations, his weakness, and wants, are all so many indubitable proofs of this intention of the Creator.

1. Society is absolutely necessary for man.

XII. Such in effect is the nature and constitution of man, that out of society he could neither preserve his life, nor display and perfect his faculties and talents, nor attain any real and solid happiness. What would become of an infant, were there not some benevolent and assisting hand to provide for his wants? He must perish, if no one takes care of him; and this state of weakness and ignorance requires even a long and continued assistance. View him when grown up to manhood, you find nothing but rudeness, ignorance, and confused ideas, which he is scarce able to convey; abandon him to himself, and you behold a savage, and perhaps a ferocious animal; ignorant of all the conveniences of life, sunk in idleness, a prey to spleen and melancholy, and almost incapable of providing against the first wants of nature. If he attains to old age, behold him relapsed into infirmities that render him almost as dependent on external aid as he was in his infancy. This dependance shews itself in a more sensible manner in accidents and maladies. What would then become of man, were he to be in a state of solitude? There is nothing but the assistance of our fellow-creatures that is able to preserve us from divers evils, or to redress them, and render life easy and happy, in whatsoever stage or situation of life.[8] <165>

---

8. Before discussing the duties of sociability, Burlamaqui provides a set of argu-

We have an excellent picture of the use of society, drawn by Seneca.*
On what, says he, *does our security depend, but on the services we render
one another? It is this commerce of benefits that makes life easy, and enables
us to defend ourselves against any sudden insults or attacks. What would be
the fate of mankind, were every one to live apart? So many men, so many
victims to other animals, an easy prey, in short, feebleness itself. In fact, other
animals have strength sufficient to defend themselves: Those that are wild
and wandering, and whose ferocity does not permit them to herd together,
are born, as it were, with arms; whereas man is on all sides encompassed
with weakness, having neither arms, nor teeth, nor claws to render him formidable. But the strength he wants by himself, he finds when united with
his equals. Nature, to make amends, has endowed him with two things,
<166> which give him a considerable force and superiority, where otherwise
he would be much inferior; I mean reason and sociability, whereby he who
alone could make no resistance, becomes master of the whole. Society gives
him an empire over other animals; society is the cause, that, not satisfied with
the element on which he was born, he extends his command over the sea. It
is this same union that supplies him with remedies in his diseases, assistance
in his old age, and comfort in his pains and anxieties; it is this that enables
him, as it were, to bid defiance to fortune. Take away society, and you destroy
the union of mankind, on which the preservation and the whole happiness
of life depends.*

---

ments to prove that man in fact needs social life in order to secure his own happiness;
much of this discussion is from DNG II.1 §8 and DHC I.3 §3.

* *Quo alio tuti sumus, quàm quòd mutuis juvamur officiis? Hoc uno instructior vita
contraque incursiones subitas munitior est, beneficiorum commercio. Fac nos singulos,
quid sumus? praeda animalium et victimae, ac imbellissimus et facillimus sanguis. Quoniam caeteris animalibus in tutelam sui satis virium est: quaecunque vaga nascuntur, &
actura vitam segregem, armata sunt. Hominem imbecillitas cingit; non unguium vis, non
dentium, terribilem caeteris fecit. Nudum & infirmum societas munit. Duas res dedit
quae illum, obnoxium caeteris, validissimum facerent, rationem & societatem. Itaque,
qui par esse nulli poterat, si seduceretur, rerum potitur. Societas illi dominium omnium
animalium dedit: Societas terris genitum, in alienae naturae transmisit imperium, &
dominari etiam in mari jussit. Haec morborum impetus arcuit, senectuti adminicula
prospexit, solatia contra dolores dedit. Haec fortes nos facit, quod licet contra fortunam
advocare. Hanc societatem tolle, & unitatem generis humani, quá vita sustinetur, scindes.*
Senec. de Benef. lib. 4. cap. 18.

2. Man by his constitution is very fit for society.

XIII. As society is so necessary to man, God has therefore given him a constitution, faculties, and talents, that render him very proper for this state. Such is, for example, the faculty of speech, which enables us to convey our thoughts with facility and readiness, and would be of no manner of use out of society. The same may be said with regard to our propensity to imitation, and of that surprising mechanism which renders all the passions and impressions of the soul so easy to be communicated. It is sufficient a man appears to be moved, in order to move and soften others.* If a person accosts us with joy painted on his countenance, he excites in us the like sentiment of joy. The tears of a stranger affect us, even before we know the cause there-<167>of;† and the cries of a man related to us only by the common tie of humanity, make us fly to his succour by a mechanical movement previous to all deliberation.

This is not all. We see that nature has thought proper to distribute differently her talents among men, by giving to some an aptitude to perform certain things, which to others are impossible; while the latter have received, in their turn, an industry denied to the former. Wherefore, if the natural wants of men render them dependent on one anther, the diversity of talents, which qualifies them for mutual aid, connects and unites them. These are so many evident signs of man's being designed for society.

3. Our natural inclinations prompt us to look out for society.

XIV. But if we consult our own inclinations, we shall likewise find, that our hearts are naturally bent to wish for the company of our equals, and to dread an intire solitude as an irksome and forlorn state. And though there have been instances of people who have thrown themselves into a solitary life, yet we cannot consider this in any other light but as the effect of superstition, or melancholy, or of a singularity extremely remote from the state of nature. Were we to investigate the cause of this social inclination, we should find it was very wisely bestowed on us by the author of our being; by reason that it is in society man finds a remedy

---

* *Homo sum; humani nihil a me alienum puto.* Ter. Heauton.
† *Ut ridentibus adrident, ita flentibus adflent*
  Humani vultus. —Hor. de Arte poet. v. 101.

for the greatest part of his wants, and an occasion for exercising <168> most of his faculties; it is in society he is capable of feeling and displaying those sensations on which nature has intailed so much satisfaction and pleasure; I mean, the sensations of benevolence, friendship, compassion, and generosity. For such are the charms of social affections, that from thence our purest enjoyments arise. Nothing in fact is so satisfactory and flattering to man, as to think he merits the esteem and friendship of others. Science acquires an additional value, when it can display itself abroad; and our joy becomes more sensible, when we have an opportunity of testifying it in public, or of pouring it into the bosom of a friend: it is redoubled by being communicated; for our own satisfaction is increased by the agreeable idea we have of giving pleasure to our friends, and of fixing them more steadily in our interest. Anxiety, on the contrary, is alleviated and softened by sharing it with our neighbour; just as a burden is eased when a good-natured person helps us to bear it.

Thus every thing invites us to the state of society; want renders it necessary to us, inclination makes it a pleasure, and the dispositions we naturally have for it, are a sufficient indication of its being really intended by our Creator.

XV. But as human society can neither subsist, nor produce the happy effects for which God has established it, unless mankind have sentiments of affection and benevolence for one another; it follows therefore, that our Creator and common Father is willing that every body should be animated with these sentiments, and do whatever lies in their power <169> to maintain this society in an agreeable and advantageous state, and to tie the knot still closer by reciprocal services and benefits.

Sociability. Principles of natural laws relative to other men.

This is the true principle of the duties which the law of nature prescribes to us in respect to other men. Ethic writers have given it the name of *Sociability*, by which they understand that disposition which inclines us to benevolence towards our fellow-creatures, to do them all the good that lies in our power, to reconcile our own happiness to that of others, and to render our particular advantage subordinate to the common and general good.

The more we study our own nature, the more we are convinced that this sociability is really agreeable to the will of God. For, beside the necessity of this principle, we find it engraved in our heart; where, if the Creator has implanted on one side the love of ourselves, the same hand has imprinted on the other a sentiment of benevolence for our fellow-creatures.[9] These two inclinations, though distinct from one another, have nothing opposite in their nature; and God who has bestowed them upon us, designed they should act in concert, in order to help, and not to destroy each other. Hence good-natured and generous hearts feel a most sensible satisfaction in doing good to mankind, because in this they follow the inclination they received from nature.

Natural laws which flow from sociability.

XVI. From the principle of sociability, as from their real source, all the laws of society, and all our general and particular duties towards other men, are derived. <170>

1. The public good ought always to be the supreme rule.

1. This union which God has established among men requires, that in every thing relating to society, the public good should be the supreme rule of their conduct, and that guided by the counsels of prudence, they should never pursue their private advantage to the prejudice of the public: For this is what their state demands, and is consequently the will of their common father.

2. The spirit of sociability ought to be universal.

2. The spirit of sociability ought to be universal. Human society embraces all those with whom we can have possibly any communication; because it is founded on the relations they all bear to one another, in consequence of their nature and state.*

3. To observe a natural equality.

3. Reason afterwards informs us, that creatures of the same rank and species, born with the same faculties to live in society, and to partake of the same advantages, have in general an equal and common right. We are therefore obliged to consider ourselves as naturally equal, and to behave as such; and it would be bidding defiance to nature, not to acknowledge this principle of equity (which by the civilians is called *aequabilitas juris*) as one of the first foundations of society. It is on this the *lex talionis*

---

* See Puffendorf, Law of nature and nations, book ii. chap. iii. § 15.

9. The emphasis on man's natural benevolence for his fellow creatures is absent in Pufendorf and Barbeyrac, but constitutes a central theme in Hutcheson's thought.

is founded, as also that simple but universal and useful rule, that we ought to have the same dispositions in regard to other men, as we desire they should have towards us, and to behave in the same manner towards them, as we are willing they should behave to us in the like circumstances.

4. Sociability being a reciprocal obligation among men, such as through malice or injustice break the <171> band of society, cannot reasonably complain, if those they have injured do not treat them as friends, or even if they proceed against them by forcible methods.

4. To preserve a benevolence even towards our enemies. Self-defence is permitted, revenge is not.

But though we have a right to suspend the acts of benevolence in regard to an enemy, yet we are never allowed to stifle its principle. As nothing but necessity can authorise us to have recourse to force against an unjust aggressor, so this same necessity should be the rule and measure of the harm we do him; and we ought to be always disposed to reconcilement so soon as he has done us justice, and we have nothing farther to apprehend.

We must therefore distinguish carefully between a just defence of one's own person, and revenge. The first does but suspend, through necessity, and for a while, the exercise of benevolence, and has nothing in it opposite to sociability. But the other stifling the very principle of benevolence, introduces, in its stead, a sentiment of hatred and animosity, a sentiment vicious in itself, contrary to the public good, and expresly condemned by the law of nature.

XVII. These general rules are very fertile of consequences.

Particular consequences.

We should do no wrong to any one, either in word or action; and we ought to repair all damages by us committed; for society could not subsist, were acts of injustice tolerated.

We ought to be sincere in our discourse, and steady to our engagements; for what trust could men repose in one another, and what security could they have in commercial life, were it lawful to violate their plighted faith? <172>

We not only ought to do to every man the good he properly deserves, but moreover we should pay him the degree of esteem and honour due to him, according to his estate and rank; because subordination is the link of society, without which there can be no order either in families, or in civil governments.

But if the public good requires that inferiors should obey, it demands also that superiors should preserve the rights of those who are subject to them, and should govern their people only in order to render them happy.

Again: men are captivated by the heart, and by favours; now nothing is more agreeable to humanity, or more useful to society, than compassion, lenity, beneficence, and generosity. This is what induced Cicero to say,* *There is nothing truer than that excellent maxim of Plato, viz. that we are not born for ourselves alone, but likewise for our country and friends: And if, according to the Stoics, the productions of the earth are for men, and men themselves for the good and assistance of one another; we ought certainly, in this respect, to comply with the <173> design of nature, and promote her intention, by contributing our share to the general interest, by mutually giving and receiving good turns, and employing all our care and industry, and even our substance, to strengthen that love and friendship which should always prevail in human society.*

Since therefore the different sentiments and acts of justice and goodness, are the only and true bonds that knit men together, and are capable of contributing to the stability, peace, and prosperity of society; we must look upon those virtues as so many duties that God imposes on us, for this reason, because whatever is necessary to his design, is of course conformable to his will.

These three principles have all the requisite characters.

XVIII. We have therefore three general principles of the laws of nature relative to the abovementioned three states of man: And these are, 1. Religion. 2. Self-love. 3. Sociability or benevolence towards our fellow-creatures.

These principles have all the characters above required. They are *true*,

---

* *Sed quoniam (ut praeclarè scriptum est a Platone) non nobis solùm nati sumus, ortusque nostri partem patria vindicat, partem amici: atque (ut placet Stoicis) quae in terris gignuntur, ad usum hominum omnia creari, homines autem hominum causa esse generatos, ut ipsi inter se aliis alii prodesse possent: in hoc naturam debemus ducem sequi, & communes utilitates in medium afferre, mutatione officiorum, dando, accipiendo: tum artibus, tum opera, tum facultatibus devincire hominum inter homines societatem.* Cic. de Offic. lib. 1. cap. 7.

because they are taken from the nature of man, in the constitution and state in which God has placed him. They are *simple,* and within every body's reach, which is an important point; because, in regard to duties, there is nothing wanting but principles that are obvious to every one; for a subtlety of mind that sets us upon singular and new ways, is always dangerous. In fine, these principles are *sufficient,* and very *fertile;* by reason they embrace all the objects of our duties, and acquaint us with the will of God in the several states and relations of man. <174>

XIX. True it is, that Puffendorf reduces the thing within a lesser compass, by establishing sociability alone as the foundation of all natural laws. But it has been justly observed, that this method is defective. For the principle of sociability does not furnish us with the proper and direct foundation of all our duties. Those which have God for their object, and those which are relative to man himself, do not flow directly and immediately from this source, but have their proper and particular principle. Let us suppose man in solitude: He would still have several duties to discharge, such as to love and honour God, to preserve himself, to cultivate his faculties as much as possible, &c. I acknowledge that the principle of sociability is the most extensive, and that the other two have a natural connexion with it; yet we ought not to confound them, as if they had not their own particular force, independent of sociability. These are three different springs, which give motion and action to the system of humanity; springs distinct from one another, but which act all at the same time pursuant to the views of the Creator.

Remarks on Puffendorf's system.

XX. Be it said nevertheless, in justification of Puffendorf, and according to a judicious observation made by Barbeyrac, that most of the criticisms on the former's system, as defective in its principle, have been pushed too far. This illustrious restorer of the study of natural law declares, his design was properly no more than to explain the natural duties <175> of man:* Now for this purpose he had occasion only for the principle of sociability. According to him, our duties towards God form a part of

The critics have carried their censures too far against him in this respect.

* See the Law of nature and nations, book ii. chap. iii. § 19. Specim. controvers. cap. 5. § 25. Spicilegium controversiarum, cap. 1. § 14.

natural theology; and religion is interwoven in a treatise of natural law, only as it is a firm support of society. With regard to the duties that concern man himself, he makes them depend partly on religion, and partly on sociability.* Such is Puffendorf's system: He would certainly have made his work more perfect, if embracing all the states of man, he had established distinctly the proper principles agreeable to each of those states, in order to deduce afterwards from thence all our particular duties: For such is the just extent we ought to give to natural law.

Of the connexion between our natural duties.

XXI. This was so much the more necessary, as notwithstanding our duties are relative to different objects, and deduced from distinct principles, yet they have, as we already hinted, a natural connexion; insomuch that they are interwoven, as it were, with one another, and by mutual assistance, the observance of some renders the practice of others more easy and certain. It is certain, for example, that the fear of God, joined to a perfect submission to his will, is a very efficacious motive to engage men to discharge what directly concerns themselves, and to do for their neighbour and for society whatever the law of nature requires. It is also certain, that the duties <176> which relate to ourselves, contribute not a little to direct us with respect to other men. For what good could the society expect from a man, who would take no care to improve his reason, or to form his mind and heart to wisdom and virtue? On the contrary, what may not we promise ourselves from those who spare no pains to perfect their faculties and talents, and are pushed on towards this noble end, either by the desire of rendering themselves happy, or by that of procuring the happiness of others? Thus whosoever neglects his duty towards God, and deviates from the rules of virtue in what concerns himself, commits thereby an injustice in respect to other men, because he subtracts so much from the common happiness. On the contrary, a person who is penetrated with such sentiments of piety, justice, and benevolence, as religion and sociability require, endeavours to make himself happy; because, according to the plan of providence, the personal felicity of every man is inseparably connected, on the one side with re-

* See the Duties of man and a citizen, book i. chap. iii. § 15.

ligion, and on the other with the general happiness of the society of which he is a member; insomuch that to take a particular road to happiness is mistaking the thing, and rambling quite out of the way. Such is the admirable harmony, which the divine wisdom has established between the different parts of the human system. What could be wanting to complete the happiness of man, were he always attentive to such salutary directions?

XXII. But as the three grand principles of our duties are thus connected, so there is likewise a natural subordination between them, that helps to decide <177> which of those duties ought to have the preference in particular circumstances or cases, when they have a kind of conflict or opposition that does not permit us to discharge them all alike.

Of the opposition that sometimes happens between these very duties.

The general principle to judge rightly of this subordination is, that the stronger obligation ought always to prevail over the weaker. But to know afterwards which is the stronger obligation, we have only to attend to the very nature of our duties, and their different degrees of necessity and utility; for this is the right way to know in that case the will of God. Pursuant to these ideas, we shall give here some general rules concerning the cases above mentioned.

1. The duties of man towards God should always prevail over any other. For of all obligations, that which binds us to our all-wise and all-bountiful Creator, is without doubt the nearest and strongest.

2. If what we owe to ourselves comes in competition with our duty to society in general, society ought to have the preference. Otherwise, we should invert the order of things, destroy the foundations of society, and act directly contrary to the will of God, who by subordinating the part to the whole, has laid us under an indispensable obligation of never deviating from the supreme law of the common good.

3. But if, every thing else equal, there happens to be an opposition between the duties of self-love and sociability, self-love ought to prevail. For man being directly and primarily charged with the care of his own preservation and happiness, it follows therefore that in a case of intire inequality, the care of ourselves ought to prevail over that of others.
<178>

4. But if, in fine, the opposition is between duties relating to ourselves, or between two duties of sociability, we ought to prefer that which is accompanied with the greatest utility, as being the most important.*

Natural law
obligatory; and
natural law of
*simple permis-
sion.* General
principle of
the law of
permission.

XXIII. What we have hitherto explained, properly regards the natural law called *obligatory,* viz. that which having for its object those actions wherein we discover a necessary agreeableness or disagreeableness to the nature and state of man, lays us therefore under an indispensable obligation of acting or not acting after a particular manner. But in consequence of what has been said above,† we must acknowledge that there is likewise a law of *simple permission,* which leaves us at liberty in particular cases to act or not; and by laying other men under a necessity of giving us no let or molestation, secures to us in this respect the exercise and effect of our liberty.

The general principle of this law of permission is, that we may reasonably, and according as we judge proper, do or omit whatever has not an absolute and essential agreeableness or disagreeableness to the nature and state of man; unless it be a thing expressly ordained or forbidden by some positive law, to which we are otherwise subject.

The truth of this principle is obvious. The Creator having invested man with several faculties, and among the rest with that of modifying his actions as he thinks proper; it is plain that in every thing <179> in which he has not restrained the use of those faculties, either by an express command or a positive prohibition, he leaves man at liberty to exercise them according to his own discretion. It is on this law of permission all those rights are founded, which are of such a nature as to leave us at liberty to use them or not, to retain or renounce them in the whole or in part; and in consequence of this renunciation, actions in themselves

---

* See Barbeyrac's fifth note on section 15. of the third chapter, book ii. of the Law of nature and nations. [Burlamaqui makes one modification to Barbeyrac's rule 2, which in Barbeyrac's text states that preference is to be given to the option which promotes more overall utility. Burlamaqui's modification results in a conflict between rules 2 and 3.]

† See part i. chap. x. § 5. and 6.

permitted, happen sometimes to be commanded or forbidden by the authority of the sovereign, and become obligatory by that means.

XXIV. This is what right reason discovers in the nature and constitution of man, in his original and primitive state. But as man himself may make divers modifications in his primitive state, and enter into several adventitious ones; the consideration of those new states fall likewise upon the object of the law of nature, taken in its full extent; and the principles we have laid down ought to serve likewise for a rule in the states in which man engages by his own act and deed.

Hence occasion has been taken to distinguish two species of natural law; the one primary, the other secondary.

The primary or primitive natural law is that which immediately arises from the primitive constitution of man, as God himself has established it, independent of any human act.

Secondary natural law is that which supposes some human act or establishment; as a civil state, property of goods, &c. <180>

It is easy to comprehend, that this secondary natural law is only a consequence of the former; or rather it is a just application of the general maxims of natural law to the particular states of mankind, and to the different circumstances in which they find themselves by their own act; as it appears in fact, when we come to examine into particular duties.

*Some perhaps will be surprized, that in establishing the principles of natural law, we have taken no notice of the different opinions of writers concerning this subject. But we judged it more adviseable to point out the true sources from whence the principles were to be drawn, and to establish afterwards the principles themselves, than to enter into a discussion which would have carried us too far for a work of this nature. If we have hit upon the true one, this will be sufficient to enable us to judge of all the rest; and if any one desires a more ample and more particular instruction, he may easily find it, by consulting Puffendorf,

Two species of natural law; one primitive, the other secondary.

* See Grotius, Rights of war and peace, book i. chap. i. § 10. and Puffendorf, Law of nature and nations, book ii. chap. iii. § 22.

who relates the different opinions of civilians, and accompanies them with very judicious reflections.* <181>

CHAPTER V

That natural laws have been sufficiently notified;
of their proper characteristics, the obligation
they produce, &c.

God has suffi-
ciently notified
the laws of
nature to man.

I. After what has been hitherto said in relation to the principles of natural laws, and the way we come to know them, there is no need to ask whether God has sufficiently notified those laws to man. It is evident we can discover all their principles, and deduce from thence our several duties, by that natural light which to no man has been ever refused. It is in this sense we are to understand what is commonly said, that this law is naturally known to all mankind. For to think with some people, that the law of nature is innate, as it were, in our minds, and actually imprinted in our souls from the first moment of our existence; is supposing a thing that is not at all necessary, and is moreover contradicted by experience.[1] All that can be said on this subject, is, that the most general and most important maxims of the law of nature, are so clear and manifest, and have such a proportion to our ideas, and such an agreeableness to our nature, that so soon as they are proposed to us, we instantly approve of them; and as we are disposed and accustomed from our infancy to feel these truths, we consider them as born with us.

Men may
assist one
another in
this respect.

II. But we must take care to observe, that when we say man may acquire the knowledge of natural <182> laws, by using his reason; we do not exclude the succours he may receive from elsewhere. Some there are, who

---

* See Puffendorf, Law of nature and nations, book ii. chap. iii. § 1–14.

1. The critique of the thesis that man's knowledge, especially moral knowledge, is based on innate ideas, imprinted in the soul or "engraved in the heart," originated with Pufendorf's remarks in DNG II.3 §13 and elsewhere. Barbeyrac also discusses the matter in his famous preface to DNG and repeatedly mentions Locke's discussions in the *Essay Concerning Human Understanding.*

having taken a particular care to cultivate their minds, are qualified to enlighten others, and to supply, by their instructions, the rudeness and ignorance of the common run of mankind. This is agreeable to the plan of providence. God having designed man for society, and given him a constitution relative to this end, the different helps which men receive of one another, ought to be equally ranked among natural means, with those which every one finds within himself, and draws from his own fund.

In effect, all men are not of themselves capable to unfold methodically the principles of natural laws, and the consequences from thence resulting.[2] It is sufficient that middling capacities are able to comprehend at least those principles, when they are explained to them, and to feel the truth and necessity of the duties that flow from thence, by comparing them with the constitution of their own nature. But if there be some capacities of a still inferior order, they are generally led by the impressions of example, custom, authority, or some present and sensible utility. Be this as it will, every thing rightly considered, the law of nature is sufficiently notified to impower us to affirm, that no man at the age of discretion, and in his right senses, can alledge for a just excuse, an invincible ignorance on this article.

III. Let us make a reflection, which presents itself here very naturally. It is, that whosoever attends seriously to the manner in which we have <183> established the principles of the laws of nature, will soon find, that the method we have followed is a fresh proof of the certainty and reality of those laws. We have waved all abstract and metaphysical speculations, in order to consult plain fact, and the nature and state of things. It is from the natural constitution of man, and from the relations he has to other beings, that we have taken our principles; and the system from thence resulting, has so strict and so necessary a connexion with this nature and state of man, that they are absolutely inseparable. If to all this we join what has been already observed in the foregoing chapters, we cannot, methinks, mistake the laws of nature, or doubt of their re-

The manner in which the principles of the laws of nature have been established, is a fresh proof of the reality of those laws.

2. This paragraph is based on DNG II.3 §13 and note 7.

ality, without renouncing the purest light of reason, and running into Pyrrhonism.

Natural laws are the effect of the divine goodness.

IV. But as the principles of the laws of nature are, through the wisdom of the Creator, easy to discover, and as the knowledge of the duties they impose on us, is within the reach of the most ordinary capacities; it is also certain, that these laws are far from being impracticable. On the contrary, they bear so manifest a proportion to the light of right reason, and to our most natural inclinations; they have also such a relation to our perfection and happiness; that they cannot be considered otherwise than as an effect of the divine goodness towards man. Since no other motive but that of doing good, could ever induce a being, who is self-existent, and supremely happy, to form creatures endowed with understanding and sense; it must have been in consequence of this same goodness that he first vouchsafed to direct <184> them by laws. His view was not merely to restrain their liberty; but he thought fit to let them know what agreed with them best, what was most proper for their perfection and happiness; and in order to add greater weight to the reasonable motives that were to determine them, he joined thereto the authority of his commands.*

This gives us to understand why the laws of nature are such as they are. It was necessary, pursuant to the views of the Almighty, that the laws he prescribed to mankind, should be suitable to their nature and state; that they should have a tendency of themselves to procure the perfection and advantage of individuals, as well as of the species; of particular people, as well as of the society. In short, the choice of the end determined the nature of the means.

The laws of nature do not depend on an arbitrary institution.

V. In fact, there are natural and necessary differences in human actions, and in the effects by them produced. Some agree of themselves with the nature and state of man, while others disagree, and are quite opposite thereto; some contribute to the production and maintenance of order, others tend to subvert it; some procure the perfection and happiness of mankind, others are attended with their disgrace and misery. To refuse

* See, part i. chap. x. § 3.

to acknowledge these differences, would be shutting one's eyes to the light, and confounding it with darkness. These are differences of a most sensible nature; and whatever a person may say to the contrary, sense and <185> experience will always refute those false and idle subtleties.

Let us not therefore seek any where else but in the very nature of human actions, in their essential differences and consequences, for the true foundation of the laws of nature, and why God forbids some things, while he commands others. These are not arbitrary laws, such as God might not have given, or have given others of a quite different nature. Supreme wisdom can no more than supreme power act any thing absurd and contradictory. It is the very nature of things that always serves for the rule of his determinations. God was at liberty, without doubt, to create or not to create man; to create him such as he is, or to give him quite a different nature. But having determined to form a rational and social being, he could not prescribe any thing unsuitable to such a creature. We may even affirm, that the supposition which makes the principles and rules of the law of nature depend on the arbitrary will of God, tends to subvert and destroy even the very idea of natural law. For if these laws were not a necessary consequence of the nature, constitution, and state of man, it would be impossible for us to have a certain knowledge of them, except by a very clear revelation, or by some other formal promulgation on the part of God. But agreed it is, that the law of nature is, and ought to be known by the mere light of reason. To conceive it therefore as depending on an arbitrary will, would be attempting to subvert it, or at least would be reducing the thing to a kind of Pyrrhonism; by reason we could have no natural means of being <186> sure that God commands or forbids one thing rather than another. Hence, if the laws of nature depend originally on divine institution, as there is no room to question; we must likewise agree, that this is not a mere arbitrary institution, but founded, on one side, on the very nature and constitution of man; and, on the other, on the wisdom of God, who cannot desire an end, without desiring at the same time the means that alone are fit to obtain it.[3]

---

3. Based on Barbeyrac, "The Judgment of an Anonymous Writer" §15 (in Samuel Pufendorf, *The Whole Duty of Man, According to the Law of Nature*, ed. Ian Hunter

Our opinion is
not very wide
from that of
Grotius. VI. It is not amiss to observe here, that the manner in which we establish the foundation of the law of nature, does not differ in the main from the principles of Grotius. Perhaps this great man might have explained his thoughts a little better. But we must own that his commentators, without excepting Puffendorf himself, have not rightly understood his meaning, and consequently have passed a wrong censure on him, by pretending, that the manner in which he established the foundation of the law of nature, is reduced to a vicious circle. *If we ask,* says Puffendorf,* *which are those things that form the matter of natural laws? the answer is, that they are those which are honest or dishonest of their own nature. If we inquire afterwards, what are those things that are honest or dishonest of their own nature? there can be no other answer given, but that they are those which form the matter of natural laws.* This is what the critics put into the mouth of Grotius. <187>

But let us see whether Grotius says really any such thing. *The law of nature,* says he,† *consists in certain principles of right reason, which inform us, that an action is morally honest or dishonest, according to the necessary agreeableness or disagreeableness it has with a rational and sociable nature; and consequently that God, who is the author of nature, commands or forbids such actions.* Here I can see no circle: For putting the question, whence comes the natural honesty or turpitude of commanded or forbidden actions? Grotius does not answer in the manner they make him; on the contrary, he says that this honesty or turpitude proceeds from the necessary agreeableness or disagreeableness of our actions with a rational and social nature.‡

---

and David Saunders [Indianapolis: Liberty Fund, 2003], pp. 267–305) and DNG II.3 §4 note 2. See also DNG I.1 §4 note 5.

* See Puffendorf, Law of nature and nations, book ii. chap. iii. § 4. Apol. § 19.
† See Grotius, Rights of war and peace, book i. chap. i. § 10.
‡ See Barbeyrac's fifth note on the Law of nature and nations, book ii. chap. iii. § 4.

VII. After having seen that the laws of nature are practicable of them-selves, evidently useful, highly conformable to the ideas which right rea-son gives us of God, suitable to the nature and state of man, perfectly agreeable to order, and, in fine, sufficiently notified; there is no longer room to question, but laws invested with all these characteristics are obligatory, and lay men under an indispensable obligation of conform-ing their conduct to them. It is even certain, that the obligation which God imposes on us by this means, is the strongest of all, by reason of its being produced by the concurrence and union of the strongest mo-tives, such as are most <188> proper to determine the will.[4] In fact, the counsels and maxims of reason oblige us, not only because they are in themselves very agreeable, and founded on the nature and immutable relations of things; but moreover by the authority of the supreme Being, who intervenes here, by giving us clearly to understand he is willing we should observe them, because of his being the author of this nature of things, and of the mutual relations they have among themselves. In fine, the law of nature binds us by an internal and external obligation at the same time; which produces the highest degree of moral necessity, and reduces liberty to the very strongest subjection, without destroying it.*

The effect of the laws of nature, is an obligation of conforming thereto our conduct.

Thus the obedience due to natural law is a sincere obedience, and such as ought to arise from a conscientious principle. The first effect of those laws is to direct the sentiments of our minds, and the motions of the heart. We should not discharge what they require of us, were we externally to abstain from what they condemn, but with regret and against our will. And as it is not allowable to desire what we are not permitted to enjoy; so it is our duty not only to practise what we are commanded, but likewise to give it our approbation, and to acknowl-edge its utility and justice.

* See part i. chap. vi. § 13.

4. While Burlamaqui's discussion of morality as a nonarbitrary institution follows Barbeyrac quite closely, the understanding of obligation as explainable in terms of motives is directly opposed to Barbeyrac; see, for example, "The Judgment of an Anonymous Writer" §6.

Natural laws are obligatory in respect to all men. VIII. Another essential characteristic of the laws of nature is, that they be universal, that is, they should oblige all men without exception. For men are not only all equally subject to God's command; but moreover, the laws of nature having their foun-<189>dation in the constitution and state of man, and being notified to him by reason, it is plain they have an essential agreeableness to all mankind, and oblige them without distinction; whatever difference there may be between them in fact, and in whatever state they are supposed. This is what distinguishes natural from positive laws; for a positive law relates only to particular persons or societies.

Grotius's opinion with regard to divine, positive, and universal law. IX. It is true that Grotius,* and after him several divines and civilians, pretend that there are divine, positive, and universal laws, which oblige all men, from the very moment they are made sufficiently known to them. But in the first place, were there any such laws, as they could not be discovered by the sole light of reason, they must have been very clearly manifested to all mankind; a thing which cannot be fully proved: And if it should be said, that they oblige only those to whom they are made known; this destroys the idea of universality attributed to them, by supposing that those laws were made for all men. Secondly, the divine, positive, and universal laws, ought to be moreover of themselves beneficial to all mankind, at all times, and in all places; and this the wisdom and goodness of God requires. But for this purpose these laws should have been founded on the constitution of human nature in general, and then they would be true natural laws.† <190>

Natural laws are immutable, and admit of no dispensation. X. We have already observed, that the laws of nature, though established by the divine will, are not the effect of an arbitrary disposition, but have their foundation in the very nature and mutual relations of things. Hence it follows, that natural laws are immutable, and admit of no dis-

---

* See Rights of war and peace, book i. chap. i. § 15. with Barbeyrac's notes.
† See Barbeyrac's sixth note on Puffendorf's Law of nature and nations, book i. chap. xi. § 18.

pensation. This is also a proper characteristic of these laws, which distinguishes them from all positive law, whether divine or human.

This immutability of the laws of nature has nothing in it repugnant to the independance, supreme power, or liberty of an all-perfect Being. Since he himself is the author of our constitution, he cannot but prescribe or prohibit such things as have a necessary agreeableness or disagreeableness to this very constitution; and consequently he cannot make any change, or give any dispensation, in regard to the laws of nature.* It is a glorious necessity in him not to contradict himself; it is a kind of impotency falsely so called, which far from limiting or diminishing his perfections, adds to their external character, and points out all their excellency.

XI. Considering the thing as has been now explained, we may say, if we will, that the laws of nature are eternal; though, to tell the truth, this expression is very uncorrect of itself, and more adapted to throw obscurity than clearness upon our <191> ideas.[5] Those who first took notice of the eternity of the laws of nature, did it very probably out of opposition to the novelty and frequent mutations of civil laws. They meant only, that the law of nature is antecedent, for example, to the laws of Moses, of Solon, or of any other legislator, in that it is coeval with mankind; and so far they were in the right. But to affirm, as a great many divines and moralists have done, that the law of nature is coeternal with God, is advancing a proposition, which reduced to its just value is not exactly true; by reason that the law of nature being made for man, its actual existence supposeth that of mankind. But if we are only to understand hereby, that God had the ideas thereof from all eternity, then we attribute nothing to the laws of nature but what is equally common to every thing that exists.†

Of the eternity of natural laws.

* See Puffendorf, Law of nature and nations, book ii. chap. iii. § 6. and Grotius, Rights of war and peace, book i. chap. i. § 10.
† The immutability of the laws of nature is acknowledged by all those who reason with any exactness. See Instit. lib. 1. tit. 2. § 11. Noodt. Probabil. Juris, lib. 2. cap. 11.
5. This discussion of the eternity of the natural laws derives from DNG I.2 §6 in fine.

We cannot finish this article better than with a beautiful passage of Cicero, preserved by Lactantius. *Right reason, says this philosopher, is indeed a true <192> law, agreeable to nature, common to all men, constant, immutable, eternal. It prompts men to their duty by its commands, and deters them from evil by its prohibitions.—It is not allowed to retrench any part of this law, or to make any alteration therein, much less to abolish it intirely. Neither the senate nor people can dispense with it; nor does it require any interpretation, being clear of itself and intelligible. It is the same at Rome and Athens; the same to-day and to-morrow. It is the same eternal and invariable law, given at all times and places, to all nations; because God, who is the author thereof, and has published it himself, is always the sole master and sovereign of mankind. Whosoever violates this law, renounces his own nature, divests himself of humanity, and will be rigorously chastised for his disobedience, though he were to escape what is commonly distinguished by the name of punishment.*

But let this suffice in regard to the law of nature considered as a rule to individuals. In order to embrace the intire system of man, and to unfold our principles in their full extent, it is necessary we say something likewise concerning the rules which nations ought to observe between each other, and are commonly called *the law of nations.* <193>

CHAPTER VI

Of the law of nations.

How civil soci-
eties are formed.

I. Among the various establishments of man, the most considerable without doubt is that of civil society, or the body politic, which is justly

---

* *Est quidem vera lex, recta ratio, naturae congruens, diffusa in omnes, constans, sempiterna, quae vocet ad officium jubendo, vetando a fraude deterreat: quae tamen neque probos frustra jubet, aut vetat; nec improbos jubendo aut vetando movet. Huic legi nec abrogari fas est, neque derogari ex hac aliquid licet; neque tota abrogari potest. Nec verò aut per senatum, aut per populum solvi hac lege possumus: neque est quaerendus explanator aut interpres ejus alius. Nec erit alia lex Romae, alia Athenis, alia nunc, alia posthac; sed omnes gentes, & omni tempore, una lex & sempiterna & immutabilis continebit; unusque erit communis quasi magister & imperator omnium Deus. Ille legis hujus inventor, disceptator, lator: cui qui non parebit ipse se fugiet, ac naturam hominis, aspernabitur; atque hoc ipso luet maximas poenas etiamsi caetera supplicia, quae putantur, effugerit.* Cicero de Republ. lib. 3. apud Lactant. Instit. Divin. lib. 6. cap. 8.

esteemed the most perfect of societies, and has obtained the name of *State* by way of preference.

Human society is simply, of itself, and with regard to those who compose it, a state of equality and independance. It is subject to God alone; no one has a natural and primitive right to command; but each person may dispose of himself, and of what he possesses, as he thinks proper, with this only restriction, that he keep within the bounds of the law of nature, and do no prejudice or injury to any man.

The civil state makes a great alteration in this primitive one. The establishing a sovereignty subverts this independance wherein men were originally with regard to one another; and subordination is substituted in its stead. The sovereign becoming the depositary as it were of the will and strength of each individual, which are united in his person, all the other members of the society become subjects, and find themselves under an obligation of obeying and conducting themselves pursuant to the laws imposed upon them by the sovereign.

II. But how great soever the change may be which government and sovereignty make in the state of nature, yet we must not imagine that the civil state <194> properly subverts all natural society, or that it destroys the essential relations which men have among themselves, or those between God and man. This would be neither physically nor morally possible: on the contrary, the civil state supposes the nature of man, such as the Creator has formed it; it supposes the primitive state of union and society, with all the relations this state includes; it supposes, in fine, the natural dependance of man with regard to God and his laws. Government is so far from subverting this first order, that it has been rather established with a view to give it a new degree of force and consistency. It was intended to enable us the better to discharge the duties prescribed by natural laws, and to attain more certainly the end for which we were created.

The civil state does not destroy but improve the state of nature.

III. In order to form a just idea of civil society, we must say, that it is no more than natural society itself modified in such a manner, as to have a sovereign that commands, and on whose will whatever concerns the happiness of society, ultimately depends; to the end that under his protec-

True ideas of civil society.

tion and through his care mankind may surely attain the felicity to which they naturally aspire.[1]

States are considered under the notion of moral persons.

IV. All societies are formed by the concurrence or union of the wills of several persons, with a view of acquiring some advantage. Hence it is that societies are considered as bodies, and receive the appellation of moral persons; by reason that those bodies are in effect animated with one sole will, which regulates all their movements. This agrees particularly with <195> the body politic or state. The sovereign is the chief or head, and the subjects the members; all their actions that have any relation to society, are directed by the will of the chief. Hence so soon as states are formed, they acquire a kind of personal properties: and we may consequently, with due proportion, attribute to them whatever agrees in particular with man; such as certain actions and rights that properly belong to them, certain duties they are obliged to fulfill, &c.

What is the law of nations.

V. This being supposed, the establishment of states introduces a kind of society amongst them, similar to that which is naturally between men; and the same reasons which induce men to maintain union among themselves, ought likewise to engage nations or their sovereigns to keep up a good understanding with one another.

It is necessary therefore there should be some law among nations, to serve as a rule for mutual commerce. Now this law can be nothing else but the law of nature itself, which is then distinguished by the name of the law of nations. *Natural law,* says Hobbes very justly, *is divided into the natural law of man, and the natural law of states:* and the latter is what we call the *law of nations.* Thus natural law and the law of nations are in reality one and the same thing, and differ only by an external denomination. We must therefore say, that the law of nations properly so called, and considered as a law proceeding from a superior, is nothing else, but the law of nature itself, not applied to men considered simply as such; <196> but to nations, states, or their chiefs, in the relations they

* *De Cive,* cap. 14. § 4.
1. Burlamaqui's discussion of Hobbes's view is taken from DNG II.3 §23.

have together, and the several interests they have to manage between each other.

VI. There is no room to question the reality and certainty of such a law of nations obligatory of its own nature, and to which nations, or the sovereigns that rule them, ought to submit. For if God, by means of right reason, imposes certain duties between individuals, it is evident he is likewise willing that nations, which are only human societies, should observe the same duties between themselves.* Certainty of this law.

VII. But in order to say something more particular concerning this subject, let us observe that the natural state of nations, in respect to each other, is that of society and peace. This society is likewise a state of equality and independance, which establishes a parity of right between them; and engages them to have the same regard and respect for one another. Hence the general principle of the law of nations is nothing more than the general law of sociability, which obliges all nations that have any intercourse with one another, to practise those duties to which individuals are naturally subject. General principle of the law of nations; what polity consists in.

These remarks may serve to give us a just idea of that art, so necessary to the directors of states, and distinguished commonly by the name of *Polity.* Polity considered with regard to foreign states, is that ability and address by which a sovereign provides for the preservation, safety, prosperity and glory of the nation he governs, by respecting the laws of justice <197> and humanity; that is, without doing any injury to other states, but rather by procuring their advantage, so much as in reason can be expected. Thus the polity of sovereigns is the same as prudence among private people; and as we condemn in the latter any art or cunning, that makes them pursue their own advantage to the prejudice of others, so the like art would be censurable in princes, were they bent upon procuring the advantage of their own people by injuring other nations. The *Reason of state,* so often alledged to justify the proceedings or enterprises of princes, cannot really be admitted for this end, but inasmuch as it is

* See chap. v. § 8.

reconcileable with the common interest of nations, or, which amounts to the same thing, with the unalterable rules of sincerity, justice, and humanity.

VIII. Grotius indeed acknowledges that the law of nature is common to all nations; yet he establishes a positive law of nations contradistinct from the law of nature; and reduces this law of nations to a sort of human law, which has acquired a power of obliging in consequence of the will and consent of all or of a great many nations.* He adds, that the maxims of this law of nations are proved by the perpetual practice of people, and the testimony of historians.

But it has been justly observed that this pretended law of nations, contradistinct from the law of nature, and invested nevertheless with a force of obliging, <198> whether the people consent to it or not, is a supposition destitute of all foundation.†

For 1. all nations are with regard to one another in a natural inde-pendance and equality. If there be therefore any common law between them, it must proceed from God their common sovereign.

2. As for what relates to customs established by an express or tacit consent among nations, these customs are neither of themselves nor uni-versally, nor always obligatory. For from this only that several nations have acted towards one another for a long time after a particular manner in particular cases, it does not follow that they have laid themselves under a necessity of acting always in the same manner for the time to come, and much less that other nations are obliged to conform to those customs.

3. Again; those customs are so much the less capable of being an oblig-atory rule of themselves, as they may happen to be bad or unjust. The profession of a corsair or pirate was, by a kind of consent, esteemed a long while lawful, between nations that were not united by alliance or

* See Grotius, Rights of war and peace: preliminary discourse, § 18. and book i. chap. i. § 14.
† See Puffendorf, Law of nature and nations, book ii. chap. iii. § 23. with Bar-beyrac's notes.

treaty. It seems likewise, that some nations allowed themselves the use of poisoned arms in time of war.* Shall we say that these were customs authorised by the law of nations, and really obligatory in respect to different people? Or shall we not rather consider them as barbarous practices; from which every just and well-governed nation ought to refrain? We can-<199>not therefore avoid appealing always to the law of nature, the only one that is really universal, whenever we want to judge whether the customs established between nations have any obligatory effect.

4. All that can be said on this subject is, that when customs of an innocent nature are introduced among nations; each of them is reasonably supposed to submit to those customs, so long as they have not made any declaration to the contrary. This is all the force or effect that can be given to received customs; but a very different effect from that of a law properly so called.

IX. These remarks give us room to conclude, that the whole might perhaps be reconciled, by distinguishing two species of laws of nations. There is certainly an universal, necessary, and self-obligatory law of nations, which differs in nothing from the law of nature, and is consequently immutable, insomuch that the people or sovereigns cannot dispense with it, even by common consent, without trangressing their duty. There is, besides, another law of nations, which we may call arbitrary and free, as founded only on an express or tacit convention; the effect of which is not of itself universal; being obligatory only in regard to those who have voluntarily submitted thereto, and only so long as they please, because they are always at liberty to change or repeal it. To which we must likewise add, that the whole force of this sort of law of nations ultimately depends on the law of nature, which commands us to be true to our engagements. Whatever really belongs to the law of nations, may be reduced to one or other of these <200> two species, and the use of this distinction will easily appear by applying it to particular questions which relate either to war, for example, to ambassadors, or to public

Two sorts of laws of nations; one of necessity and obligatory by itself; the other arbitrary and conventional.

---

* See Virgil, Aeneid, book x. ver. 139. with the 15th note of the Abbè des Fontaines.

treaties, and to the deciding of disputes which sometimes arise concerning these matters between sovereigns.*

Use of the foregoing remarks.

X. It is a point of importance to attend to the origin and nature of the law of nations, such as we have now explained them. For besides that it is al-<201>ways advantageous to form just ideas of things, this is still more necessary in matters of practice and morality. It is owing perhaps to our distinguishing the law of nations from natural law, that we have insensibly accustomed ourselves to form quite a different judgment between the actions of sovereigns and those of private people. Nothing is more usual than to see men condemned in common, for things which we praise, or at least excuse in the persons of princes. And yet it is certain, as we have already shewn, that the maxims of the law of nations have an equal authority with those of the law of nature, and are equally respectable and sacred, because they have God alike for their author. In short, there is only one sole and the same rule of justice for all mankind. Princes who infringe the law of nations, commit as great a crime as private people, who violate the law of nature: and if there be any difference

---

* Let us remark here by the way, that the ideas of the ancient Roman lawyers concerning the law of nations, are not always uniform; which creates some confusion. Some there are that understand by the LAW OF NATIONS those rules of right that are common to all men, and established amongst themselves pursuant to the light of reason; in opposition to the particular laws of each people. (See the 9th law in the Digest. de Justitia & Jure, book 1. tit. 1.) And then the law of nations signified also the law of nature. Others distinguished between these two species, as Ulpian has done in law I. of the title now mentioned. They gave the name of law of nations to that which agrees with man as such; in opposition to that which suits him as an animal. (See Puffendorf, Law of nature and nations, book 2. chap. 3. § 3. note 10.) Some, in fine, comprised the one and the other under the idea of *natural law.* (See law XI. Digest. de Justitia & Jure.) And hence it comes, that the better sort of Latin writers give indifferently the name of natural law, or the law of nations, to that which relates to either. This we find in the following passage of Cicero, where he says, that by the law of nature, that is, by the law of nations, one man is not allowed to pursue his advantage at the expence of another. *Neque vero hoc solum* NATURA, *id est,* JURE GENTIUM————*constitutum est, ut non liceat sui commodi causa, alteri nocere.* De Offic. lib. 3. cap. 5. See Mr. Noodt's commentary on the Digest, book 1. tit. 1. where this able lawyer explains very well the ambiguity of the distinction of natural law, and the law of nations, according to the different language of ancient civilians.

in the two cases, it must be charged to the prince's account,* whose unjust actions are always attended with more dreadful consequences than
those of private people.† <202>

CHAPTER VII

Whether there is any morality of actions, any obligation or duty, antecedent to the laws of nature, *and independent of the idea of a legislator?*[1]

I. The morality of human actions being founded, in general, on the
relations of agreeableness or disagreeableness between those actions and
the law, according as we have shewn in the eleventh chapter of the first
part; there is no difficulty, when once we acknowledge the laws of nature,
to affirm, that the morality of actions depends on their conformity or
opposition to those very laws. This is a point on which all civilians and
ethic writers are agreed. But they are not so unanimous in regard to the
first principle or original cause of obligation and morality.

A great many are of opinion, that there is no other principle of morality but the divine will, manifested by the laws of nature. The idea of
morality, say they, necessarily includes that of obligation; obligation sup-

Different opinions of ethic writers with respect to the first principle of morality.

---

* See part i. chap. xi. § 12.

† It is Monsieur Bernard that furnishes us with these reflections: *If a private person,*
says he, *offends without cause a person of the same station, his action is termed an injustice;
but if a prince attacks another prince without cause, if he invades his territories, and
ravages his towns and provinces, this is called waging war, and it would be temerity to
think it unjust. To break or violate contracts or agreements, is esteemed a crime among
private people: but among princes, to infringe the most solemn treaties, is prudence, is
understanding the art of government. True it is, that some pretext is always sought for,
but those who trump up these pretexts, give themselves very little trouble whether they are
thought just or not,* &c. Nouvelles de la republique des lettres, Mars 1704. page 340,
341.

1. In the original chapter title, Burlamaqui professes to provide an "Essay on this
question: whether there is any morality . . ." The word "essay" in the title may reflect
Burlamaqui's ambition to provide more than a textbook presentation of Pufendorfian natural law. The issue was hotly debated and one of the central issues that all
natural law thinkers had to have a view on.

poses law; and law a legislator. If therefore we abstract from all law, and consequently from a legislator, we shall have no such thing as right, obligation, duty, or morality, properly so called.* <203>

Others there are, who acknowledge indeed that the divine will is really a principle of obligation, and consequently a principle of the morality of human actions; but they do not stop here. They pretend, that antecedent to all law, and independent of a legislator, there are things which of themselves, and by their own nature, are honest or dishonest; that reason having once discovered this essential and specific difference of human actions, it imposes on man a necessity of performing the one and omitting the other; and that this is the first foundation of obligation, or the original source of morality and duty.

Principles relating to this question.

II. What we have already said concerning the primitive rule of human actions, and the nature and origin of obligation,† may help to throw some light on the present question. But in order to illustrate it better, let us turn back and resume the thing from its first principles, by endeavouring to assemble here, in a natural order, the principal ideas that may lead us to a just conclusion.

1. I observe in the first place, that every action considered purely and simply in itself as a natural motion of the mind or body, is absolutely indifferent, and cannot in this respect claim any share of morality.

This is what evidently appears; forasmuch as the same natural action is esteemed sometimes lawful and even good, and at other times unlawful or bad. To kill a man, for instance, is a bad action in a robber; but it is lawful or good in an executioner, or in a citizen or soldier that defends his life or coun-<204>try, unjustly attacked: a plain demonstration, that this action considered in itself, and as a simple operation of the natural faculties, is absolutely indifferent and destitute of all morality.

2. We must take care to distinguish here between the physical and moral consideration. There is undoubtedly a kind of natural goodness or malignity in actions, which by their own proper and internal virtue

---

* See Puffendorf, Law of nature and nations, book i. chap. ii. § 6.
† See part i. chap. v. & vi.

are beneficial or hurtful, and produce the physical good or evil of man. But this relation between the action and its effect is only physical; and if we stop here, we are not yet arrived at morality. It is a pity we are frequently obliged to use the same expressions for the physical and moral ideas, which is apt to create some confusion. It were to be wished that languages had a greater exactness in distinguishing the nature and different relations of things by different names.

3. If we proceed further, and suppose that there is some rule of human actions, and compare afterwards these actions to the rule; the relation resulting from this comparison is what properly and essentially constitutes morality.*

4. From thence it follows, that in order to know which is the principal or efficient cause of the morality of human actions, we must previously be acquainted with their rule.

5. Finally let us add, that this rule of human actions may in general be of two sorts, either internal or external; that is, it may be either found in man himself, or it must be sought for somewhere else.[2] Let us now make an application of these principles. <205>

III. We have already seen† that man finds within himself several principles to discern good from evil, and that these principles are so many rules of his conduct.

The first directive principle we find within ourselves is a kind of instinct, commonly called moral sense; which pointing out readily, though confusedly and without reflection, the most sensible and most striking part of the difference between good and evil, makes us love the one, and gives us an aversion for the other, by a kind of natural sentiment.

Three rules of human actions.
1. Moral sense.
2. Reason.
3. The divine will.

---

* See part i, chap. xi. § 1.
† Part i. chap. v. and part ii. chap. iii.
2. The translator gives "somewhere else" for Burlamaqui's "outside himself" ("hors de lui-même"). Burlamaqui follows Pufendorf DNG I.2 §6 very closely up to this point of the chapter. The distinction between an obligatory yet internal natural law founded in man himself without the idea of a commanding God (defined here as external natural law) is not in Pufendorf or in Barbeyrac and is even incompatible with Pufendorf's insistence that man is unable to impose obligations on himself; see DNG I.6 §7.

The second principle is reason, or the reflection we make on the nature, relations, and consequences of things; which gives us a more distinct knowledge, by principles and rules, of the distinction between
good and evil in all possible cases.

But to these two internal principles we must join a third, namely, the
divine will. For man being the handy work of God, and deriving from
the Creator his existence, his reason, and all his faculties; he finds himself
thereby in an absolute dependance on that supreme being, and cannot
help acknowledging him as his lord and sovereign. Therefore, as soon as
he is acquainted with the intention of God in regard to his creature, this
will of his master becomes his supreme rule, and ought absolutely to
determine his conduct.

These three
principles
ought to be
united.
IV. Let us not separate these three principles. They are indeed distinct
from one another, and have each their particular force; but in the actual
state of man they are necessarily united. It is sense that <206> gives us
the first notice; our reason adds more light; and the will of God, who is
rectitude itself, gives it a new degree of certainty; adding withal the
weight of his authority. It is on all these foundations united, we ought
to raise the edifice of natural law, or the system of morality.

Hence it follows, that man being a creature of God, formed with
design and wisdom, and endowed with sense and reason; the rule of
human actions, or the true foundation of morality, is properly the will
of the supreme Being, manifested and interpreted, either by moral sense
or by reason. These two natural means, by teaching us to distinguish the
relation which human actions have to our constitution, or, which is the
same thing, to the ends of the Creator, inform us what is morally good
or evil, honest or dishonest, commanded or forbidden.

Of the primi-
tive cause of
obligation.
V. It is already a great matter to feel and to know good and evil; but this
is not enough; we must likewise join to this sense and knowledge, an
obligation of doing the one, and abstaining from the other. It is this
obligation that constitutes duty, without which there would be no moral
practice, but the whole would terminate in mere speculation. But which
is the cause and principle of obligation and duty? Is it the very nature

of things discovered by reason? Or is it the divine will? This is what we must endeavour here to determine.

VI. The first reflection that occurs to us here, and to which very few, methinks, are sufficiently attentive, is, that every rule whatsoever of human <207> actions, carries with it a moral necessity of conforming thereto, and produces consequently a sort of obligation. Let us illustrate this remark.

All rules are of themselves obligatory.

The general notion of rule presents us with the idea of a sure and expeditious method to attain a particular end. Every rule supposes therefore a design, or the will of attaining to a certain end, as the effect we want to produce, or the object we intend to procure. And it is perfectly evident, that were a person to act merely for the sake of acting, without any particular design or determinate end; he ought not to trouble his head about directing his actions one way more than another; he should never mind either counsel or rule. This being premised, I affirm that every man who proposes to himself a particular end, and knows the means or rule which alone can conduct him to it, and put him in possession of what he desires, such a man finds himself under a necessity of following this rule, and of conforming his actions to it. Otherwise he would contradict himself; he would and he would not; he would desire the end, and neglect the only means which by his own confession are able to conduct him to it. Hence I conclude, that every rule, acknowledged as such, that is, as a sure and only means of attaining the end proposed, carries with it a sort of obligation of being thereby directed. For so soon as there is a *reasonable necessity* to prefer one manner of acting to another, every reasonable man, and who intends to behave as such, finds himself thereby engaged and tied, as it were, to this manner, being hindered by his reason from acting to the contrary. That is, in <208> other terms, he is really obliged; because obligation, in its original idea, is nothing more than a restriction of liberty, produced by reason, inasmuch as the counsels which reason gives us, are motives that determine us to a particular manner of acting, preferable to any other. It is therefore true, that all rules are obligatory.[3]

3. Burlamaqui's target is Pufendorf as explained by Barbeyrac in "The Judgment

Obligation may be more or less strong.

VII. This obligation, indeed, may be more or less strong, more or less strict, according as the reasons on which it is founded are more or less numerous, and have more or less power and efficacy of themselves to determine the will.

If a particular manner of acting appears to me evidently fitter than any other for my preservation and perfection, fitter to procure my bodily health and the welfare of my soul; this motive alone obliges me to act in conformity to it: And thus we have the first degree of obligation. If I find afterwards, that besides the advantage now mentioned, such a conduct will secure the respect and approbation of those with whom I converse; this is a new motive which strengthens the preceding obligation, and adds still more to my engagement. But if, by pushing my reflections still farther, I find at length that this manner of acting is perfectly agreeable to the intention of my Creator, who is willing and intends I should follow the counsels which reason gives me, as so many real laws he prescribes to me himself; it is visible, that this new consideration strengthens my engagement, ties the knot still faster, and lays me under an indispensable necessity of acting after such or such a manner. For what is there <209> more proper to determine finally a rational being, than the assurance he has of procuring the approbation and benevolence of his superior, by acting in conformity to his will and orders; and of escaping his indignation, which must infallibly pursue a rebellious creature.

Reason alone is sufficient to impose some obligation on man.

VIII. Let us follow now the thread of the consequences arising from these principles.

If it be true, that every rule is of itself obligatory, and that reason is the primitive rule of human actions; it follows, that reason only, independent of the law, is sufficient to impose some obligation on man, and

---

of an Anonymous Writer" §15 (in Samuel Pufendorf, *The Whole Duty of Man, According to the Law of Nature,* ed. Ian Hunter and David Saunders [Indianapolis: Liberty Fund, 2003], pp. 267–305), according to which reason as such can never put us under an obligation, and therefore the laws of nature remain mere speculative principles without any moral necessity until they are understood as divine commandments. See also DHC I.1 §1 note 1.

consequently to furnish room for morality and duty, commendation and censure.

There will remain no manner of doubt on this subject, if abstracting for a moment from superiority and law, we examine at first the state of man alone, considered merely as a rational being. Man proposes to himself his own good, that is, the welfare of his body and soul. He searches afterwards for the means of procuring those advantages; and so soon as he has discovered them, he approves of some particular actions, and condemns others; and consequently he approves or condemns himself, according as he acts after a manner conformable or opposite to the dictates of his reason. Does not all this evidently demonstrate, that reason puts a restraint on liberty, and lays us therefore under an obligation of doing or abstaining from particular things?

Let us proceed. Suppose that man in the forementioned state becomes the father of a family, and has a mind to act reasonably; would it be an indif-<210>ferent thing to him, to take care of, or to neglect his children, to provide for their subsistence and education, or to do neither one nor the other? Is it not, on the contrary, evident, that as this different conduct necessarily procures either the good or evil of his family; the approbation or censure which reason gives it, renders it morally good or bad, worthy of praise or blame?[4]

It would be an easy matter to pursue this way of arguing, and apply it to all the states of man. But what we have already said, shews it is sufficient to consider man as a rational being, to be convinced that reason pointing out the road which alone can lead him to the end he aims at, lays him under a necessity of following this road, and of regulating thereby his conduct: that consequently reason alone is sufficient to establish a system of morality, obligation, and duties; because when once we suppose it is reasonable to do or to abstain from certain things, this is really owning our obligation.

---

4. Burlamaqui here works with a stoic idea of rational self-interest: the rational egoist is not understood as an isolated individual, but as a self embedded in social groups. The individual's real interests cannot be defined separately from the interests of those larger wholes.

IX. "But the idea of obligation," some will say, "imports necessarily a being that obliges, and who ought to be distinct from the person obliged. To suppose that he who obliges, and he who is obliged, are one and the same person, is supposing that a man may make a contract with himself; which is quite absurd. Right reason is, in reality, nothing but an attribute of the person obliged; it cannot be therefore a principle of obligation; no body being capable of imposing on himself an indispensable necessity of acting or not acting after such or such a manner. For <211> supposing a necessity, it must not be removeable at the will and pleasure of the person subject to it; otherwise it would be void of effect. If therefore the person on whom the obligation is imposed, is the same as he who imposes it, he can disengage himself from it whenever he pleases; or rather, there is no obligation; as when a debtor inherits the estate and rights of his creditor, the debt is void. Now duty is a debt, and neither of them can be admitted but between different persons."*

Answer. X. This objection is more specious than solid. In fact, those who pretend that there is properly neither obligation nor morality without a superior and law, ought necessarily to suppose one of these two things: 1. either that there is no other rule of human actions besides law: 2. or if there be any other, none but law is an obligatory rule.

The first of these suppositions is evidently unsupportable: and after all that has been said concerning this subject, we think it quite useless to stop here to refute it. Either reason has been idly and without a design bestowed upon man, or we must allow it to be the general and primitive rule of his actions and conduct. And what is there more natural than to think that a rational being ought to be directed by reason? If we should endeavour to evade this argument, by saying, that though reason be the rule of human actions, yet there is nothing but law that can be an <212> obligatory rule; this proposition cannot be maintained, unless we con-

---

* *Nemo sibi debet* (says Seneca de Benef. lib. 5. cap. 8.) *hoc verbum* debere *non habet nisi inter duos locum.* [This is Pufendorf's view, as presented in DNG II.3 §20 and DHC I.2 §4; Barbeyrac affirms this view in "The Judgment of an Anonymous Writer" §15.]

sent to give the name of obligation to some other restriction of liberty, as well as to that which is produced by the will and order of a superior; and then it would be a mere dispute about words. Or else we must suppose, that there neither actually is, nor can even be conceived, any obligation at all, without the intervention of the will of a superior;[5] which is far from being exactly true.

The source of the whole mistake, or the cause of the ambiguity, is our not ascending to the first principles, in order to determine the original idea of obligation. We have already said, and again we say it, that every restriction of liberty, produced or approved by right reason, forms a real obligation. That which properly and formally obliges, is the dictate of our conscience, or the internal judgment we pass on such or such a rule, the observance whereof appears to us just, that is, conformable to the light of right reason.

XI. "But does not this manner of reasoning," some will reply, "contradict the clearest notions, and subvert the ideas generally received, which make obligation and duty depend on the intervention of a superior, whose will manifests itself by the law? What sort of thing is an obligation imposed by reason, or which a man imposeth upon himself? Cannot he always get rid of it, when he has a mind; and if the creditor and debtor, as we have already observed, be one and the same person; can it be properly said that there is any such thing as a debt?" <213> *A fresh objection.*

This reply is grounded on an ambiguity, or supposes the thing in question. It supposes all along, that there neither is, nor can be, any other obligation, but that which proceeds from a superior or law. I agree, that such is the common language of civilians; but this makes no manner of alteration in the nature of the thing. What comes afterwards proves nothing at all. It is true that man may, if he has a mind, withdraw himself from the obligations which reason imposes on him; but if he does, it is at his peril, and he is forced himself to acknowledge, that such a conduct *Answer.*

5. Read: ". . . this proposition cannot be maintained, unless we *refuse* to give the name of obligation to *any* other restriction of liberty than that which is produced by the will and order of a superior."

is quite unreasonable. But to conclude from thence that reason alone cannot oblige us, is going too far; because this consequence would equally invalidate the obligation imposed by a superior. For, in fine, the obligation produced by law is not subversive of liberty; we have always a power to submit to it or not, and run the hazard of the consequence. In short, the question is not concerning force or constraint, it is only in relation to a moral tie, which in what manner soever it be considered, is always the work of reason.

Duty may be taken in a loose or strict sense.

XII. True it is, that duty, pursuant to its proper and strict signification, is a debt; and that when we consider it thus, it presents the idea of an action which somebody has a right to require of us. I agree likewise, that this manner of considering duty is just in itself. Man constitutes part of a system, or whole; in consequence whereof he has necessary relations to other beings; and the actions of man viewed in this light, having always some relation to another person, the idea of duty, com-<214> monly speaking, includes this relation. And yet, as it frequently happens in morality, that we give sometimes a more extensive, and at other times a more limited sense to the same term, nothing hinders us from bestowing the more ample signification on the word *duty,* by taking it in general for an action conformable to right reason. And then, it may be very well said, that man, considered even alone, and as a separate being, has particular duties to fulfill. It is sufficient for this end, that there be some actions which reason approves, and others which it condemns. These different ideas have nothing in them that is opposite; on the contrary, they are perfectly reconciled, and receive mutual strength and assistance from each other.

Result of what has been hitherto said.

XIII. The result of what we have been now saying is as follows;

1. Reason being the first rule of man, it is also the first principle of morality, and the immediate cause of all primitive obligation.

2. Man being, by his nature and state, in a necessary dependance on the Creator, who has formed him with design and wisdom, and proposed some particular views to himself in creating him; the will of God is an-

other rule of human actions, another principle of morality, obligation, and duty.

3. We may therefore say, there are in general two sorts of morality or obligation; one antecedent to the law, and the work of reason; the other subsequent to the law, and properly the effect thereof; <215> it is on this that the forementioned distinction of internal and external obligation is founded.*

4. True it is, that those different species of obligation have not all the same force. That which arises from the law, is without doubt the most perfect; it lays the strongest restriction on liberty, and merits therefore the name of obligation by way of preference. But we must not from thence infer that it is the only one, and that there can be none of any other kind. One obligation may be real, though it be different from, and even weaker than another.

5. It is so much the more necessary to admit these two sorts of obligation and morality, as that which renders the obligation of law the most perfect, is its uniting the two species; being internal and external both at the same time.† For were there no attention given to the very nature of the laws, and were the things they command or prohibit, not to merit the approbation or censure of reason; the authority of the legislator would have no other foundation but that of power; and laws being then no more than the effect of an arbitrary will, they would produce rather a constraint, properly so called, than any real obligation.

6. These remarks are especially, and in the exactest manner, applicable to the laws of nature. The obligation these produce is of all others the most efficacious and extensive; because, on one side, the disposition of these laws is in itself very reasonable, being founded on the nature of the actions, their specific differences, and the relation or opposition <216> they have to particular ends. On the other side, the divine authority, which enjoins us to observe these rules as laws he prescribes to us, adds a new force to the obligation they produce of themselves, and

* See part i. chap. vi. § 13.
† See part i. chap. ix. § 12.

lays us under an indispensable necessity of conforming our actions to them.

7. From these remarks it follows, that those two ways of establishing morality, whereof one sets up reason and the other the will of God for its principle, ought not to be placed in opposition, as two incompatible systems, neither of which can subsist without destroying or excluding the other. On the contrary, we should join these two methods, and unite the two principles, in order to have a complete system of morality, really founded on the nature and state of man. For man, as a rational being, is subject to reason; and as a creature of God, to the will of the supreme Being. And as these two qualities have nothing opposite or incompatible in their nature, consequently these two rules, reason and the divine will, are perfectly reconciled; they are even naturally connected, and strengthened by their junction. And indeed it could not be otherwise; for, in fine, God himself is the author of the nature and mutual relations of things; and particularly of the nature of man, of his constitution, state, reason, and faculties: The whole is the work of God, and ultimately depends on his will and institution.

This manner of establishing morality does not weaken the system of natural law.
XIV. This manner of establishing the foundation of obligation and duty, is so far from weakening the system of natural law or morality, that we may affirm, it rather gives it a greater solidity and force. <217> This is tracing the thing to the very source; it is laying the foundation of the edifice. I grant, that in order to reason well on morality, we ought to take things as they are, without making abstractions; that is, we should attend to the nature and actual state of man, by uniting and combining all the circumstances that essentially enter into the system of humanity. But this does not hinder us from considering likewise the system of man in its particulars, and as it were by parts, to the end, that an exact knowledge of each of those parts may help us to understand better the whole. It is the only method we can take in order to attain this end.

Grotius's opinion examined.
XV. What has been hitherto set forth, may help to explain and justify at the same time a thought of Grotius in his preliminary discourse, § 11. This author having established, after his manner, the principles and

foundation of natural law, on the constitution of human nature, adds, *that all he has been saying would in some measure take place, were we even to grant there was no God; or that he did not concern himself about human affairs.*[6] It is obvious, by his very manner of expressing himself, that he does not intend to exclude the divine will from the system of natural law. This would be mistaking his meaning; because he himself establishes this will of the Creator as another source of right. All he means is, that independent of the intervention of God, considered as a legislator, the maxims of natural law having their foundation in the nature of things and in the human constitution; reason alone imposes already on man a necessity of following those maxims, and <218> lays him under an obligation of conforming his conduct to them. In fact, it cannot be denied but that the ideas of order, agreeableness, honesty, and conformity to right reason, have at all times made an impression on man, at least to a certain degree, and among nations somewhat civilized. The human mind is formed in such a manner, that even those who do not comprehend these ideas in their full exactness and extent, have, nevertheless, a confused notion thereof, which inclines them to acquiescence so soon as they are proposed.

XVI. But while we acknowledge the reality and certainty of those principles, we ought likewise to own, that if we proceed no farther, we are got but half way our journey; this would be unreasonably attempting to establish a system of morality independent of religion. For were we even to grant, that such a system is not destitute of all foundation; yet it is certain it could never produce of itself so effectual an obligation, as when

In order to have a perfect system of morality, we should join it with religion.

---

6. Grotius's famous dictum was severely criticized by Pufendorf in DNG I.2 §6. According to Barbeyrac, Pufendorf's critique was too severe: Grotius did not imply that natural laws are obligatory independently of the realization that they are divinely imposed; DNG II.3 §4 note 5. Grotius's dictum could thus be accepted, as long as it was taken to imply only that the laws of nature are not arbitrary as to their content, although their status as morally obligatory does depend on divine will; see DGP Prolegomena §11. Burlamaqui's position differs from both Pufendorf's and Barbeyrac's, coming closer to the views of Leibniz's critical letter, which also refers to Grotius's dictum; see "The Judgment of an Anonymous Writer" §15.

it is joined with the divine will. Since the authority of the supreme Being gives the force of laws, properly so called, to the maxims of reason, these maxims acquire thereby the highest degree of strength they can possibly have, to bind and subject the will, and to lay us under the strictest obligation. But (once more we repeat it) to pretend therefore, that the maxims and counsels of reason considered in themselves, and detached, as it were, from God's command, are not at all obligatory, is carrying the thing too far; it is concluding beyond our premises, and admitting only one species of obligation. Now this is not <219> only unconformable to the nature of things, but, as we have already observed, it is weakening even the obligation resulting from the will of the legislator. For the divine ordinances make a much stronger impression on the mind, and are followed with a greater subjection in the will, in proportion as they are approved by reason, as being in themselves perfectly agreeable to our nature, and extremely conformable to our constitution and state.

CHAPTER VIII

Consequences of the preceding chapter: reflections on the distinctions of just, honest, and useful.

There is a great deal of ambiguity and mistake concerning this subject.

I. The reflections contained in the foregoing chapter give us to understand, that there is a vast deal of ambiguity and mistake in the different sentiments of writers, in relation to morality or the foundation of natural laws. They do not always ascend to the first principles, neither do they define and distinguish exactly; they suppose an opposition between ideas that are reconcileable, and ought even to be joined together. Some reason in too abstract a manner on the human system; and following only their own metaphysical speculations, never attend sufficiently to the actual state of things, and to the natural dependance of man. Others considering principally this dependance, reduce the whole to the will and orders of the sovereign master, and seem thus to lose sight of the very nature and internal con-<220>stitution of man, from which it cannot however be separated. These different ideas are just in themselves; yet we must not establish the one, by excluding the other, or by explaining it to the other's prejudice. Reason, on the contrary, requires us to unite them, in order to find the true principles of the human system, whose foundations must be sought for in the nature and state of man.

II. It is very common to use the words *utility, justice, honesty, order,* and *fitness;* but these different notions are seldom defined in an exact manner, and some of them are frequently confounded. This want of exactness must necessarily create ambiguity and confusion; wherefore, if we intend to make things clear, we must take care to define and distinguish properly.

Of just, honest, useful, order, and fitness.

An useful action may, methinks, be defined, that which of itself tends to the preservation and perfection of man.

A just action, that which is considered as conformable to the will of a superior who commands.

An action is called honest, when it is considered as conformable to the maxims of right reason, agreeable to the dignity of our nature, deserving of the approbation of man, and consequently procuring respect and honour to the person that does it.

By order we can understand, nothing else but the disposition of several things, relative to a certain end, and proportioned to the effect we intend to produce.

Finally, as to fitness or agreeableness, it bears a very great affinity with order. It is a relation of conformity between several things, one of which is of itself proper for the preservation and perfection of the <221> other, and contributes to maintain it in a good and advantageous state.

III. We must not therefore confound the words *just, useful,* and *honest;* for they are three distinct ideas. But though distinct from one another, they have no opposition; they are three relations, which may all agree, and be applied to one single action, considered under different respects. And if we ascend so high as the first origin, we shall find that they are all derived from one common source, or from one and the same principle, as three branches from the same stock. This general principle is the approbation of reason. Reason necessarily approves whatever conducts us to real happiness: and as that which is agreeable to the preser-

Just, honest, and useful, are distinct things, and must not be confounded.

vation and perfection of man; that which is conformable to the will of the sovereign master on whom he depends; and that which procures him the esteem and respect of his equals; as all this, I say, contributes to his happiness, reason cannot but approve of each of these things separately considered, much less can it help approving, under different respects, an action in which all these properties are found united.

But though they are distinct, yet they are naturally connected.
IV. For such is the state of things, that the ideas of just, honest, and useful, are naturally connected, and as it were inseparable; at least if we attend, as we ought to do, to real, general, and lasting utility. We may say, that such an utility becomes a kind of characteristic to distinguish what is truly just, or honest, from what is so only in the erroneous opinions of men. This is a beautiful and judicious remark of <222> Cicero. *The language and opinions of men are very wide, says he, from truth and right reason, in separating the honest from the useful, and in persuading themselves that some honest things are not useful, and other things are useful but not honest. This is a dangerous notion to human life.———Hence we see that Socrates detested those sophists, who first separated those two things in opinion, which in nature are really joined.

In fact, the more we investigate the plan of divine providence, the more we find the Deity has thought proper to connect the moral good and evil with the physical, or, which is the same thing, the just with the useful. And though in some particular cases the thing seems otherwise, this is only an accidental disorder, which is much less a natural consequence of the system, than an effect of the ignorance or malice of man. Whereto we must add, that in case we do not stop at the first appearances, but proceed to consider the human system in its full extent, we shall find, that every thing well considered, and all compensations made, these

---

* In quo lapsa consuetudo deflexit de via, sensimque eò deducta est, ut honestatem ab utilitate secernens, & constituerit honestum esse aliquid quod utile non esset, & utile quod non honestum: quâ nulla pernicies major hominum vitae potuit adferri. Cic. de Offic. lib. 2. cap. 3. Itaque accepimus, Socratem exsecrari solitum eos, qui primum haec naturâ cohaerentia opinione distraxissent. Idem, lib. 3. cap. 13. See likewise Grotius, Rights of war and peace, preliminary discourse, § 17. and following; and Puffendorf, Law of nature and nations, book ii. chap. iii. § 10, 11.

irregularities will be one day or other redressed, as we shall more fully shew when we come to treat of the sanctions of natural laws. <223>

V. Here a question is sometimes proposed; whether a thing be just, be-cause God commands it, or whether God commands it, because it is just?[1]

Pursuant to our principles, the question is not at all difficult. A thing is just, because God commands it; this is implied by the definition we gave of justice. But God commands such or such things, because these things are reasonable in themselves, conformable to the order and ends he proposed to himself in creating mankind, and agreeable to the na-ture and state of man. These ideas, though distinct in themselves, are necessarily connected, and can be separated only by a metaphysical abstraction.

Whether an action is just, because God commands it?

VI. Let us, in fine, observe that this harmony or surprising agreement, which naturally occurs between the ideas of just, honest, and useful, constitutes the whole beauty of virtue, and informs us at the same time in what the perfection of man consists.

In consequence of the different systems above mentioned, moralists are divided with regard to the latter point. Some place the perfection of man in such a use of his faculties as is agreeable to the nature of his being. Others in the use of our faculties and the intention of our Cre-ator.[2] Some, in fine, pretend that man is perfect, only as his manner of thinking and acting is proper to conduct him to the end he aims at, namely, his happiness.

In what the beauty of virtue and the perfection of man consists.

1. This question is originally from Plato's *Euthyphro* 10a. The question was usually presented by critics of Pufendorfian voluntarism, who argued that Pufendorf ended up with a paradoxical claim, that good and evil are imposed by an arbitrary act of the divine will. This paragraph expresses Burlamaqui's conviction that he has found a system that can do justice to the insights of both Pufendorf (and Barbeyrac) and his (their) critics.

2. The translation is not very clear. The second option discussed by Burlamaqui is to emphasize "the relation there is between our usage of our faculties and the in-tentions of the Creator of our being."

But what we have above said sufficiently shews, that these three methods of considering the perfection of man, are very little different, and ought not to be set in opposition. As they are interwoven with <224> one another, we ought rather to combine and unite them. The perfection of man consists really in the possession of natural or acquired faculties, which enable us to obtain, and actually put us in possession of solid felicity; and this in conformity to the intention of our Creator, engraved in our nature, and clearly manifested by the state wherein he has placed us.*

A modern writer has judiciously said; *that to obey only through fear of authority, or for the hope of recompence, without esteeming or loving virtue for the sake of its own excellency; is mean and mercenary. On the contrary, to practise virtue with an abstract view of its fitness and natural beauty, without having any thought of the Creator and Conductor of the universe; is failing in our duty to the first and greatest of Beings. He only who acts jointly through a principle of reason, through a motive of piety, and with a view of his principal interest, is an honest, wise, and pious man; which constitutes, without comparison, the worthiest and completest of characters.*
<225>

CHAPTER IX

Of the application of natural laws to human actions; and first of conscience.†

What is meant by applying the laws to human actions.

I. As soon as we have discovered the foundation and rule of our duties, we have only to recollect what has been already said in the eleventh chapter of the first part of this work, concerning the morality of actions, to see in what manner natural laws are applied to human actions, and what effect ought from thence to result.

The application of the laws to human actions is nothing else, but the judgment we pass on their morality, by comparing them with the law;

* *Theory of agreeable sensations,* chap. viii.
† See the Law of nature and nations, book i. chap. iii. § 4. and following: and the Duties of man and a citizen, book i. chap. i. § 5, 6.

a judgment whereby we pronounce that those actions being either good, bad, or indifferent, we are obliged either to perform or omit them, or that we may use our liberty in this respect: and that according to the side we have taken, we are worthy of praise or blame, approbation or censure.

This is done in two different manners. For either we judge on this footing of our own actions, or of those of another person. In the first case, our judgment is called conscience: but the judgment we pass on other men's actions, is termed imputation. These are, undoubtedly, subjects of great importance, and of universal use in morality, which deserve therefore to be treated with some care and circumspection. <226>

II. Conscience is properly no more than reason itself, considered as instructed in regard to the rule we ought to follow, or to the law of nature; and judging of the morality of our own actions, and of the obligations we are under in this respect, by comparing them to this rule, pursuant to the ideas we entertain thereof.

What is conscience.

Conscience is also very frequently taken for the very judgment we pass on the morality of actions; a judgment which is the result of perfect reasoning, or the consequence we infer from two express or tacit premisses. A person compares two propositions, one of which includes the law, and the other the action; and from thence he deduces a third, which is the judgment he makes of the quality of his action. Such was the reasoning of Judas: *Whosoever delivers up an innocent man to death, commits a crime;* here is the law. *Now this is what I have done;* here is the action. *I have therefore committed a crime;* this is the consequence, or judgment which his conscience passed on the action he committed.

III. Conscience supposes therefore a knowledge of the law; and particularly of the law of nature, which being the primitive source of justice, is likewise the supreme rule of conduct. And as the laws cannot serve us for rules, but inasmuch as they are known, it follows therefore, that conscience becomes thus the immediate rule of our actions:[1] for it is evident we cannot conform to the law, but so far as we have notice thereof. <227>

Conscience supposes a knowledge of the law.

1. This is from Barbeyrac in DNG I.3 §4 note 3. Most of Burlamaqui's discussion

First rule.   IV. This being premised, the *first rule* we have to lay down concerning this matter, is, that we must enlighten our conscience, as well as consult it, and follow its counsels.

We must enlighten our conscience; that is, we must spare no care or pains to be exactly instructed with regard to the will of the legislator, and the disposition of his laws, in order to acquire just ideas of whatever is commanded, forbidden, or permited. For plain it is, that were we in ignorance or error in this respect, the judgment we should form of our actions would be necessarily vicious, and consequently lead us astray. But this is not enough. We must join to this first knowledge, the knowledge also of the action. And for this purpose, it is not only necessary to examine this action in itself; but we ought likewise to be attentive to the particular circumstances that accompany it, and the consequences that from thence may follow. Otherwise we should run a risk of being mistaken in the application of the laws, whose general decisions admit of several modifications, according to the different circumstances that accompany our actions; which necessarily influences their morality, and of course our duties. Thus it is not sufficient for a judge to be well acquainted with the tenor and purport of the law, before he pronounces sentence; he should likewise have an exact knowledge of the fact and all its different circumstances.

But it is not merely with a view of enlightening our reason, that we ought to acquire all this knowledge; it is principally in order to apply it occa-<228>sionally to the direction of our conduct. We should therefore, whenever it concerns us to act, consult previously our conscience, and be directed by its counsels. This is properly an indispensable obligation. For, in fine, conscience being, as it were, the minister and interpreter of the will of the legislator, the counsels it gives us, have all the force and authority of a law, and ought to produce the same effect upon us.

---

in this chapter is from that note and from DHC I.1 §5 notes 1–3 and DHC I.1 §7 note 1.

V. It is only therefore by enlightening our conscience, that it becomes a sure rule of conduct, whose dictates may be followed with a perfect confidence of exactly fulfilling our duty. For we should be grosly mistaken, if under a notion that conscience is the immediate rule of our actions, we were to believe that every man may lawfully do whatever he imagines the law commands or permits. We ought first to know whether this notion or persuasion is justly founded. For as Puffendorf * observes, conscience has no share in the direction of human actions, but inasmuch as it is instructed concerning the law, whose office it properly is to direct our actions. If we have therefore a mind to determine and act with safety, we must on every particular occasion observe the two following rules, which are very simple of themselves, easy to practice, and naturally follow our first rule, of which they are only a kind of elucidation.† <229>

Second rule. Before we determine to follow the dictates of conscience, we should examine thoroughly whether we have the necessary lights and helps to judge of the things before us. If we happen to want these lights and helps, we can neither decide, nor much less undertake any thing, without an inexcusable and dangerous temerity. And yet nothing is commoner than to transgress against this rule. What multitudes, for example, determine on religious disputes, or difficult questions concerning morality or politics, though they are no way capable of judging or reasoning about them?

Third rule. Supposing that in general we have necessary lights and helps to judge of the affair before us, we must afterwards see whether we have actually made use of them; insomuch, that without a new inquiry we may follow what our conscience suggests. It happens every day that for want of attending to this rule, we let ourselves be quietly prevailed upon to do a great many things, which we might easily discover to be unjust, had we given heed to certain clear principles, the justice and necessity of which is universally acknowledged.

When we have made use of the rules here laid down, we have done

* See the Law of nature and nations, book i. chap. iii. § 4.
† See Barbeyrac's first note on the Duties of man and a citizen, book i. chap. i. § 5.

whatever we could and ought; and it is morally certain, that by thus proceeding we can be neither mistaken in our judgment, nor wrong in our determinations. But if, notwithstanding all these precautions, we should happen to be mistaken, which is not absolutely impossible; this would be an infirmity, inseparable from human nature, and would carry its excuse along with it in the eye of the supreme legislator. <230>

Antecedent and subsequent conscience. Fourth rule.

VI. We judge of our actions either before, or after we have done them; wherefore there is an antecedent and a subsequent conscience.

This distinction gives us an opportunity to lay down a *fourth rule;* which is, that a prudent man ought to consult his conscience before and after he has acted.

To determine to act, without having previously examined, whether what we are going to do be good or evil, manifestly indicates an indifference for our duty, which is a most dangerous state in respect to man; a state capable of throwing him into the most fatal excesses. But as, in this first judgment, we may happen to be determined by passion, and to proceed with precipitation, or upon a very slight examen; it is therefore necessary to reflect again on what we have done, either in order to be confirmed in the right side, if we have embraced it; or to correct our mistake if possible, and to guard against the like faults for the future. This is so much the more important, as experience shews us, that we frequently judge quite differently between a past and a future transaction; and that the prejudices or passions which may lead us astray, when we are to take our resolution, oftentimes disappear either in the whole or part, when the action is over; and leave us then more at liberty to judge rightly of the nature and consequences of the action.

The habit of making this double examen, is the essential character of an honest man; and indeed nothing can be a better proof of our being seriously inclined to discharge our several duties. <231>

Subsequent conscience is either quiet, or uneasy.

VII. The effect resulting from this revisal of our conduct, is very different, according as the judgment we pass on it, absolves or condemns us. In the first case, we find ourselves in a state of satisfaction and tranquillity, which is the surest and sweetest recompence of virtue. A pure and untainted pleasure accompanies always those actions that are approved by reason; and reflection renews the sweets we have tasted, together with their remembrance. And indeed what greater happiness is there than to be inwardly satisfied, and to be able with a just confidence to promise ourselves the approbation and benevolence of the sovereign Lord on whom we depend? If, on the contrary, conscience condemns us, this condemnation must be accompanied with inquietude, trouble, reproaches, fear, and remorse; a state so dismal, that the ancients have compared it to that of a man tormented by the furies. *Every crime*, says the satyrist, *is disapproved by the very person that commits it; and the first punishment the criminal feels, is, that he cannot avoid being self-condemned, were he even to find means of being acquitted before the praetor's tribunal.*

> Exemplo quodcunque malo committitur, ipsi
> Displicet auctori: prima haec est ultio, quod, se
> Judice, nemo nocens absolvitur, improba quamvis
> Gratia fallaci praetoris vicerit urnâ.
>
> Juven. Sat. 13. ver. 1.

> *He that commits a sin, shall quickly find*
> *The pressing guilt lie heavy on his mind;*
> *Though bribes or favour shall assert his cause,*
> *Pronounce him guiltless, and elude the laws:* <232>
> *None quits himself; his own impartial thought*
> *Will damn, and conscience will record the fault.*
>
> Creech.

Hence the subsequent conscience is said to be quiet or uneasy, good or bad.

VIII. The judgment we pass on the morality of our actions is likewise susceptible of several different modifications, that produce new distinctions of conscience, which we should here point out. These distinctions may, in general, be equally applied to the two first species of conscience above mentioned; but they seem more frequently and particularly to agree with the antecedent conscience.

Decisive and dubious conscience. Fifth, sixth, and seventh rule.

Conscience is therefore either decisive or dubious, according to the degree of persuasion a person may have concerning the quality of the action.

When we pronounce decisively, and without any hesitation, that an action is conformable or opposite to the law, or that it is permitted, and consequently we ought to do or omit it, or else that we are at liberty in this respect; this is called a decisive conscience. If, on the contrary, the mind remains in suspense, through the conflict of reasons we see on both sides, and which appear to us of equal weight, insomuch that we cannot tell to which side we ought to incline; this is called a dubious conscience. Such was the doubt of the Corinthians, who did not know whether they could eat things sacrificed to idols, or whether they ought to abstain from them. On the one side, the evangelical liberty seemed to permit it; on the other, they were restrained through apprehension of seeming to give thereby a kind of consent to idolatrous acts. <233> Not knowing what resolution to take, they wrote to St. Paul to remove their doubt.

This distinction makes room also for some rules.

Fifth Rule. We do not intirely discharge our duty, by doing with a kind of difficulty and reluctance, what the decisive conscience ordains; we ought to set about it readily, willingly, and with pleasure.* On the contrary, to determine without hesitation or repugnance, against the motions of such a conscience, is shewing the highest degree of depravation and malice, and renders a person incomparably more criminal than if he were impelled by a violent passion or temptation.†

Sixth Rule. With regard to a dubious conscience, we ought to use all endeavours to get rid of our uncertainty, and to forbear acting, so long as we do not know whether we do good or evil. To behave otherwise, would indicate an indirect contempt of the law, by exposing one's self voluntarily to the hazard of violating it, which is a very bad conduct. The rule now mentioned ought to be attended to, especially in matters of great importance.

Seventh Rule. But if we find ourselves in such circumstances as necessarily oblige us to determine to act, we must then, by a new attention

* See Grotius, Rights of war and peace, book ii. chap. xx. § 19.
† See part ii. chap. v. § 7.

endeavour to distinguish the safest and most probable side, and whose consequences are least dangerous. Such is generally the opposite side to passion; it being the <234> safest way, not to listen too much to our inclinations. In like manner, we run very little risk of being mistaken in a dubious case, by following rather the dictates of charity than the suggestion of self-love.

IX. Besides the dubious conscience, properly so called, and which we may likewise distinguish by the name of irresolute, there is a scrupulous conscience, produced by slight and frivolous difficulties that arise in the mind, without seeing any solid reason for doubting.

Eighth Rule. Such scruples as these ought not to hinder us from acting, if it be necessary; and as they generally arise either from a false delicacy of conscience, or from gross superstition, we should soon get rid of them, were we to examine the thing with attention.

Scrupulous conscience. Eighth rule.

X. Let us afterwards observe, that the decisive conscience, according as it determines good or evil,[2] is either right or erroneous.

Those, for example, who imagine we ought to abstain from strict revenge, though the law of nature permits a legitimate defence, have a right conscience. On the other hand, those who think that the law which requires us to be faithful to our engagements, is not obligatory towards heretics, and that we may lawfully break through it in respect to them, have an erroneous conscience.

But what must we do in case of an erroneous conscience?

Ninth Rule. I answer, that we ought always to follow the dictates of conscience, even when it is <235> erroneous, and whether the error be vincible or invincible.

This rule may appear strange at first sight, since it seems to prescribe evil; because there is no manner of question, but that a man who acts according to an erroneous conscience, espouses a bad cause. Yet this is not so bad, as if we were to determine to do a thing, with a firm per-

Right and erroneous conscience. Ninth rule.

2. Read: "according as it determines well or badly" ("suivant qu'elle decide bien ou mal").

suasion of its being contrary to the decision of the law; for this would denote a direct contempt of the legislator and his orders, which is a most criminal disposition. Whereas the first resolution, though bad in itself, is nevertheless the effect of a laudable disposition to obey the legislator, and conform to his will.

But it does not from thence follow, that we are always excusable in being guided by the dictates of an erroneous conscience; this is true only when the error happens to be invincible. If on the contrary it is surmountable, and we are mistaken in respect to what is commanded or forbidden, we sin either way, whether we act according to, or against the decisions of conscience. This shews (to mention it once more) what an important concern it is to enlighten our conscience, because, in the case just now mentioned, the person with an erroneous conscience is actually under a melancholy necessity of doing ill, whichever side he takes. But if we should happen to be mistaken with regard to an indifferent thing, which we are erroneously persuaded is commanded or forbidden, we do not sin in that case, but when we act contrary to the light of our own conscience. <236>

Demonstrative and probable conscience. Tenth rule.

XI. In fine, there are two sorts of right conscience; the one clear and demonstrative, and the other merely probable.

The clear and demonstrative conscience is that which is founded on certain principles, and on demonstrative reasons, so far as the nature of moral things will permit; insomuch that one may clearly and distinctly prove the rectitude of a judgment made on such or such an action. On the contrary, though we are convinced of the truth of a judgment, yet if it be founded only on verisimilitude, and we cannot demonstrate its certainty in a methodical manner, and by incontestible principles, it is then only a probable conscience.

The foundations of probable conscience are in general authority and example, supported by a confused notion of a natural fitness, and sometimes by popular reasons, which seem drawn from the very nature of things. It is by this kind of conscience that the greatest part of mankind are conducted, there being very few who are capable of knowing the indispensable necessity of their duties, by deducing them from their first sources by regular consequences; especially when the point relates to maxims of morality, which being somewhat remote from the first principles, require a longer chain of reasonings. This conduct is far from being unreasonable. For those who have not sufficient light of themselves to judge properly of the nature of things, cannot do better than recur to the judgment of enlightened persons; this being the only resource left them to act with safety. We might in this respect <237> compare the persons above mentioned to young people, whose judgment has not yet acquired its full maturity, and who ought to listen and conform to the counsels of their superiors. The authority therefore, and example of sage and enlightened men, may in some cases, in default of our own lights, prove a reasonable principle of determination and conduct.

But, in fine, since those foundations of probable conscience are not so solid as to permit us absolutely to build upon them, we must therefore establish, as a *Tenth Rule,* that we ought to use all our endeavours to increase the degree of verisimilitude in our opinions, in order to approach as near as possible to the clear and demonstrative conscience; and we must not be satisfied with probability, but when we can do no better.

CHAPTER X

Of the merit and demerit of human actions; and of their imputation relative to the laws of nature.[*]

I. In explaining the nature of human actions, considered with regard to right,[†] we observed, that an essential quality of these actions is to be susceptible of imputation; that is, the agent may be reasonably looked upon as the real author thereof, <238> may have it charged to his account, and be made answerable for it; insomuch that the good or bad effects from thence arising, may be justly attributed and referred to him,

Distinction of imputability and imputation. Of the nature of a moral cause.

---

[*] See on this, and the following chapter, Puffendorf's Law of nature and nations, book i. chap. v. and chap. ix.

[†] Part i. chap. iii.

as to the efficient cause, concerning which we have laid down this principle, that every voluntary action is of an imputable nature.

We give in general the name of moral cause of an action to the person that produced it, either in the whole or part, by a determination of his will; whether he executes it himself physically and immediately, so as to be the author thereof; or whether he procures it by the act of some other person, and becomes thereby its cause. Thus whether we wound a man with our own hands, or set assassins to way-lay him, we are equally the moral cause of the evil from thence resulting.

It was observed likewise, that we must not confound the imputability of human actions with their actual imputation. The former, as has been just now mentioned, is a quality of the action; the latter is an act of the legislator, or judge, who lays to a person's charge an action that is of an imputable nature.

Of the nature of imputation. It supposes a knowledge of the law, as well as of the fact.
II. Imputation is properly therefore a judgment by which we declare, that a person being the author or moral cause of an action commanded or forbidden by the laws, the good or bad effects that result from this action, ought to be actually attributed to him; that he is consequently answerable for them, and as such is worthy of praise or blame, of recompence or punishment. <239>

This judgment of imputation, as well as that of conscience, is made by applying the law to the action, and comparing one with the other, in order to decide afterwards the merit of the fact, and to make the author consequently feel the good or evil, the punishment or recompence which the law has thereto annexed. All this necessarily supposes an exact knowledge of the law and of its right sense, as well as of the fact and such circumstances thereof, as may any way relate to the determination of the law. A want of this knowledge must render the application false, and the judgment erroneous.

Examples.
III. Let us produce a few examples. One of the *Horatii*, who remained conqueror in the combat between the brothers of this name, and the three *Curiatii*, inflamed with anger against his sister for bewailing the death of one of the Curiatii her lover, and for bitterly reproaching him

therewith, instead of congratulating him for his victory, slew her with his own hand. He was accused before the *Duumvirs;* and the question was, whether the law against murderers ought to be applied to the present case, in order to make him undergo the punishment? This was the opinion of the judges, who in fact condemned the young Roman. But an appeal being made to the people, they judged quite otherwise. Their notion was, that the law ought not to be applied to the fact; because a Roman lady, who seemed to be more concerned about her own particular interest, than sensible of the good of her country, might in some measure be considered and treated as an enemy; wherefore they pronounced the young <240> man innocent. Let us add another example of an advantageous imputation, or of a judgment of recompence. Cicero, in the beginning of his consulate, discovered the conspiracy of Catiline, which menaced the republic with ruin. In this delicate conjuncture he behaved with so much prudence and address, that the conspiracy was stifled without any noise or sedition, by the death of a few of the criminals. And yet J. Caesar, and some other enemies of Cicero, accused him before the people, for having put citizens to death contrary to rule, and before the senate or people had passed judgment against them. But the people attending to the circumstances of the fact, to the danger the republic had escaped, and to the important service Cicero had done, so far from condemning him as an infringer of the laws, decreed him the glorious title of *father of his country.*

IV. In order to settle the principles and foundations of this matter, we must observe, 1. That we ought not to conclude the actual imputation of an action merely from its imputability. An action, to merit actual imputation, must necessarily have the concurrence of these two conditions: first, that it be of an imputable nature, and secondly, that the agent be under some obligation of doing or omitting it. An example will clear up the thing. Let us suppose two young men with the same abilities and conveniences, but under no obligation of knowing algebra: one of them applies himself to this science, and the other does not; though the action of the one and the other's omission, are by themselves of an im-<241>putable nature; yet in this case they can be neither good nor bad.

Principles.
1. We ought not to infer actual imputation from imputability only.

But were we to suppose that these two young men are designed by their prince, the one for some office of state, and the other for a military employment; in this case, their application or neglect in instructing themselves in jurisprudence, for example, or in the mathematics, would be justly imputed to them. The reason is, they are both indispensibly obliged to acquire such knowledge as is necessary for discharging properly the offices or employments to which they are called. Hence it is evident, that as imputability supposeth the power of acting or not acting; actual imputation requires, moreover, that a person be under an obligation of doing either one or the other.

2. Imputation supposes some connexion between the action and its consequences.

V. 2. When we impute an action to a person, we render him, as has been already observed, answerable for the good or bad consequences of what he has done. From thence it follows, that in order to make a just imputation, there must be some necessary or accidental connexion between the thing done or omitted, and the good or bad consequences of the action or omission; and besides, the agent must have had some knowledge of this connexion, or at least he must have been able to have a probable foresight of the effects of his action. Otherwise the imputation cannot take place, as will appear by a few examples. A gunsmith sells arms to a man who has the appearance of a sensible, sedate person, and does not seem to have any bad design. And yet this man goes instantly to make an unjust attack on another person, and kills him. Here the <242> gunsmith is not at all chargeable, having done nothing but what he had a right to do; and besides, he neither could nor ought to have foreseen what happened. But if a person carelesly leaves a pair of pistols charged on a table, in a place exposed to every body, and a child insensible of the danger happens to wound or kill himself; the former is certainly answerable for the misfortune: by reason this was a clear and immediate consequence of what he has done, and he could and ought to have foreseen it.[1]

We must reason in the same manner with respect to an action productive of some good. This good cannot be attributed to a person, that

1. See especially DNG I.5 §3 note 4.

has been the cause of it without knowledge or thought thereof. But in order to merit thanks and acknowledgment, there is no necessity of our being intirely sure of success; it is sufficient there was room to reasonably presume it, and were the effect absolutely to fail, the intention would not be the less commendable.

VI. 3. But in order to ascend to the first principles of this theory, we must observe, that as man is supposed to be obliged by his nature and state to follow certain rules of conduct; the observance of those rules constitutes the perfection of his nature and state; and, on the contrary, the infringing of them forms the degradation of both. Now we are made after such a manner, that perfection and order please us of themselves; while imperfection and disorder, and whatever relates thereto, naturally displease us. Consequently, we acknowledge that those who answering the end they were designed <243> for, perform their duty, and contribute thus to the good and perfection of the human system, are deserving of our approbation, esteem, and benevolence; that they may reasonably expect these sentiments in their favour, and have some sort of a right to the advantageous effects which naturally arise from thence. We cannot, on the contrary, avoid condemning those, who, through a bad use of their faculties, degrade their own state and nature; we confess they are worthy of disapprobation and blame, and that it is agreeable to reason, the bad effects of their conduct should fall upon themselves. Such are the foundations of merit and demerit.

3. Foundations of merit and demerit.

VII. Merit therefore is a quality which intitles us to the approbation, esteem, and benevolence of our superiors or equals, and to the advantages from thence resulting. Demerit is an opposite quality, which rendering us worthy of the censure and blame of those with whom we converse, obliges us, as it were, to acknowledge that it is reasonable they should entertain those sentiments towards us; and that we are under a melancholy obligation of bearing the bad effects that flow from thence.

In what merit and demerit consists.

These notions of merit and demerit, have therefore, it is plain, their foundation in the very nature of things, and are perfectly agreeable to common sense and the notions generally received. Praise and blame, where people judge reasonably,[2] always follow the quality of actions, according as they are morally good or bad. This is clear with respect to the legislator: He must contradict himself in the grossest manner, were he not to approve what is conforma-<244>ble, and to condemn what is opposite to his laws. And as for those that depend on him, this very dependance obliges them to regulate their judgment on this subject.

4. Merit and demerit have their degrees; and so has imputation.

VIII. 4. We have already* observed, that some actions are better than others, and that bad ones may likewise be more or less so, according to the different circumstances that attend them, and the disposition of the person that does them. Merit and demerit have therefore their degrees; they may be greater or lesser. Wherefore when we are to determine exactly how far an action ought to be imputed to a person, we should have regard to these differences; and the praise or blame, the recompence or punishment, ought likewise to have their degrees in proportion to the merit or demerit. Thus, according as the good or evil proceeding from an action is more or less considerable; according as there was more or less facility or difficulty to perform or to abstain from this action; according as it was done with more or less reflection and liberty; and finally, according as the reasons that ought to have determined us thereto, or diverted us from it, were more or less strong, and the intention and motives were more or less noble and generous; the imputation is made after a more or less efficacious manner, and its effects are more or less profitable or pernicious.

5. Imputation is either simple or efficacious.

IX. 5. Imputation, as we have already hinted, may be made by different persons; and it is easy to <245> comprehend, that in those different cases, the effects thereof are not always the same; but that they must be more or less important, according to the quality of the persons, and the different right they have in this respect. Sometimes imputation is confined

* Part i. chap xi. § 12.
2. Read: "to judge reasonably of matters" ("à en juger raisonnablement").

simply to praise or blame; and at other times it goes further. This gives us room to distinguish two sorts of imputation, one simple, and the other efficacious. The first consists only in approving or disapproving the action; insomuch that no other effect arises from thence with regard to the agent. But the second is not confined to blame or praise; it produces moreover some good or bad effect with regard to the agent; that is, some real and positive good or evil that befalls him.

X. 6. Simple imputation may be made indifferently by every one, whether they have or have not a particular and personal interest in the doing or omitting of the action: it is sufficient they have a general and indirect interest. And as we may affirm that all the members of society are interested in the due observance of the laws of nature, hence they have all a right to praise or condemn another man's actions according as they are conformable or contrary to those laws. They have even a kind of obligation in this respect. The regard they owe to the legislator and his laws, requires it of them; and they would be wanting in their duty to society and to individuals, were they not to testify, at least by their approbation or censure, the esteem they have for probity and virtue, and their aversion, on the contrary, to iniquity and vice. <246>

6. Effects of one and the other.

But with regard to efficacious imputation, in order to render it lawful, we should have a particular and direct interest in the performing or omitting of the action. Now those who have such an interest, are, firstly, persons whom it concerns to regulate the actions; secondly, such as are the object thereof, namely, those towards whom we act, and to whose advantage or prejudice the thing may turn. Thus a sovereign who has enacted laws, who commands certain things with a promise of recompence, and prohibits others under a commination of punishment, ought without doubt to concern himself about the observance of his laws, and has consequently a right to impute the actions of his subjects after an efficacious manner, that is, to reward or punish them. The same may be said of a person who has received some injury or damage by another man's action: this very thing gives him a right to impute the action efficaciously to its author, in order to obtain a just satisfaction, and a reasonable indemnification.

7. If all those who are concerned, do not impute an action, it is supposed not to have been done.

XI. 7. It may therefore happen, that several persons have a right to impute each on his side, the same action to the person that did it; because this action may interest them in different respects. And in that case, if any of the persons concerned has a mind to relinquish his right, by not imputing the action to the agent so far as it concerns himself; this does not in any shape prejudice the right of the rest, which is no way in his power. When a man does me an injury, I may indeed forgive him, as to what concerns myself; but this does not diminish <247> the right the sovereign may have to take cognizance of the injury, and to punish the author, as an infringer of the law, and a disturber of the civil order and government. But if those who are interested in the action, are willing not to impute it, and all jointly forgive the injury and the crime; in this case the action ought to be morally esteemed as never committed, because it is not attended with any moral effect.

8. Difference between the imputation of good and bad actions.

XII. 8. Let us, in fine, observe, that there is some difference between the imputation of good and bad actions. When the legislator has established a certain recompence for a good action, he obliges himself to give this recompence, and he grants a right of demanding it to those who have rendered themselves worthy thereof by their submission and obedience. But with respect to penalties enacted against bad actions, the legislator may actually inflict them, if he has a mind, and has an incontestible right to do it; insomuch that the criminal cannot reasonably complain of the evil he is made to undergo, because he has drawn it upon himself through his disobedience. But it does not from thence ensue, that the sovereign is obliged to punish to the full rigour; he is always master to exercise his right, or to shew grace; to intirely remit or to diminish the punishment; and he may have very good reasons for doing either. <248>

CHAPTER XI

Application of those principles to different species of actions, in order to judge in what manner they ought to be imputed.

I. We might be satisfied with the general principles above laid down, were it not useful to make an application of them, and to point out particularly those actions or events for which we are, or are not answerable.

    1. And in the first place it follows, from what has been hitherto said, that we may impute to a person every action or omission, of which he is the author or cause, and which he could or ought to have done or omitted.

    2. The actions of those that have not the use of reason, such as infants, fools and madmen, ought not to be imputed to them. The want of knowledge hinders, in such cases, imputation. For these persons being incapable of knowing what they are doing, or of comparing it with the laws; their actions are not properly human actions, nor do they include any morality. If we scold or beat a child, it is not by way of punishment; it is only a simple correction, by which we propose principally to hinder him from contracting a bad habit.

    3. With regard to what is done in drunkenness, this state voluntarily contracted does not hinder the imputation of a bad action. <249>

II. 4. We do not impute things that are really above a person's strength; no more than the omission of a thing commanded, if there has been no opportunity of doing it. For the imputation of an omission manifestly supposes these two things; first, that a person has had sufficient strength and means to act; and secondly, that he could have made use of those means, without any prejudice to some other more indispensible duty, or without drawing upon himself a considerable evil, to which there was no obligation of being exposed. It must be understood however, that the person has not brought himself into an incapacity of acting through his own fault; for then the legislator might as lawfully punish those who

What actions are actually imputed?

Actions of such as have not the use of reason.

Of what's done in drunkenness.

Of things that are impossible. Of the want of opportunity.

have reduced themselves to this incapacity, as if they had refused to act when they were capable of complying. Such was at Rome the case of those who cut off their thumbs, in order to disable themselves from handling arms, and to be exempted from the service. In like manner a debtor is not excusable, when, through his own misconduct, he has rendered himself unable to discharge his debts. And we even become deservedly responsible for a thing in itself impossible, if we have undertaken to do it, when we knew, or might easily have known, that it surpassed our strength; in case any body happens by this means to be injured.

Of natural qualities.   III. 5. The natural qualities of body or mind cannot of themselves be imputed, either as good or evil. But a person is deserving of praise, when by his application and care these qualities are perfected, or these defects are mended; and, on the contrary, <250> one is justly accountable for the imperfections and infirmities that arise from bad conduct or neglect.

Of events produced by external causes.   6. The effects of external causes and events, of what kind soever, cannot be attributed to a person, either as good or evil, but inasmuch as he could and ought to procure, hinder, or direct them, and as he has been either careful or negligent in this respect. Thus we charge a good or bad harvest to a husbandman's account, according as he has tilled well or ill the ground, whose culture was committed to his care.

Of what is done through ignorance or error.   IV. 7. As for things done through error or ignorance, we may affirm in general, that a person is not answerable for what he has done through invincible ignorance, especially as it is involuntary in its origin and cause. If a prince travels through his own dominions disguised and *incognito,* his subjects are not to blame for not paying him the respect and honour due to him. But we should reasonably impute an unjust sentence to a judge, who neglecting to instruct himself either in the fact or the law, should happen to want the knowledge necessary to decide with equity. But the possibility of getting instruction, and the care we ought to take for this purpose, are not strictly considered in the common run of life; we only look upon what is possible or impossible in a moral sense, and with a due regard to the actual state of humanity.

Ignorance or error, in point of laws and duties, generally passes for voluntary, and does not obstruct the imputation of actions or omissions from thence <251> arising. This is a consequence of the principles* already established. But there may happen some particular cases, wherein the nature of the thing, which of itself is difficult to investigate, joined to the character and state of the person, whose faculties being naturally limited, have likewise been uncultivated for want of education and assistance, renders the error unsurmountable, and consequently worthy of excuse. It concerns the prudence of the legislator to weigh these circumstances, and to modify the imputation on this footing.

V. 8. Though temperament, habits, and passions, have of themselves a great force to determine some actions; yet this force is not such as absolutely hinders the use of reason and liberty, at least in respect to the execution of the bad designs they inspire. This is what all legislators suppose; and a very good reason they have to suppose it.† Natural dispositions, habits, and passions, do not determine men invincibly to violate the laws of nature. These disorders of the soul are not incurable; with some pains and assiduity one may contrive to remove them, according to Cicero's observation, who alledges to this purpose the example of Socrates.‡

Of the effect of temperament, habits, or passions.

But if instead of endeavouring to correct these vicious dispositions, we strengthen them by habit, this does not render us inexcusable.[1] The power of habit is, indeed, very great; it even seems to im-<252>pel us by a kind of necessity. And yet experience shews it is not impossible to master it, when we are seriously resolved to make the attempt. And were it even true that inveterate habits had a greater command over us than reason; yet as it was in our power not to contract them, they do not at all diminish the immorality of bad actions, and consequently they cannot hinder them from being imputed. On the contrary, as a virtuous

* See part i. chap. i. § 12.
† See part i. chap. ii. § 16.
‡ Tuscul. quaest. lib. 4. cap. 37.
1. Read: "does not render us excusable" ("l'on ne deviant pas excusable").

habit renders actions more commendable; so the habit of vice cannot but augment its blame and demerit. In short, if inclinations, passions, or habits, could frustrate the effect of laws, it would be needless to trouble our heads about any direction of human actions; for the principal object of laws in general is to correct bad inclinations, to prevent vicious habits, to hinder their effects, and to eradicate the passions; or at least to contain them within their proper limits.

Of forced actions.

VI. 9. The different cases hitherto exposed, contain nothing very difficult or puzzling. There are some others a little more embarrassing, which require a particular discussion.

The first question is, what we are to think of forced actions; whether they are of an imputable nature, and ought actually to be imputed?

I answer, 1. That a physical violence, and such as absolutely cannot be resisted, produces an involuntary action, which so far from meriting to be actually imputed, is not even of an imputable nature.* In this case, the author of the violence is the true and <253> only cause of the action, and as such is the only person answerable for it; whilst the immediate agent being merely passive, the fact can be no more attributed to him than to the sword, to the stick, or to any other weapon with which the blow or wound was given.

2. But if the constraint arises from the apprehension or fear of some great evil, with which we are menaced by a person more powerful than ourselves, and who is able instantly to inflict it; it must be allowed, that the action done in consequence of this fear, does not cease to be voluntary, and therefore, generally speaking, it is of an imputable nature.†

In order to know afterwards whether it ought actually to be imputed, it is necessary to inquire, whether the person on whom the constraint is laid, is under a rigorous obligation of doing or abstaining from a thing, at the hazard of suffering the evil with which he is menaced. If so, and he determines contrary to his duty, the constraint is not a sufficient reason to screen him absolutely from imputation. For generally speaking,

* See § 1.
† See part i. chap. ii. § 12.

it cannot be questioned but a lawful superior can lay us under an indispensible obligation of obeying his orders, at the hazard of bodily pain, and even at the risk of our lives.

VII. Pursuant to these principles, we must distinguish between indifferent actions, and those that are morally necessary. An action indifferent of its nature, extorted by main force, cannot be imputed to <254> the person constrained; because, not being under any obligation in this respect, the author of the violence has no right to require any thing of him. And as the law of nature expresly forbids all manner of violence, it cannot authorise it at the same time, by laying the person that suffers the violence, under a necessity of executing a thing to which he has given only a forced consent. Thus every forced promise or convention is null of itself, and has nothing in it obligatory as a promise or convention; on the contrary, it may and ought to be imputed as a crime to the author of the violence. But were we to suppose that the person who uses the constraint, exercises in this respect his own right, and pursues the execution thereof; the action, though forced, is still valid, and attended with all its moral effects. Thus a debtor, who void of any principle of honesty, satisfies his creditor only through imminent fear of imprisonment, or of execution on his goods, cannot complain against this payment, as made by constraint and violence. For being under an obligation of paying his just debts, he ought to have done it willingly and of his own accord, instead of being obliged to it by force.

> Forced actions are in themselves either good, bad, or indifferent.

As for good actions, to which a person is determined by force, and, as it were, through fear of blows or punishment, they pass for nothing, and merit neither praise nor recompence. The reason hereof is obvious. The obedience required by the law ought to be sincere; and we should discharge our duties through a conscientious principle, voluntarily, and with our own consent and free will. <255>

Finally, with regard to actions manifestly bad or criminal, to which a person is forced through fear of some great evil, and especially death; we must lay down as a general rule, that the unhappy circumstances under which a person labours, may indeed diminish the crime of a man unequal to this trial, who commits a bad action in spite of himself, and against his own inward conviction; yet the action remains intrinsically vicious, and worthy of censure; wherefore it may be, and actually is imputed, unless the exception of necessity can be alledged in the person's favour.

Why a bad action, though forced, may be imputed.

VIII. This last rule is a consequence of the principles hitherto established. A man who determines through fear of some great evil, but without suffering any physical violence, to do a thing visibly criminal, concurs in some manner to the action, and acts voluntarily, though with regret. It does not absolutely surpass the fortitude of the human mind to resolve to suffer, nay to die, rather than be wanting in our duty. We see a great many people who have a courage of this kind for very frivolous subjects, which make a lively impression on them; and though the thing be really difficult, yet it is not impossible. The legislator may therefore impose a rigorous obligation of obeying, and have just reasons for so doing. The interest of society frequently requires examples of undaunted constancy. It was never a question among civilized nations, and those that had imbibed any principles of morality, whether, for example, it was lawful to betray one's country for the preservation of life? and it is well known <256> that the opposite maxim was a received principle among the Greeks and Romans. Several heathen moralists have strongly inculcated this doctrine, namely, that the dread of pains and torments ought not to prevail upon any man to make him do things contrary to religion or justice. *If you are summoned as a witness,* says a Latin poet, *in a dubious and equivocal affair, tell the truth, and do not be afraid; tell it, were even Phalaris to menace you with his bull unless you bore false witness. Fix it as a maxim in your mind, that it is the greatest of evils to prefer life to honour; and never attempt to preserve it at the expence of the only thing that can render it desirable.*

> —Ambiguae si quando citabere testis
> Incertaeque rei; Phalaris licet imperet, ut sis
> Falsus, & admoto dictet perjuria tauro,
> Summum crede nefas animam praeferre pudori,
> Et propter vitam vivendi perdere causas.
> JUVEN. sat. 8. ver. 80.

And if a witness in a doubtful cause,
Where a brib'd judge means to elude the laws;
Though Phalaris's brazen bull were there,
And he would dictate what he'd have you swear;
Be not so profligate, but rather chuse
To guard your honour, and your life to lose,
Rather than let your virtue be betray'd,
Virtue! the noblest cause for which you're made.

STEPNEY. <257>

Such is the rule. It may happen nevertheless, as we have already hinted, that the necessity a person is under, may furnish a favourable exception, so as to hinder the action from being imputed. To explain this, we should be obliged to enter into some particulars that belong to another place. It is sufficient here to observe, that the circumstances a person is under, give us frequent room to form a reasonable presumption, that the legislator himself excuses him from suffering the evil with which he is menaced, and therefore allows him to deviate from the decision of the law; and this may be always presumed, when the side a person takes, in order to extricate himself from his perplexity, includes a lesser evil than that with which he is menaced.

IX. But Puffendorf's principles concerning this question seem to be neither just in themselves, nor well connected. He lays down as a rule, that constraint, as well as physical and actual violence, excludes all imputation, and that an action extorted through fear, ought no more to be imputed to the immediate agent, than to the sword which a person uses in giving a wound. To which he adds, that with regard to some very infamous actions, it is a mark of a generous mind to chuse rather to die than to serve as an instrument to such flagitious deeds, and that cases like these ought to be excepted.* But it has been justly observed, that this author gives too <258> great an extent to the effect of constraint; and that the example of the ax or sword, which are mere passive instruments,

Puffendorf's opinion.

* See the Duties of man and a citizen, book i. chap. i. § 24. and the Law of nature and nations, book i. chap. v. § 9. with Barbeyrac's notes.

proves nothing at all. Besides, if the general principle is solid, we don't see why he should have excepted particular cases; or at least he ought to have given us some rule to distinguish those exceptions with certainty.

Of actions in which more persons than one are concerned.

X. 10. But if the person who does a bad action through fear, is generally answerable for it, the author of the constraint is not less so; and we may justly render him accountable for the share he has had therein.

This gives us an opportunity to add a few reflections on those cases in which several persons concur to the same action; and to establish some principles whereby we may determine in what manner the action of one person is imputable to another. This subject being of great use and importance, deserves to be treated with exactness.

1. Every man, strictly speaking, is answerable only for his own actions, that is, for what he himself has done or omitted: for with regard to another person's actions, they cannot be imputed to us, but inasmuch as we have concurred to them, and as we could and ought to have procured, hindered, or at least directed them after a certain manner. The thing speaks for itself. For to impute another man's actions to a person, is declaring that the latter is the efficient, though not the only cause thereof; and consequently that this action depended in some measure on his will, either in its principle, or execution. <259>

2. This being premised, we may affirm that every man is under a general obligation of doing all he can to induce every other person to discharge his duty, and to prevent him from committing a bad action, and consequently not to contribute thereto himself, either directly or indirectly, with a premeditated purpose and will.

3. By a much stronger reason we are answerable for the actions of those over whom we have a particular inspection, and whose direction is committed to our care; wherefore the good or evil done by those persons, is not only imputable to themselves, but likewise to those to whose direction they are subject; according as the latter have taken or neglected the care that was morally necessary, such as the nature and extent of their commission and power required. It is on this footing we impute, for example, to the father of a family, the good or bad conduct of his children.

4. Let us observe likewise, that in order to be reasonably esteemed to have concurred to another man's action, it is not at all necessary for us to be sure of procuring or hindering it, by doing or omitting particular things; it is sufficient, in this respect, that we have some probability, or verisimilitude. And as, on the one side, this default of certainty does not excuse neglect; on the other, if we have done all that we ought, the want of success cannot be imputed to us; the blame in that case falls intirely upon the immediate author of the action.

5. In fine, it is proper also to remark, that in the question now before us, we are not inquiring into the degree of virtue or malice which is found <260> in the action itself, and rendering it better or worse, augments its praise or censure, its recompence or punishment. All that we want, is to make a proper estimate of the degree of influence a person has had over another man's action, in order to know whether he can be considered as the moral cause thereof, and whether this cause is more or less efficacious. To distinguish this properly, is a matter of some importance.

XI. In order to measure, as it were, this degree of influence, which decides the manner wherein we can impute to any one, another man's action, there are several circumstances and distinctions to observe, without which we should form a wrong judgment of things. For example, it is certain that a simple approbation, generally speaking, has much less efficacy to induce a person to act, than a strong persuasion, or a particular instigation. And yet the high opinion we conceive of a person, and the credit from thence arising, may occasion a simple approbation to have sometimes as great, and perhaps a greater influence over a man's action, than the most pressing persuasion, or the strongest instigation from another quarter.

Three sorts of moral causes; principal; subaltern; and collateral.

We may range under three different classes, the moral causes that influence another man's action. Sometimes it is a principal cause, insomuch that the person who executes is only a subaltern agent; sometimes the immediate agent, on the contrary, is the principal cause, while the other is only the subaltern; and at other times they are both collateral causes, which have an equal influence over the action. <261>

XII. A person ought to be esteemed the principal cause, who by doing or omitting some things, influences in such a manner another man's action or omission, that, were it not for him, this action or omission would not have happened, though the immediate agent has knowingly contributed to it. An officer, by express order of his general or prince, performs an action evidently bad: in this case the prince or general is the principal cause, and the officer only the subaltern.[2] David was the principal cause of the death of Urias, though Joab contributed thereto, being sufficiently apprized of the king's intention. In like manner Jezabel was the principal cause of the death of Naboth.*

I mentioned that the immediate agent must have contributed knowingly to the action. For suppose he could not know whether the action be good or bad, he can then be considered only as a simple instrument; but the person who gave the orders, being in that case the only and absolute cause of the action, is the only one answerable for it. Such in general is the case of subjects, who serve by order of their sovereign in an unjust war.

But the reason why a superior is deemed the principal cause of what is done by those that depend on him, is not properly their dependance; it is the order he gives them, without which it is supposed they would not of themselves have attempted the action. From whence it follows, that every other person, who has the same influence over the actions of his equals, or even of his superiors, may for the <262> same reason be considered as the principal cause. This is what we may very well apply to the counsellors of princes, or to ecclesiastics that have an ascendency over their minds, and who make a wrong use of it sometimes, in order

* See 2 Sam. chap. ii. and 1 Kings, chap. xxi.

2. Burlamaqui takes a middle position between Pufendorf and Barbeyrac. The former argued that subjects are not morally responsible for crimes committed in accordance with a command from the sovereign in the state. The subjects, especially as their safety would be threatened were they to disobey, are mere passive instruments of the sovereign's action. Barbeyrac was violently opposed to this view, referring to the experiences of the Huguenot minority in France under Louis XIV and holding that men may have both a right and a duty to disobey unjust orders. See DHC I.1 §24 note 1 and DNG I.5 §9 note 4 and especially the long footnotes 4 and 5 in DNG VIII.1 §6. See Burlamaqui's note at the end of this chapter.

to persuade them to things which they would never have determined to do of themselves. In this case, praise or blame falls principally on the author of the suggestion or counsel.*

XIII. A collateral cause is he who in doing or omitting certain things, concurs sufficiently, and as much as in him lies, to another man's action; insomuch that he is supposed to co-operate with him; though one cannot absolutely presume, that without his concurrence the action would not have been committed. Such are those who furnish succours to the immedi-<263>ate agent; or those who shelter and protect him; for example, he who while another breaks open the door, watches all the avenues of the house, in order to favour the robbery, &c. A conspiracy among several people, renders them generally all guilty alike. They are all supposed equal and collateral causes, as being associated for the same fact, and united in interest and will. And though each of them has not an equal part in the execution, yet their actions may be very well charged to one another's account.

XIV. Finally, a subaltern cause is he who has but a small influence or share in another man's action, and is only a slight occasion thereof by facilitating its execution; insomuch that the agent, already absolutely determined to act, and having all the necessary means for so doing, is only encouraged to execute his resolution; as when a person tells him the man-

---

* We shall transcribe here, with pleasure, the judicious reflections of M. Bernard (Nouvelles de la republique des lettres, August 1702. p. 291.). *In England it is very common to charge the faults of the prince to the ministers; and I own, that very often the charge is just. But the crimes of the ministers do not always excuse the faults of the sovereign; for after all, they have reason and understanding as well as other people, and are masters to do as they please. If they let themselves be too much governed by those that have the freest access to them, it is their fault. They ought on several occasions to see with their own eyes, and not to be led by the nose by a wicked and avaricious courtier. But if they are incapable to manage matters themselves, and to distinguish good from evil, they ought to resign the care of government to others that are capable: For I do not know, why we may not apply to princes who govern ill, the saying of Charles Borromeus, in respect to bishops who do not feed properly their flocks:* IF THEY ARE INCAPABLE OF SUCH AN EMPLOYMENT, WHY SO MUCH AMBITION? IF THEY ARE CAPABLE, WHY SO MUCH NEGLECT?

ner of going about it, the favourable moment, the means of escaping, &c. or when he commends his design, and animates him to pursue it.

May not we rank in the same class the action of a judge, who, instead of opposing an opinion supported by a generality of votes, but by himself adjudged erroneous, should acquiesce therein, either through fear or complaisance? Bad example must be also ranked among the subaltern causes. For generally speaking, examples of this nature make impression only on those who are otherwise inclined to evil, or subject to be easily led astray; insomuch that those who set such examples, contribute but very weakly to the evil committed by imitation. And yet there are some examples so very efficacious, <264> by reason of the character of the persons that set them, and the disposition of those who follow them, that if the former had refrained from evil, the latter would never have thought of committing it. Such are the bad examples of superiors, or of men who by their knowledge and reputation have a great ascendency over others; these are particularly culpable of all the evil which ensues from the imitation of their actions. We may reason in the same manner with respect to several other cases. According as circumstances vary, the same things have more or less influence on other men's actions, and consequently those who by so doing concur to these actions, ought to be considered sometimes as principal, sometimes as collateral, and sometimes as subaltern causes.

Application of these distinctions. XV. The application of these distinctions and principles is obvious. Supposing every thing else equal, collateral causes ought to be judged alike. But principal causes merit without doubt more praise or blame, and a higher degree of recompence or punishment than subaltern causes. I said, *supposing every thing else equal;* for it may happen through a diversity of circumstances, which augment or diminish the merit or demerit of an action, that the subaltern cause acts with a greater degree of malice than the principal one, and the imputation is thereby aggravated in respect to the subaltern. Let us suppose, for example, that a person in cool blood assassinates a man, at the instigation of one who was animated thereto by some atrocious injury he had received from his enemy. Though the instigator is the principal au-<265>thor of the murder, yet his action, done in a transport of choler, will be esteemed less heinous than that of the murderer, who, calm and serene himself, was the base instrument of the other's passion.

We shall close this chapter with a few remarks: And 1. though the distinction of three classes of moral causes, in respect to another man's action, be in itself very well founded, we must own, nevertheless, that the application thereof to particular cases is sometimes difficult. 2. In dubious cases, we should not easily charge, as a principal cause, any other person but the immediate author of the action; we ought to consider those who have concurred thereto, rather as subaltern, or at the most as collateral causes. 3. In fine, it is proper to observe, that Puffendorf, whose principles we have followed, settles very justly the distinction of moral causes; but not having exactly defined these different causes, in the particular examples he alledges, he refers sometimes to one class what properly belonged to another. This has not escaped Mons. Barbeyrac, whose judicious remarks have been here of particular use to us.* <266>

CHAPTER XII

Of the authority and sanction of natural laws† and 1. of the good or evil that naturally and generally follows from virtue or vice.

I. We understand here, by the authority of natural laws, the force they receive from the approbation of reason, and especially from their being acknowledged to have God for their author: This is what lays us under a strict obligation of conforming our conduct to them, because of the

What is meant
by the author-
ity of natural
law.

---

* See Barbeyrac's notes on the Duties of man and a citizen, book i. chap. i. § 27.

† See Puffendorf, Law of nature and nations, book ii. chap. iii. § 21. [For Burlamaqui, the authority of the natural laws and their sanction are more intimately related than for Barbeyrac or Pufendorf. Pufendorf discusses the authority of the natural laws in DNG II.3 §20 (§21, the paragraph to which Burlamaqui refers, deals only with the sanction of natural law), and his main point is that the precepts of reason cannot bind man morally without the intervention of the idea of a commanding God, a view that Burlamaqui tried to refute in chapter 7 above.]

sovereign right which God has over his creatures. What has been already explained, concerning the origin and nature, reality and certainty of those laws, is sufficient, methinks, to establish also their authority. Yet we have still some small matter to say in relation to this subject. The force of laws, properly so called, depends principally on their sanction.* This is what gives a stamp, as it were, to their authority. It is therefore a very necessary and important point, to inquire whether there be really any such thing as a sanction of natural laws, that is, whether they are accompanied with comminations and promises, punishments and rewards. <267>

The observance of natural laws forms the happiness of man and society.

II. The first reflection that presents itself to our minds, is, that the rules of conduct, distinguished by the name of natural laws, are proportioned in such a manner to our nature, to the original dispositions and natural desires of our soul, to our constitution, to our wants and actual situation in life, that it evidently appears they are made for us. For in general, and every thing well considered, the observance of those laws is the only means of procuring a real and solid happiness to individuals, as well as to the public; whereas the infraction thereof precipitates men into disorders prejudicial alike to individuals, as to the whole species. This is, as it were, the first sanction of natural laws.

Eclaircissements on the state of the question.

III. In order to prove our point, and to establish rightly the state of the question, we must observe, 1. that when the observance of natural laws is said to be capable alone of forming the happiness of man and society, we do not mean that this happiness can be ever perfect, or superior to all expectation; humanity having no pretence to any thing of this kind; and if virtue itself cannot produce this effect, it is not at all probable that vice has any advantage over her in this respect.

2. As we are inquiring which is the proper rule that man ought to go by, our question is properly reduced to this point, whether in general, and every thing considered, the observance of natural laws is not the

* See part i. chap. x. § 11.

properest and surest means to conduct man to his end, and to procure him the purest, the completest, and the most durable happiness that can possibly be enjoyed in this world; and not only with <268> regard to some persons, but to all mankind; not only in particular cases, but likewise through the whole course of life.

On this footing, it will not be a difficult task to prove, as well by reason as by experience, that the proper and ordinary effect of virtue is really such as has been mentioned, and that vice, or the irregularity of passions, produces a quite opposite effect.

IV. We have already shewn, in discoursing of the nature and state of humanity, that in what manner and light soever we consider the system of humanity, man can neither answer his end, nor perfect his talents and faculties, nor acquire any solid happiness, or reconcile it with that of his fellow-creatures, but by the help of reason; that it ought to be therefore his first care to improve his reason, to consult it, and follow the counsels thereof; that it informs him, there are some things which are fit and others unfit for him; that the former have not all an equal fitness, nor in the same manner: that he ought therefore to make a proper distinction between good and evil, in order to regulate his conduct: that true happiness cannot consist in things incompatible with his nature and state: and, in fine, that since the future ought to be equally the object of his views as the present and past, it is not sufficient, in order to attain certain happiness, to consider merely the present good or evil of each action; but we should likewise recollect what is past, and extend our views to futurity, in order to combine the whole, and see what ought to be the result thereof in the intire duration of our being. These are so many <269> evident and demonstrable truths. Now the laws of nature are no more than consequences of these primitive truths; whence it appears that they have necessarily, and of themselves, a great influence on our happiness. And how is it possible to call this in question, after having seen in the course of this work, that the sole method to discover the principles of those laws, is to set out with the study of the nature and state of man, and to inquire afterwards into what is essentially agreeable to his perfection and happiness.

Proof of the above-mentioned truth, by reason.

Proofs by
experience.
1. Virtue is of
itself the prin-
ciple of an
inward satis-
faction; and
vice a principle
of disquiet and
trouble.

V. But that which appears so clear and so well established by reason, is rendered incontestible by experience. In fact, we generally observe, that virtue, that is, the observance of the laws of nature, is of itself a source of internal satisfaction, and that it is infinitely advantageous in its effects, whether in particular to individuals, or to human society in general, whereas vice is attended with quite different consequences.

Whatever is contrary to the light of reason and conscience, cannot but be accompanied with a secret disapprobation of mind, and afford us vexation and shame. The heart is afflicted with the idea of the crime, and the remembrance thereof is always bitter and sorrowful. On the contrary, every conformity to right reason is a state of order and perfection, which the mind approves; and we are framed in such a manner, that a good action becomes the seed, as it were, of a secret joy; and we always recollect it with pleasure. And indeed, what can be sweeter or more comfortable, than to be able to bear an inward <270> testimony to ourselves, that we are what we ought to be, and that we perform what is reasonably our duty, what fits us best, and is most conformable to our natural destination? Whatever is natural, is agreeable; and whatever is according to order, is a subject of satisfaction and content.

Of external
goods and
evils, which are
the conse-
quence of
virtue and vice.

VI. Besides this internal principle of joy, which attends the practice of natural laws, we find it produces externally all sorts of good effects. It tends to preserve our health, and to prolong our days; it exercises and perfects the faculties of the mind; it renders us fit for labour, and for all the functions of domestic and civil life; it secures to us the right use and possession of all our goods and property; it prevents a great number of evils, and softens those it cannot prevent; it procures us the confidence, esteem, and affection of other men; from whence result the greatest comforts of social life, and the most effectual helps for the success of our undertakings.

Observe on what the public security, the tranquillity of families, the prosperity of states, and the absolute welfare of every individual are founded. Is it not on the grand principles of religion, temperance, modesty, beneficence, justice, and sincerity? Whence arise, on the contrary, the greatest part of the disorders and evils that trouble society, and break in upon the happiness of man? Whence, but from the neglect of those very principles? Besides the inquietude and infamy that generally accompanies irregularity and debauch, vice is likewise attended with a multitude of external evils, such as the infeebling of <271> the body and mind, distempers and untoward accidents, poverty very often and misery, violent and dangerous parties, domestic jars, enmities, continual fears, dishonour, punishments, contempt, hatred, and a thousand crosses and difficulties in every thing we undertake. One of the ancients has very elegantly said,* *that malice drinks one half of her own poison.*

VII. But if such are the natural consequences of virtue and vice in respect to the generality of mankind, these effects are still greater among those who by their condition and rank have a particular influence on the state of society, and determine the fate of other men. What calamities might not the subjects apprehend, if their sovereigns were to imagine themselves superior to rule, and independent of all law; if directing every thing to themselves, they were to listen only to their own whims and caprice, and to abandon themselves to injustice, ambition, avarice, and cruelty? What good, on the contrary, must not arise from the government of a wise and virtuous prince; who considering himself under a particular obligation of never deviating from the rules of piety, justice, moderation, and beneficence, exercises his power with no other view, but to maintain order within, and security without, and places his glory in ruling his subjects uprightly, that is, in making them wise and happy?[1] We need only have recourse to history, and consult experience, to be <272> convinced that these are real truths, which no reasonable person can contest.

These different effects of virtue and vice are still greater among those who are invested with power and authority.

---

* Seneca, ep. 82. *Quemadmodum Attalus noster dicere solebat, malitia ipsa maximam partem veneni sui bibit.*

1. Burlamaqui's conception of the aims of good governance differs noticeably from that of Barbeyrac and Pufendorf. Barbeyrac quite explicitly denied that the civil laws exist in order to render the subjects virtuous. The laws exist to guarantee a tranquil public order. Barbeyrac, "Discourse on What Is Permitted by the Laws," in Samuel Pufendorf, *The Whole Duty of Man, According to the Law of Nature,* ed. Ian Hunter and David Saunders (Indianapolis: Liberty Fund, 2003), p. 317.

Confirmation
of this truth
by the confes-
sion of all
nations.

VIII. This is a truth so generally acknowledged, that all the institutions which men form among themselves for their common good and advantage, are founded on the observance of the laws of nature; and that even the precautions taken to secure the effect of these institutions, would be vain and useless, were it not for the authority of those very laws. This is what is manifestly supposed by all human laws in general; by the establishments for the education of youth; by the political regulations which tend to promote the arts and commerce; and by public as well as private treaties. For of what use would all those things be, or what benefit could accrue from thence, were we not previously to establish them on justice, probity, sincerity, and the sacred inviolability of an oath, as on their real foundation and basis?

Confirmation
of the same
truth by the
absurdity of
the contrary.

IX. But in order to be more sensibly satisfied of this truth, let any one try, that pleases, to form a system of morality on principles directly opposite to those we have now established. Let us suppose that ignorance and prejudice take place of knowledge and reason; that caprice and passion are substituted instead of prudence and virtue: let us banish justice and benevolence from society, and from the commerce of mankind, to make room for unjust self-love, which calculating every thing for itself, takes no notice of other people's interest, or of the public advantage. Let us extend and apply these principles to the particular conditions of human life, and <273> we shall see what must be the result of a system of this kind, were it ever to be received and pass for a rule. Can we imagine it would be able to produce the happiness of society, the good of families, the advantage of nations, and the welfare of mankind? No one has ever yet attempted to maintain such a paradox; so evident and glaring is the absurdity thereof.

Answer to
some par-
ticular
objections.

X. I am not ignorant, that injustice and passion are capable in particular cases of procuring some pleasure or advantage. But not to mention that virtue produces much oftener and with greater certainty the same effects; reason and experience inform us, that the good procured by injustice is not so real, so durable, nor so pure, as that which is the fruit of virtue. This is because the former being unconformable to the state of a rational and social being, is defective in its principle, and has only a deceitful appearance.* It is a flower which having no root, withers and falls almost as soon as it blossoms.

With regard to such evils and misfortunes as are annexed to humanity, and to which it may be said, that virtuous people are exposed as well as others; certain it is, that virtue has here also a great many advantages. In the first place, it is very proper of itself to prevent or remove several of those evils; and thus we observe that wise and sober people actually escape a great many precipices and snares into which the vicious and inconsiderate are hurried. 2. In cases wherein wisdom and prudence cannot prevent those evils, yet it gives the soul a sufficient vigour to <274> support them, and counterbalances them with sweets and consolations which contribute to abate in great measure their impression. Virtue is attended with an inseparable contentment, of which nothing can bereave us; and our essential happiness is very little impaired by the transitory, and, in some measure, external accidents that sometimes disturb us.

Surprised I am, (says Isocrates),† *that any one should imagine, that those who adhere constantly to piety and justice, must expect to be more unhappy*

---

* See part i. chap. vi. § 3.

† Θαυμάζω δ' εἴ τις οἴεται τοὺς τὴν εὐσέβειαν καὶ τὴν δικαιοσύνην ἀσκοῦντας, καὶ καρτερεῖν καὶ μένειν ἐν τούτοις ἐθέλοντας, ἔλαττον ἕξειν τῶν πονηρῶν. ἀλλ' οὐχ ἡγουμένους καὶ παρὰ θεοῖς καὶ παρὰ ἀνθρώποις πλέον οἴσεσθαι, τῶν ἄλλων. ἐγὼ μὲν γὰρ οἴομαι τούτους μόνους, ὧν δεῖ πλεονεκτεῖν, τοὺς δ' ἄλλους οὐδὲ γινώσκειν οὐδὲν ὧν βελτίον ἐστίν. ὁρῶ γὰρ τοὺς μὲν τὴν ἀδικίαν προτιμῶντας, καὶ τὸ λαβεῖν τι τῶν ἀλλοτρίων μέγιστον ἀγαθὸν νομίζοντας, ὅμοια πάσχοντας τοῖς δελεαζομένοις τῶν ζώων, καὶ καταρχὰς μὲν ἀπολαύοντας ὧν ἂν λάβωσιν, ὀλίγῳ δ' ὕστερον ἐν τοῖς μεγίστοις κακοῖς ὄντας. τοὺς δὲ μετ' εὐσεβείας καὶ δικαιοσύνης ζῶντας, ἔν τε τοῖς παροῦσι χρόνοις ἀσφαλῶς διάγοντας, καὶ περὶ τοῦ σύμπαντος αἰῶνος ἡδίους τὰς ἐλπίδας ἔχοντας. καὶ ταῦτ' εἰ μὴ κατὰ πάντων οὕτως εἴθισται συμβαίνειν, ἀλλὰ τό γ' ὡς ἐπὶ τὸ πολὺ τοῦτον γίγνεται τὸν τρόπον. χρὴ δὲ τοὺς εὖ φρονοῦντας, ἐπειδὴ τὸ μέλλον ἀεὶ συνοίσειν οὐ καθορῶμεν, τὸ πολλάκις ὠφέλουν τοῦτο φαίνεσθαι προαιρουμένους. πάντων δ' ἀλογώτατον πεπόνθασιν, ὅσοι κάλλιον μὲν ἐπιτήδευμα νομίζουσιν εἶναι, καὶ θεοφιλέστερον τὴν δικαιοσύνην τῆς ἀδικίας, χεῖρον δ' οἴονται βιώσεσθαι τοὺς ταύτῃ χρωμένους, τῶν τὴν πονηρίαν προῃρημένων. Isocrat. Orat. de Permutatione §§ 33–35. [The text is today known as "On peace"; for a modern edition, see *Isocrates,* vol. 2, trans. George Norlin. Loeb Classical Series. (Cambridge: Harvard University Press, 1962), pp. 28–31.]

than the unrighteous, and have not a right to promise themselves greater advantages from the gods and men. For my part, I am of opinion, that the virtuous alone abundantly enjoy whatever is worthy of our pursuit; and the wicked, on the contrary, are entirely ignorant of their real interests. He that prefers injustice to justice, and makes his sovereign good consist in depriving another <275> man of his property, is like, methinks, to those brute creatures that are caught by the bait: the unjust acquisition flatters his senses at first, but he soon finds himself involved in very great evils. Those on the contrary who take up with justice and piety, are not only safe for the present, but have likewise reason to conceive good hopes for the remainder of their lives. I own, indeed, that this does not always happen; yet it is generally confirmed by experience. Now in things whose success cannot be infallibly foreseen, it is the business of a prudent man to embrace that side which most generally turns out to his advantage. But nothing is more unreasonable than the opinion of those, who believing that justice has something in it more beautiful and more agreeable to the gods than injustice, imagine nevertheless that those who embrace the former are more unhappy than such as abandon themselves to the latter.

The advantage always ranges itself on the side of virtue; and this is the first sanction of the laws of nature.

XI. Thus every thing duly considered, the advantage is without comparison on the side of virtue. It manifestly appears, that the scheme of the divine wisdom was to establish a natural connexion between physical and moral evil, as between the effect and the cause; and, on the contrary, to intail physical good, or the happiness of man, on moral good, or the practice of virtue: insomuch, that generally speaking, and pursuant to the original institution of things, the observance of natural laws is as proper and necessary to advance both the public and particular happiness, as temperance and good regimen is naturally conducive to the preservation of health. And as these natural rewards and punishments of virtue and vice, are an effect of the divine institution; <276> they may be really considered, as a kind of sanction of the laws of nature, which adds a considerable authority to the maxims of right reason.

XII. And yet we must acknowledge, that this first sanction does not as yet seem sufficient to give all the authority and weight of real laws, to the counsels of reason. For if we consider the thing strictly, we shall find, that by the constitution of human things, and by our natural dependance upon one another, the general rule above mentioned is not so fixt and invariable, but it admits of divers exceptions, by which the force and effect thereof must certainly be weakened.

General difficulty drawn from the exceptions, which render this first sanction insufficient.

1. Experience, in general, shews us, that the degree of happiness or misery which every one enjoys in this world, is not always exactly proportioned and measured to the degree of virtue or vice of each particular person. Thus health, the goods of fortune, education, situation of life, and other external advantages, generally depend on a variety of conjunctures, which render their distribution very unequal; and these advantages are frequently lost by accidents, to which all men are equally subject. True it is, that the difference of rank or riches does not absolutely determine the happiness or misery of life: yet agree we must, that extreme poverty, the privation of all necessary means of instruction, excessive labour, afflictions of the mind, and pains of the body, are real evils, which a variety of casualties may bring as well upon virtuous as other men.

The goods and evils of nature and fortune, are distributed unequally, and not according to each person's merit.

2. Besides this unequal distribution of natural goods and evils, honest men are no more sheltered than <277> others from divers evils arising from malice, injustice, violence, and ambition. Such are the persecutions of tyrants, the horrors of war, and so many other public or private calamities to which the good and the bad are indiscriminately subject. It even frequently happens, that the authors of all those miseries are those who feel least their effects, either because of their extraordinary success and good fortune, or because their insensibility is arrived to that pitch, as to let them enjoy, almost without trouble and remorse, the fruit of their iniquities.

The evils produced by injustice fall as well upon the innocent as the guilty.

3. Again. It is not unusual to see innocence exposed to calumny, and virtue itself become the object of persecution. Now in those particular cases, in which the honest man falls, as it were, a victim to his own virtue, what force can the laws of nature be said to have, and how can their authority be supported? Is the internal satisfaction arising from the tes-

Sometimes even virtue itself is the cause of persecution.

timony of a good conscience, capable alone to determine man to sacrifice his property, his repose, his honour, and even his life? And yet those delicate conjunctures frequently happen; and the resolution then taken, may have very important and extensive consequences in relation to the happiness and misery of society.

The means which human prudence employs to remedy those disorders, are likewise insufficient.

XIII. Such is indeed the actual state of things. On the one side we see, that in general the observance of natural laws is alone capable of establishing some order in society, and of constituting the happiness of man; but on the other it appears, that virtue and vice are not always sufficiently characterised by their effects, and by their common and natural conse-<278>quences, to make this order on all occasions prevail.

Hence arises a considerable difficulty against the moral system by us established. All laws, some will say, ought to have a sufficient sanction to determine a reasonable creature to obey, by the prospect of its own good and interest, which is always the primum mobile of its actions. Now though the moral system you have spoke of, gives in general a great advantage to its followers, over those who neglect it; yet this advantage is neither so great, nor so sure, as to be capable to indemnify us sufficiently in each particular case for the sacrifices we are obliged to make in the discharge of our duty. This system is not therefore as yet supported with all the authority and force necessary for the end that God proposes; and the character of law, especially of a law proceeding from an all-wise being, requires still a more distinct, surer, and more extensive sanction.

That legislators and politicians have been sensible of this deficiency, is manifest, by their endeavouring to supply it in the best manner they are able. They have published a civil law, which tends to strengthen the law of nature; they have denounced punishments against vice, promised rewards to virtue, and erected tribunals. This is undoubtedly a new support of justice, and the best human method that could be contrived to prevent the forementioned inconveniences. And yet this method does not provide against every disorder, but leaves still a great vacuum in the moral system.

For 1. there are several evils, as well natural as arising from human injustice, from which all the <279> power of man cannot preserve even the most virtuous. 2. Human laws are not always drawn up in conformity to justice and equity. 3. Let them be supposed never so just, they cannot extend to every case. 4. The execution of those laws is sometimes committed to weak, ignorant, or corrupt men. 5. How great soever the integrity of a magistrate may be, still there are many things that escape his vigilance: he cannot see and redress every grievance. 6. It is not an unexampled case, that virtue instead of finding a protector in its judge, meets with an implacable enemy. What resource shall be left to innocence in that case? To whom shall she fly for succour, if the very person that ought to undertake her protection and defence, is armed against her?

XIV. Thus the difficulty still subsists; a difficulty of very great consequence, because on the one side it makes against the plan of a divine providence, and on the other it may contribute to invalidate what we have said in respect to the empire of virtue, and its necessary connexion with the felicity of man.

The difficulty proposed, is of great consequence.

So weighty an objection that has been started in all ages, deserves we should carefully endeavour to remove it. But the greater and more real it is, the more probably we may presume it has a proper solution. For how is it to be imagined, that the Divine Wisdom could have left such an imperfection, such an enigma in the moral order, after having regulated every thing so well in the physical world?

Let us therefore see whether some new reflections on the nature and destination of man, will not direct us to a different place from the present life, for <280> the solution we are here inquiring. What has been said concerning the natural consequences of virtue and vice on this earth, already shews us a demi-sanction of the laws of nature: let us try whether we cannot find an intire and proper one, whose species, degree, time, and manner, depend on the good will of the legislator, and are sufficient to make all the compensations required by strict justice, and to place in this, as in every other respect, the system of the divine laws much above those of human institution.

CHAPTER XIII

Proofs of the immortality of the soul. That there is a
sanction, properly so called, in respect to natural law.[1]

State of the
question.

I. The difficulty we have been speaking of, and which we attempt here to illustrate, supposes, as every one may see, that the human system is absolutely limited to the present life, that there is no such thing as a future state, and consequently that there is nothing to expect from the Divine Wisdom in favour of the laws of nature, beyond what is manifested in this life.

Were it possible, on the contrary, to prove that the present state of man is only the commencement of a more extensive system; and moreover, that the supreme Being has really been pleased to invest the rules of conduct prescribed to us by reason, with all the authority of laws, by strengthening them <281> with a sanction properly so called; we might in fine conclude, that there is nothing wanting to complete the moral system.

Division of
opinions. How
it is possible to
know the will
of God in
respect to this
point.

II. The learned are divided in their opinions with respect to these important questions. Some there are who maintain, that reason alone affords clear and demonstrative proofs, not only of the rewards and punishments of a future life; but likewise of a state of immortality. Others on the contrary pretend, that by consulting reason alone, we meet with nothing but obscurity and uncertainty, and that so far from finding any demonstration this way, we have not even a probability of a future life.

It is carrying the thing too far, perhaps, on both sides, to reason after this manner. Since the question is concerning a point which depends

---

1. While the foregoing chapter elaborated on Pufendorf's views in DNG II.3 §21, the present chapter agrees with Barbeyrac in insisting that reason alone can establish reasonable grounds for taking sanctions in the afterlife into account; see Barbeyrac in DNG II.3 §21 note 6; DHC préface de l'auteur §4 note 1; "The Judgment of an Anonymous Writer," §6, in Samuel Pufendorf, *The Whole Duty of Man, According to the Law of Nature,* ed. Ian Hunter and David Saunders (Indianapolis: Liberty Fund, 2003), pp. 267–305. Burlamaqui's discussion of immortality is much more elaborate than Barbeyrac's.

intirely on the will of the Deity, the best way undoubtedly to know this will, would be an express declaration on his side. But confining ourselves within the circle of natural knowledge, let us try whether independently of this first method, reason alone can afford us any sure light in relation to this subject, or furnish us with conjectures and presumptions sufficiently strong, to infer from thence with any certainty the will of God. With this view, let us investigate a little closer the nature and present state of man, let us consult the ideas which right reason gives us of the perfection of the supreme Being, and of the plan he has formed with respect to mankind; in order to know, in fine, the necessary consequences of the natural laws he has been pleased to prescribe. <282>

III. With regard to the nature of man, we are first of all to inquire whether death be really the last term of our existence, and the dissolution of the body be necessarily followed with the annihilation of the soul; or whether the soul is immortal, that is, whether it subsists after the death of the body?

Whether the soul is immortal?

Now the immortality of the soul is so far from being in itself impossible, that reason supplies us with the strongest conjectures, that this is in reality the state for which it was designed.

First proof. The nature of the soul seems intirely distinct from that of the body.

The observations of the ablest philosophers distinguish absolutely the soul from the body, as a being in its nature essentially different. 1. In fact, we do not find that the faculties of the mind, the understanding, the will, liberty, with all the operations they produce, have any relation to those of extension, figure and motion, which are the properties of matter. 2. The idea we have of an extended substance, as purely passive, seems to be absolutely incompatible with that proper and internal activity which distinguishes a thinking being. The body is not put into motion of itself, but the mind finds inwardly the principle of its own movements; it acts, it thinks, it wills, it moves the body; it turns its operations, as it pleases; it stops, proceeds, or returns the way it went. 3. We observe likewise, that our thinking part[2] is a simple, single, and indivis-

2. The original uses the more amorphous expression "that which thinks in us" ("ce qui pense en nous").

ible being; because it collects all our ideas and sensations, as it were, into one point, by understanding, feeling, and comparing them, &c. which cannot be done by a being composed of various parts. <283>

Death does not therefore necessarily imply the annihilation of the soul. IV. The soul seems therefore to be of a particular nature, to have nothing in common with gross and material beings, but to be a pure spirit, that participates in some measure of the nature of the supreme Being. This has been very elegantly expressed by Cicero: *We cannot find, says he,* *on earth the least trace of the origin of the soul. For there is nothing mixt or compound in the mind; nothing that seems to proceed from the earth, water, air, or fire. These elements have nothing productive of memory, understanding, reflection; nothing that is able to recall the past, to foresee the future, and to embrace the present. We shall never find the source from whence man has derived those divine qualities, but by tracing them up to God. It follows therefore, that the soul is endowed with a singular nature, which has nothing in it common with those known and familiar elements. Hence, let the nature of a being that has sensation, understanding, will, and principle of life, be what it will, this being is surely heavenly, divine, and consequently immortal.* <284>

This conclusion is very just. For if the soul be essentially distinct from the body, the destruction of the one is not necessarily followed with the annihilation of the other; and thus far nothing hinders the soul from subsisting, notwithstanding the destruction of its ruinous habitation.[3]

---

* *Animorum nulla in terris origo inveniri potest: nihil enim in animis mixtum atque concretum, aut quod ex terrâ natum atque fictum esse videatur: nihil ne aut humidum quidem aut flabile aut igneum. His enim in naturis nihil inest, quod vim memoriae, mentis, cogitationis habeat; quod et praeterita teneat, & futura provideat, & complecti possit praesentia: quae sola divina sunt; nec invenietur unquam, unde ad hominem venire possint nisi a Deo. Singularis est igitur quaedam natura atque vis animi, sejuncta ab his usitatis notisque naturis. Ita quicquid est illud, quod sentit, quod sapit, quod vivit, quod viget, caeleste et divinum ob eamque rem aeternum sit necesse est.* Cic. Tuscul. disput. lib. 1. cap. 27.

3. The original talks of the destruction not of our "ruinous" but of our "fragile" habitation ("la ruine du bâtiment fragile où il habitait").

V. Should it be said, that we are not sufficiently acquainted with the *Objection.* intrinsic nature of substances, to determine that God could not com- *Answer.* municate thought to some portion of matter; I should answer, that we cannot however judge of things but according to their appearance and our ideas; otherwise, whatever is not founded on a strict demonstration, must be uncertain, and this would terminate in a kind of pyrrhonism. All that reason requires is, that we distinguish properly between what is dubious, probable, or certain; and since all we know in relation to matter, does not seem to have any affinity with the faculties of the soul; and as we even find in one and the other, qualities that seem incompatible; it is not prescribing limits to the Divine Power, but rather following the notions that reason has furnished us, to affirm it is highly probable, that the thinking part of man is essentially distinct from the body.

VI. But let the nature of the soul be what it will, and be it even, though *Confirmation* contrary to all appearance, supposed corporeal; still it would no ways *of the pre-* follow, that the death of the body must necessarily bring on the anni- *ceding truth.* hilation of the soul. For we do not find an instance of any annihilation *Nothing in* properly so called. The body itself, <285> how inferior soever to the *nature is* mind, is not annihilated by death. It receives, indeed, a great alteration; *annihilated.* but its substance remains always essentially the same, and admits only a change of modification or form. Why therefore should the soul be an- nihilated? It will undergo, if you please, a great mutation; it will be de- tached from the bonds that unite it to the body, and will be incapable of operating in conjunction with it: But is this an argument that it can- not exist separately, or that it loses its essential quality, which is that of understanding? This does not at all appear; for one does not follow from the other.

Were it therefore impossible for us to determine the intrinsic nature of the soul, yet it would be carrying the thing too far, and concluding beyond what we are authorised by fact to maintain, that death is nec- essarily attended with a total destruction of the soul. The question is therefore reducible to this point: Is God willing to annihilate, or to pre- serve the soul? But if what we know in respect to the nature of the soul, does not incline us to think it is destined to perish by death; we shall see likewise, that the consideration of its excellency is a very strong presumption in favour of its immortality.

Second proof. The excellency of the soul. VII. And indeed it is not at all probable, that an intelligent being, capable of knowing such a multitude of truths, of making so many discoveries, of reasoning upon an infinite number of things, of discerning their proportions, fitness, and beauties; of contemplating the works of the Creator, of tracing them up to him, of observing his designs, and penetrating into their causes; of raising himself a-<286>bove all sensible things to the knowledge of spiritual and divine subjects; that has a power to act with liberty and discernment, and to array himself with the most beautiful virtues; it is not, I say, at all probable, that a being adorned with qualities of so excellent a nature, and so superior to those of brute animals, should have been created only for the short space of this life. These considerations made a lively impression upon the ancient philosophers. *When I consider,* says Cicero,* *the surprizing activity of the mind, so great a memory of what's past, and such an insight into futurity; when I behold such a number of arts and sciences, and such a multitude of discoveries from thence arising; I believe, and am firmly persuaded, that a nature which contains so many things within itself, cannot be mortal.*

Confirmation. Our faculties are always susceptible of a greater degree of perfection. VIII. Again: Such is the nature of the human mind, that it is always capable of improvement, and of perfecting its faculties. Though our knowledge is actually confined within certain limits, yet we see no bounds to that which we are capable of acquiring, to the inventions we are able to make, to the progress of our judgment, prudence, and virtue. Man is in this respect always susceptible of some new degree of perfection and maturity. Death overtakes him before he has finished, as it were, his progress, and when he was capable of proceeding a great deal farther. *How can it enter,* says a celebrated English <287> writer,† *into the thoughts*

---

* *Quid multa? Sic mihi persuasi, sic sentio, cum tanta celeritas animorum sit, tanta memoria praeteritorum futurorumque prudentia, tot artes, tantae scientiae, tot inventa, non posse eam naturam, quae res eas contineat, esse mortalem.* Cic. de Senec. cap. 2.
† Spectator, Vol. II. N° 117.

of man, that the soul, which is capable of such immense perfections, and of receiving new improvements to all eternity, shall fall away into nothing almost as soon as it is created? Are such abilities made for no purpose? A brute arrives at a point of perfection that he can never pass: In a few years he has all the endowments he is capable of; and were he to live ten thousand more, would be the same thing he is at present. Were a human soul thus at a stand in her accomplishments, were her faculties to be full blown, and incapable of further enlargements, I could imagine it might fall away insensibly, and drop at once into a state of annihilation. But can we believe a thinking being, that is in a perpetual progress of improvements, and travelling on from perfection to perfection, after having just looked abroad into the works of its Creator, and made a few discoveries of his infinite goodness, wisdom, and power, must perish at her first setting out, and in the very beginning of her enquiries?

IX. True it is, that most men debase themselves in some measure to an animal life, and have very little concern about the improvement of their faculties. But if those people voluntarily degrade themselves, this ought to be no prejudice to such as chuse to support the dignity of their nature; neither does it invalidate what we have been saying in regard to the excellency of the soul. For to judge rightly of things, they ought to be considered in themselves, and in their most perfect state. <288>

Objection. Answer.

X. It is undoubtedly in consequence of the natural sense of the dignity of our being, and of the grandeur of the end we are designed for, that we naturally extend our views to futurity; that we concern ourselves about what is to happen after our death; that we seek to perpetuate our name and memory, and are not insensible to the judgment of posterity. These sentiments are far from being the illusion of self-love or prejudice. The desire and hope of immortality is an impression we receive from nature. And this desire is so very reasonable in itself, so useful, and so closely connected with the system of humanity, that we may at least infer from thence a very probable induction in favour of a future state. How great soever the vivacity of this desire may be in itself, still it increases in proportion as we take more care to cultivate our reason, and as we

Third proof, drawn from our natural dispositions and desires.

advance in the knowledge of truth and the practice of virtue. This sentiment becomes the surest principle of noble, generous, and public-spirited actions; and we may affirm, that were it not for this principle, all human views would be low, mean, and sordid.

All this seems to point out to us clearly, that by the institution of the Creator, there is a kind of natural proportion and relation between the soul and immortality. For it is not by deceit and illusion that the Supreme Wisdom conducts us to his proposed end: a principle so reasonable and necessary; a principle that cannot but be productive of good effects, that raises man above himself, and renders him not only capable of the sublimest undertakings, but superior to the most delicate temptations, and such as are most dan-<289>gerous to virtue; such a principle, I say, cannot be chimerical.*

Thus every thing concurs to persuade us that the soul must subsist after death. The knowledge we have of the nature of the mind; its excellence and faculties ever susceptible of a higher degree of perfection; the disposition which prompts us to raise ourselves above the present life, and to desire immortality; are all so many natural indications, and form the strongest presumption, that such indeed is the intention of the Creator.

The sanction of natural laws will shew itself in a future life.   XI. The clearing up of this first point is of great importance in regard to our principal question, and solves already, in part, the difficulty we are examining. For when once the soul is supposed to subsist after the dissolution of the body, nothing can hinder us from saying, that whatever is wanting in the present state to complete the sanction of

---

* Cicero gives an admirable picture of the influence which the desire and hope of immortality has had in all ages, to excite men to great and noble actions. *"Nemo unquam,"* says he, *"sine magna spe immortalitatis se pro patria offerret ad mortem. Licuit esse otioso Themistocli; licuit Epaminondae; licuit, ne et vetera et externa quaeram, mihi: sed nescio quo modo inhaeret in mentibus quasi saeculorum quoddam augurium futurorum; idque in maximis ingeniis altissimisque animis existit maxime, et apparet facillimè. Quoquidem dempto, quis tam esset amens, qui semper in laboribus et periculis viveret?"* Tuscul. Quaest. lib. 1. cap. 15.

natural law, will be executed hereafter, if so it be agreeable to the Divine Wisdom.

We come now from considering man on the physical side, which opens us already a passage towards <290> finding the object of our present pursuit. Let us see now whether by viewing man on the moral side, that is, as a being capable of rule, who acts with knowledge and choice, and whether raising ourselves afterwards to God, we cannot discover new reasons and still stronger presumptions of a future life, of a state of rewards and punishments.

Here we cannot avoid repeating part of those things which have been already mentioned in this work, because we are upon the point of considering their intire result; the truth we intend here to establish being, as it were, the conclusion of the whole system. It is thus a painter, after having worked singly upon each part of his piece, thinks it necessary to retouch the whole, in order to produce what is called the *total effect and harmony.*

XII. Man, we have seen, is a rational and free agent, who distinguishes justice and honesty, who finds within himself the principles of conscience, who is sensible of his dependance on the Creator, and born to fulfill certain duties. His greatest ornament is reason and virtue; and his chief task in life is to advance in that path, by embracing all the occasions that offer, to improve, to reflect, and to do good. The more he practises and confirms himself in such laudable occupations, the more he accomplishes the views of the Creator, and proves himself worthy of the existence he has received. He is sensible he can be reasonably called to an account for his conduct, and he approves or condemns himself according to his different manner of acting. <291>

From all these circumstances it evidently appears, that man is not confined, like other animals, to a mere physical oeconomy, but that he is included in a moral one, which raises him much higher, and is attended with greater consequences. For what appearance or probability is there, that a soul which advances daily in wisdom and virtue, should tend to annihilation, and that God should think proper to extinguish this light in its greatest lustre? Is it not more reasonable to think, that the good or

First proof, drawn from the nature of man considered on the moral side.

bad use of our faculties will be attended with future consequences; that we shall be accountable to our Creator, and finally receive the just retribution we have merited? Since therefore this judgment of God does not display itself sufficiently in this world, it is natural to presume, that the plan of the Divine Wisdom, with regard to us, embraces a duration of a much greater extent.

Second proof, drawn from the perfections of God.

XIII. Let us ascend from man to God, and we shall be still further convinced, that such, in reality, is the plan he formed.

If God is willing (a point we have already proved) that man should observe the rules of right reason, in proportion to his faculties and the circumstances he is under; this must be a serious and positive will. It is the will of the Creator, of the Governor of the world, of the sovereign Lord of all things. It is therefore a real command, which lays us under an obligation of obeying. It is moreover the will of a Being supremely powerful, wise and good, who proposing always, both with respect to himself and to his creatures, the most excellent ends, cannot fail to esta-<292>blish the means, which in the order of reason, and pursuant to the nature and state of things, are necessary for the execution of his design. No one can reasonably contest these principles; but let us see what consequences may be drawn from thence.

1. If it actually became the Divine Wisdom to give laws to man, this same wisdom requires these laws should be accompanied with necessary motives to determine rational and free agents to conform thereto in all cases. Otherwise we should be obliged to say, either that God does not really and seriously desire the observance of the laws he has enacted, or that he wants power or wisdom to procure it.

2. If through an effect of his goodness, he has not thought proper to let men live at random, or to abandon them to the capriciousness of their passions; if he has given them a light to direct them; this same goodness must, undoubtedly, induce him to annex a perfect and durable happiness to the good use that every man makes of this light.

3. Reason informs us afterwards, that an all-powerful, all-wise, and all-bountiful Being is infinitely fond of order; that these same perfections make him desire that this order should reign among his intelligent and

free creatures, and that it was for this very reason he subjected them to laws. The same reasons that induced him to establish a moral order, engage him likewise to procure their observance. It must be therefore his satisfaction and glory, to render all men sensible of the difference he makes between those who disturb, and those who conform to order. He cannot be indifferent in this respect: on the contrary, he is determined, by the love he <293> has for himself and his perfections, to invest his commands with all the efficacy necessary to render his authority respected: This imports an establishment of future rewards and punishments; either to keep man within rule, as much as possible, in the present state, by the potent motives of hope and fear; or to give afterwards an execution worthy of his justice and wisdom to his plan, by reducing every thing to the primitive order he has established.

4. The same principle carries us yet further. For if God be infinitely fond of the order he has established in the moral world, he cannot but approve of those, who with a sincere and constant attachment to this order, endeavour to please him by concurring to the accomplishment of his views; and he cannot but disapprove of such as observe an opposite conduct:* for the former are, as it were, his friends, and the latter declare themselves his enemies. But the approbation of the Deity imports his protection, benevolence, and love; whereas his disapprobation cannot but be attended with quite contrary effects. If so, how can any one imagine, that God's friends and enemies will be confounded, and no difference made between them? Is it not much more consonant to reason to think, that the Divine Justice will manifest at length, some way or other, the extreme difference he places between virtue and vice, by rendering finally and perfectly happy those, who by a submission to his will are become the objects of his benevolence; and, on the contrary, by making the wicked feel his just severity and resentment? <294>

XIV. This is what our clearest notions of the perfections of the supreme Being induce us to judge concerning his views, and the plan he has formed. Were not virtue to meet surely and inevitably with a final rec-

---

* See part ii. chap. x. § 7.

ompence, and vice with a final punishment, and this in a general and complete manner, exactly proportioned to the degree of merit or demerit of each person; the plan of natural laws would never answer our expectation from a supreme Legislator, whose prescience, wisdom, power, and goodness, are without bounds. This would be leaving the laws divested of their principal force, and reducing them to the quality of simple counsels; it would be subverting, in fine, the fundamental part of the system of intelligent creatures, namely, that of being induced to make a reasonable use of their faculties, with a view and expectation of happiness. In short, the moral system would fall into a state of imperfection, which could be reconciled neither with the nature of man, nor with the state of society, nor with the moral perfections of the Deity. It is otherwise, when we acknowledge a future life. The moral system is thereby supported, connected, and finished, so as to leave nothing wanting to render it complete: It is then a plan really worthy of God, and useful to man. The supreme Being does all he ought to do with free and rational creatures, to induce them to behave as they should; the laws of nature are thus established on the most solid foundations; and nothing is wanting to bind men by such motives as are properest to make an impression.

Hence if this plan be without comparison the most beautiful and the best; if it be likewise the <295> most worthy of God, and the most connected with what we know of the nature, wants, and state of man; how can any one doubt of its being that which the Divine Wisdom has actually chosen?

The objection drawn from the present state of things serves to prove the sentiment it opposes.

XV. I acknowledge, indeed, that could we find in the present life a sufficient sanction of the laws of nature, in the measure and plenitude above mentioned, we should have no right to press this argument; for nothing could oblige us to search into futurity for an intire unravelling of the divine plan. But we have seen in the preceding chapter, that though by the nature of things, and even by the various establishments of man, virtue has already its reward, and vice its punishment; yet this excellent and just order is accomplished only in part, and that we find a great number of exceptions to this rule in history, and the experience of human life. Hence arises a very puzzling objection against the au-thority of natural laws. But as soon as mention is made of another life, the difficulty disappears; every thing is cleared up and set to right; the system appears connected, finished, and supported; the Divine Wisdom is justified: we find all the necessary supplements and compensations to redress the present irregularities; virtue acquires a firm and unshaken prop, by furnishing the virtuous man with a motive capable to support him in the most dangerous difficulties, and to render him triumphant over the most delicate temptations.

Were this only a simple conjecture, it might be considered rather as a convenient than solid supposition. But we have seen that it is founded also <296> on the nature and excellence of the soul; on the instinct that inclines us to raise ourselves above the present life; and on the nature of man considered on the moral side, as a creature accountable for his ac-tions, and obliged to conform to a certain rule. When besides all this we behold that the same opinion serves to support, and perfectly crowns the whole system of natural law, it must be allowed to be no less probable than it is beautiful and engaging.

XVI. Hence this same opinion has been received more or less at all times, and by all nations, according as reason has been more or less cultivated, or as people have inquired closer into the origin of things. It would be an easy matter to alledge divers historical proofs, and to produce also several beautiful passages from the ancient philosophers, in order to shew that the reasons which strike us, made the like impressions on the wisest of the Pagans. But we shall be satisfied with observing, that these tes-timonies, which have been collected by other writers, are not indifferent on this subject; because this shews, either the vestiges of a primitive tra-dition, or the voice[4] of reason and nature, or both; which adds a con-siderable weight to our argument. <297>

The belief of a future state has been received by all nations.

4. The original has a more dramatic "cri" or "cry" of reason and nature.

CHAPTER XIV

That the proofs we have alledged have such a
probability and fitness, as renders them sufficient to
fix our belief, and to determine our conduct.

The proofs we have given of the sanction of natural laws are sufficient.

I. We have seen how far our reason is capable of conducting us with regard to the important question of the immortality of the soul, and a future state of rewards and punishments. Each of the proofs we have alledged, has without doubt its particular force; but joining to the assistance of one another, and acquiring a greater strength by their union, they are certainly capable of making an impression on every attentive and unprejudiced mind, and ought to appear sufficient to establish the authority and sanction of natural law in as full an extent as we desire.

Objection. These proofs contain no more than a fit or suitable reason. General answer.

II. If any one should say, that all our reasonings on this subject are only probability and conjecture, and properly reducible to a plausible reason or fitness, which leaves the thing still at a great distance from demonstration; I shall agree, if he pleases, that we have not here a complete evidence; yet the probability, methinks, is so very strong, and the fitness so great and so well established, that this is sufficient to make it prevail over the contrary opinion, and consequently to determine us.
<298>

For we should be strangely embarrassed, if in every question that arises, we should refuse to be determined by any thing but a demonstrative argument. Most commonly we are obliged to be satisfied with an assemblage of probabilities, which, in a conjunct consideration, very seldom deceive us, and ought to supply the place of evidence in subjects unsusceptible of demonstration. It is thus that in natural philosophy, in physic, criticism, history, politics, commerce, and generally in all the affairs of life, a prudent man is determined by a concurrence of reasons, which, every thing considered, he judges superior to the opposite arguments.

III. In order to render the force of this kind of proof more obvious, it will not be amiss to explain here at first what we mean by a *plausible reason* or *fitness;* to inquire afterwards into the general principle on which this sort of reasoning is founded; and to see in particular what constitutes its force when applied to the law of nature. This will be the right way to know the just value of our arguments, and what weight they ought to have in our determinations.

A plausible reason or fitness is that which is drawn from the necessity of admitting a point as certain, for the perfection of a system in other respects solid, useful, and well connected, but which would be defective without this point; when there is no reason to suppose that it has any essential defect.* For example: upon beholding a great and magnificent palace, we remark an admirable symmetry and propor-<299>tion; where all the rules of art, which form the solidity, convenience, and beauty of a building, are strictly observed. In short, all that we see of the building denotes an able architect. May it not therefore be reasonably supposed, that the foundation which we do not see is equally solid and proportioned to the great mass it bears? Can it be imagined that the architect's ability and knowledge should have forsaken him in so important a point? In order to form such a supposition, we should have certain proofs of this deficiency, or have seen that in fact the foundation is imperfect; otherwise we could not presume so improbable a thing. Who is it, that on a mere metaphysical possibility of the architect's having neglected to lay the foundation, would venture to wager that the thing is really so?

IV. Such is the nature of fitness. The general foundation of this manner of reasoning is, that we must not consider only what is possible, but what is probable; and that a truth of itself very little known, acquires a probability by its natural connexion with other truths more obvious. Thus natural philosophers do not question but they have discovered the truth, when an hypothesis happily explains all the phenomena; and an

What is meant by a suitable reason.

General foundation of this manner of reasoning.

* See chap. viii. § 2.

event very little known in history, appears no longer doubtful, when we see it serves for a key and basis to many other indubitable events. It is on this principle in great measure that moral certainty is founded,* which is so much used <300> in most sciences, as well as in the conduct of life, and in things of the greatest importance to individuals, families, and to the whole society.

This kind of fitness is very strong in respect to natural law.

V. But if this manner of judging and reasoning takes place so frequently in human affairs, and is in general founded on so solid a principle; it is still much surer when we are to reason on the works of God, to discover his plan, and to judge of his views and designs. For the whole universe, with the several systems that compose it, and particularly the system of man and society, are the work of a supreme understanding. Nothing has been done by chance; nothing depends on a blind, capricious, or impotent cause; every thing has been calculated and measured with a profound wisdom. Here therefore, more than any where else, we have a right to judge, that so powerful and so wise an author, has omitted nothing necessary for the perfection of his plan; and that consistent with himself he has fitted it with all the essential parts, for the design he proposed. If we ought to presume reasonably such a care in an able architect, who is nothing more than a man subject to error; how much more ought we to presume it in a being of infinite wisdom?

This fitness has different degrees. Principles to judge of it.

VI. What we have been now saying, shews that this fitness is not always of the same weight, but may be more or less strong, in proportion to the greater or lesser necessity on which it is established. And to lay down rules on this subject, we may say in general, 1. That the more we know the views and design of the author; 2. The more we <301> are assured of his wisdom and power; 3. The more this power and wisdom are perfect; 4. The more considerable are the inconveniences that result from the opposite system; the more they border upon the absurd; and the

---

* See M. Boullier's philosophical essay on the souls of brutes, &c. second edition; to which has been joined a treatise of the true principles that serve as a foundation to moral certainty. Amst. 1737.

more pressing we find the consequences drawn from this sort of considerations. For then we have nothing to set in opposition to them by way of counterbalance; and consequently it is on that side we are determined by right reason.

VII. These principles are of themselves applicable to our subject, and this in so just and complete a manner, that the reason drawn from probability or fitness cannot be carried any farther. After what has been said in the preceding chapters, it would be entering into useless repetitions, to attempt to prove here all the particulars: the thing sufficiently proves itself. Let us be satisfied with observing, that the fitness in favour of the sanction of natural laws, is so much the stronger and more pressing, as the contrary opinion throws into the system of humanity an obscurity and confusion, which borders very much upon the absurd, if it does not come quite up to it. The plan of the Divine Wisdom becomes in respect to us an insoluble enigma; we are no longer able to account for any thing; and we cannot tell why so necessary a thing should be wanting in a plan so beautiful in other respects, so useful, and so perfectly connected.

Application of these principles to our subject.

VIII. Let us draw a comparison between the two systems, to see which is most conformable to order, most suitable to the nature and state of man, and, in short, most reasonable and worthy of God. <302>

Comparison of the two opposite systems.

Suppose, on one side, that the Creator proposed the perfection and felicity of his creatures, and in particular the good of man and society. That for this purpose, having invested man with understanding and liberty, and rendered him capable of knowing his end, of discovering and following the road that can alone conduct him to it, he lays him under a strict obligation of walking constantly in this road, and of ever following the light of reason, which ought always to direct his steps. That in order to guide him the better, he has given him all the principles[1] necessary to serve him as a rule. That this direction, and these principles, coming from a powerful, wise, and good superior, have all the charac-

---

1. In the original, God is said to have given man all the *sentiments* and principles necessary, etc.

teristics of a real law. That this law carries already along with it, even in this life, its reward and punishment; but that this first sanction being insufficient, God, in order to give to a plan so worthy of his wisdom and goodness, its full perfection, and to furnish mankind in all possible cases with necessary motives and helps, has moreover established a proper sanction in respect to natural law, which will be manifested in a future life: and that attentive to the conduct of man, he proposes to make him give an account of his actions, to recompence virtue, and to punish vice, by a retribution exactly proportioned to the merit or demerit of each person.

Let us set now in opposition to this first system the other, which supposes that every thing is limited, in respect to man, to the present life, and that he has nothing to hope or fear beyond this term: that God after having created man and instituted society, concerns himself no more about them: that <303> after giving us a power of discerning good and evil by the help of reason, he takes no manner of notice of the use we make thereof, but leaves us in such a manner to ourselves, that we are absolutely at liberty to do as we please: that we shall have no account to give to our Creator, and that notwithstanding the unequal and irregular distribution of the goods and evils of this life, notwithstanding the disorders caused by the malice or injustice of mankind, we have no redress or compensation ever to expect from God.

The system of the sanction of natural laws is far preferable to the opposite system.

IX. Can any one say that this last system is comparable to the first? Does it set the divine perfections in so great a light? Is it so worthy of the divine wisdom, bounty, and justice? Is it so proper to stem the torrent of vice and to support virtue, in delicate and dangerous conjunctures? Does it render the structure of society as solid, and invest the laws of nature with such an authority as the glory of the supreme Legislator and the good of humanity requires? Were we to chuse between two societies, one of which admitted the former system, while the other acknowledged only the latter, is there a prudent man but would highly prefer to live in the first of those societies?

There is, certainly, no comparison between those two systems, in respect to beauty and fitness: the first is a work of the most perfect reason;

the second is defective, and provides no manner of remedy against a great many disorders. Now even this alone points out sufficiently on which side the truth lies; because the business is to judge and reason of the designs and works of the Deity, who does every thing with infinite wisdom. <304>

X. Let no one say, that limited as we are, it is temerity to decide after this manner; and that we have too imperfect ideas of the divine nature and perfections, to be able to judge of his plan and designs with any certainty. This reflection, which is in some measure true, and in some cases just, proves too much, if applied to our subject, and consequently has no weight. Let us but reflect a little, and we shall find that this thought leads us insensibly to a kind of pyrrhonism, which would be the subversion of all order and social oeconomy. For in fine there is no medium; we must chuse one of the two systems above explained. To reject the first, is admitting the second with all its inconveniences. This remark is of some importance, and alone is almost sufficient to shew us the force of fitness in this case; because not to acknowledge the solidity of this reason, is to lay one's self under a necessity of receiving a defective system; a system loaded with inconveniences, and whose consequences are very far from being reasonable.

Objection. Answer.

XI. Such are the nature and force of the fitness, on which the proofs of the sanction of natural laws are established. All that remains now, is to see what impression these proofs united, ought to make on our minds, and what influence they should have over our conduct. This is the capital point in which the whole ought to terminate.

Of the influence which those proofs ought to have over our conduct. We should act in this world on the foundation of the belief of a future state.

1. In the first place I observe, that though all that can be said in favour of the sanction of natural laws, were still to leave the question undecided; yet it <305> would be reasonable even in this very uncertainty to act, as if it had been determined in the affirmative. For it is evidently the safest side, namely, that in which there is less at all events to lose, and more to gain. Let us state the thing as dubious. If there be a future state, it is not only an error not to believe it, but likewise a dangerous irregularity to act as if there were no such thing: an error of this kind is

attended with pernicious consequences; whereas if there is no such thing, the mistake in believing it, produces in general none but good effects; it is not subject to any inconveniences hereafter, nor does it, generally speaking, expose us to any great difficulties for the time present. Be it therefore as it may, and let the case be ever so unfavourable to natural laws, a prudent man will never hesitate which side he is to embrace, whether the observance, or the violation of those laws: virtue will certainly have the preference of vice.

2. But if this side of the question is the most prudent and eligible, even under a supposition of doubt and uncertainty, how much more will it be so, if we acknowledge, as we cannot avoid, that this opinion is at least more probable than the other? A first degree of verisimilitude, or a simple though slight probability, becomes a reasonable motive of determination, in respect to every man that calculates and reflects. And if it be prudent to conduct ourselves by this principle in the ordinary affairs of life, does prudence permit us to deviate from this very road in the most important affairs, such as essentially interest our felicity? <306>

3. But, in fine, if proceeding still further, and reducing the thing to its true point, it is agreed that we have actually, if not a strict demonstration of a future life, at least a probability founded on many reasonable presumptions, and so great a fitness as borders very near upon certainty; it is still more evident, that in the present state of things, we ought to act on this footing, and are not reasonably allowed to form any other rule of conduct.*

It is a necessary consequence of our nature and state.

XII. Nothing, indeed, is more worthy of a rational being, than to seek for evidence on every subject, and to be determined only by clear and certain principles. But since all subjects are not susceptible thereof, and yet we are obliged to determine; what would become of us, if we were always to wait for a perfect demonstration? In failure of the highest degree of certainty, we must take up with the next to it; and a great probability becomes a sufficient reason of acting, when there is none of equal weight to oppose it. If this side of the question be not in itself evidently

* See part i. chap. vi. § 6.

certain, it is at least an evident and certain rule, that in the present state of things, it ought to have the preference.

This is a necessary consequence of our nature and condition. As we have only a limited knowledge, and yet are under a necessity of determining and acting; were it requisite for this purpose to have a perfect certainty, and were we to refuse to accept of probability as a principle of determi-<307>nation; we should be either obliged to determine in favour of the least probable side, and contrary to verisimilitude (which no body, methinks, will attempt to maintain) or we should be forced to spend our days in dubiousness and uncertainty, to fluctuate continually in a state of irresolution, and to remain ever in suspence, without acting, without resolving upon any thing, or without having any fixt rule of conduct; which would be a total subversion of the system of humanity.

XIII. But if it be reasonable in general to admit of fitness and probability as the rule of conduct, for want of evidence; this rule becomes still more necessary and just, in particular cases, in which, as hath been already observed, a person runs no risk in following it. When there is nothing to lose, if we are mistaken; and a great deal to win, if we are not; what can we desire more for a rational motive of acting? Especially when the opposite side exposes us to very great danger, in case of error; and affords us no manner of advantage, supposing we are in the right. Under such circumstances there is no room for hesitating; reason obliges us to embrace the safest side; and this obligation is so much the stronger, as it arises from a concurrence of motives of the greatest weight and solidity.

Reason lays us under an obligation of so doing.

In short, if it be reasonable to embrace this side, even in case of an intire uncertainty, it is still more so when there is some probability in its favour; it becomes necessary if these probabilities are co-<308>gent and numerous; and, in fine, the necessity still increases, if, at all events, this is the safest and most advantageous party. What can any one desire more, in order to produce a real obligation,* according to the principles we have established in regard to the internal obligation imposed by reason.

* See part i. chap. vi. § 9, and 13.

It is a duty that God himself imposes on us.

XIV. Again. This internal and primitive obligation is confirmed by the Divine Will itself, and consequently rendered as strong as possible. In fact, this manner of judging and acting being, as we have seen, the result of our constitution, such as the Creator has formed it; this alone is a certain proof, that it is the will of God we should be directed by those principles, and consider it as a point of duty. For whatever, as we have already observed,* is inherent in the nature of man, whatever is a consequence of his original constitution and state, acquaints us clearly and distinctly with the will of the Creator, with the use he expects we should make of our faculties, and the obligations to which he has thought proper to subject us. This is a point that merits great attention. For if we may affirm, without fear of mistake, that the Deity is actually willing that man should conduct himself in this life on the foundation of the belief of a future state, and as having every thing to hope or to fear on his side, according as he has acted justly or unjustly; does there not arise from thence a more than probable proof of the reality of this state, and <309> of the certainty of rewards and punishments? Otherwise we should be obliged to say, that God himself deceives us, because this error was necessary for the execution of his designs, as a principle essential to the plan he has formed in respect to humanity. But to speak after this manner of the most perfect Being, of a Being, whose power, wisdom, and goodness, are infinite, would be using a language equally absurd and indecent. For this very reason, that as the abovementioned article of belief is necessary to mankind, and enters into the views of the Creator, it cannot be false. Whatever the Deity sets before us as a duty, or as a reasonable principle of conduct, must be certainly true.

Conclusion.

XV. Thus every thing concurs to establish the authority of natural laws. 1. The approbation they receive from reason. 2. The express command of God. 3. The real advantages which their observance procures us in this world; and, in fine, the great hopes and just fears we ought to have in respect to futurity, according as we have observed or despised those laws. Thus it is that God binds us to the practice of virtue by such strong

* See part ii. chap. iv. § 5.

and so numerous connexions, that every man who consults and listens to reason, finds himself under an indispensible obligation of rendering them the unvariable rule of his conduct.

XVI. Some perhaps will object, that we have been too diffusive in respect to the sanction of natural laws. True it is, that most of those who have written concerning the law of nature, are more con-<310>cise on this article, and Puffendorf himself does not say much about it.* This author, without absolutely excluding the consideration of a future life from this science, seems nevertheless to confine the law of nature within the bounds of the present life, as tending only to render us sociable.† And yet he acknowledges that man is naturally desirous of immortality, and that this has induced heathens to believe the soul immortal; that this belief is likewise authorised by an ancient tradition concerning the Goddess of revenge; to which he adds, that in fact it is very probable God will punish the violation of the laws of nature; but that there is still a great² obscurity in this respect, and nothing but revelation can put the thing out of doubt.‡

But were it even true, that reason affords us nothing but probabilities in regard to this question, yet we must not exclude from the law of nature all considerations of a future state; especially if these probabilities are so very great, as to border upon certainty. The above article enters neces-

That which is already probable by reason only, is set in full evidence by revelation.

---

* The reader may see in a small treatise, intitled, Judgment of an anonymous, &c. and inserted in the 5th edition of the Duties of man and a citizen, the remarks that Mr. Leibnitz, author of that treatise, makes against Puffendorf upon this score. Barbeyrac, who has joined his own remarks to Mr. Leibnitz's work justifies Puffendorf pretty well. And yet an attentive observer will find there is still something wanting to the entire justification of this author's system. [The translator abbreviates this note by omitting Burlamaqui's judgment. The sentence continues ". . . of this author's system, which, on this point, is in fact somewhat weak." Most of Pufendorf's numerous commentators agreed with Leibniz on this point and held that sanctions in the afterlife form a crucial part in a system of natural law. However, Burlamaqui is far more insistent on providing explicit arguments for the immortality of the soul and for sanctions in the afterlife than, for example, Barbeyrac.]

† See Puffendorf's preface on the Duties of man and a citizen, § 6, 7.

‡ See the Law of nature and nations, book ii. chap. iii. § 21.

2. "Some" rather than "a great" ("quelque obscurité").

sarily into <311> the system of this science, and forms a part thereof so much the more essential, that were it not for this, the authority of natural law would be weakened, as we have already demonstrated; and it would be difficult (to say nothing more) to establish on any solid grounds several important duties, which oblige us to sacrifice our greatest advantages to the good of society, or to the support of equity and justice. Necessary therefore it was, to examine with some care, how far our natural light may lead us in respect to this question, and to shew the force of the proofs that our reason affords us, and the influence those proofs ought to have over our conduct.

True it is, as we have already observed, that the best way to know the will of God in this respect, would be an express declaration on his part. But if reasoning, as mere philosophers, we have not been able to make use of so decisive a proof, nothing can hinder us, as christian philosophers, to avail ourselves of the advantage we have from revelation, in order to strengthen our conjectures. Nothing, indeed, can be a better argument that we have reasoned and conjectured right, than the positive declaration of the Deity on this important point. For since it appears in fact that God is willing to recompense virtue, and to punish vice in another life, it is no longer possible to doubt of what we have advanced, namely, that this is extremely conformable to his wisdom, goodness, and justice. The proofs we have drawn from the nature of man, from God's designs in his favour, from the wisdom and equity with which he governs the world, and from the present state of things, are not a work of the imagina-<312>tion, or an illusion of self-love; no, they are reflections dictated by right reason: and when revelation comes up to their assistance, it sets then in full evidence what already had been rendered probable by the sole light of nature.

But the reflection we have here made, regards not only the sanction of natural laws, it may be equally extended to the other parts of this work. It is to us a great pleasure to see that the principles we have laid down, are exactly those that the christian religion adopts for its basis, and on which the whole structure of religion and morality is raised.[3] If

3. Read: "on which she [the Christian religion] raises the whole structure of religion and morality."

on one side this remark serves to confirm us in these principles, by assuring us that we have hit upon the true system of nature; on the other, it ought to dispose us to have an infinite esteem for a revelation which perfectly confirms the law of nature, and converts moral philosophy into a religious and popular doctrine; a doctrine founded on facts, and in which the authority and promises of the Deity manifestly intervene in the fittest manner to make an impression upon man. This happy agreement between natural and revealed light, is equally honourable to both.

Finis.

VOLUME 2

THE PRINCIPLES OF POLITIC LAW

THE

PRINCIPLES

OF

NATURAL and POLITIC

LAW,

IN TWO VOLUMES,

By *J. J. BURLAMAQUI,*

Counsellor of State, and late Professor of NATURAL
and CIVIL LAW at GENEVA.

Translated into ENGLISH by Mr. NUGENT.

The SECOND EDITION, revised and corrected.

VOL. II.

LONDON,
Printed for J. NOURSE, Bookseller in Ordinary to his
MAJESTY.

MDCCLXIII.

CONTENTS[1]

1. The page numbers in the Contents are those of the 1763 edition.

PART II

In which are explained the different forms of government,
the ways of acquiring or losing sovereignty, and the
reciprocal duties of sovereigns and subjects.

PART III

A more particular examination of the essential parts of sovereignty, or of the different rights of the sovereign, with respect to the internal administration of the state, such as the legislative power, the supreme power in matters of religion, the right of inflicting punishments, and that which the sovereign has over the *Bona Reipublicae,* or the goods contained in the commonwealth.

2. This chapter is, both in Burlamaqui's original and in Nugent's translation, numbered the eighth instead of the seventh (there is no chapter seven).

PART IV

In which are considered the different rights of sovereignty with respect to foreign states; the right of war, and every thing relating to it; public treaties, and the right of ambassadors.

THE
PRINCIPLES
OF
POLITIC LAW;

Being a SEQUEL to[1] the
PRINCIPLES of the LAW of NATURE.

∞ PART I ∞

Which treats of the origin and nature of civil
society, of sovereignty in general, of its peculiar
characteristic, limitations, and essential parts.

CHAPTER I

Containing a few general and preliminary reflections,
which serve as an introduction to this and the
following parts.

I. Whatever has been hitherto explained concerning the rights and duties
of man, relates to the natural and primitive society, established by God
himself, independent of human institution:[2] We must now treat of civil

---

1. "Being a sequal . . ." was added by the translator in order to strengthen the
impression that the *Principles of Politic Law* was a genuine sequel and second part of
the *Principles of Natural Law*. See the introduction.
2. The first sentence, referring to the contents of the *Principles of Natural Law,*
was added by the translator. The French original starts "Civil society, or the body
politic . . ." ("La société civile ou le corps politique . . .").

society, or the body politic, which is deservedly esteemed the com-
<2>pletest of societies, and to which the name of *State* has been given
by way of preference.

II. For this purpose we shall repeat here the substance of some principles
established in the preceding volume,[3] and we shall give a further explication of others relative to this subject.

　　1°. Human society is originally and in itself a state of equality and
independence.

　　2°. The institution of sovereignty destroys this independence.

　　3°. This institution does not subvert natural society.

　　4°. On the contrary, it contributes to strengthen and cement it.

III. To form therefore a just idea of civil society, we must call it natural
society itself, modified in such a manner, that there is a sovereign pre-
siding over it, on whose will whatever relates to the welfare[4] of the society
ultimately depends; to the end that, by these means, mankind[5] may attain, with greater certainty, that happiness to which they all do naturally
aspire.

IV. The institution of civil societies produces some new relations
amongst mankind; I mean such as subsist between those different bodies
or communities, which are called states or nations, from whence the law
of nations and civil polity are derived.

V. In fact, so soon as states are formed, they acquire, in some measure,
personal properties; and con-<3>sequently we may attribute the same
rights and obligations to them, as are attributed to individuals, considered as members of society. And indeed it is evident, that if reason im-

　　3. References to "established in the preceding volume" are again added by the
translator. He has supplanted these words for the original's "concerning the natural
and primitive society that God himself established and which is independent of human facts."

　　4. The original has "happiness" rather than "welfare."

　　5. Burlamaqui's "les hommes" could also be translated "men."

poses certain duties on individuals towards each other, it prescribes likewise those very same rules of conduct to nations, (which are composed only of men) in the intercourse which they may have with each other.

VI. We may therefore apply to kingdoms and nations the several maxims of natural law hitherto explained; and the same law, which is called natural, when speaking of individuals, is distinguished by the name of the law of nations, when applied to men, considered as members forming those different bodies, known by the name of states or nations.[6]

VII. To enter into this subject, we must observe, that the natural state of nations, with respect to each other, is that of society and peace. This society is likewise a state of equality and independence, which establishes between them a right of equality, by which they are obliged to have the same regard for each other. The general principle therefore of the law of nations, is nothing more than the general law of sociability, which obliges nations to the same duties as are prescribed to individuals.

VIII. Thus the law of natural equality, that which prohibits our injuring any person, and commands the reparation of damage done, the law likewise of beneficence, of fidelity to our engagements, &c. < 4 > are so many laws in regard to nations, which impose both on the people and on their respective sovereigns the same duties as are prescribed to individuals.

IX. It is a point of some importance to attend to the nature and origin of the law of nations, such as hath been here explained; for it follows from thence, that the law of nations is of equal authority with the law

---

6. This understanding derives from DNG II.3 §23, where Pufendorf identifies Hobbes (*De Cive* XIV §§4–5) as his source. Burlamaqui's main modifications of the Hobbesian picture (e.g., his argument that the state of nature is a state of peace) are central features in Pufendorf's critique of Hobbes. The shared consensus is that, contrary to what Grotius had claimed in DGP I.1 §14, arbitrary law of nations is a mere chimera, and that all principles of the law of nations that are valid gain their validity from being applications of natural law.

of nature itself, of which it constitutes a part, and that they are equally sacred and venerable, since both have the Deity for their author.

X. There cannot even be any other law of nations really obligatory, and intrinsically invested with the force of a law. For since all nations are in respect to each other in a state of perfect equality,[7] it is beyond contradiction, that if there be any common law betwixt them, it must necessarily have God, their common sovereign, for its author.

XI. As to what concerns the tacit consent or customs of nations, on which some doctors establish a law of nations, they cannot of themselves produce a real obligation. For from this only, that several nations have behaved towards each other for some time after a certain manner, it does not follow that they have laid themselves under a necessity of acting constantly so for the future, and much less that every other nation is obliged to conform to this custom.[8] <5>

XII. All that can be said is, that when once a particular usage or custom is introduced between nations that have a frequent intercourse with each other, these nations are, and may reasonably be, supposed to submit to this usage, unless they have, in express terms, declared that they will not conform to it any longer; and this is all the effect that can be attributed to the received usages between nations.

XIII. This being premised, we may distinguish two sorts of laws of nations, one necessary, which is obligatory of itself, and no way differs from the law of nature; the other arbitrary and free, founded only on a kind of tacit convention, and deriving all its force from the law of nature, which commands us to be faithful to our engagements.

---

7. "An equality of right" might be a better translation for "égalité de droit." Barbeyrac declares in DNG II.3 §23 note 2 that all nations are equal and unable to impose laws on each other.

8. See DGP I.1 §14 note 3.

XIV. What has been said concerning the law of nations, furnishes princes with several important reflections; among others, that since the law of nations is, in reality, nothing else but the law of nature itself, there is but one and the same rule of justice for all mankind, insomuch that those princes who violate them are as guilty of as great a crime as private people, especially as their wicked actions are generally attended with more unhappy consequences than those of private people.

XV. Another consequence that may be drawn from the principles we have established relating to the law of nature and nations, is to form a just idea of that <6> science so necessary to the directors of nations, which is called *Policy:* By policy therefore is meant that knowledge or ability by which a sovereign provides for the preservation, security, prosperity, and glory of the nation he governs, without doing any prejudice to other people, but rather consulting their advantage as much as possible.

XVI. In short, that which is called prudence, in respect to private persons, is distinguished by the name of policy when applied to sovereigns; and as that mischievous ability, by which a person seeks his own advantage to the detriment of others, and which is called artifice or cunning, is deserving of censure in individuals, it is equally so in those princes, whose policy aims at procuring the advantage of their own nation, to the prejudice of what they owe to other people, in virtue of the laws of humanity and justice.[9]

XVII. From what has been said of the nature of civil society in general, it is easy to comprehend that, among all human institutions, there is none more considerable than this; and that, as it embraces whatever is interesting to the happiness of society, it is a very extensive subject, and consequently that it is important alike both to princes and people to have proper instructions upon this head.

9. Pufendorf asserts that the science of politics is a prudential type of knowledge; DNG I.2 §4.

XVIII. That we may reduce the several articles relative to this matter into some order, we shall divide our work into four parts.

The first will treat of the origin and nature of civil societies, of the manner in which states are <7> formed, of sovereignty in general, its proper characteristics, its limitations, and essential parts.

In the second we shall explain the different forms of government, the various ways of acquiring or losing sovereignty, and the reciprocal duties of sovereigns and subjects.

The third will contain a more particular inquiry into those essential parts of sovereignty which are relative to the internal administration of the state, such as the legislative power, the supreme power in respect to religion, the right of inflicting punishments, that which the sovereign has over the estates and effects contained in his dominions, &c.

In the fourth, in fine, we shall explain the rights of sovereigns with regard to foreigners, where we shall treat of the right of war, and of whatever is relative to that subject, of alliances, and other public treaties, and likewise of the rights of ambassadors.[10]

CHAPER II

Of the real origin of civil societies.

I. Civil society is nothing more than the union of a multitude of people, who agree to live in subjection to a sovereign, in order to find, through his protection and care, the happiness to which they naturally aspire.

II. Whenever the question concerning the origin of civil society is started, it may be considered two different ways; for either I am asked my opinion <8> concerning the origin of governments in reality and in fact; or else in regard to the right of congruity and fitness; that is, what

10. The separation of natural law and politic law follows Pufendorf's division of tasks between the two books of the DHC. The first fourth delineated above corresponds (*grosso modo*) to DHC II chapters 5–7; the second fourth to chapters 8, 10, and 11; the third to chapters 12, 13, 15, and 18; the fourth to chapters 16 and 17.

are the reasons which should induce mankind to renounce their natural
liberty, and to prefer a civil state to that of nature? Let us see first what
can be said in regard to the fact.[1]

III. As the establishment of society and civil government is almost coeval
with the world, and there are but very few records extant of those first
ages; nothing can be advanced with certainty concerning the real origin
of civil societies. All that political writers say upon this subject is reduced
to conjectures that have more or less probability.

IV. Some attribute the origin of civil societies to paternal authority.
These observe that all the ancient traditions inform us, that the first men
lived a long time; by this longevity, joined to the multiplicity of wives,
which was then permitted, a great number of families saw themselves
united under the authority of one grandfather; and as it is difficult that
a society, any thing numerous, can maintain itself without a supreme
authority, it is natural to imagine that their children, accustomed from
their infancy to respect and obey their fathers, voluntarily resigned the
supreme command into their hands, so soon as they arrived to a full
maturity of reason.[2]

V. Others suppose that the fear and diffidence which mankind had of
one another, was their inducement to unite together under a chief, in
order to shelter themselves from those mischiefs which <9> they apprehended.[3] From the iniquity of the first men, say they, proceeded war, as

---

1. Burlamaqui thus makes a clear separation between the question of the de facto
origin of civil societies and the question of the de jure legitimacy of government.
The social contract is a reply to the question concerning the legitimacy of power
relations, but it does not furnish a credible account of the historical origin of the
same. This observation was discussed in detail by Barbeyrac in DNG VII.1 §7 note 1.

2. This covert reference to Filmer together with the Lockean critique is from DNG
VI.2 §10 note 2.

3. By this, Burlamaqui means Pufendorf (and probably Hobbes). Barbeyrac summarizes Pufendorf's view as being "that the mere fear of the insults of others" was
the historical reason for the establishment of all civil societies, DNG VII.1 §7 note 1.

also the necessity to which they were reduced of submitting to masters, by whom their rights and privileges might be determined.

VI. Some there are, in fine, who pretend that the first beginnings of civil societies are to be attributed to ambition supported by force or abilities. The most dexterous, the strongest, and the most ambitious reduced at first the simplest and weakest into subjection; those growing states were afterwards insensibly strengthened by conquests, and by the concurrence of such as became voluntary members of those societies.[4]

VII. Such are the principal conjectures of political writers in regard to the origin of societies; to which let us add a few reflections.

The first is, that in the institution of societies, mankind in all probability thought rather of redressing the evils which they had experienced, than of procuring the several advantages resulting from laws, from commerce, from the arts and sciences, and from all those other improvements so frequently mentioned in history.

2°. The natural disposition of mankind, and their general manner of acting, do not by any means permit us to refer the institution of all governments to a general and uniform principle. More natural it is to think that different circumstances gave rise to different states. <10>

3°. We behold without doubt the first image of government in democratic society, or in families; but there is all the probability in the world, that it was ambition, supported by force or abilities, which first subjected the several fathers of families under the dominion of a chief. This appears very agreeable to the natural disposition of mankind, and seems

---

4. This is Barbeyrac's account. Barbeyrac builds on Bayle's observation, that men in the state of nature would be unable to formulate complex accounts of the advantages to be had through forming a political community. The history of the birth of states, as Barbeyrac depicts it, is rather a history of manipulative individuals striving for immediate advantages and for power—the Biblical example he draws on is Nimrod. See DNG VII.1 §7 note 1. Burlamaqui's comments in the following paragraphs are from the same (very long) note.

further supported by the manner in which the scripture speaks of Nimrod,* the first king mentioned in history.

4°. When such a body politic was once framed, several others joined themselves to it afterwards, through different motives; and other fathers of families being afraid of insults or oppression from those growing states, determined to form themselves into the like societies, and to chuse to themselves a chief.

5°. Be this as it may, we must not imagine that those first states were such as exist in our days. Human institutions are ever weak and imperfect in their beginnings, there is nothing but time and experience that can gradually bring them to perfection.

The first states were in all probability very small: Kings in those days were only a kind of chieftains, or particular magistrates, appointed for deciding disputes, or for the command of armies. Hence we find by the most ancient histories, that there were sometimes several kings in one and the same nation.

VIII. But to conclude, whatever can be said in regard to the original of the first governments, consists, according to what we have already observed, in mere conjectures, that have only more or <11> less probability. Besides, this is a question rather curious than useful or necessary; the point of importance, and that particularly interesting to mankind, is to know whether the establishment of government, and of a supreme authority, was really necessary, and whether mankind derive from thence any considerable advantages: This is what we call the right of congruity or fitness, and what we are going now to examine.

* See Genesis, c. x. v. 8, & seq.

CHAPTER III

Of the right of congruity or fitness with regard to the institution of civil society, and the necessity of a supreme authority: of civil liberty; that it is far preferable[1] to natural liberty, and that the state is of all human conditions the most perfect, the most reasonable, and consequently the natural state of man.

I. We are here to inquire, whether the establishment of civil society, and of a supreme authority, was absolutely necessary to mankind, or whether they could not live happy without it? And whether sovereignty, whose original is owing perhaps to usurpation, ambition, and violence, does not include an attempt against the natural equality and independency of man? These are without doubt questions of importance, and which merit the utmost attention.[2] <12>

II. I grant, at first setting out, that the primitive and original society which nature has established amongst mankind, is a state of equality and independence; it is likewise true, that the law of nature is that to which all men are obliged to conform their actions; and in fine it is certain, that this law is in itself most perfect, and the best adapted for the preservation and happiness of mankind.

III. It must likewise be granted, that if mankind, during the time they lived in natural society, had exactly conformed to nature's laws, nothing would have been wanting to complete their happiness, nor would there have been any occasion to establish a supreme authority upon earth. They would have lived in a mutual intercourse of love and beneficence,

---

1. Another possible translation of Burlamaqui's "qu'elle l'emporte de beaucoup sur la liberté naturelle" would be "which is of considerably larger extent than natural liberty."

2. For Burlamaqui, and for the elite in general, the Genevan citizens who reacted against the growing influence of the small council were basically troublemakers who pursued chaos and anarchy.

in a simplicity without state or pomp, in an equality without jealousy, strangers to all superiority but that of virtue, and to every other ambition than that of being disinterested and generous.[3]

IV. But mankind were not long directed by so perfect a rule; the vivacity of their passions soon weakened the force of nature's law, which ceased now to be a bridle sufficient for them, so that they could no longer be left to themselves thus weakened and blinded by their passions. Let us explain this a little more particularly.

V. Laws are incapable of contributing to the happiness of society, unless they be sufficiently known. The laws of nature cannot be known otherwise to man, than as he makes a right use of his reason; but as the greatest part of mankind, abandoned to themselves, listen rather to the prejudices of passion than <13> to reason and truth, it thence follows, that in the state of natural society, the laws of nature were known but very imperfectly, and consequently that in this condition of things man could not lead an happy life.

VI. Besides, the state of nature wanted another thing necessary for the happiness and tranquillity of society, I mean a common judge, acknowledged as such, whose business it is to decide the differences that every day arise betwixt individuals.

VII. In this state, as every one would be supreme arbiter of his own actions, and would have a right of being judge himself, both of the laws

---

3. Burlamaqui's picture of a paradise-like golden age of innocence and of obedience to natural law contrasts sharply with the standard modern natural law account of matters presented by Hobbes and Pufendorf. Burlamaqui's defense of civil authority is at least as strong as theirs, however, and this constitutes an important difference from Barbeyrac, who presented his not-so-pessimistic views on the state of nature in notes to DNG II.2 §2. The state could in some cases, Barbeyrac claimed, be worse than the state of nature: men in the state of nature would not therefore have been ready to renounce to their natural liberty completely and unconditionally. Burlamaqui passes over Barbeyrac's criticism in silence.

of nature and of the manner in which he ought to apply them, this independence and excessive liberty could not but be productive of disorder and confusion, especially in cases where there happened to be any clashing of interests or passions.

VIII. In fine, as in the state of nature no one had a power of enforcing the execution of the laws, nor an authority to punish the violation of them, this was a third inconveniency of the state of primitive society, by which the efficacy of natural laws was almost intirely destroyed. For as men are framed, the laws derive their greatest force from the coercive power, which, by exemplary punishments, intimidates the wicked, and balances the superior force of pleasure and passion.[4]

IX. Such were the inconveniencies that attended the state of nature. By the excessive liberty and in-<14>dependence which mankind enjoyed, they were hurried into perpetual troubles: for which reason they were under an absolute necessity of quitting this state of independence, and of seeking a remedy against the evils of which it was productive; and this remedy they found in the establishment of civil society and a sovereign authority.[5]

X. But this could not be obtained without effecting two things equally necessary; the first was to unite together by means of a more particular society; the second to form this society under the dependence of a person invested with an uncontrolable power,[6] to the end that he might maintain order and peace.

---

4. This is Pufendorf's view in DNG VIII.3 §4: note that Barbeyrac, in note 3 to that paragraph, opposes Pufendorf on this point, drawing on Locke and on Grotius in support of a general right to punish crimes in the state of nature. The absence of efficient sanctions is another argument in favor of a strong need for political community.

5. This can be contrasted with Barbeyrac in DNG II.2 §2 note 17.

6. "A right to command in the last instance" ("en dernier resort") in the original.

XI. By these means they remedied the inconveniencies above-mentioned. The sovereign, by promulgating his laws, acquaints his subjects with the rules which they ought to follow. We then cease to be judges in our own cause, our whims and passions are checked, and we are obliged to contain ourselves within the limits of that regard and respect which we owe to each other.

XII. This might be sufficient to prove the necessity of government, and of a supreme authority in society, and to establish the right of congruity or fitness in this respect: But as it is a question of the utmost importance; as mankind have a particular interest in being well acquainted with their state; as they have a natural passion for independence, and generally frame false notions of liberty;[7] it will <15> not be improper to continue our reflections on this subject.

XIII. Let us therefore examine into natural and civil liberty;[8] let us afterwards endeavour to shew, that civil liberty is far preferable to that of nature, and consequently, that the state which it produces, is of all human conditions the most perfect, and, to speak with exactness, the true natural state of man.

XIV. The reflections we have to make upon this subject are of the last importance, affording useful lessons both to princes and subjects. The greatest part of mankind are strangers to the advantages of civil society, or at least they live in such a manner, as to give no attention to the beauty or excellence of this salutary institution. On the other hand, princes often lose sight of the end for which they were appointed, and instead of thinking that the supreme authority was established for no other purpose than for the maintenance and security of the liberty of mankind,

7. A reference to the Genevan bourgeoisie's demands; see, for example, Helena Rosenblatt, *Rousseau and Geneva: From the First Discourse to the Social Contract, 1749–1762* (Cambridge: Cambridge University Press, 1997), pp. 154–55.

8. Barbeyrac refers to Locke's distinction between natural and civil liberty in DNG II.5 §19 note 2.

that is, to make them enjoy a solid happiness, they frequently direct it to a different end, and to their own private advantage. Nothing therefore is more necessary than to remove the prejudices both of sovereigns and subjects in regard to this article.

XV. Natural liberty is the right which nature gives to all mankind, of disposing of their persons and property, after the manner they judge most convenient to their happiness, on condition of their act-<16>ing within the limits of the law of nature, and of their not abusing it to the prejudice of other men. To this right of liberty there is a reciprocal obligation corresponding, by which the law of nature binds all mankind to respect the liberty of other men, and not to disturb them in the use they make of it, so long as they do not abuse it.

XVI. The laws of nature are therefore the rule and measure of liberty; and in the primitive and natural state, mankind have no liberty but what the laws of nature give them; for which reason it is proper to observe here, that the state of natural liberty is not that of an intire independence. In this state, men are indeed independent with regard to one another, but they are all in a state of dependence on God and his laws. Independence, generally speaking, is a state unsuitable to man, because by his very nature he holds it of a superior.

XVII. Liberty and independence of any superior, are two very distinct things, which must not be confounded. The first belongs essentially to man, the other cannot suit him. And so far is it from being true, that human liberty is of itself inconsistent with dependence on a sovereign and submission to his laws, that, on the contrary, it is this power of the sovereign, and the protection which men derive from thence, that forms the greatest security of their liberty.

XVIII. This will be still better understood by recollecting what we have already settled, when <17> speaking of natural liberty. We have shewn that the restrictions which the law of nature makes to the liberty of man, far from diminishing or subverting it, on the contrary constitutes its

perfection and security. The end of natural laws is not so much to restrain the liberty of man, as to make him act agreeably to his real interests; and moreover, as these very laws are a check to human liberty, in
whatever may be of pernicious consequence to others, it secures, by these
means, to all mankind, the highest, and the most advantageous degree
of liberty they can reasonably desire.[9]

XIX. We may therefore conclude, that in the state of nature man could
not enjoy all the advantages of liberty, but inasmuch as this liberty was
made subject to reason, and the laws of nature were the rule and measure
of the exercise of it. But if it be true in fact, that the state of nature was
attended with the several inconveniencies already mentioned, inconveniences which almost effaced the impression and force of natural laws,
it is a plain consequence, that natural liberty must have greatly suffered
thereby, and that by not being restrained within the limits of the law of
nature, it could not but degenerate into licentiousness, and reduce mankind to the most frightful and the most melancholy of situations.

XX. As they were perpetually divided by contentions, the strongest oppressed the weakest; they possessed nothing with tranquillity; they enjoyed no repose: and what we ought particularly to observe is, that all
these evils were owing chiefly to that very <18> independence which
mankind were possessed of in regard to each other, and which deprived
them of all security of the exercise of their liberty; insomuch that by
being too free, they enjoyed no freedom at all; for freedom there can be
none, when it is not subject to the direction of laws.

XXI. If it be therefore true, that the civil state gives a new force to the
laws of nature, if it be true also, that the establishment of sovereignty
secures, in a more effectual manner, the observance of those laws, we

---

9. Burlamaqui's sentence runs: ". . . it secures for them the highest degree of freedom that they can reasonably aspire to, namely that which is most to their advantage."
His intention is to reaffirm that a reasonable man strives for only as much freedom
as is advantageous to him.

must conclude, that the liberty, which man enjoys in this state, is far more perfect, more secure, and better adapted to procure his happiness, than that which he was possessed of in the state of nature.

XXII. True it is that the institution of government and sovereignty is a considerable limitation to natural liberty, for man must renounce that[10] power of disposing of his own person and actions, in a word, his independence. But what better use could mankind make of their liberty, than to renounce every dangerous tendency it had in regard to themselves, and to preserve no more of it than was necessary to procure their own real and solid happiness?

XXIII. Civil liberty is therefore, in the main, nothing more than natural liberty, divested of that part of it which formed the independence of individuals, by the authority which they have conferred on their sovereign. <19>

XXIV. This liberty is still attended with two considerable advantages, which natural liberty had not. The first is, the right of insisting that their sovereign shall make a good use of his authority, agreeably to the purposes for which he was intrusted with it. The second is the security which prudence requires that the subjects should reserve to themselves for the execution of the former right, a security absolutely necessary, and without which the people can never enjoy any solid liberty.

XXV. Let us therefore conclude, that to give an adequate definition of civil liberty, we must say, that it is natural liberty itself, divested of that part, which constituted the independence of individuals, by the authority which it confers on sovereigns, and attended with a right of insisting on his making a good use of his authority, and with a moral security that this right will have its effect.

---

10. The translator omits the word "arbitrary."

XXVI. Since civil liberty therefore is far preferable to that of nature, we may safely conclude, that the civil state, which procures this liberty to mankind, is of all human states the most perfect, the most reasonable, and of course the true natural state of man.[11]

XXVII. And indeed, since man, by his nature, is a free and intelligent being, capable of discovering his state by himself, as well as its ultimate end, and of taking the necessary measures to attain it, it is properly in this point of view that we must consider his natural state; that is, the natural state of man <20> must be that, which is most agreeable to his nature, to his constitution, to reason, to the good use of his faculties, and to his ultimate end; all which circumstances perfectly agree with the civil state. In short, as the institution of government and supreme authority brings men back to the observance of the laws of nature, and consequently to the road of happiness, it makes them return to their natural state, from whence they had strayed by the bad use which they made of their liberty.

XXVIII. The reflections we have here made on the advantages which men derive from government, deserve very great attention.

1°. They are extremely proper for removing the false notions which most people have upon this subject; as if the civil state could not be established but in prejudice to their natural liberty, and as if government had been invented only to satisfy the ambition of designing men,[12] contrary to the interest of the rest of the community.

2°. They inspire mankind with a love and respect for so salutary an institution, disposing them thus to submit voluntarily to whatever the

11. Pufendorf and Barbeyrac discuss the view that the civil state is the true state of nature since it is the state that conforms to God's intentions, but neither adopts this language; see, for example, DNG II.2 §4.

12. Burlamaqui's original "of the most considerable amongst them" ("des plus considérables d'entr'eux") carries a different message than the translated text. Burlamaqui is here opposed to what he understands as the bourgeois view of government, that it was introduced merely in order to favor the interests of the aristocracy rather than the people as a whole.

civil society requires of them, from a conviction that the advantages from thence derived are very considerable.

3°. They may likewise contribute greatly to the increase of the love of one's country, the first seeds of which nature herself has implanted, as it were, in the hearts of all mankind, in order to promote, as it most effectually does, the happiness of society. Sextus Empiricus relates, "that it was a custom among the ancient Persians, upon the death of a king, <21> to pass five days in a state of anarchy, as an inducement to be more faithful to his successor, from the experience they acquired of the inconveniences of anarchy, of the many murders, robberies, and every other mischief, with which it is pregnant."*

XXIX. As these reflections are proper for removing the prejudices of private people, so they likewise contain most excellent instructions even for sovereigns. For is there any thing better adapted for making princes sensible of the full extent of their duty, than to reflect seriously on the ends which the people proposed to themselves in intrusting them with their liberty, that is, with whatever is most valuable to them; and on the engagements into which they entered, by charging themselves with so sacred a deposit? When mankind renounced their independence and natural liberty, by giving masters to themselves, it was in order to be sheltered from the evils with which they were afflicted, and in hopes, that under the protection and care of their sovereign, they should meet with solid happiness. Thus have we seen, that by civil liberty mankind acquired a right of insisting upon their sovereign's using his authority agreeably to the design with which he was entrusted with it, which was to render their subjects wise and virtuous, and thereby to promote their real felicity. In a word, whatever has been said concerning the advantages of the civil state preferably <22> to that of nature, supposes this state in its due perfection; and that both subjects and sovereign discharge their duties towards each other.

* Advers. Mathemat. lib. 2. § 33. Vid. Herodot. lib. 1. cap. 96, & seq.

CHAPTER IV

Of the essential constitution of states, and of the manner in which they are formed.

I. After treating of the original of civil societies, the natural order of our subject leads us to examine into the essential constitution of states, that is, into the manner in which they are formed, and the internal frame of those surprizing[1] structures.

II. From what has been said in the preceding chapter it follows, that the only effectual method which mankind could employ in order to skreen themselves from the evils with which they were afflicted in the state of nature, and to procure to themselves all the advantages wanting to their security and happiness, must be drawn from man himself, and from the assistance of society.

III. For this purpose, it was necessary that a multitude of people should unite in so particular a manner, that their preservation must depend on each other, to the end that they remain under a necessity of mutual assistance, and by this junction of strength and interests, be able not only to repel the insults <23> against which each individual could not guard so easily, but also to contain those who should attempt to deviate from their duty, and to promote, more effectually, their common advantage. Let us explain more particularly how this could be effected.

IV. Two things were necessary for this purpose.[2]
  1°. It was necessary to unite for ever the wills of all the members of the society, in such a manner, that from that time forward they should never desire but one and the same thing in whatever relates to the end and purpose of society. 2°. It was requisite afterwards to establish a supreme power supported by the strength of the whole body (by which

---

1. Read: ". . . of those wonderful structures" ("merveilleux").
2. Burlamaqui's account draws heavily on DNG VII.2 and on DHC II.6 §§3–6.

means they might over-awe those who should be inclinable to disturb the peace) and to inflict a present and sensible evil on such as should attempt to act contrary to the public good.

V. It is from this union of wills and of strength, that the body politic or state results, and without it we could never conceive a civil society. For let the number of confederates be ever so great, if each man was to follow his own private judgment in things relating to the public good, they would only embarrass one another, and the diversity of inclinations and judgments, arising from the levity and natural inconstancy of man, would soon demolish all concord, and mankind would thus relapse into the inconveniencies of the state of nature. Besides, a society of that kind could never act long in concert, and for the same end, nor maintain itself in that harmony which constitutes its whole strength, without a supe-<24>rior power, whose business it is to serve as a check to the inconstancy and malice of man, and to oblige each individual to direct all his actions to the public utility.

VI. All this is performed by means of covenants; for this union of wills in one and the same person could never be so effected, as to actually destroy the natural diversity of inclinations and sentiments; but it is done by an engagement which every man enters into, of submitting his private will to that of a single person, or of an assembly; insomuch that every resolution of this person or assembly, concerning things relative to the public security or advantage, must be considered as the positive will of all in general, and of each in particular.

VII. With regard to the union of strength, which produces the sovereign power, it is not formed by each man's communicating physically his strength to a single person, so as to remain utterly weak and impotent; but by a covenant or engagement, whereby all in general, and each in particular, oblige themselves to make no use of their strength, but in such a manner as shall be prescribed to them by the person on whom they have, with one common accord, conferred the supreme authority.

VIII. By this union of the body politic under one and the same chief, each individual acquires, in some measure, as much strength as the whole society united. Suppose, for instance, there are a million of men in the commonwealth, each man is able to resist this <25> million, by means of their subjection to the sovereign, who keeps them all in awe, and hinders them from hurting one another. This multiplication of strength in the body politic resembles that of each member in the human body; take them asunder, and their vigor is no more; but by their mutual union the strength of each increases, and they form, all together, a robust and animated body.

IX. The state may be defined, a society by which a multitude of people unite together, under the dependence of a sovereign, in order to find, through his protection and care, the happiness to which they naturally aspire. The definition which Tully gives, amounts pretty near to the same. *Multitudo juris consensu, & utilitatis communione sociata.* A multitude of people united together by a common interest, and by common laws, to which they submit with one accord.[3]

X. The state is therefore considered as a body, or as a moral person, of which the sovereign is the chief or head, and the subjects are the members; in consequence of which we attribute to this person certain actions peculiar to him, certain rights, privileges, and possessions, distinct from those of each citizen, and to which neither each citizen, nor many, nor even all together, can pretend, but only the sovereign.

XI. It is moreover this union of several persons in one body, produced by the concurrence of the wills and the strength of every individual in one and the same person, that distinguishes the state from a mul-

3. Barbeyrac quoted Cicero's definition with some approval in DNG VII.2 §13 note 1. The central difference from Pufendorf's Hobbesian definition concerns the aims of the state: Burlamaqui differs from Hobbes, Pufendorf, and Barbeyrac in stressing happiness as a goal that the state should secure. The Pufendorfian and Barbeyracian understanding is that the state aims at securing external peace. See DNG VII.2 §13 and DHC II.6 §10.

<26>titude. For a multitude is only an assemblage of several persons, each of whom has his own private will, with the liberty of judging according to his own notions of whatever is proposed to him, and of determining as he pleases; for which reason they cannot be said to have only one will. Whereas the state is a body, or a society, animated by only one soul, which directs all its motions, and makes all its members act after a constant and uniform manner, with a view to one and the same end, namely, the public utility.

XII. But it will be here objected, that if the union of the will and of the strength of each member of the society, in the person of the sovereign, destroys neither the will nor the natural force of each individual; if they always continue in possession of it; and if they are able, in fact, to employ it against the sovereign himself, what does the force of the state consist in, and what is it that constitutes the security of this society? I answer, that two things contribute chiefly to maintain the state, and the sovereign, who is the soul of it.

The first is the engagement itself, by which individuals have subjected themselves to the command of a sovereign, an engagement which derives a considerable force both from divine authority, and from the sanction of an oath. But as to vicious and ill-disposed minds, on whom these motives make no impression, the strength of the government consists chiefly in the fear of those punishments which the sovereign may inflict upon them, by virtue of the power with which he is invested. <27>

XIII. Now since the means, by which the sovereign is enabled to compel rebellious and refractory persons to their duty, consists in this, that the rest of the subjects join their strength with him for this end (for, were it not for this, he would have no more power than the lowest of his subjects) it follows from thence, that it is the ready submission of good subjects that furnishes the sovereign with the means of repressing the insolent, and of maintaining his authority.

XIV. But provided a sovereign shews never so small an attachment to his duty, he will always find it easy to fix the better part of his subjects in his interest, and of course to have the greatest part of the strength of the state in his hands, and to maintain the authority of the government. Experience has always shewn that princes only need a common share of virtue to be adored by their subjects. We may therefore affirm, that the sovereign is capable of deriving from himself the means necessary for the support of his authority, and that a prudent exercise of the sovereignty, pursuant to the end for which it was designed, constitutes at the same time the happiness of the people, and, by a necessary consequence, the greatest security of the government in the person of the sovereign.

XV. Tracing the principles here established in regard to the formation of states, &c. were we to suppose that a multitude of people, who had lived hitherto independent of each other, wanted to establish a civil society, we shall find a ne-<28>cessity for different covenants, and for a general decree.[4]

1°. The first covenant is that by which each individual engages with all the rest to join for ever in one body, and to regulate, with one common consent, whatever regards their preservation and their common security. Those who do not enter into this first engagement, remain excluded from the new society.

2°. There must afterwards be a decree made for settling the form of government; otherwise they could never take any fixt measures for promoting, effectually and in concert, the public security and welfare.

3°. In fine, when once the form of government is settled, there must be another covenant, whereby, after having pitched upon one or more persons to be invested with the power of governing, those on whom this supreme authority is conferred, engage to consult most carefully the common security and advantage, and the others promise fidelity and allegiance to the sovereign. This last covenant includes a submission of the strength and will of each individual to the will of the head of the society, as far as the public good requires; and thus it is that a regular state and perfect government are formed.

4. The account of the two covenants and the decree needed in order to establish a state are from Pufendorf; see, for example, DHC II.6 §§7–9.

XVI. What we have hitherto delivered may be further illustrated by the account we have in history concerning the foundation of the Roman state.[5] At first we behold a multitude of people, who flock together with a view of settling on the banks of the Tiber; afterwards they consult about what form of <29> government they shall establish, and the party for monarchy prevailing, they confer the supreme authority on Romulus.*

XVII. And though we are strangers to the original of most states, yet we must not imagine that what has been here said, concerning the manner in which civil societies are formed, is a mere fiction. For since it is certain, that all civil societies had a beginning, it is impossible to conceive, how the members, of which they are composed, could agree to live together, dependent on a supreme authority, without supposing the covenants above-mentioned.

XVIII. And yet all political writers do not explain the origin of states after our manner. Some there are † who pretend, that states are formed merely by the covenant of the subjects with one another, by which each man enters into an engagement with all the rest not to resist the will of the sovereign, upon condition that the rest on their side submit to the same engagement; but they pretend that there is no original compact between the sovereign and the subjects.[6]

XIX. The reason why these writers give this explication of the matter, is obvious. Their design is to give an arbitrary and unlimited authority to sovereigns, and to deprive the subjects of every means of withdrawing their allegiance upon any pretext whatever, notwithstanding the bad use the sovereign <30> may make of his authority. For this purpose it was

* See Dionysius Halicarn. lib. 2. in the beginning.

† A. Hobbes, de Cive, cap. v. § 7.

5. Rome was suggested as an example in DNG VII.2 §8, a paragraph from which Burlamaqui's following paragraph also draws heavily.

6. Burlamaqui's critical exposition of Hobbes's view, which forms the rest of this chapter, is from DNG VII.2 §§9–12.

absolutely necessary to free kings from all restraint of compact or covenant between them and their subjects, which, without doubt, is the chief instrument of limiting their power.

XX. But notwithstanding it is of the utmost importance to mankind, to support the authority of kings, and to defend it against the attempts of restless or mutinous spirits, yet we must not deny evident truths, or refuse to acknowledge a covenant, in which there is manifestly a mutual promise, of performing things to which they were not before obliged.

XXI. When I submit voluntarily to a prince, I promise him allegiance, on condition that he will protect me; the prince on his side promises me his protection, on condition that I will obey him. Before this promise, I was not obliged to obey him, nor was he obliged to protect me, at least by any *perfect* obligation; it is therefore evident, that there must be a mutual engagement.

XXII. But there is still something more; for so far is the system we are here refuting, from strengthening the supreme authority, and from screening it from the capricious invasions of the subject, that, on the contrary, nothing is of a more dangerous consequence to sovereigns, than to fix their right on such a foundation. For if the obligation of the subjects towards their princes is founded merely on the mutual covenant between the subjects, by which each <31> man engages for the sake of the rest to obey the sovereign, on condition that the rest do the same for his sake; it is evident, that at this rate every subject makes the force of his engagement depend on the execution of that of every other fellow-subject; and consequently if any one refuses to obey the sovereign, all the rest stand released from their allegiance. Thus by endeavouring to extend the rights of sovereigns beyond their just limits, instead of strengthening, they rather inadvertently weaken them.

CHAPTER V

Of the sovereign, sovereignty, and the subjects.

I. The sovereign in a state, is that person who has a right of commanding in the last resort.

II. As to the sovereignty we must define it, the right of commanding civil society in the last resort, which right the members of this society have conferred on one and the same person, with a view to preserve order and security in the commonwealth, and, in general, to procure, under his protection and through his care, their own real happiness, and especially the sure exercise of their liberty.

III. I say, in the first place, that sovereignty is the right of commanding civil society in the last resort, to shew that the nature of sovereignty consists chiefly in two things. <32>

The first is, the right of commanding the members of the society, that is, of directing their actions with authority, or with a power of compelling.

The second is, that this right ought to be that of commanding in the last resort in such a manner, that every private person be obliged to submit, without a power left to any man of resisting. Otherwise, if this authority was not superior to every other upon earth, it could establish no order or security in the commonwealth, though these are the ends for which it was established.

IV. In the second place, I say, that it is a right conferred upon a person, and not upon a man, to denote that this person may be, not only a single man, but likewise a multitude of men, united in council, and forming only one will, by means of a plurality of suffrages, as we shall more particularly explain hereafter.

V. Thirdly, I say, to one and the same person, to shew that sovereignty can admit of no share or partition, that there is no sovereign at all when there are many, because there is no one who commands then in the last resort, and none of them being obliged to give way to the other, their competition must necessarily throw every thing into disorder and confusion.[1]

VI. I add, in fine, to procure their own happiness, &c. in order to point out the end of sovereignty, that is, the welfare[2] of the people. When sovereigns once lose sight of this end, when they pervert it to <33> their private interests, or caprices, sovereignty then degenerates into tyranny, and ceases to be a legitimate authority. Such is the idea we ought to form of a sovereign and of sovereignty.

VII. All the other members of the state are called subjects, that is, they are under an obligation of obeying the sovereign.

VIII. Now a person becomes a member or subject of a state two ways, either by an express or by a tacit covenant.[3]

IX. If by an express covenant, the thing admits of no difficulty. But, with regard to a tacit covenant, we must observe that the first founders of states, and all those who afterwards became members thereof, are supposed to have stipulated, that their children and descendants should, at their coming into the world, have the right of enjoying those advantages which are common to all the members of the state, provided nevertheless that these descendants, when they attain to the use of reason, be on their part willing to submit to the government, and to acknowledge the authority of the sovereign.

1. Barbeyrac insists in DNG VII.4 §1 note 1 that it is a mistake to stress the indivisibility of sovereignty. Burlamaqui introduces the formula "in the last resort" and insists strongly on this indivisibility in order to counter any argument to the effect that the sovereign power is wielded by the small council and the general council conjointly. For more details, see the introduction.

2. Here Burlamaqui uses the word "felicity" rather than "welfare."

3. This and the following paragraphs are from DNG VII.2 §20.

X. I said, provided the descendants acknowledged the authority of the sovereign; for the stipulation of the parents cannot, in its own nature, have the force of subjecting the children against their will to an authority, to which they would not of themselves chuse to submit: Hence the authority of the sovereign over the children of the members of the state, and the <34> right, on the other hand, which these children have to the protection of the sovereign, and to the advantages of the government, are founded on mutual consent.

XI. Now if the children of members of the state, upon attaining to the years of discretion, are willing to live in the place of their parentage, or in their native country, they are by this very act supposed to submit themselves to the power that governs the state, and consequently they ought to enjoy, as members of that state, the advantages naturally arising from it. This is the reason likewise, that when once the sovereign is acknowledged, he has no occasion[4] to tender the oath of allegiance to the children, who are afterwards born in his dominions.

XII. Besides, it is a maxim which has been ever considered as a general law of government, that whosoever merely enters upon the territories of a state, and by a much stronger reason, those who are desirous of enjoying the advantages which are to be found there, are supposed to renounce their natural liberty, and to submit to the established laws and government, so far as the public and private safety requires. And if they refuse to do this, they may be considered as enemies, in this sense at least, that the government has a right to expel them the country; and this is likewise a tacit covenant, by which they make a temporary submission to the government.

XIII. Subjects are sometimes called *cives,* or members of the civil state; some indeed make no di-<35>stinction between these two terms, but I think it is better to distinguish them. The appellation of *civis* ought to be understood only of those who share in all the advantages and privi-

---

4. "No need" rather than "no occasion" ("pas besoin").

leges of the association, and who are properly members of the state, either by birth, or in some other manner. All the rest are rather inmates, strangers, or temporary inhabitants, than members.[5] As to women and servants, the title of member is applicable to them only, inasmuch as they enjoy certain rights, in virtue of their dependence on their domestic governor, who is properly a member of the state; and all this depends on the laws and particular customs of each government.

XIV. To proceed; members, besides the general relation of being united in the same civil society, have likewise many other particular relations, which are reducible to two principal ones.

The first is, when private people compose particular bodies or corporations.

The second is, when sovereigns entrust particular persons with some share of the administration.

XV. Those particular bodies are called *Companies, Chambers, Colleges, Societies, Communities.* But it is to be observed, that all these particular societies are finally subordinate to the sovereign.

XVI. Besides, we may consider some as more ancient than the establishment of civil states, and others as formed since. <36>

XVII. The latter are likewise either public, such as are established by the authority of the sovereign, and then they generally enjoy some particular

---

5. The translation replaces "simple" with "temporary" here, thus transforming the sense of what Burlamaqui is saying. When Burlamaqui says "simple habitants," he means immigrants who have been granted a right to live in Geneva, a right that should not be confused with citizenship but that also does not refer to temporary residents. Full civic rights (including the right to participate and vote in the general council) were the privilege of a minority in eighteenth-century Geneva. See Helena Rosenblatt, *Rousseau and Geneva: From the First Discourse to the Social Contract, 1749–1762* (Cambridge: Cambridge University Press, 1997), p. 18. Because of its engagement in Genevan politics, Burlamaqui's discussion of citizenship deviates a little from Pufendorf's language, but apart from this, the paragraph is still a faithful rendering of Pufendorf's DNG VII.2 §20. The rest of this chapter repeats paragraphs 21, 23, and 24 without deviating substantially from Pufendorf's views.

privileges, agreeably to their patents: or private, such as are formed by private people.

XVIII. In fine, these private bodies are either lawful or unlawful. The former are those, which, having nothing in their nature contrary to good order, good manners, or the authority of the sovereign, are supposed to be approved of by the state, though they have not received any formal sanction. With respect to unlawful bodies, we mean not only those whose members unite for the open commission of any crime, such as gangs of robbers, thieves, pirates, banditti, but likewise all other kinds of confederacy, which the subjects enter into, without the consent of the sovereign, and contrary to the end of civil society. These engagements are called cabals, factions, conspiracies.

XIX. Those members whom the sovereign entrusts with some share of the administration, which they exercise in his name and by his authority, have in consequence thereof particular relations to the rest of the members, and are under stronger engagements to the sovereign; these are called ministers, public officers, or magistrates.

XX. Such are the regents of a kingdom, during a minority, the governors of provinces and towns, the commanders of armies, the directors of the treasury, the presidents of courts of justice, ambassadors, <37> or envoys to foreign powers, &c. As all these persons are entrusted with a share of the administration, they represent the sovereign, and it is they that have properly the name of public ministers.

XXI. Others there are, who assist merely in the execution of public business, such as counsellors, who only give their opinion, secretaries, receivers of the public revenue, soldiers, subaltern officers, &c.

CHAPTER VI

Of the immediate source, and foundation
of sovereignty.

I. Though what has been said in the fourth chapter concerning the structure of states, is sufficient to shew the original and source of sovereignty, as well as its real foundation; yet as this is one of those questions on which political writers are greatly divided, it will not be amiss to examine it somewhat more particularly; and what remains still to be said upon this subject, will help to give us a more complete idea of the nature and end of sovereignty.

II. When we inquire here into the source of sovereignty, our intent is to know the nearest and immediate source of it; now it is certain, that the supreme authority, as well as the title on which this power is established, and which constitutes its right, is derived immediately from the very covenants <38> which constitute civil society, and give birth to government.[1]

III. And indeed, upon considering the primitive state of man, it appears most certain, that the appellations of sovereigns and subjects, masters and slaves, are unknown to nature. Nature has made us all of the same species, all equal, all free and independent of each other; in short, she was willing that those, on whom she has bestowed the same faculties, should have all the same rights. It is therefore beyond all doubt, that, in this primitive state of nature, no man has of himself an original right of commanding others, or any title to sovereignty.

IV. There is none but God alone that has, in consequence of his nature and perfections, a natural, essential, and inherent right of giving laws to

---

1. This is from DNG VII.2 §1.

mankind,[2] and of exercising an absolute sovereignty over them. The case is otherwise between man and man; they are in their own nature as independent of one another, as they are dependent on God. This liberty and independance is therefore a right naturally belonging to man, of which it would be unjust to deprive him against his will.

V. But if this be the case, and there is yet a supreme authority subsisting amongst mankind, whence can this authority arise, unless it be from the compacts or covenants, which men have made amongst themselves upon this subject? For as we have a right of transferring our property to another by a covenant; so, by a voluntary submission, a person may convey <39> to another, who accepts of the renunciation, the natural right he had of disposing of his liberty and natural strength.[3]

VI. It must therefore be agreed, that sovereignty resides originally in the people, and in each individual with regard to himself; and that it is the transferring and uniting the several rights of individuals in the person of the sovereign,[4] that constitutes him such, and really produces sovereignty. It is beyond all dispute, for example, that when the Romans chose Romulus and Numa for their kings, they must have conferred upon them, by this very act, the sovereignty, which those princes were not possessed of before, and to which they had certainly no other right than what was derived from the election of the people.

2. The original states that only God has a natural and inherent right to give laws to men ("aux hommes"). Burlamaqui would certainly agree with the translator, that only God can give laws to mankind as a whole, but he is also saying that only God's right to impose laws on even a single human being is natural and inherent.

3. Burlamaqui thus subscribes to the standard picture, which compares the social contract with a person's act of selling himself into slavery—a parallel made more explicit in Pufendorf's DNG VII.3 §1 in fine.

4. Unlike Pufendorf, Burlamaqui explicitly insists on popular sovereignty, but he also argues that the contract results in the transfer of "all the rights of every individual" ("tous les droits de tous les particuliers"). The translation makes Burlamaqui's view less transparent.

VII. Nevertheless, though it be evident, that the immediate original of sovereignty is owing to human covenants, yet nothing can hinder us from affirming, with good ground, that it is of divine as well as human right.[5]

VIII. And indeed, right reason having made it plainly appear, after the multiplication of mankind, that the establishment of civil societies and of a supreme authority, was absolutely necessary for the order, tranquillity, and preservation of the species, it is as convincing a proof that this institution is agreeable to the designs of Providence, as if God himself had declared it to mankind by a positive revelation. And since God is essentially fond of order, he is doubtless willing that there should be a supreme <40> authority upon earth, which alone is capable of procuring and supporting that order amongst mankind, by enforcing the observance of the laws of nature.

IX. There is a beautiful passage of Cicero's to this purpose.* *Nothing is more agreeable to the supreme Deity, that governs this universe, than civil societies lawfully established.*

X. When therefore we give to sovereigns the title of God's vicegerents upon earth, this does not imply that they derive their authority immediately from God; but it signifies only, that by means of the power lodged in their hands, and with which the people have invested them, they maintain, agreeably to the views of the Deity, both order and peace, and thus procure the felicity of mankind.[6]

---

* *Nihil est illi principi Deo, qui omnem hunc mundum regit, quod quidem in terris fiat acceptius, quam consilia coetusque hominum jure sociati, quae civitates appellantur.* Somn. Scip. cap. 3.

5. This and the following paragraphs are almost verbatim from DNG VII.3 §2.

6. This paragraph is drawn word for word from DNG VII.3 §2, with the exception of an added "and thus procure the felicity of mankind." The following paragraph on happiness is Burlamaqui's.

XI. But if these magnificent titles add a considerable lustre to sovereignty, and render it more respectable, they afford likewise, at the same time, an excellent lesson to princes. For they cannot deserve the title of God's vicegerents upon earth, but inasmuch as they make use of their authority, pursuant to the views and purposes for which they were intrusted with it, and agreeably to the intention of the Deity, that is, for the happiness of the people, by using all their endeavours to inspire them with virtuous principles.[7] <41>

XII. This, without doubt, is sufficient to make us look upon the original of government as sacred, and to induce subjects to shew submission and respect to the person of the sovereign. But there are political writers who carry the thing further, and maintain that it is God who confers immediately the supreme power on princes, without any intervention or concurrence of man.[8]

XIII. For this purpose, they make a distinction betwixt the cause of the state, and the cause of the sovereignty. They confess indeed that states are formed by covenants, but they insist that God himself is the immediate cause of the sovereignty. According to their notions, the people, who chuse to themselves a king, do not, by this act, confer the supreme authority upon him, they only point out the person whom heaven is to entrust with it. Thus the consent of the people to the dominion of one or more persons, may be considered as a channel, through which the supreme authority flows, but is not its real source.

XIV. The principal argument which these writers adopt, is, that as neither each individual amongst a number of free and independent people, nor the whole collective multitude, are in any wise possessed of the supreme authority, they cannot confer it on the prince. But this argument proves nothing: it is true that neither each member of the society, nor

7. The original ends ". . . to make them wise and virtuous" (". . . à les rendre sages & vertueux").
8. This discussion of the divine right of kings is from DNG VII.3 §§3–4.

the whole multitude collected, are formally invested with the supreme authority, such as we behold it in the sovereign, but it is sufficient that they possess it vir-<42>tually, that is, that they have within themselves all that is necessary to enable them, by the concurrence of their free will and consent, to produce it in the sovereign.

XV. Since every individual has a natural right of disposing of his natural freedom according as he thinks proper, why should he not have a power of transferring to another that right which he has of directing himself? Now is it not manifest, that if all the members of this society agree to transfer this right to one of their fellow-members, this cession will be the nearest and immediate cause of sovereignty? It is therefore evident, that there are, in each individual, the seeds, as it were, of the supreme power. The case is here very near the same as in that of several voices, collected together, which, by their union, produce a harmony, that was not to be found separately in each.

XVI. But it will be here objected, that the scripture itself says, that every man ought to be subject to the supreme powers, because they are established by God.* I answer, with Grotius, that men have established civil societies, not in consequence of a divine ordinance, but of their voluntary motion, induced by the experience they had had of the incapacity which separate families were under, of defending themselves against the insults and attacks of human violence. From thence (he adds) arises the civil power, which St. Peter, for this <43> reason, calls a *human* power,† though in other parts of scripture it bears the name of a divine institution,‡ because God has approved of it as an establishment useful⁹ to mankind.§

---

* Rom. xiii.

† Ep. i. chap. ii. v. 13.

‡ Rom. xiii. 1.

§ Grotius on the right of war and peace, book i. chap. iv. § 7, No. 3. See above, No. 7, and following.

9. Burlamaqui's original reads (like Barbeyrac's translation of Grotius in note 1 on page 307) "felicitous" ("salutaire") rather than "useful."

XVII. The other arguments, in favour of the opinion we have been here refuting, do not even deserve our notice. In general, it may be observed, that never were more wretched reasons produced upon this subject, as the reader may be easily convinced by reading Puffendorf on the law of nature and nations, who, in the chapter corresponding to this, gives these arguments at length, and fully refutes them.*

XVIII. Let us therefore conclude, that the opinion of those, who pretend that God is the immediate cause of sovereignty, has no other foundation than that of adulation and flattery, by which, in order to render the authority of sovereigns more absolute, they have attempted to render it independent of all human compact, and dependent only on God. But were we even to grant, that princes hold their authority immediately of God, yet the consequences, which some political writers want to infer, could not be drawn from this principle.

XIX. For since it is most certain, that God could never entrust princes with this supreme authority, <44> but for the good of society in general, as well as of individuals, the exercise of this power must necessarily be limited by the very intention which the Deity had in conferring it on the sovereign; insomuch that the people would still have the same right of refusing to obey a prince, who, instead of concurring with the views of the Deity, would, on the contrary, endeavour to cross and defeat them, by rendering his people miserable, as we shall prove more particularly hereafter.

* See the Law of nature and nations, book vii. chap. iii.

CHAPTER VII

Of the essential characters of sovereignty, its modifications, extent, and limits.

1°. Of the characteristics of sovereignty.

I. Sovereignty we have defined to be a right of commanding in the last resort in civil society, which right the members of this society have conferred upon some person, with a view of maintaining order and security in the commonwealth. This definition shews us the principal characteristics of the power that governs the state, and this is what it will be proper to explain here in a more particular manner.

II. The first characteristic, and that from which all the others flow, is its being a supreme and independent power, that is, a power that judges in the last resort of whatever is susceptible of human direction, and relates to the welfare[1] and advantage <45> of society; insomuch that this power acknowledges no other superior power on earth.

III. It must be observed however, that when we say the civil power is, of its own nature, supreme and independent, we do not mean thereby, that it does not depend, in regard to its original, on the human will:* all that we would have understood is, that, when once this power is established, it acknowledges no other upon earth, superior or equal to it, and consequently that whatever it ordains in the plenitude of its power, cannot be reversed by any other human will, as superior to it.

IV. That in every government there should be such a supreme power, is a point absolutely necessary; the very nature of the thing requires it, otherwise it is impossible for it to subsist. For since powers cannot be multiplied to infinity, we must necessarily stop at some degree of au-

---

* See above, chap. iv, &c. where we have proved the contrary.
1. The original reads "felicity" ("salut") rather than "welfare."

thority superior to all other: and let the form of government be what it will, monarchical, aristocratical, democratical, or mixt, we must always submit to a supreme decision; since it implies a contradiction to say, that there is any person above him, who holds the highest rank in the same order of beings.

V. A second characteristic, which is a consequence of the former, is that the sovereign, as such, is not accountable to any person upon earth for his conduct, nor liable to any punishment from man; for both suppose a superior.[2] <46>

VI. There are two ways of being accountable.

One as to a superior, who has a right of reversing what has been done, if he does not find it to his liking, and even of inflicting some punishment, and this is inconsistent with the idea of a sovereign.

The other as to an equal, whose approbation we are desirous of having; and in this sense a sovereign may be accountable, without any absurdity. And even they who have a right idea of honour, endeavour by such means to acquire the approbation and esteem of mankind, by letting all the world see, that they act with prudence and integrity: but this does not imply any dependance.

VII. I said that the sovereign, as such, was neither accountable nor punishable; that is, so long as he continues really a sovereign, and has not forfeited his right. For it is past all doubt, that if the sovereign, utterly forgetful of the end for which he was entrusted with the sovereignty, applied it to a quite contrary purpose, and thus became an enemy to the state; the sovereignty returns (*ipso facto*) to the nation, who, in that case, can act towards the person, who was their sovereign, in the manner they think most agreeable to their security and interests. For, whatever notion we may entertain of sovereignty, no man, in his senses, will pretend to say, that it is an undoubted title to follow the impulse of our irregular passions with impunity, and thus to become an enemy to society.

2. This and the following paragraph are from DNG VII.6 §2.

VIII. A third characteristic essential to sovereignty, considered in itself, is, that the sovereign, as such, be <47> above all human or civil law. I say, all human law; for there is no doubt but the sovereign is subject to the divine laws, whether natural or positive.[3]

> Regum timendorum in proprios greges,
> Reges in ipsos imperium est Jovis.[4]
>
> HOR. lib. 3. Od. 1.

IX. But with regard to laws merely human, as their whole force and obligation ultimately depends on the will of the sovereign, they cannot, with any propriety of speech, be said to be obligatory in respect to him: for obligation necessarily supposeth two persons, a superior and an inferior.[5]

X. And yet natural equity requires sometimes, that the prince should conform to his own laws, to the end that his subjects may be more effectually induced to observe them. This is extremely well expressed in these verses of Claudian.*

> In commune jubes si quid, censesve tenendum,
> Primus jussa subi; tunc observantior aequi
> Fit populus, nec ferre negat, cum viderit ipsum
> Auctorem parêre sibi: componitur orbis
> Regis ad exemplum; nec sic inflectere sensus
> Humanos edicta valent, ut vita regentis.
>
> *Would you your public laws should sacred stand,*
> *Lead first the way, and act what you command.*
> *The crowd grow mild and tractable to see*

---

* De IV. Consul. Honor. v. 296, & seq.

3. Burlamaqui follows Pufendorf in DNG VII.6 §3.

4. "Kings o'er their flocks the sceptre wield; E'en kings beneath Jove's sceptre bow." *The Odes and Carmen Saeculare of Horace,* translated by John Conington, Project Gutenberg, 2004, http://www.gutenberg.org/etext/5432.

5. This and the following paragraph, including the quote, are from DNG VII.6 §3.

The author governed by his own decree.
The world turns round, as its great matter draws,
And princes lives bind stronger than their laws. <48>

XI. To proceed; in treating here of sovereignty, we suppose that it is really and absolutely such in its own nature,[6] and that the establishment of civil laws ultimately depends on the sole will of the person who enjoys the honours and title of sovereign, insomuch that his authority, in this respect, cannot be limited: otherwise this superiority of the prince above the laws is not applicable to him in the full extent in which we have given it him.

XII. This sovereignty, such as we have now represented it, resided originally in the people. But when once the people have transferred their right to a sovereign, they cannot, without contradiction, be supposed to continue still masters of it.

XIII. Hence the distinction which some political writers make between *real sovereignty,* which always resides in the people, and *actual sovereignty,*[7] which belongs to the king, is equally absurd and dangerous. For it is ridiculous to pretend, that after the people have conferred the supreme authority on the king, they should still continue in possession of that very authority, superior to the king himself.

XIV. We must therefore observe here a just medium, and establish principles that neither favour tyranny, nor the spirit of mutiny and rebellion.

1°. It is certain, that so soon as a people submit to a king, really such, they have no longer the supreme power.

2°. But it does not follow, from the people's having conferred the supreme power in such a manner, that they have reserved to themselves in no case the right of resuming it. <49>

---

6. Read: ". . . we here suppose sovereignty to be such as it is by its own intrinsic nature, . . ." (". . . nous supposons la Souveraineté telle qu'elle est en elle-même, . . .").

7. The terms are from Barbeyrac's note 1 to DNG VII.6 §4; the point, from the paragraph itself.

3°. This reservation is sometimes explicit; but there is always a tacit one, the effect of which discloses itself, when the person, entrusted with the supreme authority, perverts it to an use directly contrary to the end for which it was conferred upon him, as will better appear hereafter.

XV. But though it be absolutely necessary, that there should be a supreme and independent authority in the state, there is nevertheless some difference, especially in monarchies and aristocracies,[8] with regard to the manner in which those who are entrusted with this power, exercise it. In some states the prince governs as he thinks proper; in others, he is obliged to follow some fixt and constant rules, from which he is not allowed to deviate; this is what I call the modifications of sovereignty, and from thence arises the distinction of absolute and limited sovereignty.

2°. Of absolute sovereignty.

XVI. Absolute sovereignty is therefore nothing else but the right of governing the state as the prince thinks proper, according as the present situation of affairs seems to require, and without being obliged to consult any person whatever, or to follow any fixt and perpetual rules.

XVII. Upon this head we have several important reflections to make.

1°. The word *absolute power* is generally very odious to republicans; and I must confess, that when it is misunderstood, it is apt to make the most dangerous impression on the minds of princes, especially in the mouths of flatterers. <50>

2°. In order to form a just idea of it, we must trace it to its principle. In the state of nature, every man has an absolute right to act after what manner he thinks most conducive to his happiness, and without being obliged to consult any person whatever, provided however that he does

---

8. This paragraph and the following are from DNG VII.6 §7, with the words "and aristocracies" being added here. The same matter is discussed more briefly in DHC II.9 §5.

nothing contrary to the laws of nature: consequently when a multitude of men unite together, in order to form a state, this body hath the same liberty in regard to matters in which the public good is concerned.

3°. When therefore the whole body of the people confer the sovereignty upon a prince, with this extent and absolute power, which originally resided in themselves, and without adding any particular limitation to it, we call that sovereignty absolute.

4°. Things being thus constituted, we must not confound an absolute power with an arbitrary, despotic, and unlimited authority. For, from what we have here advanced concerning the original and nature of absolute sovereignty, it manifestly follows, that it is limited, from its very nature, by the intention of those who conferred it on the sovereign, and by the very laws of God. This is what we must explain more at large.[9]

XVIII. The end which mankind proposed to themselves in renouncing their natural independance, and establishing government and sovereignty, was doubtless to redress the evils which they laboured under, and to secure their happiness. If so, how is it possible to conceive, that those, who, with this view, granted an absolute power to the sovereign, should have intended to give him an arbitrary and unlimited autho-<51>rity, so as to intitle him to gratify his caprice and passions, to the prejudice of the life, property, and liberty of the subject? On the contrary, we have shewn above, that the civil state must necessarily empower the subjects to insist upon the sovereign's using his authority for their advantage, and according to the purposes for which he was entrusted with it.

XIX. It must therefore be acknowledged, that it never was the intention of the people to confer absolute sovereignty upon a prince, but with this express condition, that the public good should be the supreme law to direct him; consequently so long as the prince acts with this view, he is authorized by the people; but, on the contrary, if he makes use of his power merely to ruin and destroy his subjects, he acts intirely of his own

9. Burlamaqui uses slightly stronger (antiabsolutist) language here at the end of his paragraph than Pufendorf does in DNG VII.6 §7 in fine.

head, and not in virtue of the power with which he was entrusted by the people.

XX. Still further, the very nature of the thing does not allow absolute power to be extended beyond the bounds of public utility; for absolute sovereignty cannot confer a right upon the sovereign, which the people had not originally in themselves. Now before the establishment of civil society, surely no man had a power of injuring either himself or others; consequently absolute power cannot give the sovereign a right to hurt and abuse his subjects.

XXI. In the state of nature every man was absolute master of his own person and actions, provided he confined himself within the limits of the law of <52> nature. Absolute power is formed only by the union of all the rights of individuals in the person of the sovereign; of course the absolute power of the sovereign is confined within the same bounds, as those by which the absolute power of individuals was originally limited.

XXII. But I go still further, and affirm that, supposing even a nation had been really willing to grant their sovereign an arbitrary and unlimited power, this concession would of itself be void and of no effect.

XXIII. No man can divest himself so far of his liberty as to submit to an arbitrary prince, who is to treat him absolutely according to his fancy. This would be renouncing his own life, which he is not master of; it would be renouncing his duty, which is never permitted: and if thus it be with regard to an individual who should make himself a slave, much less hath an entire nation that power, which is not to be found in any of its members.[10]

XXIV. By this it appears most evident, that all sovereignty, how absolute soever we suppose it, hath its limits; and that it can never imply an ar-

---

10. Burlamaqui's Lockean rejection of absolutism derives from Barbeyrac's note 2 to DNG VII.8 §6, where Barbeyrac draws on Locke and on Algernon Sidney.

bitrary power in the prince of doing whatever he pleases, without any other rule or reason than his own despotic will.

XXV. For how indeed should we attribute any such power to the creature, when it is not to be found in the supreme Being himself? His absolute domi-<53>nion is not founded on a blind will; his sovereign will is always determined by the immutable rules of wisdom, justice, and beneficence.

XXVI. In short, the right of commanding, or sovereignty, ought always to be established ultimately on a power of doing good, otherwise it cannot be productive of a real obligation; for reason cannot approve or submit to it; and this is what distinguishes empire and sovereignty from violence and tyranny. Such are the ideas we ought to form of absolute sovereignty.

3°. Of limited sovereignty.

XXVII. But although absolute power, considered in itself, and such as we have now represented it, implies nothing odious or unlawful, and, in that sense, people may confer it upon the sovereign; yet we must allow, that the experience of all ages has informed mankind, that this is not the form of government which suits them best, nor the fittest for procuring them a state of tranquillity and happiness.[11]

XXVIII. Whatever distance there may be between the subjects and the sovereign, in whatsoever degree of elevation the latter may be placed above the rest, still he is a human creature like themselves; their souls are all cast, as it were, in the same mould, they are all subject to the same prejudices, and susceptible of the same passions. <54>

---

11. Burlamaqui's treatment of limited sovereignty draws heavily on Pufendorf's in DNG VII.6 §10.

XXIX. Again, the very station, which sovereigns occupy, exposes them to temptations, unknown to private people. The generality of princes have neither virtue nor courage sufficient to moderate their passions, when they find they may do whatever they list. The people have therefore great reason to fear, that an unlimited authority will turn out to their prejudice, and that if they do not reserve some security to themselves, against the sovereign's abusing it, he will some time or other abuse it.

XXX. It is these reflections, justified by experience, that have induced most, and those the wisest, nations, to set bounds to the power of their sovereigns, and to prescribe the manner in which the latter are to govern; and this has produced what is called limited sovereignty.

XXXI. But though this limitation of the supreme power be advantageous to the people, it does no injury to the princes themselves; nay it may rather be said, that it turns out to their advantage, and forms the greatest security to their authority.

XXXII. It does no injury to princes; for if they could not be satisfied with a limited authority, their business was to refuse the crown; and when once they have accepted of it upon these conditions, they are no longer at liberty to endeavour afterwards to break through them, or to strive to render themselves absolute.

XXXIII. It is rather advantageous to princes, because those who are invested with absolute power, <55> and are desirous of discharging their duty, are obliged to a far greater vigilance and circumspection, and exposed to more fatigue, than those who have their task, as it were, marked out to them, and are not allowed to deviate from certain rules.

XXXIV. In fine, this limitation of sovereignty forms the greatest security to the authority of princes; for, as they are less exposed hereby to temptation, they avoid that popular fury, which is sometimes discharged on those, who, having been invested with absolute authority, abuse it to the public prejudice. Absolute power easily degenerates into despotism, and despotism paves the way for the greatest and most fatal revolutions that can happen to sovereigns. This is what the experience of all ages has verified: it is therefore a happy incapacity in kings not to be able to act contrary to the laws of their country.[12]

XXXV. Let us therefore conclude, that it intirely depends upon a free people, to invest the sovereigns, whom they place over their heads, with an authority either absolute, or limited by certain laws, provided these laws contain nothing contrary to justice, nor to the end of government. These regulations, by which the supreme authority is kept within bounds, are called, *The fundamental laws of the state.*

4°. *Of fundamental laws.*

XXXVI. The fundamental laws of a state, taken in their full extent, are not only the decrees by which the entire body of the nation determine the form of <56> government, and the manner of succeeding to the crown; but are likewise the covenants betwixt the people and the person on whom they confer the sovereignty, which regulate the manner of governing, and by which the supreme authority is limited.

XXXVII. These regulations are called fundamental laws, because they are the basis, as it were, and foundation of the state, on which the structure of the government is raised, and because the people look upon those regulations as their principal strength and support.

XXXVIII. The name of laws however has been given to these regulations in an improper and figurative sense; for, properly speaking, they are real covenants. But as those covenants are obligatory between the contracting parties, they have the force of laws themselves. Let us explain this more at large.

---

12. See DNG VII.6 §9 note 1.

XXXIX. 1°. I observe in the first place, that there is a kind of fundamental law, essential to all governments, even in those states where the most absolute sovereignty prevails. This law is that of the public good, from which the sovereign can never depart, without being wanting in his duty; but this alone is not sufficient to limit the sovereignty.

XL. Hence those promises, either tacit or express, by which princes bind themselves even by oath, when they come to the crown, of governing according to the laws of justice and equity, of consulting the public good, of oppressing no man, of protecting <57> the virtuous, and of punishing evil doers, and the like, do not imply any limitation to their authority, nor any diminution of their absolute power. It is sufficient that the choice of the means for procuring the advantage of the state, and the method of putting them in practice, be left to the judgment and disposal of the sovereign; otherwise the distinction of absolute and limited power would be utterly abolished.

XLI. 2°. But with regard to fundamental laws, properly so called, they are only more particular precautions taken by the people, to oblige sovereigns more strongly to employ their authority, agreeably to the general rule of the public good. This may be done several ways; but still these limitations of the sovereignty have more or less force, according as the nation has taken more or less precautions, that they shall have their due effect.

XLII. Hence, 1°. a nation may require of a sovereign, that he will engage, by a particular promise, not to make any new laws, nor to levy new imposts, to tax only some particular things, to give places and employments only to a certain set of people, and not to take any foreign troops into his pay, &c. Then indeed the supreme authority is limited in those different respects, insomuch that whatever the king attempts afterwards, contrary to the formal engagement he entered into, shall be void and of no effect. But if there should happen to be an extraordinary case, in which the sovereign thought it conducive to the public good, to deviate from the fundamental <58> laws, he is not allowed to do it of his own head, in contempt of his solemn engagement, but in that case he ought to consult the people themselves, or their representatives. Otherwise, under pretence of some necessity or utility, the sovereign might easily break his word, and frustrate the effect of the precautions taken by the nation to limit his power. And yet Puffendorf thinks otherwise.* But, for a still greater security of the performance of the engagements into which the sovereign entered, and which limit his power, it is proper to require explicitly of him, that he shall convene a general assembly of the people, or of their representatives, or of the nobility of the country, when any matters happen to fall under debate, which it was thought improper to leave to his decision. Or else the nation may previously establish a council, a senate, or parliament, without whose consent the prince shall be rendered incapable of acting in regard to things which the nation did not think fit to submit to his will.

XLIII. 2°. History informs us, that some nations have carried their precautions still further, by inserting, in plain terms, in their fundamental laws, a condition or clause, by which the king was declared to have forfeited his crown, if he broke through those laws. Puffendorf gives an example of this, taken from the oath of allegiance which the people of Aragon formerly made to their kings. *We, who have as much power as you, make you our king, upon condition that you maintain inviolably our rights and liberties, and not otherwise.* <59>

XLIV. It is by such precautions as these, that a nation really limits the authority she confers on the sovereign, and secures her liberty. For, as we have already observed, civil liberty ought to be accompanied not only with a right of insisting on the sovereign's making a due use of his authority, but moreover with a moral certainty that this right shall have its effect. And the only way to render the people thus certain, is to use proper precautions against the abuse of the sovereign power, in such a manner as these precautions shall not be easily eluded.

* See the Law of nature and nations, book vii. chap. vi. § 10.

XLV. Besides, we must observe, that these limitations of the sovereign power do not render it defective, nor make any diminution in the supreme authority; for a prince, or a senate, who has been invested with the supreme power upon this footing, may exercise every act of it as well as in an absolute monarchy. All the difference is, that in the latter the prince alone determines ultimately according to his private judgment; but in a limited monarchy, there is a certain assembly, who, in conjunction with the king, take cognizance of particular affairs, and whose consent is a necessary condition, without which the king can determine nothing. But the wisdom and virtue of good sovereigns, are strengthened by the concurring assistance of those who have a share in the authority. Princes always do what they incline to, when they incline to nothing but what is just and good; and they ought to esteem themselves happy in having it put out of their power to act otherwise.

XLVI. 3°. In a word, as the fundamental laws, <60> which limit the sovereign authority, are nothing else but the means which the people use to assure themselves that the prince will not recede from the general law of the public good in the most important conjunctures, it cannot be said that they render the sovereignty imperfect or defective. For if we suppose a prince invested with absolute authority, but at the same time blessed with so much wisdom and virtue, that he will never, even in the most trifling case, deviate from the laws which the public good requires, and that all his determinations shall be subjected to this superior rule, can we, for that reason, say, that his power is in the least weakened or diminished? No, certainly; for the precautions, which the people take against the weakness or the wickedness inseparable from human nature, in limiting the power of their sovereigns to hinder them from abusing it, do not in the least weaken or diminish the sovereignty; but, on the contrary, they render it more perfect, by reducing the sovereign to a necessity of doing good, and consequently by putting him, as it were, out of a capacity of misbehaving.

XLVII. Neither are we to believe that there are two distinct wills in a state, whose sovereignty is limited in the manner we have explained; for the state wills or determines nothing but by the will of the king. Only it is to be observed, that when a condition stipulated happens to be broken, the king cannot decree at all, or at least he must do so in vain in certain points; but he is not, for this reason, less a sovereign than he was before. Because a prince cannot do every thing according to his humour, it <61> does not follow from this, that he is not the sovereign. Sovereign and absolute power ought not to be confounded; and, from what has been said, it is evident, that the one may subsist without the other.

XLVIII. 4°. Lastly, there is still another manner of limiting the authority of those to whom the sovereignty is committed; which is not to trust all the different rights included in the sovereignty to one single person, but to lodge them in separate hands, or in different bodies, that they may modify or restrain the sovereignty.

XLIX. For example, if we suppose that the body of the nation reserves to itself the legislative power, and that of creating the principal magistrates; that it gives the king the military and executive powers, &c. and that it trusts to a senate composed of the principal men, the judiciary power, that of laying taxes, &c. it is easily conceived, that this may be executed in different manners, in the choice of which prudence must determine us.

L. If the government is established on this footing, then, by the original compact of association, there is a kind of partition in the rights of the sovereignty, by a reciprocal contract or stipulation between the different bodies of the state. This partition produces a balance of power, which places the different bodies of the state in such a mutual dependance, as retains every one, who has a share in the sovereign authority, within the bounds which the law prescribes to them; by which means the public liberty is secured. For ex-<62>ample, the regal authority is balanced by the power of the people, and a third order serves as a counter-balance to the two former, to keep them always in an equilibrium, and hinder the one from subverting the other. And this is sufficient, concerning the distinction between absolute and limited sovereignty.

5°. Of patrimonial, and usufructuary kingdoms.

LI. In order to finish this chapter, let us observe, that there is still another accidental difference in the manner of possessing the sovereignty, especially with respect to kings. Some are masters of their crown in the way of patrimony, which they are permitted to share, transfer, or alienate to whom they have a mind; in a word, of which they can dispose as they think proper: others hold the sovereignty in the way of *use* only, not of property; and this either for themselves only, or with the power of transmitting it to their descendants according to the laws established for the succession. It is upon this foundation that the learned distinguish kingdoms into patrimonial, and usufructuary or not patrimonial.

LII. We shall here add, that those kings possess the crown in full property, who have acquired the sovereignty by right of conquest; or those to whom a people have delivered themselves up without reserve, in order to avoid a greater evil; but that, on the contrary, those kings, who have been established by a free consent of the people, possess the crown in the way of *use* only. This is the manner in <63> which Grotius explains this distinction, in which he has been followed by Puffendorf, and by most of the other commentators or writers.*

LIII. On this we may make the following remarks.
1°. There is no reason to hinder the sovereign power, as well as every other right, from being alienated or transferred. In this there is nothing contrary to the nature of the thing; and if the agreement between the prince and the people bears that the prince shall have full right to dispose

* See Grotius on the right of war and peace, lib. i. chap. iii. § 11 and 12, &c. Puffendorf on the law of nature and nations, lib. vii. chap. vi. § 14, 15.

of the crown as he shall think proper, this will be what we call a patrimonial kingdom.

2°. But examples of such agreements are very rare; and we hardly find
any other except that of the Egyptians with their king, mentioned in
Genesis.*

3°. The sovereign power, however absolute, is not, of itself, invested
with the right of property, nor consequently with the power of alienation. These two ideas are intirely distinct, and have no necessary connection with each other.

4°. It is true, some alledge a great many examples of alienations made
in all ages by sovereigns: but either those alienations had no effect; or
they were made with an express or tacit consent of the people; or, lastly,
they were founded on no other title but that of force. <64>

5°. Let us therefore take it for an incontestable principle, that, in dubious cases, every kingdom ought to be judged not patrimonial, so long
as it cannot be proved, that a people submitted themselves on that footing to a sovereign.

CHAPTER VIII

*Of the parts of sovereignty, or of the different
essential rights which it includes.*

I. In order to finish this first part, nothing remains but to treat of the
different parts of sovereignty. We may consider sovereignty as an assemblage of various rights and different powers, which, though distinct, are
nevertheless conferred for the same end; that is to say, for the good of
the society, and which are all essentially necessary for this same end: these
different rights and powers are called the essential parts of sovereignty.[1]

II. To be convinced that these are the parts of sovereignty, we need only
attend to its nature and end.

* Chap. xlvii. v. 18, &c.
1. The first three paragraphs are from DNG VII.4 §§1–2.

The end of sovereignty is the preservation, the tranquillity, and the happiness of the state, as well within itself, as with respect to its interests abroad; so that sovereignty must include every thing that is essentially necessary for procuring this twofold end.

III. 1°. As this is the case, the first part of sovereignty, and that which is, as it were, the founda-<65>tion of all the rest, is the legislative power, by virtue of which the sovereign establishes general and perpetual rules, which are called *laws*. By these means every one knows how he ought to conduct himself for the preservation of peace and good order, what share he retains of his natural liberty, and how he ought to exert his rights, so as not to disturb the public tranquillity.

It is by means of laws that we contrive so nobly to unite the prodigious diversity of sentiments and inclinations observable among men, and establish that concert and harmony so essential to society, since they direct the different actions of individuals to the general good and advantage. But it must be supposed that the laws of the sovereign contain nothing opposite to the divine laws, whether natural or revealed.

IV. 2°. To the legislative we must join the coercive power, that is to say, the right of ordaining punishments against those who molest the community by their irregularities, and the power of actually inflicting them. Without this power, the establishment of civil society and of laws, would be absolutely useless, and we could not propose to live in peace and safety. But that the dread of punishments may make a sufficient impression on the minds of the people, the right of punishing must extend to the power of inflicting the greatest of natural evils, which is death; otherwise the dread of punishment would not be always capable of counter-balancing the force of pleasure, and the impulse of passion. In a word, the subjects must have a stronger interest to observe, <66> than to violate the law. Thus the vindicative power is certainly the highest degree of authority which one man can hold over another.[2]

2. This paragraph summarizes DNG VII.4 §3.

V. 3°. Further, it is necessary for the preservation of peace, that the sovereign should have a right to take cognizance of the different quarrels between the subjects, and to decide them in the last resort; as also to examine the accusations laid against any person, in order to absolve or punish him by his sentence, conformably to the laws: this is what we call *jurisdiction,* or the *judiciary power.* To this we must also refer the right of pardoning criminals when the public utility requires it.[3]

VI. 4°. Besides, as the ways of thinking, or opinions embraced by the subject, may have a very great influence on the welfare of the commonwealth, it is necessary that sovereignty should include a right of examining the doctrines taught in the state, so that nothing may be publicly advanced but what is conformable to truth, and conducive to the advantage of society. Hence it is, that it belongs to the sovereign to establish professors, academies, and public schools; and the supreme power, in matters of religion, is as much his right, as the nature of the thing will permit. After having secured the public repose at home, it is necessary to guard the people against strangers, and to procure to them, by leagues with foreign states, all the necessary aids and advantages, whether in the seasons of peace or war.[4]

VII. 5°. In consequence of this, the sovereign <67> ought to be invested with the power of assembling and arming his subjects, or of raising other troops in as great a number as is necessary for the safety and defence of the state, and of making peace when he shall judge proper.[5]

VIII. 6°. Hence also arises the right of contracting public engagements, of making treaties and alliances with foreign states, and of obliging all the subjects to observe them.

3. See DNG VII.4 §4.
4. See DNG VII.4 §8.
5. For this and the next paragraph, see DNG VII.4 §5.

IX. 7°. But as the public affairs, both at home and abroad, cannot be conducted by a single person, and as the sovereign is incapable of discharging all these duties, he must certainly have a power to create ministers and subordinate magistrates, whose business it is to take care of the public welfare, and transact the affairs of the state in his name, and under his authority. The sovereign, who has entrusted them with those employments, may, and ought to compel them to discharge them, and oblige them to give an exact account of their administration.[6]

X. 8°. Lastly, the affairs of the state necessarily demand, both in times of peace and war, considerable expences, which the sovereign himself neither can, nor ought to furnish. He must therefore have a right of reserving to himself a part of the goods or products of the country, or of obliging the subjects to contribute either by their purse, or by their labour and personal service, as much as the public necessities demand, and this is called the *right of subsidies or taxes.*[7] <68>

To this part of the sovereignty we may refer the prerogative of coining money, the right of hunting, with that of fishing, &c. These are the principal parts essential to sovereignty.

The End of the First Part. <69>

6. See DNG VII.4 §6.
7. See DNG VII.4 §7.

PART II

In which are explained the different forms of
government, the ways of acquiring or losing
sovereignty, and the reciprocal duties of
sovereigns and subjects.

CHAPTER I

Of the various forms of government.

I. Nations have been sensible, that it was essential to their happiness and
safety, to establish some form of government. They have all agreed in
this point, that it was necessary to institute a supreme power, to whose
will every thing should be ultimately submitted.

II. But, the more the establishment of a supreme power is necessary, the
more important is the choice <70> of the person invested with that high
dignity. Hence it is that, in regard to this article, nations are extremely
divided, having entrusted the supreme power in different hands, according as they judged it most conducive to their safety and happiness;
neither have they taken this step without making several systems and
restrictions, which may vary greatly. This is the origin of the different
forms of government.

III. There are therefore various forms of government, according to the
different subjects in whom the sovereignty immediately resides, and according as it is inherent either in a single person, or in a single assembly,
more or less compounded; and this is what forms the constitution of the
state.

IV. These different forms of government may be reduced to two general classes, namely, to the simple forms, or to those which are compounded or mixed.[1]

V. There are three simple forms of government; Democracy, Aristocracy, and Monarchy.

VI. Some nations, more diffident than others, have placed the sovereign power in the multitude itself, that is to say, in the heads of families assembled and met in council, and such governments are called Popular or Democratic.

VII. Other nations of a bolder turn, passing to the opposite extreme, have established Monarchy, <71> or the government of a single man. Thus Monarchy is a state in which the supreme power, and all the rights essential to it, reside in a single person, who is called *King, Monarch,* or *Emperor.*

VIII. Others have kept a due medium between those two extremes, and lodged the whole sovereign authority in a council composed of select members, and this is termed an Aristocracy, or the government of the Nobles.

IX. Lastly, other nations have been persuaded, that it was necessary, by a mixture of the simple forms, to establish a compound government, and, making a division[2] of the sovereignty, to entrust the different parts of it into different hands; to temper, for example, Monarchy with Aristocracy; and at the same time to give the people a share in the sovereignty: this may be executed different ways.

1. This distinction is discussed in DNG VII.5 §§12–13, where Pufendorf explains his preference for the terms "regular"/"irregular." Burlamaqui's discussion of the three simple forms of government summarizes DNG VII.5 §4 onward.
2. Read: ". . . of making a kind of division of the sovereignty . . ." ("une espèce de partage").

X. In order to have a more particular knowledge of the nature of these different forms of government, we must observe, that as in Democracies the sovereign is a moral person, formed by the reunion of all the heads of families into a single will, there are three things absolutely necessary for the constitution of this form of government.

1°. That there be a certain place, and regulated times for deliberating in common on the public affairs; the members of the sovereign council might assemble at different times, or places, whence factions <72> would arise, which would interrupt the union essential to the state.

2°. It must be established for a rule, that the plurality of suffrages shall pass for the will of the whole; otherwise no affair could be determined, it being impossible that a great number of people should be always of the same opinion. We must therefore esteem it the essential quality of a moral body, that the resolution of the majority shall pass for the will of the whole.

3°. Lastly, it is essential that magistrates should be appointed to convene the people in extraordinary cases, to dispatch ordinary affairs, in their name, and to see that the decrees of the assembly be executed; for since the sovereign council cannot always sit, it is evident that it cannot take the direction of every thing itself.

XI. With regard to Aristocracies, since the sovereignty resides in a council or senate, composed of the principal men of the nation, it is absolutely necessary that the conditions essential to the constitution of a Democracy, and which we have above mentioned, should also concur to establish an Aristocracy.

XII. Further, Aristocracy may be of two kinds, either by birth and hereditary, or elective. The Aristocracy by birth, and hereditary, is that which is confined to a certain number of families, to which birth alone gives right, and which passes from parents to their children, without any choice, and to the <73> exclusion of all others. On the contrary, the elective Aristocracy is that in which a person arrives at the government by election only, and without receiving any right from birth.

XIII. In a word, it may be equally observed of Aristocracies and Democracies, that, whether in a popular state, or in a government of the nobles, every citizen, or every member of the supreme council, has not the supreme power, nor even a part of it; but this power resides either in the general assembly of the people, convened according to the laws, or in the council of the nobles; for it is one thing to have a share in the sovereignty, and another to have the right of suffrage in an assembly invested with the sovereign power.

XIV. As to Monarchy, it is established when the whole body of the people confer the sovereign power on a single person, which is done by an agreement betwixt the king and his subjects, as we have before explained.

XV. There is therefore this essential difference between Monarchy and the two other forms of government, that, in Democracies and Aristocracies, the actual exercise of the sovereign authority depends on the concurrence of certain circumstances of time and place; whereas in a Monarchy, at least when it is simple and absolute, the prince can give his orders at all times, and in all places: *It is Rome wherever the Emperor resides.*[3] <74>

XVI. Another remark, which very naturally occurs on this occasion, is, that in a Monarchy, when the king orders any thing contrary to justice and equity, he is certainly to blame, because in him the civil and natural wills are the same thing. But when the assembly of the people, or a senate, form an unjust resolution, only those citizens or senators, who carried the point, render themselves really accountable, and not those who were of the opposite sentiment.[4] Let this suffice for the simple forms of government.

3. For Pufendorf, this is a reason for preferring monarchy to other forms of government; see DNG VII.5 §9.

4. This point and the distinction between natural and civil will were made by Hobbes, quoted by Pufendorf in DNG VII.5 §9 in fine. Barbeyrac and Burlamaqui used "volonté physique" for the former.

XVII. As to mixed or compound governments, they are established, as we have observed, by the concurrence of the three simple forms, or only of two; when, for example, the king, the nobles, and the people, or only the two latter, share the different parts of the sovereignty between them, so that one administers some parts of it, and the others the remainder. This mixture may be made various ways, as we observe in most republics.

XVIII. It is true, to consider sovereignty in itself, and in the height of plenitude and perfection, all the rights, which it includes, ought to belong to a single person, or to one body, without any partition; so that there be but one supreme will to govern the subject. There cannot, properly speaking, be several sovereigns in a state, who shall act as they please, independently of each other. This is morally impossible, and besides would manifestly tend to the ruin and destruction of society. <75>

XIX. But this union of the supreme power does not hinder the whole body of the nation, in whom this power originally resides, from regulating the government by a fundamental law, in such a manner as to commit the exercise of the different parts of the supreme power to different persons or bodies, who may act independently of each other, in regard to the rights committed to them, but still subordinate to the laws from which those rights are derived.

XX. And provided the fundamental laws, which establish this species of partition in the sovereignty, regulate the respective limits of the different branches of the legislature, so that we may easily see the extent of their jurisdiction; this partition produces neither a plurality of sovereigns, nor an opposition between them, nor any irregularity in the government.[5]

---

5. In the following paragraphs, Burlamaqui strives to prove this claim, which is contrary to Pufendorf's view. To show that a mixed state does not need to be an irregular state, Burlamaqui must argue that the sovereign power remains essentially undivided even when, as in Geneva, the sovereign power is exercised by two distinct instances (or even three: Geneva was ruled in the eighteenth century by the small council of twenty-five, the council of two hundred, and the general council of all citizens).

XXI. In a word, in this case there is, properly speaking, but one sovereign, who in himself is possessed of the fulness of power. There is but one supreme will. This sovereign is the body of the people, formed by the union of all the orders of the state; and this supreme will is the very law, by which the whole body of the nation makes its resolutions known.

XXII. They, who thus share the sovereignty among them, are properly no more than the executors of the law, since it is from the law itself that they hold their power. And as these fundamental <76> laws are real covenants, or what the civilians call *pacta conventa,* between the different orders of the republic,* by which they mutually stipulate, that each shall have such a particular part of the sovereignty, and that this shall establish the form of government, it is evident that, by these means, each of the contracting parties acquires a right not only of exercising the power granted to it, but also of preserving that original right.

XXIII. Such party cannot even be divested of its right in spite of itself, and by the will of the rest, so long at least as it conducts itself in a manner conformable to the laws, and not manifestly opposite to the public welfare.[6]

XXIV. In a word, the constitution of those governments can be changed only in the same manner, and by the same methods, by which it was established, that is to say, by the unanimous concurrence of all the contracting parties who have fixed the form of government by the original contract.

---

* See part i. chap. vii. No. 35, &c. [in this second volume, i.e., *The Principles of Politic Law,* (henceforth *PPL*).]

6. The translator omits some words here. Burlamaqui holds that the party cannot be divested of its right "by the sole will of the others, so long at least as it wields this right in a manner that accords with the laws, or that is not manifestly or totally contrary to the public welfare." The translation loses sight of both the fact that the party in question (Burlamaqui is here thinking of the small council) can indeed be divested of its power by the will of the rest, although not at any time and in any way whatsoever (not by the "sole" will, as it were, of the rest), and of the fact that this can happen only when the party's actions are not only against the law but also manifestly or totally against the welfare of the people.

XXV. This constitution of the state by no means destroys the union of a moral body composed of several persons, or of several bodies, really distinct in themselves, but joined by a fundamental law in a mutual engagement.[7]

XXVI. From what has been said on the nature of mixed or compound governments it follows, that in all such states, the sovereignty is limited; for as <77> the different branches are not committed to a single person, but lodged in different hands, the power of those, who have a share in the government, is thereby restrained; and as they are thus a check to each other, this produces such a balance of authority, as secures the public weal, and the liberty of individuals.

XXVII. But with respect to simple governments; in these the sovereignty may be either absolute or limited. Those who are possessed of the sovereignty, exercise it sometimes in an absolute, and sometimes in a limited manner, by fundamental laws, which prescribe bounds to the sovereign, with regard to the manner in which he ought to govern.

XXVIII. On this occasion it is expedient to observe, that all the accidental circumstances, which can modify simple Monarchies or Aristocracies, and which, in some measure, may be said to limit sovereignty, do not, for that reason, change the form of government, which still continues the same. One government may partake somewhat of another, when the manner, in which the sovereign governs, seems to be borrowed from the form of the latter; but it does not, for that reason, change its nature.

XXIX. For example, in a Democratic state, the people may entrust the care of several affairs either to a principal member, or to a senate. In an

---

7. The translation omits some words. The sentence should begin: "This economy of government, this constitution of the state. . . ." The end of the sentence should read: ". . . but joined together by a reciprocal agreement, by a fundamental law, which makes them into one whole."

Aristocracy, there may be a chief magistrate invested with a particular authority, or an assembly of the people to be consulted on some occasions. Or lastly, in a Mo-<78>narchic state, important affairs may be laid before a senate, &c. But these accidental circumstances do by no means change the form of the government; neither is there a partition of the sovereignty on this account; the state still continues purely either Democratic, Aristocratic, or Monarchic.

XXX. In a word, there is a wide difference between exercising a proper power, and acting by a foreign and precarious authority, which may every minute be taken away by him who conferred it. Thus what constitutes the characteristic of mixed or compound commonwealths, and distinguishes them from simple governments, is, that the different orders of the state, who have a share in the sovereignty, possess the rights which they exercise by an equal title, that is to say, in virtue of the fundamental law, and not under the title of commission, as if the one was only the minister or executor of the other's will. We must therefore be sure to distinguish between the form of government, and the manner of governing.

XXXI. These are the principal observations with respect to the various forms of government. Puffendorf explains himself in a somewhat different manner, and calls those governments irregular, which we have stiled mixed; and he gives the name of regular to the simple governments.*

XXXII. But this regularity is only in idea; the true rule of practice ought to be that which is most conformable to the end of civil society, supposing <79> men to be in their usual state, and taking the general course of things into the account, according to the experience of all countries and ages. Now on this footing, the states, in which the whole depends on a single will, are so far from being[8] happy, that it is certain their sub-

---

* See Law of nature and nations, book vii. chap. v. [Apart from the important discussion of mixed governments, most of this chapter is quite close to Pufendorf's text.]

8. Read: "so far from being the most happy, that . . ."

jects have the most frequent reason to lament the loss of their natural independency.

XXXIII. Besides, it is with the body politic, as with the human body; there is a difference between a sound and a cachectic state.

XXXIV. These disorders arise either from the abuse of the sovereign power, or from the bad constitution of the state; and the causes thereof are to be sought for either in the defects of the governors, or in those of the government itself.

XXXV. In Monarchies, the defects of the person are, when the king has not the qualifications necessary for reigning, when he has little or no attachment to the public good, and when he delivers his subjects up as a prey, either to the avarice or ambition of his ministers, &c.

XXXVI. With regard to Aristocracies, the defects of the persons are, when, by intrigue and other sinister methods, they introduce into the council, either wicked men, or such as are incapable of business, while persons of merit are excluded; when factions and cabals are formed; and when the nobles treat the populace as slaves, &c. <80>

XXXVII. In fine, we sometimes see also in Democracies, that their assemblies are disturbed with intestine broils, and merit is oppressed by envy, &c.

XXXVIII. In regard to the defects of government, they are of various kinds. For example, if the laws of the state be not conformable to the natural genius of the people,[9] tending to engage in a war a nation, that is not naturally warlike, but inclined to the peaceful arts; or if not, they

---

9. Read: "if they tend, for example, to engage in a war . . ." and later "if its laws are not agreeable to the situation and the qualities of the country, one does badly, for example . . . ." This is not a particularly well-built sentence in the original, but it remains coherent as a list of different examples of bad government.

should be agreeable to the situation and the natural products of the country; thus it is bad conduct, not to promote commerce and manufactures, in a province well situated for that purpose, and abounding with the materials of trade. It is also a defect of government, if the constitution of the state renders the dispatch of affairs very slow or difficult, as in Poland, where the opposition of a single member dissolves the diet.

XXXIX. It is customary to give particular names to these defects in government. Thus the corruption of Monarchy is called Tyranny. Oligarchy is the abuse of Aristocracy; and the abuse of Democracy is called Ochlocracy. But it often happens that these words denote less a defect or disorder in the state, than some particular passion or disgust in those who use them.

XL. To conclude this chapter, we have only to take some notice of those compound forms of government[10] which are formed by the union of several particular states. These may be defined an assem-<81>blage of perfect governments strictly united by some particular bond, so that they seem to make but a single body with respect to the affairs which interest them in common, though each preserves its sovereignty full and entire, independently of the others.

XLI. This assemblage is formed either by the union of two or more distinct states, under one and the same king; as for instance, England, Scotland, and Ireland, before the union lately made between England and Scotland; or when several independent states agree among themselves to form but a single body: such are the united provinces of the Netherlands, and the Swiss cantons.

XLII. The first kind of union may happen, either by marriage, or by succession, or when a people chuse for their king the sovereign of an-

---

10. The original has "états" ("states") rather than "governments." Further down in this paragraph, the translator omits "in other respects" ("d'ailleurs") from the sentence "though each preserves its sovereignty full and entire in other respects, independently of the others."

other country; so that those different states come to be united under a prince who governs each in particular by its fundamental laws.

XLIII. As to the compound governments, formed by the perpetual confederacy of several states, it is to be observed, that this is the only method by which several small governments, too weak to maintain themselves separately against their enemies, are enabled to preserve their liberties.[11]

XLIV. These confederate states engage to each other only to exercise, with common consent, certain parts of the sovereignty, especially those which relate to their mutual defence against foreign enemies. <82> But each of the confederates retains an entire liberty of exercising, as it thinks proper, those parts of the sovereignty, which are not mentioned in the treaty of union, as parts that ought to be exercised in common.

XLV. Lastly, it is absolutely necessary, in confederate states, to ascertain a time and place for assembling when occasion requires, and to invest some member with a power of convening the assembly for extraordinary affairs, and such as will not admit of delay. Or they may establish a perpetual assembly, composed of the deputies of each state, for dispatching common affairs according to the orders of their superiors.

CHAPTER II

An essay on this question, Which is the best form
of government?

I. It is certainly one of the most important questions in politics, and has most exercised the men of genius, to determine *the best form of government.*

II. Every form of government has its advantages and inconveniencies inseparable from it. It would be in vain to seek for a government abso-

---

11. ". . . preserve their liberty" ("liberté").

lutely perfect; and however perfect it might appear in speculation, yet it is certain, that in practice, and under the ad-<83>ministration of men, it will ever be attended with some particular defects.

III. But though we cannot arrive at the summit of perfection in this respect, it is nevertheless certain, that there are different degrees, which prudence must determine. That government ought to be accounted the most complete, which best answers the end of its institution, and is attended with fewest inconveniencies. Be this as it may, the examination of this question furnishes very useful instructions both to subjects and sovereigns.

IV. Disputes on this subject are of a very ancient date; and there is nothing more interesting upon the topic, than what we read in the father of history, Herodotus, who relates what passed in the council of the seven chiefs of Persia, when the government was to be re-established after the death of Cambyses, and the punishment of the Magus, who had usurped the throne under the pretext of being Smerdis the son of Cyrus.[1]

V. Otanes was of opinion, that Persia should be formed into a republic, and spoke nearly in the following strain. "I am not of opinion that we should lodge the government in the hands of a single person. You know to what excess Cambyses proceeded, and to what degree of insolence the Magus arrived: how can the state be well governed in a monarchy, where a single person is permitted to act according to his pleasure? <84> An authority uncontrolled corrupts the most virtuous man, and defeats his best qualities. Envy and insolence flow from riches and prosperity; and all other vices are derived from those two sources.[2] Kings hate virtuous

---

1. There is a reference to Herodotus's account of this discussion in DNG VII.5 §22, where Pufendorf provides a very brief discussion of the best form of government. In the present chapter Burlamaqui does not follow Pufendorf but provides a justification of the Genevan (mixed) system.

2. The translator omits the end of the sentence: ". . . when one is master over all things."

men who oppose their unjust designs, but caress the wicked who favour them. A single person cannot see every thing with his own eyes; he often lends a favourable ear to false accusations; he subverts the laws and customs of the country; he attacks the chastity of women, and wantonly puts the innocent to death. When the people have the government in their own hands, the equality among the members prevents all those evils. The magistrates are, in this case, chosen by lot; they render an account of their administration, and they form all their resolutions in common with the people. I am therefore of opinion, that we ought to reject Monarchy and introduce a popular government, because we rather find these advantages in a multitude, than in a single person." Such was the harangue of Otanes.

VI. But Megabyses spoke in favour of Aristocracy. "I approve (said he) of the opinion of Otanes with respect to exterminating Monarchy, but I believe he is wrong in endeavouring to persuade us to trust the government to the discretion of the people;[3] for surely nothing can be imagined more stupid and insolent than the giddy multitude. Why should we reject the power of a single man, to deliver up ourselves to the tyranny of a blind and disorderly populace? If a king sets about <85> an enterprize, he is at least capable of listening to advice; but the people are a blind monster, devoid of reason and capacity. They are strangers to decency, virtue, and their own interests. They do every thing precipitately, without judgment, and without order, resembling a rapid torrent, which cannot be stemmed. If therefore you desire the ruin of the Persians, establish a popular government. As to myself, I am of opinion, that we should make choice of virtuous men, and lodge the government in their hands." Such was the sentiment of Megabyses.

VII. After him, Darius spoke in the following terms. "I am of opinion, that there is a great deal of good sense in the speech which Megabyses has made against a popular state; but I also think, that he is not entirely

---

3. Here the translator gives "people" for "multitude" and "giddy multitude" for "rabble" ("populace").

in the right, when he prefers the government of a small number to Monarchy. It is certain, that nothing can be imagined better, or more perfect, than the administration of a virtuous man. Besides, when a single man is master, it is more difficult for the enemy to discover his secret counsels and resolutions. When the government is in the hands of many, it is impossible but enmity and hatred must arise among them; for as every one desires his opinion to be followed, they gradually become mutual enemies. Emulation and jealousy divide them, and then their aversions run to excess. From hence arise seditions; from seditions, murders; and from murders, a monarch insensibly becomes necessary. Thus the government at length is sure to fall <86> into the hands of a single person. In a popular state, there must needs be a great store of malice and corruption. It is true, equality does not generate hatred; but it foments friendship among the wicked, who support each other, till some person or other, who by his behaviour has acquired an authority over the multitude, discovers the frauds, and exposes the perfidy of those villains. Such a man shews himself really a monarch; and hence we know that Monarchy is the most natural government, since the seditions of Aristocracy, and the corruption of Democracy, are equal inducements for our uniting the supreme power in the hands of a single person."

The opinion of Darius was approved, and the government of Persia continued monarchic. We thought this passage of history sufficiently interesting to be related on this occasion.

VIII. To determine this question, we must trace matters to their very source. Liberty, under which we must comprehend all the most valuable enjoyments,[4] has two enemies in civil society. The first is licentiousness, and confusion; and the second is oppression arising from tyranny.

IX. The first of those evils arises from liberty itself, when it is not kept within due bounds.

The second is owing to the remedy which mankind have contrived against the former evil, that is, to sovereignty. <87>

---

4. The translator gives "enjoyment" for Burlamaqui's simple "goods" ("biens").

X. The height of human felicity and prudence is to know how to guard against those two enemies: the only method is to have a well-constituted government,[5] formed with such precautions, as to banish licentiousness, and yet be no way introductive to tyranny.

XI. It is this happy temperament that alone can give us the idea of a good government. It is evident, that the political constitution which avoids those extremes, is so justly adapted for the preservation of order,[6] and for providing against the necessities of the people, that it leaves them a sufficient security, that this end shall be perpetually held in view.

XII. But here we shall be asked, Which government is it that approaches nearest to this perfection? Before we answer this question, it is proper to observe, that it is very different from our being asked, Which is the most legitimate government?

XIII. As for the latter question, it is certain, that governments of every kind, which are founded on the free acquiescence of the people, whether express or justified by a long and peaceable possession, are all equally legitimate, so long at least as, by the intention of the sovereign, they tend to promote the happiness of the people: thus no other cause can subvert a government, but an open and actual violence, either in its establishment, or in its exercise; I mean usurpation, or tyranny. <88>

XIV. To return to the principal question, I affirm, that the best government is neither absolute Monarchy, nor that which is entirely popular: the former is too violent,[7] encroaches on liberty, and inclines too much to tyranny; the latter is too weak, leaves the people too much to themselves, and tends to confusion and licentiousness.

---

5. Read: ". . . a sovereign in the true sense of the word, a government formed with such precautions, . . ."

6. Read: ". . . preservation of order internally and externally, that it leaves at the same time to the people sufficient guarantees, that this end . . ."

7. Burlamaqui writes ". . . the former is too harsh [fort], encroaches too heavily on liberty . . ."

XV. It were to be wished, for the glory of sovereigns and for the happiness of the people, that we could contest the fact above asserted with respect to absolute governments. We may venture to affirm, that nothing can be compared to an absolute government, in the hands of a wise and virtuous prince. Order, diligence, secrecy,[8] expedition, the greatest enterprizes, and the most happy execution, are the certain effects of it. Dignities, honours, rewards and punishments, are all dispensed under it with justice and discernment. So glorious a reign is the era of the golden age.

XVI. But to govern in this manner, a superior genius, perfect virtue, great experience, and uninterrupted application, are necessary. Man, in so high an elevation, is rarely capable of so many accomplishments. The multitude of objects diverts his attention, pride seduces him, pleasure tempts him, and flattery, the bane of the great, does him more injury than all the rest. It is difficult to escape so many snares; and it generally happens, that an absolute prince becomes an easy prey to his passions, and consequently renders his subjects miserable. <89>

XVII. Hence proceeds the disgust of people to absolute governments, and this disgust sometimes is worked up to aversion and hatred. This has also given occasion to politicians to make two important reflections.

The first is, that, in an absolute government, it is rare to see the people interest themselves in its preservation. Oppressed with their burdens, they long for a revolution, which cannot render their situation more uncomfortable.

The second is, that it is the interest of princes to engage the people in the support of their government, and to give them a share therein, by privileges tending to secure their liberty. This is the best expedient to promote the safety of princes at home, together with their power abroad, and their glory in every respect.

---

8. The translator omits one characteristic in Burlamaqui's list of the wonders of absolute government: subordination.

XVIII. It has been said of the Romans, that, so long as they fought for their own interests, they were invincible; but, as soon as they became slaves under absolute masters, their courage failed, and they asked for no more than bread and public diversions, *panem & circenses.*

XIX. On the contrary, in states where the people have some share in the government, every individual interests himself in the public good, because each, according to his quality or merit, partakes of the general success, or feels the loss sustained by the state. This is what renders men active and generous, what inspires them with an ardent love of their country, and with an invincible courage, so as to be proof against the greatest misfortunes. <90>

XX. When Hannibal had gained four victories over the Romans, and killed more than two hundred thousand of that nation, when, much about the same time, the two brave Scipios perished in Spain, not to mention several considerable losses at sea, and in Sicily, who could have thought that Rome could have withstood her enemies? Yet the virtue of her citizens, the love they bore their country, and the interest they had in the government, augmented the strength of that republic in the midst of her calamities, and at last she surmounted every difficulty. Among the Lacedaemonians and Athenians we find several examples to the same point.

XXI. These advantages are not found in absolute governments. We may justly affirm, that it is an essential defect in them not to interest the people in their preservation, that they are too violent,[9] tending too much to oppression, and very little to the good of the subject.

XXII. Such are absolute governments: those of the popular kind are no better, and we may say they have no advantage but liberty, and their leaving the people at their option to choose a better.

---

9. For "violent" read "harsh" or "hard" ("fort").

XXIII. Absolute governments have at least two advantages: the first is, that they have happy intervals when in the hands of good princes: the second is, that they have a greater degree of force, activity, and expedition.

XXIV. But a popular government has none of those <91> advantages; formed by the multitude, it bears a strong resemblance to that many-headed monster. The multitude is a mixture of all kinds of people; it contains a few men of parts, some of whom may have honest intentions; but far the greater number cannot be depended on, as they have nothing to lose, and consequently can hardly be trusted. Besides, a multitude always acts with slowness and confusion. Secrecy and precaution are advantages unknown to them.

XXV. Liberty is not wanting in popular states; nay, they have rather too much of it, since it degenerates into licentiousness. Hence it is that they are ever tottering and weak. Intestine commotions, or foreign attacks, often throw them into consternation: it is their ordinary fate to fall a prey to the ambition of their fellow-citizens, or to foreign usurpation, and thus to pass from the highest liberty to the lowest slavery.

XXVI. This is proved by the experience of different nations. Even at present, Poland is a striking example of the defects of popular government, from the anarchy and disorder which reigns in that republic. It is the sport of its own inhabitants and of foreign nations, and is frequently the seat of intestine war; because, under the appearance of Monarchy, it is indeed too popular a government.[10]

XXVII. We need only read the histories of Florence and Genoa, to behold a lively exhibition of the misfortunes which republics suffer from the mul-<92>titude, when the latter attempt to govern. The ancient re-

---

10. The example of Poland is discussed in Barbeyrac in DHC II.8 §10 note 5 but without any emphatic rejection of democratic or "popular" government.

publics, especially Athens, the most considerable in Greece, are capable of setting this truth in a stronger light.

XXVIII. In a word, Rome perished in the hands of the people; and monarchy gave birth to it. The patricians, who composed the senate, by freeing it from the regal dignity, had rendered it mistress of Italy. The people, by the encroachment of the tribunes, gradually usurped the authority of the senate. From that time discipline was relaxed, and gave place to licentiousness. At length the republic was reduced, by the people themselves, to the most abject slavery.

XXIX. It is not therefore to be doubted, but popular governments are the weakest and worst of all others. If we consider the education of the vulgar, their laborious employments, their ignorance and brutality, we must quickly perceive, that they are made to be governed; and that good order, and their own advantage, forbid them to interfere with that province.[11]

XXX. If therefore neither the government of the multitude, nor the absolute will of a single person, are fit to procure the happiness of a nation,[12] it follows, that the best governments are those which are so tempered, as to secure the happiness of the subjects, by avoiding tyranny and licentiousness.

XXXI. There are two ways of finding this temperament. <93>
    The first consists in lodging the sovereignty in a council so composed, both as to the number and choice of persons, that there shall be a moral certainty of their having no other interests than those of the community, and of their being always ready to give a faithful account of their conduct. This is what we see happily practised in most republics.

---

11. Read: ". . . forbid them from taking upon themselves that task."
12. For "nation" read "people" ("peuple").

XXXII. The second is, to limit the sovereignty of the prince in monarchic states, by fundamental laws, or to invest the person, who enjoys the honours and title of sovereignty, with only a part of the supreme authority, and to lodge the other in different hands, for example, in a council or parliament. This is what gives birth to limited monarchies.*

XXXIII. With regard to Monarchies, it is proper, for example, that the military and legislative powers, together with that of raising taxes, should be lodged in different hands, to the end that they may not be easily abused. It is easy to conceive, that these restrictions may be made different ways. The general rule, which prudence directs, is to limit the power of the prince, so that no danger may be apprehended from it; but at the same time not to carry things to excess, for fear of weakening the government.

XXXIV. By following this just medium, the people will enjoy the most perfect liberty, since they have all the moral securities that the prince will not abuse his power. The prince, on the other hand, <94> being, as it were, under a necessity of doing his duty, considerably strengthens his authority, and enjoys a high degree of happiness and solid glory; for as the felicity of the people is the end of government, it is also the surest foundation of the throne. See what has been already said on this subject.

XXXV. This species of Monarchy, limited by a mixed government, unites the principal advantages of absolute Monarchy, and of the Aristocratic and popular governments; at the same time it avoids the dangers and inconveniencies peculiar to each. This is the happy temperament which we have been endeavouring to find.

XXXVI. The truth of this remark has been proved by the experience of past ages. Such was the government of Sparta: Lycurgus, knowing that each of the three sorts of simple governments had very great inconveniencies; that Monarchy easily fell into arbitrary power and tyranny; that

* See part i. chap. vii. § 26, &c. [*PPL.*]

Aristocracy degenerated into the oppressive government of a few individuals, and Democracy into a wild and lawless dominion, thought it expedient to combine those three governments in that of Sparta, and mix them, as it were, into one, so that they might serve as a remedy and counterpoise to each other. This wise legislator was not deceived, and no republic preserved its laws, customs, and liberty, longer than that of Sparta.

XXXVII. It may be said, that the government of the Romans, under the republic, united in some mea-<95>sure, as that of Sparta, the three species of authority. The consuls held the place of kings, the senate formed the public council, and the people had also some share in the administration.

XXXVIII. If modern examples are wanted, is not England at present a proof of the excellency of mixed governments?[13] Is there a nation, every thing considered, that enjoys a higher degree of prosperity or reputation?

XXXIX. The northern nations, which subverted the Roman empire, introduced into the conquered provinces that species of government, which was then called Gothic. They had kings, lords, and commons; and experience shews, that the states, which have retained that species of government, have flourished more than those which have devolved the whole government into the hands of a single person.

XL. As to Aristocratic governments, we must first distinguish Aristocracy by birth, from that which is elective. The former has several advantages, but is also attended with very great inconveniencies. It inspires the nobility with pride, and entertains, between the grandees and the people, division, contempt, and jealousy, which are productive of considerable evils.

13. Read: ". . . governments, and of limited monarchy?"

XLI. But the latter has all the advantages of the former, without its defects. As there is no privilege of exclusion, and as the door to preferment is open to all the citizens, we find neither pride nor di-<96>vision among them. On the contrary, a general emulation glows in the breasts of all the members, converting every thing to the public good, and contributing infinitely to the preservation of liberty.

XLII. Thus if we suppose an elective Aristocracy, in which the sovereignty is in the hands of a council so numerous, as to comprehend the chief property[14] of the republic, and never to have any interest opposite to that of the state. If besides, this council be so small, as to maintain order, harmony and secrecy; if it be chosen from among the wisest, and most virtuous citizens; and lastly, if its authority be limited and kept within rule,[15] there can be no doubt but such a government is very well adapted to promote the happiness of a nation.

XLIII. The most difficult point in these governments, is to temper them in such a manner, that, while the people are assured of their liberty, by giving them some share in the government, these assurances shall not be carried too far, so as to make the government approach too near to Democracy: for the preceding reflections sufficiently evince the inconveniencies which would result from this step.

XLIV. Let us therefore conclude, from this inquiry into the different forms of government, that the best are either a limited Monarchy, or an Aristocracy tempered with Democracy, by some privileges in favour of the body of the people.

14. The translation is interpretative here. Burlamaqui writes: "a council sufficiently numerous to comprehend the most important interests of the nation, & never to have interests opposed to these." The translator could be right that Burlamaqui is thinking mainly of economic interests.

15. The translator omits ". . . by reserving to the people some portion of the sovereignty, . . ."

XLV. It is true, there are always some deductions <97> to be made from the advantages which we have ascribed to those governments; but this is owing to the infirmity of human nature, and not to the establishments. The constitution above described is the most perfect that can be imagined, and if we adulterate it by our vices and follies, this is the fate of all sublunary affairs; and since a choice must be made, the best is that attended with the fewest inconveniencies.

XLVI. In a word, should it still be asked, which government is best? I would answer, that every species of government is not equally proper for every nation, and that, in this point, we must have a regard to the humour and character of the people, and to the extent of the country.

XLVII. Great states can hardly admit of republican governments; hence a monarchy, wisely limited, suits them better. But as to states, of an ordinary extent, the most advantageous government for them, is an elective aristocracy, tempered with some privileges in favour of the body of the people.

CHAPTER III

Of the different ways of acquiring sovereignty.

I. The only just foundation of all acquisition of sovereignty, is the consent, or will of the people.* But as this consent may be given different <98> ways, according to the different circumstances attending it; hence we distinguish the several ways of acquiring sovereignty.[1]

II. Sometimes a people are constrained, by force of arms, to submit to the dominion of a conqueror; at other times, the people, of their own accord, confer the supreme authority on some particular person. Sov-

---

* On this subject, see part i. chap. vi. [*PPL.*]
    1. The first three paragraphs are based on DHC II.10 §1, the fourth repeats §2, the fifth repeats §3.

ereignty may therefore be acquired either by force and violence, or in a free and voluntary manner.

III. These different acquisitions of sovereignty may agree in some measure to all sorts of governments; but as they are most remarkable in monarchies, it shall be principally with respect to the latter, that we shall examine this question.

1°. *Of conquest.*

IV. Sovereignty is sometimes acquired by force, or rather is seized by conquest or usurpation.

V. Conquest is the acquisition of sovereignty, by the superiority of a foreign prince's arms, who reduces the vanquished to submit to his government. Usurpation is properly made by a person naturally submitted to him from whom he wrests the supreme power; but custom often confounds these two terms.[2]

VI. There are several remarks to be made on conquest, considered as a method of acquiring the sovereignty. <99>
    1°. Conquest, in itself, is rather the occasion of acquiring the sovereignty, than the immediate cause of this acquisition. The immediate cause is the consent of the people, either tacit or expressed. Without this consent the state of war always subsists between two enemies, and one is not obliged to obey the other. All that can be said is, that the consent of the vanquished is extorted by the superiority of the conqueror.

VII. 2°. Lawful conquest supposes, that the conqueror has had just reason to wage war against the vanquished. Without this, conquest is by no means, of itself, a just title; for a man cannot acquire a sovereignty over a nation, by bare seizure, as over a thing which belongs to no proprietor.

2. This paragraph and the three following are based on DNG VII.7 §3; see also DHC II.10 §2.

Thus when Alexander waged war against distant nations, who had never heard of his name, certainly such a conquest was no more a lawful title to the sovereignty over those people, than robbery is a lawful manner of becoming rich. The quality and number of the persons do not change the nature of the action, the injury is the same, and the crime equal.

VIII. But if the war be just, the conquest is also the same: for, in the first place, it is a natural consequence of the victory; and the vanquished, who deliver themselves to the conqueror, only purchase their lives by the loss of their liberties. Besides, the vanquished having, through their own fault, engaged in an unjust war, rather than grant the satisfaction they owed, are supposed to have tacitly consented to the conditions which the con-<100>queror should impose on them, provided they were neither unjust nor inhuman.

IX. 3°. But what must we think of unjust conquests, and of submission extorted by mere violence? Can it give a lawful right? I answer, we should distinguish whether the usurper has changed the government from a republic into a monarchy, or dispossessed the lawful monarch. In the latter case, he is obliged to restore the crown to the right owner, or to his heirs, till it can be presumed that they have renounced their pretension; and this is always presumed, when a considerable time is elapsed without their being willing or able to make any effort to recover the crown.[3]

X. The law of nations therefore admits of a kind of prescription with respect to sovereignty. This is requisite for the interest and tranquillity of societies; a long and quiet possession of the supreme power, must establish the legality of it, otherwise there would never be an end of disputes in regard to kingdoms and their limits; this would be a source of perpetual quarrels, and there would hardly be any such thing as a sovereign lawfully possessed of the supreme authority.

---

3. This and the four following paragraphs are from DNG VII.7 §4.

XI. It is, indeed, the duty of the people, in the beginning, to resist the usurper with all their might, and to continue faithful to their prince; but if, in spite of their utmost efforts, their sovereign is defeated, and is no longer able to assert his right, <101> they are obliged to no more, but may lawfully take care of their own preservation.

XII. The people cannot live in a state of anarchy, and as they are not obliged to expose themselves to perpetual wars, in defence of the rights of their former sovereign, their consent may render the right of the usurper lawful;[4] and in this case the sovereign dethroned ought to rest contented with the loss of his dominions, and consider it as a misfortune.

XIII. With regard to the former case, when the usurper has changed the republic into a monarchy; if he governs with moderation and equity, it is sufficient that he has reigned peaceably for some time, to afford reason to believe, that the people consent to his dominion, and to efface what was defective in the manner of his acquiring it. This may be very well applied to the reign of Augustus. But if, on the contrary, the prince, who has made himself master of the republic, exercises his power in a tyrannical manner, and oppresses his subjects, they are not then obliged to obey him. In these circumstances the longest possession imports no more than a long continuation of injustice.

2°. Of the election of sovereigns.

XIV. But the most legitimate way of acquiring sovereignty, is founded on the free consent of the people. This is effected either by the way of election, or by the right of succession; for which reason kingdoms are distinguished into elective and hereditary.[5] <102>

---

4. Read: ". . . they may by their consent render the right of the usurper lawful . . ." If they do give their consent, then the usurper not only may but in fact does become lawful, on Burlamaqui's principles. The people have a right to give their consent to the usurper's rule in order to avoid "perpetual wars."

5. For this and the next paragraph, see DHC II.10 §3 and DNG VII.7 §6.

XV. Election is that act, by which the people design or nominate a certain person, whom they judge capable of succeeding the deceased king, to govern the state; and so soon as this person has accepted the offer of the people, he is invested with the sovereignty.

XVI. We may distinguish two sorts of elections, one entirely free, and the other limited in certain respects; the former when the people can chuse whom they think proper, and the latter when they are obliged, for example, to chuse a person of a certain nation, a particular family, religion, &c. Among the ancient Persians, no man could be king unless he had been instructed by the Magi.*

XVII. The time between the death of the king and the election of his successor, is called an *Interregnum.*

XVIII. During the *Interregnum* the state is, as it were, an imperfect body without a head; yet the civil society is not dissolved. The sovereignty then returns to the people, who, till they chuse a new king to exercise it, have it even in their power to change the form of government.[6]

XIX. But it is a wise precaution, to prevent the troubles of an *Interregnum,* to nominate beforehand those, who, during that time, are to hold the reins of government. Thus in Poland the archbishop of <103> Gnesna, with the deputies of great and little Poland, are appointed for that purpose.[7]

XX. The persons, invested with this employment, are called *Regents of the kingdom;* and the Romans stiled them *Interreges.* They are temporary, and, as it were, provisional magistrates, who, in the name, and by the authority of the people, exercise the acts of sovereignty, so that they are

* See Cic. de Divin. lib. i. cap. iv.
6. Burlamaqui is less ambiguous about the power returning to the people than Pufendorf in DNG VII.7 §7, the paragraph on which Burlamaqui draws here.
7. This paragraph and the next are from DNG VII.7 §8.

obliged to give an account of their administration. This may suffice for
the way of election.

3°. *Of succession to the crown.*

XXI. The other manner of acquiring sovereignty, is the right of succession, by which princes, who have once acquired the crown, transmit it
to their successors.

XXII. It may seem at first that elective kingdoms have the advantage over
those which are hereditary, because, in the former, the subjects may always chuse a prince of merit, and capable of governing. However, experience shews, that, taking all things into the account, the way of succession is more conducive to the welfare of the state.

XXIII. For, 1°. by this method we avoid the vast inconveniencies, both
foreign and domestic, which arise from frequent elections. 2°. There is
less contention and uncertainty, with respect to the title of the successor.
3°. A prince, whose crown is hereditary, all other circumstances being
equal, will <104> take greater care of his kingdom, and spare his subjects
more, in hopes to leave the crown to his children, than if he only possessed it for life. 4°. A kingdom, where the succession is regulated, has
greater stability and force. It can form mightier projects, and pursue
them more vigorously, than if it were elective. 5°. In a word, the person
of the prince strikes the people with greater reverence, and they have
reason to hope, that the splendor of his descent, and the impressions of
his education, will inspire him with the necessary qualities for holding
the reins of government.[8]

XXIV. The order of succession is regulated either by the will of the last
king, or by that of the people.

---

8. From DNG VII.7 §12 in fine.

XXV. In kingdoms, truly patrimonial, every king has a right to regulate the succession, and to dispose of the crown as he has a mind; provided the choice he makes of his successor, and the manner in which he settles the state, be not manifestly opposite to the public good, which, even in patrimonial kingdoms, is ever the supreme law.[9]

XXVI. But if the king, prevented perhaps by death, has not named his successor, it seems natural to follow the laws or customs established in that country, concerning private inheritances, so far at least as the safety of the state will admit.* But it is certain that, in those cases, the most approved and powerful candidate will always carry it. <105>

XXVII. In kingdoms, which are not patrimonial, the people regulate the order of succession: and although they may establish the succession as they please, yet prudence requires they should follow the method most advantageous to the state, best adapted to maintain order and peace, and most expedient to promote the public security.

XXVIII. The usual methods are, a succession, simply hereditary, which follows nearly the rules of common inheritances; and the lineal succession, which receives more particular limitations.[10]

XXIX. The good of the state therefore requires that a succession, simply hereditary, should vary in several things from private inheritances.

   1°. The kingdom ought to remain indivisible, and not be shared among several heirs, in the same degree; for, in the first place, this would considerably weaken the state, and render it less proper to resist the attacks of a foreign enemy. Besides, the subjects, having different masters, would no longer be so closely united among themselves: and lastly, this might lay a foundation for intestine wars, as experience has too often evinced.[11]

---

* See the Law of nature and nations, book vii. chap. vii. § 11.
9. From DHC II.10 §6. Burlamaqui adds the clause concerning public good.
10. From DHC II.10 §8.
11. From DHC II.10 §9 and DNG VII.7 §12. The latter paragraph furnishes the material for the next eight paragraphs as well.

XXX. 2°. The crown ought to remain in the posterity of the first possessor, and not to pass to his relations in a collateral line, and much less
to those who have only connections of affinity with him. This is, no
doubt, the intention of a people who <106> have rendered the crown
hereditary in any one family. Thus, unless it is otherwise determined, in
default of the descendants of the first possessor, the right of disposing
of the kingdom returns to the nation.

XXXI. 3°. Those only ought to be admitted to the succession, who are
born of a marriage conformable to the laws of the nation. For this there
are several reasons. 1°. This was, no doubt, the intention of the people,
when they settled the crown on the descendants of the king. 2°. The
people have not the same respect for the king's natural or base sons, as
for his lawful children. 3°. The father of natural children is not known
for certain, there being no sure method of ascertaining the father of a
child born out of wedlock; and yet it is of the last importance that there
should be no doubt about the birth of those who are to reign, in order
to avoid the disputes which might embroil the kingdom. Hence it is,
that, in several countries, the queen is delivered in public, or in the presence of several persons.

XXXII. 4°. Adopted children, not being of the royal blood, are also excluded from the crown, which ought to revert to the people so soon as
the royal line fails.

XXXIII. 5°. Among those who are in the same degree, whether really or
by representation, the males are to be preferred to the females, because
they are presumed more proper for the command of armies, <107> and
for exercising the other functions of government.

XXXIV. 6°. Among several males, or several females in the same degree,
the eldest ought to succeed. It is birth which gives this right; for the
crown being at the same time indivisible and hereditary, the eldest, in
consequence of his birth, has a preference, of which the younger cannot
deprive him. But it is just that the eldest should give his brothers a suf-

ficiency to support themselves decently, and in a manner suitable to their rank. What is allotted them for this purpose is distinguished by the name of *Appennage.*

XXXV. 7°. Lastly, we must observe, that the crown does not pass to the successor in consequence of the pleasure of the deceased king, but by the will of the people, who have settled it on the royal family. Hence it follows, that the inheritance of the particular estate of the king, and that of the crown, are of a quite different nature, and have no connection with each other; so that, strictly speaking, the successor may accept of the crown, and refuse the private inheritance; and, in this case, he is not obliged to pay the debts due upon this particular estate.

XXXVI. But it is certain, that honour and equity hardly permit a prince, who ascends the throne, to use this right, and that, if he has the glory of his royal house at heart, he will, by oeconomy and frugality, be enabled to pay the debts of his predecessor. But this ought not to be done at the expence of the <108> public.[12] These are the rules of succession simply hereditary.

XXXVII. But since in this hereditary succession, where the next heir to the deceased king is called to the crown, terrible disputes may happen concerning the degree of proximity, when those who remain are a little distant from the common stem; several nations have established the lineal succession from branch to branch, the rules of which are these following.

1°. All those descended from the royal founder are accounted so many lines or branches, each of which has a right to the crown according to the degree of its proximity.

2°. Among those of this line, who are in the same degree, in the first place sex, and then age, gives the preference.

---

12. The translator omits the word "treasury" from "public treasury." The paragraph itself is based on Grotius in DGP II.7 §19, a passage referred to by Barbeyrac in note 6 to DNG VII.7 §12.

3°. We must not pass from one line to another, so long as there remains one of the preceding, even though there should be another line of relations nearer to the deceased king. For example: <109>

A king leaves three sons, Lewis, Charles, and Henry. The son of Lewis, who succeeds him, dies without children; Charles leaves a grandson; Henry is still living, and is the uncle of the deceased king; the grand-child of Charles is only his cousin-german: and yet this grand-child will have the crown, as being transmitted to him by his grand-father, whose line has excluded Henry and his descendants, till it be quite extinct.

4°. Every one has therefore a right to succeed in his rank, and transmits this right to his descendants, with the same order of succession, though he has never reigned himself; that is to say, the right of the deceased passes to the living, and that of the living to the deceased.

5°. If the last king has died without issue, we make choice of the nearest line to his, and so on.[13]

XXXVIII. There are two principal kinds of lineal <110> succession, namely, *Cognatic* and *Agnatic.* These names come from the Latin words *Cognati* and *Agnati,* the former of which, in the Roman law, signifies

13. This and the next three paragraphs are from DNG VII.7 §13.

the relations on the mother's side, and the latter those on the father's side.

XXXIX. The *Cognatic* lineal succession is that which does not exclude women from the succession, but only calls them after the males in the same line; so that, when only women remain, there is no transition made to another line, but the succession runs back to the female again, in case the males, who were superior or equal to them in other respects, shall happen to fail with all their descendants. This succession is also called *Castilian*. Hence it follows, that the daughter of the son of the last king, is preferred to the son of the daughter of the same prince, and the daughter of one of his brothers to the son of one of his sisters.

XL. The *Agnatic* lineal succession is that in which only the male issue of males succeeds, so that women, and all those descending from them, are perpetually excluded. It is also called the *French* succession. This exclusion of women and their descendants is principally established to hinder the crown from devolving to a foreign race, by the marriage of princesses of the blood royal.

XLI. These are the principal kinds of succession in use, and may be tempered in different manners by the people; but prudence directs us to prefer those which are subject to the least difficulty; and in this respect <111> the lineal succession has the advantage over that which is simply hereditary.

XLII. Several questions, equally curious and important, may be started with regard to the succession of kingdoms. On this subject the reader may consult Grotius.* We shall only examine, who has a right to decide the disputes that may arise between two or more pretenders to a crown?

1°. If the kingdom be patrimonial, and disputes arise after the death of the king, the best method is to refer the cause to arbitrators of the

---

* The Right of war and peace, book ii. chap. vii. § 25, &c. [Burlamaqui also draws on Barbeyrac's note 4 to DGP II.7 §27.]

royal family. The welfare and peace of the kingdom recommend this conduct.

2°. But if in kingdoms established by the voluntary act of the people, the dispute arises even in the king's life-time, he is not a competent judge of it; for then the people must have invested him with the power of regulating the succession according to his own pleasure, which is not to be supposed. It therefore belongs to the people to decide the dispute, either by themselves or by their representatives.

3°. The same holds true, if the dispute does not arise till after the death of the king: in this case it is either necessary to determine which of the pretenders is nearest to the deceased sovereign; and this is a matter of fact which the people only ought to determine, because they are principally interested in it.

4°. Or the point is to know, what degree, or line, ought to have the preference according to the order of succession established by the people; and then it is a matter of right. Now who can deter-<112>mine better this point than the people themselves, who have established the order of succession? Otherwise there would be no method of deciding the dispute but by force of arms, which would be entirely opposite to the good of the society.

XLIII. But to avoid every perplexity of this kind, it would be proper that the people should, by a fundamental law, expressly reserve to themselves the right of judging in the above cases. What has been said is sufficient on the different ways of acquiring sovereignty.

CHAPTER IV

Of the different ways of losing sovereignty.

I. Let us now enquire how sovereignty may be lost; and in this there is no great difficulty, after the principles we have established on the ways of acquiring it.[1]

---

1. For the first four paragraphs, see DGP II.7 §25 and Barbeyrac's notes 1 and 2 to the same.

II. Sovereignty may be lost by abdication, that is, when the reigning prince renounces the sovereignty, so far as it regards himself. Of this the history even of latter ages furnishes us with remarkable examples.

III. As sovereignty derives its original from a covenant between the king and his subjects; if, for plausible reasons, the king thinks proper to renounce the supreme dignity, the people have not properly a right to constrain him to keep it. <113>

IV. But such an abdication must not be made at an unseasonable juncture: as for instance, when the kingdom is like to sink into a minority, especially if it be threatened with a war; or when the prince, by his bad conduct, has thrown the state into a dangerous convulsion, in which he cannot abandon it without betraying his trust, and ruining his country.

V. But we may safely say, that a prince very rarely finds himself in such circumstances, as should engage him to renounce the crown. However his affairs may be situated, he may ease himself of the drudgery of government, and still retain the superior command. A king ought to die upon the throne; and it is a weakness unworthy of him, to divest himself of his authority. Besides, experience has shewn, that abdication is too frequently attended with unhappy catastrophes.[2]

VI. It is therefore certain, that a prince may, for himself, renounce the crown, or the right of succession. But there is great difficulty whether he can do it for his children.

VII. To judge rightly of this point, which has embarrassed so many politicians, we must establish the following principles.

1°. Every acquisition of right or power over another, and consequently of sovereignty, supposes the consent of him over whom this right is to be acquired, and the acceptance of him who is to acquire it. Till this acceptance is settled, the intention of the former does not produce, in

---

2. ". . . an unhappy and miserable end" (". . . une fin de vie triste & misérable").

favour of the latter, <114> an absolute and irrevocable right: It is only a simple designation, which he is at liberty to accept of or not.

VIII. 2°. Let us apply these principles. The princes of the blood royal, who have accepted the will of the people, by which the crown has been conferred on them, have certainly thereby acquired an absolute and irrevocable right, of which they cannot be stripped without their own consent.

IX. 3°. With regard to those who are not yet born, as they have not accepted of the designation of the people, they have not as yet acquired any right. Hence it follows, that, in relation to them, this designation is only an imperfect act, a kind of expectancy, the completion of which intirely depends on the will of the people.

X. 4°. But it may be said, the ancestors of those, who are not yet born, have consented and stipulated for them, and consequently received the engagement of the people in their behalf. But this is rather an argument in favour of renunciation, which it effectually establishes; for as the right of those, who are not yet born, has no other foundation than the concurrence of the will of the people and of their ancestors, it is evident that this right may be taken from them, without injustice, by those very persons, from the single will of whom they hold it.[3]

XI. 5°. The single will of a prince, without the consent of the nation, cannot effectually exclude his children from the crown to which the people have called them. In like manner, the single will of the <115> people, without the consent of the prince, cannot deprive his children of an expectancy which their father has stipulated with the people in their favour. But if these two wills unite, they may, without doubt, alter what they have established.

---

3. The argument is from DGP II.4 §10.

XII. 6°. It is true, this renunciation ought not to be made without a cause, and through inconstancy and levity. Under these circumstances it cannot be justified, and the good of the state does not permit, that, without necessity, an alteration should be made in the order of the succession.

XIII. 7°. If, on the other hand, the nation be so situated, that the renunciation of a prince, or a princess, is absolutely necessary to its tranquillity and happiness, then the supreme law of the public good, which has established the order of the succession, requires it should be set aside.

XIV. 8°. Let us add, that it is for the general good of nations, such renunciations be valid, and the parties interested should not attempt to disannul them. For there are times and conjunctures in which they are necessary for the welfare of the state; and if those with whom we are treating, should come to think that the renunciation would afterwards be set aside, they certainly would have nothing to do with us. Now this must be productive of bloody and cruel wars. Grotius decides this question nearly in the same manner. The reader may see what he says of it.*
<116>

XV. 9°. Since war or conquest is a method of acquiring sovereignty, as we have seen in the preceding chapter, it is evidently also a means of losing it.

XVI. With regard to tyranny and the deposing of sovereigns, both which are also ways of losing the supreme power, as these two articles bear some relation to the duties of subjects towards their sovereigns, we shall treat of them in the next chapter more particularly, after we have considered those duties.

---

* Book ii. chap. vii. § 26. and book ii. chap. iv. § 10. [The text in Burlamaqui's paragraph is from Barbeyrac's footnote 2 to DGP II.7 §26.]

CHAPTER V

Of the duties of subjects in general.

I. According to the plan we have laid down, we must here treat of the duties of subjects. Puffendorf has given us a clear and distinct idea of them, in the last chapter of his *Duties of a Man and a Citizen.*[1] We shall follow him step by step.

II. The duties of subjects are either general or particular; and both flow from their state and condition.

III. All subjects have this in common, that they live under the same sovereign and the same government, and that they are members of the same state. From these relations the general duties arise. <117>

IV. But as they have different employments, enjoy different posts in the state, and follow different professions; hence also arise their particular duties.

V. It is also to be observed, that the duties of subjects suppose and include those of man, considered simply as such, and as a member of human society in general.

VI. The general duties of subjects have, for their object, either the governors of the state, or the whole body of the people, viz. their country, or the individuals among their fellow-subjects.[2]

VII. As to sovereigns and governors of the state, every subject owes them that respect, fidelity, and obedience, which their character demands.

---

1. It is DHC II.18. Paragraphs 2, 3, and 4 are from the first paragraph of that chapter. Barbeyrac provides a short version of the chapter, with commentary, in DNG VII.8 §10 note 3.
    2. From DHC II.18 §2.

Hence it follows, that we ought to be contented with the present government, and to form no cabals nor seditions, but to be attached to the interest of the reigning prince, more than to that of any other person, to pay him honour, to think favourably of him, and to speak with respect of him and his actions. We ought even to have a veneration for the memory of good princes, &c.[3]

VIII. With respect to the whole body of the state, a good subject makes it his rule to prefer the public welfare to every thing else, bravely to sacrifice his fortune, and his private interests, and even his life, for the preservation of the state; and to employ all his abilities and his industry to advance the honour, and to procure the advantage of his native country.[4]
<118>

IX. Lastly, the duty of a subject to his fellow-subjects consists in living with them, as much as he possibly can, in peace and strict union, in being mild, complaisant, affable, and obliging to each of them, in creating no trouble by a rude or litigious behaviour, and in bearing no envy or prejudice against the happiness of others, &c.[5]

X. As to the particular duties of subjects, they are connected with the particular employments which they follow in society. We shall here lay down some general rules in regard to this matter.

1°. A subject ought not to aspire after any public employment, nor even to accept of it, when he is sensible that he is not duly qualified for it. 2°. He ought not to accept of more employments than he can discharge. 3°. He should not use unlawful means to obtain public offices. 4°. It is even sometimes a kind of justice not to seek after certain employments, which are not necessary to us, and which may be as well filled

---

3. From DHC II.18 §3 with the exception of the last remark, that we ought to venerate the memory of good princes, which is from Barbeyrac in DNG VII.8 §10 note 3.

4. This is DHC II.18 §4.

5. This is DHC II.18 §5.

by others, for whom they are perhaps more adapted. 5°. He ought to discharge the several functions of the employments he has obtained, with the utmost application, exactness, and fidelity.[6]

XI. Nothing is more easy than to apply these general maxims to the particular employments of society, and to draw inferences proper to each of them; as for instance, with respect to ministers and counsellors of state, ministers of religion, public professors, magistrates and judges, officers in the army and soldiers, receivers of taxes, ambassadors, &c. <119>

XII. The particular duties of subjects cease with the public charges from whence they arise. But as to the general duties, they subsist so long as a person remains subject to the state. Now a man ceases to be a subject, principally three ways. 1°. When he goes to settle elsewhere. 2°. When he is banished from a country for some crime, and deprived of the rights of a subject. 3°. And lastly, when he is reduced to a necessity of submitting to the dominion of a conqueror.[7]

XIII. It is a right inherent in all free people, that every man should have the liberty of removing out of the commonwealth, if he thinks proper. In a word, when a person becomes member of a state, he does not thereby renounce the care of himself and his own private affairs. On the contrary, he seeks a powerful protection, under the shelter of which he may procure to himself both the necessaries and conveniencies of life. Thus the subjects of a state cannot be denied the liberty of settling elsewhere, in order to procure those advantages which they do not enjoy in their native country.[8]

6. Based on DHC II.18 §6, but Burlamaqui does not follow Pufendorf and Barbeyrac in enumerating the duties incumbent on different kinds of state functionaries, a topic that he mentions in the following paragraph.
7. From DHC II.18 §15.
8. For this paragraph, see DHC II.18 §15 note 1 and DNG VIII.11 §6.

XIV. On this occasion there are however certain maxims of duty and decency, which cannot be dispensed with.

1°. In general, a man ought not to quit his native country without the permission of his sovereign: But his sovereign ought not to refuse it him, without very important reasons.

2°. It would be contrary to the duty of a good subject to abandon his native country at an unseason-<120>able juncture, and when the state has a particular interest that he should stay at home.*

3°. If the laws of the country have determined any thing in this point, we must be determined by them; for we have consented to those laws in becoming members of the state.

XV. The Romans forced no person to continue under their government, and Cicero † highly commends this maxim, calling it the surest foundation of liberty, "which consists in being able to preserve or renounce our right as we think proper."

XVI. Some propose a question, whether subjects can go out of the state in great companies? In this point Grotius and Puffendorf are of opposite sentiments.‡ As for my own part, I am of opinion that it can hardly happen, that subjects should go out of the state in large companies, except in one or other of these two cases; either when the government is tyrannical, or when a multitude of people cannot subsist in the country; as when manufacturers, <121> for example, or other tradesmen, cannot find the means of making or distributing their commodities. Under these circumstances, the subjects may retire if they will, and they are authorized so to do by virtue of a tacit exception. If the government be

---

* See Grotius on the Right of war and peace, book ii. chap. v. § 24.

† *O excellent and divine laws, enacted by our ancestors in the beginning of the Roman empire———Let no man change his city against his will, nor let him be compelled to stay in it. These are the surest foundations of our liberty, that every one should have it in his power either to preserve or relinquish his right.* Orat. pro L. Corn. Balb. cap. 13. adde Leg. 12. § 9. Digest. de cap. diminut. *&* postlim. lib. 49. tit. 15.

‡ See Grotius, *ubi supra,* and Puffendorf on the Law of nature and nations, book viii. chap. xi. § 4.

tyrannical, it is the duty of the sovereign to change his conduct; for no subject is obliged to live under tyranny.[9] If misery forces them to remove, this is also a reasonable exception against the most express engagements, unless the sovereign furnishes them with the means of subsistence. But, except in those cases, were the subjects to remove in great companies, without a cause, and by a kind of general desertion, the sovereign may certainly oppose their removal, if he finds that the state suffers great prejudice by it.

XVII. A man ceases to be a subject of the state when he is for ever banished, in punishment for some crime: for the moment that the state will not acknowledge a man to be one of its members, but drives him from its territories, he is released from his engagements as a subject. The civilians call this punishment a civil death. But it is evident that the state, or sovereign, cannot expel a subject from their territories whenever they please, unless he has deserved it by the commission of some crime.

XVIII. Lastly, a man may cease to be a subject by the superior force of an enemy, by which he is reduced to a necessity of submitting to his dominion: and this necessity is founded on the right which every man has to take care of his own preservation. <122>

CHAPTER VI

Of the inviolable rights of sovereignty, of the deposing of sovereigns, of the abuse of the supreme power, and of tyranny.

I. What we have said in the preceding chapter, concerning the duties of subjects to their sovereigns, admits of no difficulty. We are agreed in general upon the rule, that the person of the sovereign should be sacred and inviolable. But the question is, whether this prerogative of the sov-

9. Read: ". . . for no subject has consented to living under tyranny."

ereign be such, that it is never lawful for the people to rise against him, to cast him from the throne, or to change the form of government?[1]

II. In answer to this question, I observe in the first place, that the nature and end of government lay an indispensable obligation on all subjects not to resist their sovereign, but to respect and obey him, so long as he uses his power with equity and moderation, and does not exceed the limits of his authority.

III. It is this obligation to obedience in the subjects, that constitutes the whole force of civil society and government, and consequently the intire felicity of the state. Whoever therefore rises against the sovereign, or makes an attack upon his person or authority, renders himself manifestly guilty of the greatest crime which a man can commit, since he endeavours to subvert the first foundations of the public felicity, in which that of every individual is included. <123>

IV. But if this maxim be true with respect to individuals, may we also apply it to the whole body of the nation, of whom the sovereign originally holds his authority? If the people think fit to resume, or to change the form of government, why should they not be at liberty to do it? Cannot they who make a king, also depose him?[2]

V. Let us endeavour to solve this difficulty. I therefore affirm, that the people themselves, that is, the whole body of the nation, have not a right to depose the sovereign, or to change the form of government, without any other reason than their own pleasure, and purely from inconstancy or levity.

VI. In general, the same reasons which establish the necessity of government and supreme authority in society, also prove that the government ought to be stable, and that the people should not have the power

1. This is the theme in DNG VII.8, especially from §5 onward.
2. This and the three following paragraphs are based on DNG VII.8 §6.

of deposing their sovereigns, whenever, through caprice or levity, they are inclined so to act, and when they have no sound reason to change the form of government.

VII. Indeed, it would be subverting all government, to make it depend on the caprice or inconstancy of the people. It would be impossible for the state to be ever settled amidst those revolutions, which would expose it so often to destruction; for we must either grant that the people cannot dispossess their sovereign, and change the form of government;[3] or we must give them, in this respect, a liberty without controll. <124>

VIII. An opinion which saps the foundation of all authority, which destroys all power, and consequently all society, cannot be admitted as a principle of reasoning, or of conduct in politics.

IX. The law of congruity or fitness is in this case of the utmost force. What should we say of a minor, who, without any other reason than his caprice, should withdraw from his guardian, or change him at pleasure? The present case is in point the same. It is with reason that politicians compare the people to minors; neither being capable of governing themselves. They must be subject to tuition,[4] and this forbids them to withdraw from their authority, or to alter the form of government, without very substantial reasons.

X. Not only the law of congruity forbids the people wantonly to rise against their sovereign or the government; but justice also makes the same prohibition.

XI. Government and sovereignty are established by mutual agreement betwixt the governor and the governed; and justice requires that people

3. The translator omits "without considerable and important reasons," thus giving the sentence a meaning quite different from the original.
4. Instead of ". . . they must be subject to tuition, . . ." read: ". . . they must give themselves masters, . . ."

should be faithful to their engagements. It is therefore the duty of the subjects to keep their word, and religiously to observe their contract with their sovereign, so long as the latter performs his engagements.

XII. Otherwise the people would do a manifest injustice to the sovereign, in depriving him of a right <125> which he has lawfully acquired, which he has not used to their prejudice, and for the loss of which they cannot indemnify him.

XIII. But what must we think of a sovereign, who, instead of making a good use of his authority, injures his subjects, neglects the interest of the state, subverts the fundamental laws, drains the people by excessive taxes, which he squanders away in foolish and useless expences, &c? Ought the person of such a king to be sacred to the subjects? Ought they patiently to submit to all his extortions? Or, can they withdraw from his authority?[5]

XIV. To answer this question, which is one of the most delicate in politics, I observe, that disaffected, mutinous, or seditious subjects, often make things, highly innocent, pass for acts of injustice in the sovereign. The people are apt to murmur at the most necessary taxes; others seek to destroy the government, because they have not a share in the administration. In a word, the complaints of subjects oftener denote the bad humour and seditious spirit of those who make them, than real disorders in the government, or injustice in those who govern.

XV. It were indeed to be wished, for the glory of sovereigns, that the complaints of subjects never had juster foundations. But history and experience teach us that they are too often well founded. Under these circumstances, what is the duty of subjects? <126> Ought they patiently to suffer? Or, may they resist their sovereign?

5. For this and the next paragraph, see DNG VII.8 §6.

XVI. We must distinguish between the extreme abuse of sovereignty, which degenerates manifestly into tyranny, and tends to the entire ruin of the subjects; and a moderate abuse of it, which may be attributed to human weakness, rather than to an intention of subverting the liberty and happiness of the people.

XVII. In the former case, I think the people[6] have a right to resist their sovereign, and even to resume the sovereignty which they have given him, and which he has abused to excess. But if the abuse be only moderate, it is their duty to suffer something, rather than to rise in arms against their sovereign.

XVIII. This distinction is founded on the nature of man, and the nature and end of government. The people must patiently bear the slight injustices of their sovereign, or the moderate abuse of his power, because this is no more than a tribute due to humanity. It is on this condition they have invested him with the supreme authority. Kings are men as well as others, that is to say, liable to be mistaken, and, in some instances, to fail in point of duty. Of this the people cannot be ignorant, and on this footing they have treated with their sovereign.

XIX. If, for the smallest faults, the people had <127> a right to resist or depose their sovereign, no prince could maintain his authority, and the community would be continually distracted; such a situation would be directly contrary both to the end and institution of government, and of sovereignty.

XX. It is therefore right to overlook the lesser faults of sovereigns, and to have a regard to the laborious and exalted office with which they are invested for our preservation. Tacitus beautifully says: "We must endure the luxury and avarice of sovereigns, as we endure the barrenness of a soil, storms, and other inconveniencies of nature. There will be vices as

6. The translator omits "always."

long as there are men; but these are not continual, and are recompensed by the intermixture of better qualities."*

XXI. But if the sovereign should push things to the last extremity, so that his tyranny becomes insupportable, and it appears evident that he has formed a design to destroy the liberty of his subjects, then they have a right to rise against him, and even to deprive him of the supreme power.[7]

XXII. This I prove, 1°. by the nature of tyranny, which of itself degrades the sovereign of his dignity. Sovereignty always supposes a beneficent power: we must indeed make some allowance for the weakness <128> inseparable from humanity; but beyond that, and when the people are reduced to the last extremity, there is no difference between tyranny and robbery. The one gives no more right than the other, and we may lawfully oppose force to violence.

XXIII. 2°. Men have established civil society and government for their own good, to extricate themselves from troubles, and to be rescued from the evils of a state of nature. But it is highly evident, that if the people were obliged to suffer every oppression from their sovereigns, and never to resist their encroachments, this would be reducing them to a far more deplorable state, than that from which they wanted to avoid, by the institution of sovereignty. It can never surely be presumed, that this was the intention of mankind.[8]

XXIV. 3°. Even a people, who have submitted to an absolute government, have not thereby forfeited the right of asserting their liberty, and

---

* *Quomodo sterilitatem, aut nimios imbres, et caetera naturae mala, ita luxum vel avaritiam dominantium tolerate. Vitia erunt, donec homines; sed neque haec continua, et meliorum interventu pensantur.* Hist. lib. iv. cap. lxxiv. N. 4. [The quote is from DNG VII.8 §5. Many of Burlamaqui's quotations from ancient and other sources are from Grotius or Pufendorf, or from Barbeyrac's footnotes.]

7. This and the following paragraph are from DNG VII.8 §6.

8. This point was made by Barbeyrac, for example, in DNG II.2 §2 note 17.

taking care of their preservation, when they find themselves reduced to the utmost misery. Absolute sovereignty, in itself, is no more than the highest power of doing good; now the highest power of procuring the good of a person, and the absolute power of destroying him at pleasure, have no connection with each other. Let us therefore conclude, that never any nation had an intention to submit their liberties to a sovereign in such a manner, as never to have it in their power to resist him, not even for their own preservation. <129>

XXV. "Suppose," says Grotius,* "one had asked those who first formed the civil laws, whether they intended to impose on all the subjects the fatal necessity of dying, rather than taking up arms to defend themselves against the unjust violence of their sovereign? I know not whether they would have answered in the affirmative. It is rather reasonable to believe they would have declared, that the people ought not to endure all manner of injuries, except perhaps when matters are so situated, that resistance would infallibly produce very great troubles in the state, or tend to the ruin of many innocent people."

XXVI. We have already proved,† that no person can renounce his liberty to such a degree as that here mentioned. This would be selling his own life, that of his children, his religion, in a word, every advantage he enjoys, which it is not certainly in any man's power to do. This may be illustrated by the comparison of a patient and his physician.[9]

XXVII. If therefore the subjects have a right to resist the manifest tyranny even of an absolute prince, they must, for a stronger reason, have the same power with respect to a prince who has only a limited sovereignty, should he attempt to invade the rights and properties of his people.‡ <130>

---

* Book i. chap. iv. § 7. N. 2.
† Part i. chap. vii. N. 22, &c. [*PPL*.]
‡ Grotius on the Right of war and peace, book i. chap. iv. § 8.
9. From Barbeyrac's Lockean footnote 2 to DNG VII.8 §6. The comparison is from a long quote from Algernon Sidney in the same note.

XXVIII. We must indeed patiently suffer the caprice and austerity of our masters, as well as the bad humour of our fathers and mothers;[10] but, as Seneca says, "Though a person ought to obey a father in all things, yet he is not obliged to obey him when his commands are of such a nature, that he ceases thereby to be a father."

XXIX. But it is here to be observed, that when we say the people have a right to resist a tyrant, or even to depose him, we ought not, by the word people, to understand the vile populace or dregs of a country, nor the cabal of a small number of seditious persons, but the greatest and most judicious part of the subjects of all orders in the kingdom. The tyranny, as we have also observed, must be notorious, and accompanied with the highest evidence.[11]

XXX. We may likewise affirm, that, strictly speaking, the subjects are not obliged to wait till the prince has entirely rivetted their chains, and till he has put it out of their power to resist him. It is high time to think of their safety, and to take proper measures against their sovereign, when they find that all his actions manifestly tend to oppress them, and that he is marching boldly on to the ruin of the state.

XXXI. These are truths of the last importance. It is highly proper they should be known, not only for the safety and happiness of nations, but also for the advantage of good and wise kings. <131>

XXXII. They, who are well acquainted with the frailty of human nature, are always diffident of themselves; and wishing only to discharge their duty, are contented to have bounds set to their authority, and by such means to be hindered from doing what they ought to avoid. Taught by reason and experience, that the people love peace and good government, they will never be afraid of a general insurrection, so long as they take

10. This is from DNG VII.8 §5.
11. This paragraph and the following are from Barbeyrac in note 1 to DNG VII.8 §6.

care to govern with moderation, and hinder their officers from committing injustice.

XXXIII. However, the abettors of despotic power and passive obedience, start several difficulties on this subject.

First Objection. A revolt against the supreme power includes a contradiction; for if this power is supreme, there is none superior to it. By whom then shall it be judged? If the sovereignty still inheres in the people, they have not transferred their right; and if they have transferred it, they are no longer masters of it.

Answer. This difficulty supposes the point in question, namely, that the people have divested themselves so far of their liberty, that they have given full power to the sovereign to treat them as he pleases, without having in any case reserved to themselves the power of resisting him. This is what no people ever did, nor ever could do. There is therefore no contradiction in the present case. A power given for a certain end, is limited by that very end. The supreme power acknowledges none above itself, so long as the sovereign has not forfeit-<132>ed his dignity. But if he has degenerated into a tyrant, he can no longer claim a right which he has forfeited by his own misconduct.

XXXIV. *Second Objection.* But who shall judge, whether the prince performs his duty, or whether he governs tyrannically? Can the people be judges in their own cause?

Answer. It certainly belongs to those who have given any person a power, which he had not of himself, to judge whether he uses it agreeably to the end for which it was conferred on him.[12]

XXXV. *Third Objection.* We cannot, without imprudence, grant this right of judging to the people. Political affairs are not adapted to the

---

12. This is Locke's argument, quoted by Barbeyrac in DNG VII.8 §6 note 1. Burlamaqui's arguments against absolute monarchy rely heavily on this footnote throughout.

capacity of the vulgar, but are sometimes of so delicate a nature, that even persons of the best sense cannot form a right judgment of them.

Answer. In dubious cases, the presumption ought ever to be in favour of the sovereign, and obedience is the duty of subjects. They ought even to bear a moderate abuse of sovereignty. But in cases of manifest tyranny, every one is in a condition to judge whether he is highly injured or not.[13]

XXXVI. *Fourth Objection.* But do we not expose the state to perpetual revolutions, to anarchy, and to certain ruin, by making the supreme authority depend on the opinion of the people, and by granting them the liberty to rise on particular occasions against their sovereign? <133>

Answer. This objection would be of some force, if we pretended that the people had a right to oppose their sovereign, or to change the form of government, through levity or caprice, or even for a moderate abuse of the supreme power. But no inconveniency will ensue, while the subjects only use this right with all the precautions, and in the circumstances above supposed. Besides, experience teaches us that it is very difficult to prevail on a nation to change a government to which they have been accustomed. We are apt to overlook not only slight, but even very considerable mistakes in our governors.[14]

XXXVII. Our hypothesis does not tend more than any other, to excite disturbances in a state; for a people, oppressed by a tyrannic government, will rebel as frequently as those who live under established laws.[15] Let the abettors of despotic power cry up their prince as much as they please, let them say the most magnificent things of his sacred person, yet the people, reduced to the last misery, will trample these specious reasons under foot, as soon as they can do it with any appearance of success.

13. Pufendorf in DNG VII.8 §6.

14. This is from Barbeyrac, whose Lockean footnote 1 contrasts with Pufendorf's expressions in the main text of the DNG VII.8 §6.

15. The translator omits the end of the sentence: ". . . that he does not want violated." The text is word for word from Barbeyrac's Locke quotation in DNG VII.8 §6 note 1.

XXXVIII. In fine, though the subjects might abuse the liberty which we grant them, yet less inconveniency would arise from this, than from allowing all to the sovereign, so as to let a whole nation perish, rather than grant it the power of checking the iniquity of its governors. <134>

CHAPTER VIII

Of the duty[1] *of sovereigns.*

I. There is a sort of commerce, or reciprocal return of the duties of the subjects to the sovereign, and of his to them. Having treated of the former, it remains that we take a view of the latter.

II. From what has been hitherto explained concerning the nature of sovereignty, its end, extent and boundaries, the duty of sovereigns may easily be gathered. But since this is an affair of the last importance, it is necessary to say something more particular on it, and to collect the principal heads of it as it were into one view.

III. The higher a sovereign is raised above the level of other men, the more important are his duties: if he can do a great deal of good, he can also do a great deal of mischief. It is on the good or evil conduct of princes that the happiness or misery of a whole nation or people depends. How happy is the situation, which, on all instances, furnishes occasions of doing good to so many thousands! But at the same time, how dangerous is the post which exposes every moment to the injuring of millions! Besides, the good which princes do, sometimes extends to the most remote ages; as the evils they commit are multiplied to latest posterity. This sufficiently discovers the importance of their duties. <135>

1. The translator transforms the original's duties into a singular duty. Note also that there is no chapter 7 in the translation: the same is true of the French original. This chapter is on the whole a striking example of how Burlamaqui sometimes takes his text word for word from Barbeyrac's French edition of Pufendorf. In this lengthy chapter, almost nothing can be attributed to Burlamaqui himself.

IV. In order to have a proper knowledge of the duty of sovereigns, we need only attentively consider the nature and end of civil societies, and the exercise of the different parts of sovereignty.

V. 1°. The first general duty of princes, is carefully to inform themselves of every thing that falls under the complete discharge of their trust: for a person cannot well acquit himself in that which he has not first rightly learnt.[2]

VI. It is a great mistake to imagine that the knowledge of government is an easy affair; on the contrary, nothing is more difficult, if princes would discharge their duty.[3] Whatever talents or genius they may have received from nature, this is an employment that requires the whole man. The general rules of governing well are few in number; but the difficulty is to make a just application of them to times and circumstances; and this demands the greatest efforts of diligence and human prudence.

VII. 2°. When a prince is once convinced of the obligation he is under to inform himself exactly of all that is necessary for the discharge of his trust, and of the difficulty of getting this information, he will begin with removing every obstacle which may oppose it. And first it is absolutely necessary, that princes should retrench their pleasures and useless diversions, so far as these may be a hinderance to the knowledge and practice of their duty. Then they ought to endeavour to have wise, prudent and experienced <136> persons about them; and, on the contrary, to remove flatterers, buffoons, and others, whose whole merit consists in things that are frivolous and unworthy the attention of a sovereign. Princes ought not to choose for favourites those who are most proper to divert them, but such as are most capable of governing the state.

---

2. This and the next six paragraphs are from DNG VII.9 §2, including note 3, which forms the basis for Burlamaqui's eighth paragraph. See also DHC II.11 §2.

3. The translator omits "with dignity" here.

VIII. Above all things, they cannot guard too much against flattery. No human condition has so great an occasion[4] for true and faithful advice, as that of kings. And yet princes, corrupted by flattery, take every thing, that is free and ingenuous, to be harsh and austere. They are become so delicate, that every thing, which is not adulation, offends them: But nothing ought they to be so greatly afraid of as this very adulation, since there are no miseries into which they may not be hurried by its poisonous insinuation. On the contrary, the prince is happy, even if he has but a single subject, who is so generous as to speak the truth to him; such a man is the treasure of the state. Prudent sovereigns, who have their true interests at heart, ought continually to imagine that court sycophants only regard themselves and not their master; whereas a sincere counsellor, as it were, forgets himself, and thinks only on the advantage of his master.

IX. 3°. Princes ought to use all possible application to understand the constitution of the state, and the natural temper of their subjects. They ought not in this respect to be contented with a general and superficial knowledge. They should enter into par-<137>ticulars, and carefully examine into the constitution of the state, into its establishment and power, whether it be old or of late date, successive or elective, acquired by legal methods or by arms; they should also see how far this jurisdiction reaches, what neighbours are about them, what allies, and what strength and what conveniences the state is provided with. For according to these considerations the scepter must be swayed, and the rider must take care to keep a stiffer or slacker rein.

X. 4°. Sovereigns ought also to endeavour to excel in such virtues as are most necessary to support the weight of so important a charge, and to regulate their outward behaviour in a manner worthy of their rank and dignity.

---

4. The translator replaces "need" ("besoin") with "occasion."

XI. We have already shewn that virtue in general consists in that strength of mind, which enables us not only to consult right reason on all occasions, but also to follow her counsels with ease, and effectually to resist every thing capable of giving us a contrary biass. This single idea of virtue is sufficient to shew how necessary it is to all men. But none have more duties to fulfil, none are more exposed to temptation, than sovereigns; and none of course have a greater necessity for the assistance of virtue. Besides, virtue in princes has this advantage, that it is the surest method of inspiring their subjects with the like principles. For this purpose they need only shew the way. The example of the prince has a greater force than the law.[5] It is, as it were, a living law, of more efficacy than precept. But to descend to particulars. <138>

XII. The virtues most necessary to sovereigns are, 1°. *Piety,* which is certainly the foundation of all other virtues; but it must be a solid and rational piety, free from superstition and bigotry. In the high situation of sovereigns, the only motive, which can most surely induce them to the discharge of their duty, is the fear of God. Without that, they will soon run into every vice which their passions dictate; and the people will become the innocent victims of their pride, ambition, avarice and cruelty. On the contrary, we may expect every thing that is good from a prince, who fears and respects God, as a supreme Being on whom he depends, and to whom he must one day give an account of his administration. Nothing can be so powerful a motive as this to engage princes to perform their duty, nothing can so well cure them of that dangerous mistake, that being above other men, they may act as absolute lords, as if they were not to render an account of their conduct, and be judged in their turn, after having passed sentence on others.

5. A similar remark is made in DNG VII.9 §2 and §4 in fine. The list of the sovereign's virtues in Burlamaqui's paragraphs 12 to 21 (including the quote from Cicero) is from Barbeyrac in DNG VII.9 §2 note 8.

XIII. 2°. The love of *Equity* and *Justice.* The principal end a prince was made for, is to take care that every one should have his right.[6] This ought to engage him to study not only the science of those great civilians who ascend to the first principles of law, which regulate human society, and are the basis, as it were, of government and politics; but also that part of the law, which descends to the affairs of particular persons. This branch is generally left for the gentlemen of the long robe, and not admitted into the education of princes, though they are every day to < 139 > pass judgment upon the fortunes, liberties, lives, honour and reputation of their subjects. Princes are continually talked to of valour and liberality; but if justice does not regulate these two qualities, they degenerate into the most odious vices: Without justice, valour does nothing but destroy; and liberality is only a foolish profuseness. Justice keeps all in order, and contains within bounds him who distributes it, as well as those to whom it is distributed.

XIV. 3°. *Valour.* But it must be set in motion by justice, and conducted by prudence. A prince should expose his person to the greatest perils as often as it is necessary. He dishonours himself more by being afraid of danger in time of war, than by never taking the field. The courage of him who commands others, ought not to be dubious; but neither ought he to run headlong into danger. Valour can no longer be a virtue than as it is guided by prudence, otherwise it is a stupid contempt of life, and a brutal ardour. Inconsiderate valour is always insecure. He, who is not master of himself in dangers, is rather fierce than brave; if he does not fly, he is at least confounded. He loses that presence of mind which would be necessary for him to give proper orders, to take advantage of opportunities, and to rout the enemy. The true way of finding glory, is calmly to wait for the favourable occasion. Virtue is the more revered, as she shews herself plain, modest, and averse to pride and ostentation.

---

6. ". . . in order to ensure that each is rendered what belongs to him" ("ce qui lui appartient"). In the next sentence, Burlamaqui writes about "the science of those great jurisconsults who ascend to the primary justice [à la première Justice] that regulates human society and determines the principles of government and of politics."

In proportion as the necessity of exposing yourself to danger augments, your foresight and courage ought also to increase. <140>

XV. 4°. Another virtue, very necessary in princes, is to be extremely reserved in discovering their thoughts and designs. This is evidently necessary to those who are concerned in government: It includes a wise diffidence, and an innocent dissimulation.

XVI. 5°. A prince must, above all things, accustom himself to moderate his desires. For as he has the power of gratifying them, if he once gives way to them, he will run to the greatest excess, and by destroying his subjects, will at last complete his own ruin. In order to form himself to this moderation, nothing is more proper than to accustom himself to patience. This is the most necessary of all virtues for those who are to command. A man must be patient to become master of himself and others. Impatience, which seems to be a vigorous exertion of the soul, is only a weakness and inability of suffering pain. He who cannot wait and suffer, is like a person that cannot keep a secret. Both want resolution to contain themselves. The more power an impatient man has, the more fatal his impatience will be to him. He will not wait; he gives himself no time to judge; he forces every thing to please himself; he tears off the boughs, to gather the fruit before it is ripe; he breaks down the gates, rather than stay till they are opened to him.

XVII. 6°. *Goodness* and *Clemency* are also virtues very necessary to a prince: His office is to do good, and it is for this end the supreme power is lodged in his hand. It is also principally by this that he ought to distinguish himself. <141>

XVIII. 7°. *Liberality*, well understood and well applied, is so much the more essential to a prince, as avarice is a disgrace to a person to whom it costs almost nothing to be liberal. To take it exactly, a king, as a king, has nothing properly his own; for he owes his very self to others. But on the other hand, no person ought to be more careful in regulating the exercise of this noble virtue. It requires great circumspection, and supposes, in the prince, a just discernment and a good taste to know how to bestow and dispense favours on proper persons. He ought, above all things, to use this virtue for rewarding merit and virtue.

XIX. But liberality has its bounds, even in the most opulent princes. The state may be compared to a family. The want of foresight, profusion of treasure, and the voluptuous inclination of princes, who are the masters of it, do more mischief than the most skilful ministers can repair.

XX. To reimburse his treasures, squandered away without necessity, and often in criminal excesses, he must have recourse to expedients which are fatal to the subjects and the state. He loses the hearts of the people, and causes murmurs and discontents, which are ever dangerous, and of which an enemy may take advantage. These are inconveniencies that even common sense might point out, if the strong propensity to pleasure, and the intoxication of power, did not often extinguish the light of reason in princes. To what cruelty and injustice did not the extravagant profusions of Nero carry him? A prudent oeconomy, <142> on the contrary, supplies the deficiencies of the revenue, maintains families and states, and preserves them in a flourishing condition. By oeconomy princes not only have money in time of need, but also possess the hearts of their subjects, who freely open their purses upon any unforeseen emergency, when they see that the prince has been sparing in his expences; the contrary happens when he has squandered away his treasures.

XXI. This is a general idea of the virtues most necessary to a sovereign, besides those which are common to him with private people, and of which some are included even in those we have been mentioning. Cicero follows almost the same ideas in the enumeration he makes of the royal virtues.*

---

* *Fortem, justum, severum, gravem, magnanimum, largum, beneficum, liberalem dici, hae sunt regiae laudes.* Orat. pro rege Dejotaro, cap. 9.

XXII. It is by the assistance of these virtues, of which we here have given an idea, that sovereigns are enabled to apply themselves with success to the functions of government, and to fulfil the different duties of it. Let us say something more particular on the actual exercise of those duties.

XXIII. There is a general rule which includes all the duties of a sovereign, and by which he may easily judge how to proceed under every circumstance. *Let the safety of the people be the supreme law.* This ought to be the chief end of all his actions. The supreme authority has been conferred <143> upon him with this view;[7] and the fulfilling of it is the foundation of his right and power. The prince is properly the servant of the public. He ought, as it were, to forget himself, in order to think only on the advantage and good of those whom he governs. He ought not to look upon any thing as useful to himself, which is not so to the state. This was the idea of the heathen philosophers. They defined a good prince, one who endeavours to render his subjects happy; and a tyrant, on the contrary, one who aims only at his own private advantage.

XXIV. The very interest of the sovereign demands, that he should direct all his actions to the public good. By such a conduct he wins the hearts of his subjects, and lays the foundation of solid happiness and true glory.[8]

XXV. Where the government is most despotic, there sovereigns are least powerful. They ruin every thing, and are the sole possessors of the whole country; but then the state languishes, because it is exhausted of men and money; and this first loss is the greatest and most irreparable. His subjects seem to adore him, and to tremble at his very looks: But see what will be the consequence upon the least revolution; then we find that this monstrous power, pushed to excess, cannot long endure, because it has no resource in the hearts of the people. On the first blow,

7. The translator omits "only" here. This paragraph is from DNG VII.9 §3.
8. This and the next paragraph are from DNG VII.9 §3 note 2.

the idol tumbles down and is trampled under foot. The king, who, in his prosperity, found not a man who durst tell him the truth, shall not find one, in his adversity, that will vouchsafe either to ex-<144>cuse, or defend him against his enemies. It is therefore equally essential to the happiness of the people and of sovereigns, that the latter should follow no other rule in their manner of governing, than that of the public welfare.

XXVI. It is not difficult, from this general rule, to deduce those of a more particular nature. The functions of the government relate either to the domestic interests of the state, or to its foreign concerns.

XXVII. As for the domestic interests of the state, the first care of the sovereign ought to be, 1°. to form his subjects to good manners. For this purpose the duty of supreme rulers is, not only to prescribe good laws, by which every one may know how he ought to behave, in order to promote the public good; but especially to establish the most perfect manner of public instruction, and of the education of youth. This is the only method of making the subjects conform to the laws both by reason and custom, rather than through fear of punishment.[9]

XXVIII. The first care of a prince therefore ought to be to erect public schools for the education of children, and for training them betimes[10] to wisdom and virtue. Children are the hope and strength of a nation. It is too late to correct them when they are spoiled. It is infinitely better to prevent the evil, than to be obliged to punish it. The king, who is the father of all his people, is more particularly the father of all the youth, who are, as it were, the flower of the whole nation. And as it is in the <145> flower, that fruits are prepared, so it is one of the principal duties of the sovereign to take care of the education of youth, and the instruc-

9. This and the next paragraph are from DNG VII.9 §4 and from note 1 to that paragraph.
10. Read: "from early on" ("de bonne heure").

tion of his subjects,[11] to plant the principles of virtue early in their minds, and to maintain and confirm them in that happy disposition. It is not laws and ordinances, but good morals, that properly regulate the state.

> Quid leges sine moribus
> Vanae proficiunt.*
>
> *And what are laws, unless obey'd*
> *By the same moral virtues they were made?*
>
> Francis.

Those who have had a bad education, make no scruple to violate the best political constitutions;[12] whereas they who have been properly trained up, chearfully conform to all good institutions. In fine, nothing is more conducive to so good an end in states, than to inspire the people in the earlier part of life with the principles of the Christian religion, purged from all human invention. For this religion includes the most perfect scheme of morality, the maxims of which are[13] extremely well adapted for promoting the happiness of society.

XXIX. 2°. The sovereign ought to establish good laws for the settling of such affairs, as the subjects have most frequent occasion to transact with each other. These laws ought to be just, equitable, clear, without ambiguity and contradiction, useful, accommodated to the condition and the genius of the <146> people, at least so far as the good of the state

---

* Horat. lib. iii. Od. 24. v. 35, 36.

11. The translator gives "subject" for Burlamaqui's "citizen." The gardening metaphor is from Plato and is presented by Barbeyrac in DNG VII.9 §4 note 1. The Horace quote is in DNG VII.9 §4 note 2.

12. Read : ". . . to violate the most precise laws . . ." ("les loix les plus précises") and add ". . . institutions, as if by themselves" ("comme d'eux-mêmes").

13. Add "in themselves." This addition shows how Burlamaqui understands the moral maxims of the Christian religion to provide good guidance even when we abstract from their religious function. Burlamaqui's text abbreviates Pufendorf and omits the argument that the purified (i.e., protestant) Christian religion is the true path to salvation.

will permit, that, by their means, differences may be easily determined: But they are not to be multiplied without necessity.[14]

XXX. I said, that laws ought to be *accommodated to the condition and genius of the people;* and for this reason I have before observed, that the sovereign ought to be thoroughly instructed in this article; otherwise one of these two inconveniencies must happen, either that the laws are not observed, and then it becomes necessary to punish an infinite number of people, while the state reaps no advantage from it; or that the authority of the laws is despised, and then the state is on the brink of destruction.

XXXI. I mentioned also, that *laws ought not to be multiplied without necessity;* for this would only tend to lay snares for the subject, and expose him to inevitable punishments, without any advantage to the society. In fine, it is of great importance to regulate what relates to the administration and ordinary forms of justice, so that every subject may have it in his power to recover his right, without losing much time, or being at a great expence.

XXXII. 3°. It would be of no use to make good laws, if people were suffered to violate them with impunity. Sovereigns ought therefore to see them properly executed, and to punish the delinquents without exception of persons, according to the quality and degree of the offence. It is even sometimes proper to punish severely at first. There are circum-<147>stances in which it is clemency to make such early examples, as shall stop the course of iniquity. But what is chiefly necessary, and what justice and the public good absolutely require, is, that the severity of the laws be exercised not only upon the subjects of moderate fortune and condition, but also upon the wealthy and powerful. It would be unjust that reputation, nobility, and riches, should authorize any one to insult

14. This paragraph and the two following are from DNG VII.9 §5.

those who are destitute of these advantages. The populace are often reduced by oppression to despair, and their fury at last throws the state into convulsions.[15]

XXXIII. 4°. Since men first joined in civil societies to skreen themselves from the injuries and malice of others, and to procure all the sweets and pleasures which can render life commodious and happy; the sovereign is obliged to hinder the subjects from wronging each other, to maintain order and peace in the community by a strict execution of the laws, to the end that his subjects may obtain the advantages which mankind can reasonably propose to themselves by joining in society. When the subjects are not kept within rule, their perpetual intercourse easily furnishes them with opportunities of injuring one another. But nothing is more contrary to the nature and end of civil government, than to permit subjects to do themselves justice, and, by their own private force, to revenge the injuries they think they have suffered. We shall here add a beautiful passage from Mr. de la Bruiere upon this subject.* <148> "What would it avail me, or any of my fellow-subjects, that my sovereign was successful and crowned with glory, that my country was powerful and the terror of neighbouring nations, if I were forced to lead a melancholy and miserable life under the burthen of oppression and indigence? If, while I was secured from the incursions of a foreign enemy, I found myself exposed at home to the sword of an assassin, and was less in danger of being robbed or massacred in the darkest nights, and in a thick forest, than in the public streets? If safety, cleanliness, and good order, had not rendered living in towns so pleasant, and had not only furnished them with the necessaries, but moreover with all the sweets and conveniencies of life? If, being weak and defenceless, I were encroached upon in the country, by every neighbouring great man? If so good a provision had not been made to protect me against his injustice? If I had not at hand so many, and such excellent masters, to educate my children in those arts

---

* Characters and manners of the present age, chap. x. of the sovereign.
15. Based on VII.9 §6.

and sciences which will one day make their fortune? If the conveniency of commerce had not made good substantial stuffs for my cloathing, and wholesome food for my nourishment, both plentiful and cheap? If, to conclude, the care of my sovereign had not given me reason to be as well contented with my fortune, as his princely virtues must needs make him with his?"[16]

XXXIV. 5°. Since a prince can neither see nor do every thing himself, he must have the assistance of ministers: But these, as they derive their whole <149> authority from their master, all the good or evil they do is finally imputed to him. It is therefore the duty of sovereigns to chuse persons of integrity and ability for the employments with which they entrust them. They ought often to examine their conduct, and to punish or recompense them, according to their merits. In fine, they ought never to refuse to lend a patient ear to the humble remonstrances and complaints of their subjects, when they are oppressed and trampled on by ministers and subordinate magistrates.[17]

XXXV. 6°. With regard to subsidies and taxes, since the subjects are not obliged to pay them, but as they are necessary to defray the expences of the state, in war or peace; the sovereign ought to exact no more than the public necessities, or the signal advantage of the state, shall require. He ought also to see that the subjects be incommoded as little as possible by the taxes laid upon them. There should be a just proportion in the tax of every individual, and there must be no exception or immunity which may turn to the disadvantage of others. The money collected ought to be laid out in the necessities of the state, and not wasted in luxury, debauchery, foolish largesses, or vain magnificence. Lastly, the expences ought to be proportioned to the revenue.[18]

16. From DNG VII.9 §8. The quote from de la Bruyère is from Barbeyrac, note 1 to the paragraph in question.
   17. From DNG VII.9 §9.
   18. From DNG VII.9 §10.

XXXVI. 7°. It is the duty of a sovereign to draw no farther supplies from his subjects than he really stands in need of:[19] The wealth of the subjects forms the strength of the state, and the advantage of fami-<150>lies and individuals. A prince therefore ought to neglect nothing that can contribute to the preservation and increase of the riches of his people. For this purpose he should see that they draw all the profit they can from their lands and waters, and keep themselves always employed in some industrious exercise or other. He ought to further and promote the mechanic arts, and give all possible encouragement to commerce. It is likewise his duty to bring his subjects to a frugal method of living by good sumptuary laws, which may forbid superfluous expences, and especially those by which the wealth of the natives is translated to foreigners.

XXXVII. 8°. Lastly, it is equally the interest and duty of a supreme governor, to guard against factions and cabals, from whence seditions and civil wars easily arise. But, above all, he ought to take care that none of his subjects place a greater dependance, even under the pretext of religion, on any other power, either within or without the realm, than on his lawful sovereign. This in general is the law of the public good in regard to the domestic interests, or internal tranquillity of the state.

XXXVIII. As to foreign concerns, the principal duties of the king are,

1°. To live in peace with his neighbours as much as he possibly can.

2°. To conduct himself with prudence in regard to the alliances and treaties he makes with other powers.

3°. To adhere faithfully to the treaties he has made. <151>

4°. Not to suffer the courage of his subjects to be enervated, but, on the contrary, to maintain and augment it by good discipline.

5°. In due and seasonable time to make the preparations necessary to put himself in a posture of defence.

6°. Not to undertake any unjust or rash war.

19. Read: "The sovereign can draw the funds that he has need of only from the goods of his subjects: The wealth . . ." The paragraph is from DNG VII.9 §11. The next paragraph is from §12.

7°. Lastly, even in times of peace to be very attentive to the designs and motions of his neighbours.[20]

XXXIX. We shall say no more of the duties of sovereigns. It is sufficient at present to have pointed out the general principles, and collected the chief heads: what we have to say hereafter concerning the different parts of sovereignty, will give the reader a more distinct idea of the particular duties attending it.

The End of the Second Part. <152>

---

20. This paragraph is based on DNG VII.9 §13.

∞ PART III ∞

A more particular examination of the essential parts of
sovereignty, or of the different rights of the sovereign,
with respect to the internal administration of the state,
such as the legislative power, the supreme power in
matters of religion, the right of inflicting punishments,
and that which the sovereign has over the
Bona Reipublicae,[1] or the goods contained
in the commonwealth.

CHAPTER I

*Of the legislative power, and the civil laws
which arise from it.*

I. We have hitherto explained what[2] relates to the nature of civil society
in general, of government, and of sovereignty, which is the soul of it.
Nothing remains to compleat the plan we laid down, but more par-
<153>ticularly to examine the different parts of sovereignty, as well those
which directly regard the internal administration of the state, as those
which relate to its interests abroad, or to its concerns with foreign powers, which will afford us an opportunity of explaining the principal questions relating to those subjects; and to this purpose we design this and
the subsequent part.

---

1. The Latin was added by the translator.
2. Read: ". . . explained all that relates to the nature of civil society in general, . . ."

II. Among the essential parts of sovereignty, we have given the first rank to the *legislative power,* that is to say, the right which the sovereign has of giving laws to his subjects, and of directing their actions, or of prescribing the manner in which they ought to regulate their conduct; and it is from hence the civil laws are derived. As this right of the sovereign is, as it were, the essence of sovereignty, order requires that we should begin with the explication of whatever relates to it.

III. We shall not here repeat what we have elsewhere said of the nature of laws in general: But, supposing the principles we have established on that head, we shall only examine the nature and extent of the legislative power in society, and that of the civil laws and decrees of the sovereign from thence derived.

IV. *Civil Laws* then are all those ordinances by which the sovereign binds his subjects.[3] The assemblage or body of those ordinances is what we call the *Civil Law.* In fine, civil jurisprudence is that science[4] or art, by which the civil laws are not only established, <154> but explained in case of obscurity, and are properly applied to human actions.

V. The establishment of civil society ought to be fixed, so as to make a sure and undoubted provision for the happiness and tranquillity of man. For this purpose it was necessary to establish a constant order, and this could only be done by fixed and determinate laws.

VI. We have already observed, that it was necessary to take proper measures to render the laws of nature as effectual as they ought to be, in order to promote the happiness of society; and this is effected by means of the civil laws.[5]

---

3. Read: "The *Civil Laws* then are all those laws that the sovereign of the society imposes on his subjects . . ."

4. The translator adds the idea that jurisprudence is a science: in this connection, Burlamaqui states only that it is an art.

5. Most of Burlamaqui's observations in this paragraph are from DHC II.12 §§6–8 or from DNG VIII.1 §1 notes 2 and 3.

For, 1°. They serve to make the laws of nature better known.

2°. They give them a new degree of force, and render the observance of them more secure, by means of their sanction, and of the punishments which the sovereign inflicts on those who despise and violate them.

3°. There are several things which the law of nature prescribes only in a general and indeterminate manner; so that the time, the manner, and the application to persons, are left to the prudence and discretion of every individual. It was however necessary, for the order and tranquillity of the state, that all this matter should be regulated; which is done by the civil laws.

4°. They also serve to explain any obscurity that may arise in the maxims of the law of nature.

5°. They qualify or restrain, in various ways, the use of those rights which every man naturally possesses. <155>

6°. Lastly, they determine the forms that are to be observed, and the precautions which ought to be taken, to render the different engagements that people enter into with each other effectual and inviolable; and they ascertain the manner in which a man is to prosecute his rights in the civil court.

VII. In order therefore to form a just idea of the civil laws, we must say, that as civil society is no other than natural society itself, qualified or restrained by the establishment of a sovereign whose business it is to maintain peace and order; in like manner the civil laws are those of nature, perfected in a manner suitable to the state and advantages of society.

VIII. As this is the case, we may very properly distinguish two sorts of civil laws. Some are such with respect to their authority only, and others with regard to their original. To the former class, we refer all the natural laws which serve as rules in civil courts, and which are also confirmed by a new sanction of the sovereign. Such are all laws which determine the crimes that are to be punished by the civil justice; and the obligations upon which an action may commence in the civil court, &c.

As to the civil laws, so called, because of their original, these are arbitrary decrees, which, for their foundation, have only the will of the sovereign, and suppose certain human establishments; or which regulate things relating to the particular advantage of the state, though indifferent in themselves, and undetermined by the law of nature. Such are the laws which prescribe the necessary forms in contracts <156> and testaments, the manner of proceeding in courts of justice, &c. But it must be observed, that all those regulations should tend to the good of the state as well as of individuals, so that they are properly appendages to the law of nature.[6]

IX. It is of great importance carefully to distinguish in the civil laws, what is natural and essential in them, from what is only adventitious. Those laws of nature, the observance of which is essentially conducive to the peace and tranquillity of mankind, ought certainly to have the force of law in all states; neither is it in the power of the prince to abrogate them. As to the others, which do not so essentially interest the happiness of society, it is not always expedient to give them the force of law, because the controversies about the violation of them would often be very perplexed and intricate, and likewise lay a foundation for an infinite number of litigious suits. Besides, it was proper to give the good and virtuous an opportunity of distinguishing themselves by the practice of those duties, the violation of which incurs no human penalties.

X. What we have said of the nature of civil laws sufficiently shews, that though the legislative be a *supreme,* yet it is not an *arbitrary,* power; but, on the contrary, it is limited in several respects.

1°. And as the sovereign holds the legislative power originally of the will of each member of the society, it is evident, that no man can confer on another a right which he has not himself; and consequently the legislative power cannot be extended beyond this <157> limit. The sovereign therefore can neither command nor forbid any other actions than such as are either voluntary or possible.

2°. Besides, the natural laws dispose of human actions antecedently to the civil laws, and men cannot recede from the authority of the for-

6. This and the following paragraph are mainly based on DNG VIII.1 §1.

mer. Therefore, as those primitive laws limit the power of the sovereign, he can determine nothing so as to bind the subject contrary to what they either expressly command or forbid.

XI. But we must be careful not to confound two things entirely distinct, I mean the *State of Nature,* and the *Laws of Nature.* The primitive and natural state of man may admit of different changes and modifications, which are left to the disposal of man, and have nothing contrary to his obligations and duties. In this respect, the civil laws may produce a few changes in the natural state, and consequently make some regulations unknown to the law of nature, without containing any thing contrary to that law, which supposes the state of liberty in its full extent, but nevertheless permits mankind to limit and restrain that state, in the manner which appears most to their advantage.

XII. We are however far from being of the opinion of those writers,* who pretend that it is impossible the civil laws should be repugnant to that of nature, *because,* say they, *there is nothing either just or unjust antecedently to the establishment of those laws.* What we have above advanced, and the principles <158> we have established in the whole course of this work, sufficiently evince the absurdity of this opinion.[7]

XIII. It is as ridiculous to assert, that before the establishment of civil laws and society, there was no rule of justice to which mankind were subject, as to pretend that truth and rectitude depend on the will of man, and not on the nature of things. It would have even been impossible for mankind to found societies of any durability, if, antecedently to those societies, there had been neither justice nor injustice, and if they had not, on the contrary, been persuaded that it was just to keep their word, and unjust to break it.

---

* Hobbes.

7. Pufendorf presents and refutes Hobbes's view in DNG VIII.1 §§2ff. Burlamaqui uses the reply in §5 of Pufendorf's account in the next paragraph.

XIV. Such in general is the extent of the legislative power, and the nature of the civil laws, by which that power exerts itself. Hence it follows, that the whole force of civil laws consists in two things, namely, in their *Justice* and in their *Authority.*

XV. The authority of the laws consists in the force given them by the person, who, being invested with the legislative power, has a right to enact those laws; and in the Divine Will which commands us to obey him. With regard to the justice of civil laws, it depends on their relation to the good order of society, of which they are the rule, and on the particular advantage of establishing them, according as different conjunctures may require.

XVI. And since the sovereignty, or right of com-<159>manding, is naturally founded on a *beneficent Power,* it necessarily follows, that the *Authority* and *Justice* of laws are two characteristics essential to their nature, in default of which they can produce no real obligation. The power of the sovereign constitutes the authority of his laws, and his beneficence permits him to make none but such as are conformable to equity.

XVII. However certain and incontestable these general principles may be, yet we ought to take care not to abuse them in the application. It is certainly essential to every law that it should be equitable and just; but we must not from thence conclude, that private subjects have a right to refuse obedience to the commands of the sovereign, under a pretence that they do not think them altogether just. For, besides that some allowance is to be made for human infirmity, the opposing the legislative power which constitutes the whole safety of the public, must evidently tend to the subversion of society; and subjects are obliged to suffer the inconveniencies which may arise from some unjust laws, rather than expose the state to ruin by their disobedience.

XVIII. But if the abuse of the legislative power proceeds to excess, and to the subversion of the fundamental principles of the laws of nature, and of the duties which it enjoins, it is certain that, under such circumstances, the subjects are, by the laws of God, not only authorized, but even obliged to refuse obedience to all laws of this kind. <160>

XIX. But this is not sufficient. That the laws may be able to impose a real obligation, and reckoned just and equitable, it is necessary the subjects should have a perfect knowledge of them; now they cannot of themselves know the civil laws, at least those of an arbitrary nature; these are, in some measure, facts of which the people may be ignorant. The sovereign ought therefore to declare his will, and to administer laws and justice, not by arbitrary and hasty decrees, but by mature regulations, duly promulgated.

XX. These principles furnish us with a reflection of great importance to sovereigns. Since the first quality of laws is, that they be known, sovereigns ought to publish them in the clearest manner. In particular, it is absolutely necessary that the laws be written in the language of the country; nay, it is proper that public professors should not use a foreign language in their lectures on jurisprudence. For what can be more repugnant to the principle which directs, that the laws should be perfectly known, than to make use of laws, written in a dead language, which the generality of the people do not understand; and to render the knowledge of those laws attainable only in that language? I cannot help saying, that this is an absurd practice,[8] equally contrary to the glory of sovereigns, and to the advantage of subjects.

XXI. If we therefore suppose the civil laws to be accompanied with the conditions above-mentioned, they have certainly the force of obliging the subjects <161> to observe them. Every individual is bound to submit to their regulations, so long as they include nothing contrary to the divine law, whether natural or revealed; and this not only from a dread of the punishments annexed to the violation of them, but also from a prin-

---

8. The translator replaces Burlamaqui's exclamation "it is a vestige of barbarity" ("c'est là un reste de barbarie") with "this is an absurd practice."

ciple of conscience, and in consequence of a maxim of natural law, which commands us to obey our lawful sovereign.[9]

XXII. In order rightly to comprehend this effect of the civil laws, it is to be observed, that the obligation, which they impose, extends not only to external actions, but also to the inward sentiments. The sovereign, by prescribing laws to his subjects, proposes to render them wise and virtuous. If he commands a good action, he is willing it should be done from principle; and when he forbids a crime, he not only prohibits the external action, but also the design or intention.

XXIII. In fact, man being a free agent, is induced to act only in consequence of his judgment, by a determination of his will. As this is the case, the most effectual means, which the sovereign can employ to procure the public happiness and tranquillity, is to work upon the mind, by disposing the hearts of his subjects to wisdom and virtue.

XXIV. Hence it is that public establishments are formed for the education of youth. Academies and professors are appointed for this purpose. The end of these institutions is to inform and instruct man-<162>kind, and to make them early acquainted with the rules of a happy and virtuous life. Thus the sovereign, by means of instruction, has an effectual method of instilling just ideas and notions into the minds of his subjects; and by these means his authority has a very great influence upon the internal actions, the thoughts, and inclinations of those who are subjected to the direction of his laws, so far at least as the nature of the thing will permit.

XXV. We shall close this chapter with the discussion of a question, which naturally presents itself in this place.[10]

---

9. The translator modifies the passage, which is taken directly from Barbeyrac in DNG VIII.1 §1 note 3 in fine.

10. Barbeyrac was strongly opposed to Pufendorf's contention that a citizen may innocently perform inhuman actions commanded by his sovereign; Burlamaqui's

Some ask, whether a subject can innocently execute the unjust commands of a sovereign, or if he ought not rather to refuse absolutely to obey him, even at the hazard of his life? Puffendorf seems to answer this question with a kind of hesitation, but at length he declares for the opinion of Hobbes in the following manner. We must distinguish, he says, whether the sovereign commands us in our own name to do an unjust action, which may be accounted our own; or, whether he orders us to perform it in his name, as instruments in the execution of it, and as an action which he accounts his own. In the latter case, he pretends that we may, without scruple, execute the action ordered by the sovereign, who is then to be considered as the only author of it. Thus, for example, soldiers ought[11] to execute the orders of their prince, because they do not act in their own name, but as instruments and in the name of their master. <163> But, on the contrary, it is never lawful to do in our own name, an action that our conscience tells us is unjust or criminal. Thus, for instance, a judge, whatever orders he may have from the prince, ought never to condemn an innocent person, nor a witness depose against the truth.

XXVI. But, in my opinion, this distinction does not remove the difficulty; for in whatever manner we pretend that a subject acts in those cases, whether in his own name, or in that of his prince, his will concurs in some manner or other to the unjust and criminal action, which he executes by order of the sovereign. We must therefore impute either both actions partly to him, or else none at all.

---

presentation of the issue in this paragraph is borrowed from Pufendorf in *DNG* VIII.1 §6. Burlamaqui, in the three following paragraphs, presents Barbeyrac's criticisms from note 4 and adds a quote from note 1. Finally, in paragraph 29, Burlamaqui returns to Pufendorf's criticized view, which he presents using Barbeyrac's disapproving characterization from *DNG* VIII.1 §6 note 4. Yet in Burlamaqui's text, the passage with which Barbeyrac rejected Pufendorf becomes a sentence with which Burlamaqui endorses Pufendorf's position—without responding to the Barbeyracian criticisms that had just been presented.

11. The translator omits "always."

XXVII. The surest way then, is to distinguish between a case where the prince commands a thing evidently unjust, and where the matter is doubtful. As to the former, we must generally, and without any restriction, maintain, that the greatest menaces ought never to induce us, even by the order and in the name of the sovereign, to do a thing which appears to us evidently unjust and criminal; and though we may be very excusable in the sight of man for having been overcome by such a severe trial, yet we shall not be so before the Divine tribunal.

XXVIII. Thus a parliament, for instance, commanded by the prince to register an edict manifestly unjust, ought certainly to refuse it. The same I say <164> of a minister of state, whom a prince would oblige to execute a tyrannical or iniquitous order; of an ambassador whose master gives him instructions contrary to honour and justice; or of an officer, whom the sovereign should command to kill a person whose innocence is as clear as the noon-day. In those cases we should nobly exert our courage, and with all our might resist injustice, even at the peril of our lives. *It is better to obey God than men.* For, in promising obedience to the sovereign, we could never do it but on condition, that he should not order any thing manifestly contrary to the laws of God, whether natural or revealed. To this purpose there is a beautiful passage in a tragedy written by Sophocles. "I did not believe (says Antigone to Creon king of Thebes) that the edicts of a mortal man, as you are, could be of such force, as to supersede the laws of the gods themselves, laws not written indeed, but certain and immutable; for they are not of yesterday or to-day, but established perpetually and for ever, and no one knows when they began. I ought not therefore, for fear of any man, to expose myself, by violating them, to the punishment of the gods."*

XXIX. But in cases where the matter is doubtful, the best resolution is certainly to obey. The duty of obedience, being a clear obligation, ought

* Sophocl. Antigon. v. 463, &c.

to supersede all doubt.[12] Otherwise, if the obligation of the subjects, to comply with the commands of their sovereign, permitted them to suspend their <165> obedience till they were convinced of the justice of his commands; this would manifestly annihilate the authority of the prince, and subvert all order and government. It would be necessary that soldiers, executioners, and other inferior officers of court, should understand politics and the civil law, otherwise they might excuse themselves from their duty of obedience, under the pretence that they are not sufficiently convinced of the justice of the orders given them; and this would render the prince incapable of exercising the functions of government. It is therefore the duty of the subject to obey in those circumstances; and if the action be unjust in itself, it cannot be imputed to him, but the whole blame falls on the sovereign.

XXX. Let us here collect the principal views which the sovereign ought to have in the enacting of laws.

1°. He should pay a regard to those primitive rules of justice which God himself has established, and take care that his laws be perfectly conformable to those of the Deity.

2°. The laws should be of such a nature, as to be easily followed and observed. Laws, too difficult to be put in execution, are apt to shake the authority of the magistrate, or to lay a foundation for insurrections.

3°. No laws ought to be made in regard to useless and unnecessary things.

4°. The laws ought to be such, that the subjects may be inclined to observe them rather of their own accord than through necessity. For this reason, the <166> sovereign should only make such laws as are evidently useful, or at least he should explain and make known to the subjects, the reasons and motives that have induced him to enact them.

5°. He ought not to be easily persuaded to change the established laws. Frequent changes in the laws certainly lessens their authority, as well as that of the sovereign.

12. Read: ". . . ought to prevail in case of doubt" (". . . doit l'emporter dans le doute").

6°. The prince ought not to grant dispensations without very good reason; otherwise he weakens the laws, and lays a foundation for jealousies, which are ever prejudicial to the state and to individuals.

7°. Laws should be so contrived as to be assisting to each other, that is to say, some should be preparatory to the observance of others, in order to facilitate their execution. Thus, for example, the sumptuary laws, which prescribe bounds to the expences of the subject, contribute greatly to the execution of those ordinances, which impose taxes and public contributions.

8°. A prince, who would make new laws, ought to be particularly attentive to time and conjunctures.

On this principally depends the success of a new law, and the manner in which it is received.

9°. In fine, the most effectual step a sovereign can take to enforce his laws, is to conform to them himself, and to shew the first example, as we have before observed. <167>

CHAPTER II

Of the right of judging the doctrines taught in the state: Of the care which the sovereign ought to take to form the manners of his subjects.

I. In the enumeration of the essential parts of sovereignty, we have comprehended the right of judging of the doctrines taught in the state, and particularly of every thing relating to religion. This is one of the most considerable prerogatives of the sovereign, which it behoves him to exert according to the rules of justice and prudence. Let us endeavour to shew the necessity of this prerogative, to establish its foundations, and to point out its extent and boundaries.

II. The first duty of the sovereign ought to be to take all possible pains to form the hearts and minds of his people. In vain would it be for him to enact the best laws, and to prescribe rules of conduct in every thing relative to the good of society, if he did not moreover take proper measures to convince his people of the justice and necessity of those rules, and of the advantages naturally arising from the strict observance of them.

III. And indeed, since the principle of all human actions is the will, and the acts of the will depend on the ideas we form of good and evil, as well as of the rewards and punishments, which must follow <168> those acts, so that every one is determined by his own judgment; it is evident that the sovereign ought to take care[1] that his subjects be properly instructed from their infancy, in all those principles which can form them to an honest and sober life, and in such doctrines as are agreeable to the end and institution of society. This is the most effectual means of inducing men to a ready and sure obedience, and of forming their manners. Without this, the laws would not have a sufficient force to restrain the subject within the bounds of his duty. So long as men do not obey the laws from principle, their submission is precarious, and uncertain; and they will be ever ready to withdraw their obedience, when they are persuaded they can do it with impunity.

IV. If therefore people's manner of thinking, or the ideas and opinions commonly received, and to which they are accustomed, have so much influence on their conduct, and so strongly contribute either to the good or evil of the state; and if it be the duty of the sovereign to attend to this article, he ought to neglect nothing that can contribute to the education of youth, to the advancement of the sciences, and to the progress of truth. If this be the case, we must needs grant him a right of judging of the doctrines publicly taught, and of proscribing all those which may be opposite to the public good and tranquillity.

V. It belongs therefore to the sovereign alone to establish academies and public schools of all kinds, and to authorize the respective professors. It

---

1. Read: ". . . each acts in accordance with the opinion he entertains; . . ." and ". . . ought to make it his first care that . . ." This paragraph and the two following are from DNG VII.4 §8 and DNG VII.9 §4, including notes 1 and 2.

is his <169> business to take care that nothing be taught in them, under any pretext, contrary to the fundamental maxims of natural law, to the principles of religion or good politics; in a word, nothing capable of producing impressions prejudicial to the happiness of the state.

VI. But sovereigns ought to be particularly delicate as to the manner of using this prerogative, and not to exert it beyond its just bounds, but to use it only according to the rules of justice and prudence, otherwise great abuses will follow. Thus a particular point or article may be misapprehended, as detrimental to the state, while, in the main, it no way prejudices, but rather is advantageous to society; or princes, whether of their own accord, or at the instigation of wicked ministers, may erect inquisitions with respect to the most indifferent and even the truest opinions, especially in matters of religion.[2]

VII. Supreme rulers cannot therefore be too much on their guard, against suffering themselves to be imposed on by wicked men, who, under a pretext of public good and tranquillity, seek only their own particular interests, and who use their utmost efforts to render opinions obnoxious, only with a view to ruin men of greater probity than themselves.

VIII. The advancement of the sciences, and the progress of truth, require that a reasonable liberty should be granted to all those who busy themselves in such laudable pursuits, and that we should not <170> condemn a man as a criminal, merely because on certain subjects he has ideas different from those commonly received. Besides, a diversity of ideas and opinions, is so far from obstructing, that it rather facilitates, the progress of truth; provided however that sovereigns take proper measures to oblige men of letters to keep within the bounds of moderation, and that just respect which mankind owe to one another; and that they exert their authority in checking those who grow too warm in their disputes, and break through all rules of decency, so as to injure, calumniate, and render suspected every one that is not in their way of thinking. We

2. This paragraph is from Barbeyrac in DNG VII.4 §8 note 3.

must admit, as an indubitable maxim, that truth is of itself very advantageous to mankind, and to society, that no true opinion is contrary to peace and good order, and that all those notions, which, of their nature, are subversive of good order, must certainly be false; otherwise we must assert, that peace and concord are repugnant to the laws of nature. <171>

CHAPTER III

Of the power of the sovereign in matters of religion.

I. The power of the sovereign, in matters of religion, is of the last importance. Every one knows the disputes which have long subsisted on this topic between the empire and the priesthood, and how fatal the consequences of it have been to states. Hence it is equally necessary, both to sovereigns and subjects, to form just ideas on this article.

II. My opinion is, that the supreme authority in matters of religion, ought necessarily to belong to the sovereign; and the following are my reasons for this assertion.

III. I observe, 1°. that if the interest of society requires that laws should be established in relation to human affairs, that is, to things which properly and directly interest only our temporal happiness; this same interest cannot permit, that we should altogether neglect our spiritual concerns, or those which regard religion, and leave them without any regulation. This has been acknowledged in all ages, and among all nations; and this is the origin of the *civil Law* properly so called, and of the *sacred* or *ecclesiastic Law*. All civilized nations have established these two sorts of law.

IV. But if matters of religion have, in several respects, need of human regulation, the right of deter-<172>mining them in the last resort can belong only to the sovereign.

First Proof. This is incontestably proved by the very nature of sovereignty, which is no more than the right of determining in the last resort, and consequently admits of no power in the society it governs, either superior to, or exempt from, its jurisdiction, but embraces, in its full extent, every thing that can interest the happiness of the state, both *sacred* and *profane*.

V. The nature of sovereignty cannot permit any thing, susceptible of human direction, to be withdrawn from its authority; for what is withdrawn from the authority of the sovereign, must either be left independent, or subjected to some other person different from the sovereign himself.

VI. Were no rule established in matters of religion, this would be throwing it into a confusion and disorder, quite contrary to the good of society, the nature of religion, and the views of the Deity, who is the author of it. But, if we submit these matters to an authority independent of that of the sovereign, we fall into another inconveniency, since thus we establish, in the same society, two sovereign powers independent of each other, which is not only incompatible with the nature of sovereignty, but a contradiction in itself.[1]

VII. And indeed, if there were several sovereigns in the same society, they might also give contrary orders. But who does not perceive that opposite <173> orders, with respect to the same affair, are manifestly repugnant to the nature of things, and cannot have their effect, nor produce a real obligation? How would it be possible, for instance, that a man, who receives different orders at the same time from two superiors, such as to repair to the camp, and to go to church, should be obliged to obey both? If it be said that he is not obliged to comply with both, there must therefore be some subordination of the one to the other, the inferior will yield to the superior, and it will not be true that they are both sovereign and independent. We may here very properly apply the words

---

1. Burlamaqui's argument in this and the following paragraph follows Pufendorf's in DNG VII.4 §8 and especially in §11 in fine.

of *Christ. No man can serve two masters; and a kingdom divided against itself cannot stand.*

VIII. *Second Proof.* I draw my second proof from the end of civil society and sovereignty. The end of sovereignty is certainly the happiness of the people, and the preservation of the state. Now, as religion may several ways either injure or benefit the state, it follows, that the sovereign has a right over religion, at least so far as it can depend on human direction. He, who has a right to the *end,* has, undoubtedly, a right also to the *means.*

IX. Now that religion may several ways injure or benefit the state, we have already proved in the first volume of this work.[2]

1°. All men have constantly acknowledged, that the Deity makes his favours to a state depend principally on the care which the sovereign takes to induce his subjects to honour and serve him. <174>

2°. Religion can of itself contribute greatly to render mankind more obedient to the laws, more attached to their country, and more honest towards one another.

3°. The doctrines and ceremonies of religion have a considerable influence on the morals of people, and on the public happiness. The ideas which mankind imbibed of the Deity, have often misled them to the most preposterous forms of worship, and prompted them to sacrifice human victims. They have even, from those false ideas, drawn arguments in justification of vice, cruelty, and licentiousness, as we may see by reading the ancient poets. Since religion therefore has so much influence over the happiness or misery of society, who can doubt but it is subject to the direction of the sovereign?

---

2. This is another addition by the translator, meant to strengthen the impression that the *Principles of Politic Law* constitutes a genuine second part of a single *Principles of Natural and Politic Law* (see the introduction). Burlamaqui simply says "is incontestable." The first argument below does not seem to be in Pufendorf or Barbeyrac, but the two others are similar to arguments in DNG VII.4 §11 or in DNG VII.9 §4 and in note 3 to the same.

X. *Third Proof.* What we have been affirming evinces, that it is incumbent on the sovereign to make religion, which includes the most valuable interests of mankind, the principal object of his care and application. He ought to promote the eternal, as well as the present and temporal happiness of his subjects: This is therefore a point properly subject to his jurisdiction.[3]

XI. *Fourth Proof.* In fine, we can in general acknowledge only two sovereigns, God and the prince. The sovereignty of God is a transcendent, universal, and absolute supremacy, to which even princes themselves are subject; the sovereignty of the prince holds the second rank, and is subordinate to that of God, but in such a manner, that the prince <175> has a right to regulate every thing, which interests the happiness of society, and by its nature is susceptible of human direction.

XII. After having thus established the right of the sovereign in matters of religion, let us examine into the extent and bounds of this prerogative; whereby it will appear, that these bounds are not different from those which the sovereignty admits in all other matters. We have already observed, that the power of the sovereign extended to every thing susceptible of human direction. Hence it follows, that the first boundary we ought to fix to the authority of the sovereign, but which indeed is so obvious as scarce needs mentioning, is, that he can order nothing impossible in its nature, either in religion, or any thing else; as for example, to fly into the air, to believe contradictions, &c.

XIII. The second boundary, but which does not more particularly interest religion than every thing else, is deduced from the Divine laws: for it is evident, that all human authority being subordinate to that of God; whatever the Deity has determined by some law, whether *natural* or *positive,* cannot be changed by the sovereign. This is the foundation of that maxim, *It is better to obey God than men.*

3. Burlamaqui's view is opposite to Barbeyrac's and Pufendorf's; see DNG VII.4 §11 note 2 and DHC II.12 §3.

XIV. It is in consequence of these principles, that no human authority can, for example, forbid the preaching of the gospel, or the use of the sacraments, nor establish a new article of faith, nor intro-<176>duce a new worship: for God having given us a rule of religion, and forbidden us to alter this rule, it is not in the power of man to do it; and it would be absurd to imagine that any person whatever can either believe or practice a thing as conducive to his salvation, in opposition to the Divine declaration.

XV. It is also on the footing of the limitations here established, that the sovereign cannot lawfully assume to himself an empire over consciences, as if it were in his power to impose the necessity of believing such or such an article in matters of religion. Nature itself and the divine laws are equally contrary to this pretension. It is therefore no less absurd than impious to endeavour to constrain consciences, and to propagate religion by force of arms. The natural punishment of those who are in an error is to be taught.* As for the rest, we must leave the care of the success to God.

XVI. The authority of the sovereign, in matters of religion, cannot therefore extend beyond the bounds we have assigned to it; but these are the only bounds, neither do I imagine it possible to think of any others. But what is principally to be observed, is, that these limits of the sovereign power, in matters of religion, are not different from those he ought to acknowledge in every other matter; on the contrary, they are precisely the same; and equally agree with all the parts of the sove-<177>reignty, being no less applicable to common subjects than to those of religion. For example, it would be no more lawful for a father to neglect the education of his children, though the prince should order him to neglect it, than it would be for pastors or Christians to abandon the service of God, even if they had been commanded so to do by an impious sovereign. The reason of this is, because the law of God prohibits both, and this law is superior to all human authority.

* Errantis poena est doceri.

XVII. However, though the power of the sovereign, in matters of religion, cannot change what God has determined, we may affirm, that those very things are, in some measure, submitted to the authority of the sovereign. Thus, for example, the prince has certainly a right to remove the external obstacles[4] which may prevent the observance of the laws of God, and to make such an observance easy. This is even one of his principal duties. Hence also arises his prerogative of regulating the functions of the clergy and the circumstances of external worship, that the whole may be performed with greater decency, so far, at least, as the law of God has left these things to human direction. In a word, it is certain that the supreme magistrate may also give an additional degree of force and obligation to the divine laws, by temporal rewards and punishments. We must therefore acknowledge the right of the sovereign in regard to religion, and that this right cannot belong to any[5] power on earth. <178>

XVIII. Yet the defenders of the rights of the priesthood start many difficulties on this subject, which it will be proper to answer. If God, say they, delegates to men the authority he has over his church, it is rather to his pastors and ministers of the gospel, than to sovereigns and magistrates. The power of the magistrate does not belong to the essence of the church. God, on the contrary, has established pastors over his church, and regulated the functions of their ministry; and in their office they are so far from being the vicegerents of sovereigns, that they are not even obliged to pay them an unlimited obedience. Besides, they exercise their functions on the sovereign, as well as on private persons; and the scripture, as well as church history, attribute a right[6] of government to them.

Answer. When they say that the power of the magistrate does not belong to the essence of the church, they would explain themselves more

---

4. This argument was famously defended by Augustine, whose views were used in the French forced conversions of the Huguenots to Catholicism. Huguenot thinkers like Pierre Bayle and Barbeyrac were very critical of this argument; see, for example, Barbeyrac's préface du traducteur §9 in DNG.

5. The translator omits "other."

6. The translator replaces "duty" ("devoir") with "right."

properly, if they said that the church may subsist though there were no magistrates. This is true, but we cannot from hence conclude, that the magistrate has no authority over the church; for, by the same reason, we might prove that merchants, physicians, and every person else, do not depend on the sovereign; because it is not essential to merchants, physicians, and mankind in general, to be governed by magistrates. However, reason and scripture subject them to the *superior powers.*

XIX. 2°. What they add is very true, that God has established pastors, and regulated their functions, <179> and that in this quality they are not the vicegerents of human powers; but it is easy to convince them by examples, that they can draw no consequence from thence to the prejudice of the supreme authority. The function of a physician is from God as the Author of nature; and that of a pastor is derived also from the Deity as the Author of religion. This however does not hinder the physician from having a dependance on the sovereign. The same may be said of agriculture, commerce, and all the arts. Besides, the judges hold their offices and places from the prince, yet they do not receive all the rules they are to follow from him. It is God himself who orders them to take no bribe, and to do nothing through hatred or favour, &c. Nothing more is requisite to shew how unjust a consequence it is to pretend, that, because a thing is established by God, it should be independent of the sovereign.

XX. 3°. But, say they, pastors are not always obliged to obey the supreme magistrate. We agree, but we have observed that this can only take place in matters directly opposite to the law of God; and we have shewn that this right is inherent in every person in common affairs as well as in religion, and consequently does not derogate from the authority of the sovereign.

XXI. 4°. Neither can we deny that the pastoral functions are exercised on kings, not only as members of the church, but also in particular as possessed of the regal power. But this proves nothing; for what function is there that does not regard the sovereign? <180> In particular, does the physician less exercise his profession on the prince, than on other people? Does he not equally prescribe for him a regimen and the medicines necessary for his health? Does not the office of a counsellor regard also the sovereign, and even in his quality of chief magistrate? And yet who ever thought of exempting those persons from a subjection to the supreme authority?

XXII. 5°. But lastly, say they, is it not certain, that scripture and ancient history ascribe the government of the church to pastors? This is also true, but we need only examine into the nature of the government belonging to the ministers of religion, to be convinced that it does not at all diminish the authority of the sovereign.

XXIII. There is a government of *simple direction,* and a government of *authority.* The former consists in giving counsel, or teaching the rules which ought to be followed. But it supposes no authority in him who governs, neither does it restrain the liberty of those who are governed, except in as much as the laws inculcated on that occasion imply an obligation of themselves. Such is the government of physicians concerning health, of lawyers with regard to civil affairs, and of counsellors of state with respect to politics. The opinions of those persons are not obligatory in regard to indifferent things; and in necessary affairs they are not binding of themselves, but only so far as they inculcate the laws established by nature, or by the sovereign, and this is the species of government belonging to pastors. <181>

XXIV. But there is also a government of *jurisdiction and authority,* which implies the right of establishing regulations, and really obliges the subject. This government, arising from the sovereign authority, obliges by the nature of the authority itself, which confers the power of compulsion. But it is to be remarked, that real authority is inseparable from the right of compelling and obliging. These are the criterion by which alone it may be distinguished. It is this last species of government which we ascribe to the sovereign; and of which we affirm that it does not belong to pastors.*

XXV. We therefore say, that the government, belonging to pastors, is that of counsel, instruction and persuasion, whose entire force and authority consists in the word of God, which they ought to teach the people; and by no means in a personal authority. Their power is to declare the orders of the Deity, and goes no farther.

XXVI. If at present we compare these different species of government, we shall easily perceive that they are not opposite to each other, even in matters of religion. The government of simple direction, which we give to pastors, does not clash with the sovereign authority; on the contrary, it may find an advantage in its aid and assistance. Thus there is no contradiction in saying, that the so-<182>vereign governs the pastors, and that he is also governed by them, provided we attend to the different species of government. These are the general principles of this important doctrine, and it is easy to apply them to particular cases.

CHAPTER IV

Of the power of the sovereign over the lives and fortunes of his subjects in criminal cases.

I. The principal end of civil government and society, is to secure to mankind all their natural advantages, and especially their lives. This end necessarily requires that the sovereign should have some right over the lives of his subjects, either in an *indirect manner,* for the defence of the state, or in a *direct manner,* for the punishment of crimes.[1]

---

* See the gospel according to St. Luke, chap. xii. v. 14. first epistle to the Corinthians, chap. x. v. 4. Ephes. chap. vi. v. 17. Philip. iii. v. 20.
    1. The first paragraph is from DNG VIII.2 §1.

II. The power of the prince over the lives of the subjects, with respect to the defence of the state, regards the right of war, of which we shall treat hereafter. Here we intend to speak only of the power of inflicting punishments.

III. The first question which presents itself, is to know the origin and foundation of this part of the sovereign power; a question, which cannot be answered without some difficulty. Punishment, it is said, is an evil which a person suffers in a compulsive way: A man cannot punish himself; and consequently <183> it seems that individuals could not transfer to the sovereign a right which they had not over themselves.[2]

IV. Some civilians pretend, that when a sovereign inflicts punishments on his subjects, he does it by virtue of their own consent; because, by submitting to his authority, they have promised to acquiesce in every thing he should do with respect to them; and in particular a subject, who determines to commit a crime, consents thereby to suffer the punishment established against the delinquent.

V. But it seems difficult to determine the right of the sovereign on a presumption of this nature, especially with respect to capital punishments; neither is it necessary to have recourse to this pretended consent of criminals, in order to establish the vindicative power. It is better to say that the right of punishing malefactors, derives its origin from that which every individual originally had in the society of nature, to repel the injuries committed against himself, or against the members of the society, which right has been yielded and transferred to the sovereign.[3]

VI. In a word, the right of executing the laws of nature, and of punishing those who violate them, belongs originally to society in general, and to

2. This and the following paragraph are from DNG VIII.3 §1.
3. Burlamaqui sides with Barbeyrac, Locke, and Grotius against Pufendorf here in his views concerning punishment. This paragraph and the next two are from DNG VIII.3 §4 note 3.

each individual in particular; otherwise the laws which nature and reason impose on man, would be entirely useless in a state of nature, if no body had the power of putting them in execution, or of punishing the violation of them. <184>

VII. Whoever violates the laws of nature, testifies thereby, that he tramples on the maxims of reason and equity, which God has prescribed for the common safety; and thus he becomes an enemy of mankind. Since therefore every man has an incontestable right to take care of his own preservation and that of society, he may, without doubt, inflict on such a person punishments capable of producing repentance in him, of hindering him from committing the like crimes for the future, and even of deterring others by his example. In a word, the same laws of nature which prohibit vice, do also confer a right of pursuing the perpetrator of it, and of punishing him in a just proportion.

VIII. It is true, in a state of nature, these kinds of chastisements are not inflicted by authority, and the criminal might happen to shelter himself from the punishments he has to dread from other men, or even repel their attacks. But the right of punishment is not for that either less real or less founded. The difficulty of putting it in execution does not destroy it: This was one of the inconveniencies of the primitive state, which men have efficaciously remedied by the establishment of sovereignty.

IX. By following these principles, it is easy to comprehend that the right of a sovereign, to punish crimes, is no other than that natural right which human society and every individual had originally to execute the law of nature, and to take care of their own safety; this natural right has been yielded and transferred to the sovereign, who, by means of <185> the authority with which he is invested, exercises it in such a manner, as it is difficult for wicked men to evade it. Besides, whether we call this natural right of punishing crimes the vindicative power, or whether we refer it to a kind of *right of war,* is a matter of indifference, neither does it change its nature on that account.

X. This is the true foundation of the right of the sovereign with respect to punishments. This being granted, I define punishment an evil, with which the prince threatens those who are disposed to violate his laws, and which he really inflicts, in a just proportion, whenever they violate them, independently of the reparation of the damage, with a view to some future good, and finally for the safety and peace of society.

XI. I say, 1°. that punishment is an evil, and this evil may be of a different nature, according as it affects the life of a person, his body, his reputation, or his estate. Besides, it is indifferent whether this evil consists in hard and toilsome labour, or in suffering something painful.

XII. I add, in the second place, that it is the sovereign who awards punishments; not that every punishment in general supposes sovereignty, but because we are here speaking of the right of punishing in society, and as a branch of the supreme power. It is therefore the sovereign alone that is empowered to award punishments in society; but individuals cannot do themselves justice, without encroaching on the rights of the prince. <186>

XIII. I say, 3°. *with which the sovereign threatens, &c.* to denote the chief intention of the prince. He threatens first, and then punishes, if menaces be not sufficient to prevent the crime. Hence it also appears that punishment ever supposes guilt, and consequently we ought not to reckon among punishments, properly so called, the different evils to which men are exposed, without having antecedently committed a crime.

XIV. I add, 4°. that punishment is inflicted *independently of the reparation of the damage,* to shew that these are two things very distinct, and ought not to be confounded. Every crime is attended with two obligations; the first is, to repair the injury committed; and the second, to suffer the punishment; therefore the delinquent ought to satisfy both. It is also to be observed on this occasion, that the right of punishment in civil society is transferred to the magistrate, who may by his own authority pardon a criminal; but this is not the case with respect to the right of satisfaction or reparation of damages. The magistrate cannot acquit the offender in this article, and the injured person always retains his right; so that he is wronged, if he be hindered from obtaining due satisfaction.[4]

XV. Lastly, 5°. by saying, *that punishment is inflicted with a view to some good;* we point out the end which the prince ought to propose to himself in inflicting punishments, and this we shall more particularly explain. <187>

XVI. The sovereign, as such, has not only a right, but is also obliged to punish crimes. The use of punishment is so far from being contrary to equity, that it is absolutely requisite for the public tranquillity. The supreme power would be useless, were it not invested with a right, and armed with a force, sufficient to deter the wicked by the apprehension of some evil, and to make them suffer that evil, when they injure society. It was even necessary that this power should extend so far, as to make them suffer the greatest of natural evils, which is *death;* in order effectually to repress the most daring audaciousness, and, as it were, to balance the different degrees of human wickedness by a sufficient counterpoise.

XVII. Such is the right of the sovereign. But if he has a right to punish, the criminal must be also under some obligation in this respect; for we cannot possibly conceive a right without an obligation corresponding to it. But wherein does this obligation of the criminal consist? Is he obliged to betray himself, and voluntarily expose himself to punishment? I answer, that this is not necessary for the end proposed in the establishment of punishments; nor can we reasonably require that a man should thus betray himself; but this does not hinder him from being under a real obligation.[5]

4. This paragraph is based on DNG VIII.3 §4 note 3.
5. Pufendorf discusses Hobbes's view, which is here in question, in DNG VIII.3 §4; Burlamaqui's discussion in the next four paragraphs is based on that paragraph and on Barbeyrac's comments in note 8 to the same.

XVIII. 1°. It is certain, that when there is a simple pecuniary punishment, to which a man has been lawfully condemned, he ought to pay <188> it without being forced by the magistrate; not only prudence requires it, but also the rules of justice, according to which we are bound to repair any injury we have committed, and to obey lawful judges.

XIX. 2°. What relates to corporal, and especially to capital, punishments, is attended with greater difficulty. Such is our natural fondness for life,[6] and aversion to infamy, that a criminal cannot be under an obligation of accusing himself voluntarily, and presenting himself to punishment; and indeed neither the public good, nor the rights of the person intrusted with the supreme authority, demand it.

XX. 3°. In consequence of this same principle, a criminal may innocently seek his safety in flight, and is not obliged to remain in prison if he perceives the doors open, or if he can easily force them. But it is not lawful for him to procure his liberty by the commission of a new crime, as by cutting the throats of the jailors, or by killing those sent to apprehend him.

XXI. 4°. But, in fine, if we suppose that the criminal is known, that he is taken, that he cannot make his escape from prison, and that, after a mature examination or trial, he is convicted of the crime, and consequently condemned to condign punishment; he is in this case certainly obliged to undergo the punishment, and to acknowledge the lawfulness of his sentence; so that there is no injury <189> done him, nor can he reasonably complain of any one but himself: Much less can he withdraw from punishment by violence, and oppose the magistrate in the exercise of his right. In this properly consists the obligation of the criminal with respect to punishment. Let us now enquire more particularly into the end the sovereign ought to propose to himself in inflicting them.

---

6. Read: "Such is the natural instinct that attaches man to life, . . ."

XXII. In general, it is certain that the prince never ought to inflict punishments but with a view to some public advantage. To make a man suffer merely because he has done a thing, and to attend only to what has passed, is a piece of cruelty condemned by reason; for, after all, it is impossible that the fact should be undone. In short, the right of punishing is a part of sovereignty: now sovereignty is founded ultimately on a beneficent power: it follows therefore, that even when the chief ruler makes use of his power of the sword, he ought to aim at some advantage, or future good, agreeably to what is required of him by the very nature and foundation of his authority.[7]

XXIII. The principal end of punishment is therefore the welfare[8] of society; but as there may be different means of arriving at this end, according to different circumstances, the sovereign also, in inflicting punishments, proposes different and particular views, ever subordinate, and all finally reducible to the principal end above-mentioned. What we have said, agrees with the ob-<190>servation of Grotius.* "In punishments, we must either have the good of the criminal in view, or the advantage of him whose interest it was that the crime should not have been committed, or the good of all indifferently."

XXIV. Hence the sovereign sometimes proposes to correct the criminal, and make him lose the vicious habit, so as to cure the evil by its contrary, and to take away the sweets of the crime by the bitterness of the punishment. This punishment, if the criminal is reformed by it, tends to the public good. But if he should persevere in his wickedness, the sovereign must have recourse to more violent remedies, and even to death.

---

* Lib. ii. cap. xx. § 6. N. 2.

7. This paragraph is based on DNG VIII.3 §8, but the observation that sovereignty is founded on a beneficent power is added by Burlamaqui.

8. For "welfare," read "safety and tranquillity." The quote from Grotius in this paragraph is from DNG VIII.3 §9, which is also the source for Burlamaqui's next paragraph.

XXV. Sometimes the chief ruler proposes to deprive criminals of the means of committing new crimes; as for example, by taking from them the arms which they might use, by shutting them up in prison, by banishing them, or even by putting them to death. At the same time he takes care of the public safety, not only with respect to the criminals themselves, but also with regard to those inclined to commit the like crime, in deterring them by those examples. For this reason, nothing is more agreeable to the end of punishment, than to inflict it with such a solemnity[9] as is most proper to make an impression on the minds of the vulgar.

XXVI. All these particular ends of punishment <191> ought to be constantly subordinate, and referred to the principal end, namely, the safety of the public, and the sovereign ought to use them all as means of obtaining that end; so that he should not have recourse to the most rigorous punishments, till those of greater lenity are insufficient to procure the public tranquillity.

XXVII. But here a question arises, whether all actions, contrary to the laws, can be lawfully punished? I answer, that the very end of punishment, and the constitution of human nature, evince there may be actions, in themselves evil, which however it is not necessary for human justice to punish.[10]

XXVIII. And, 1°. acts purely internal, or simple thoughts which do not discover themselves by any external acts prejudicial to society; for example, the agreeable idea of a bad action, the desire of committing it,

---

9. For "inflict it with such a solemnity . . ." read: "inflict it publicly, and with such arrangements as are most proper to make an impression . . ." This paragraph is from DNG VIII.3 §11.

10. The discussion in this and the next four paragraphs is based on DNG VIII.3 §14, although Burlamaqui's insistence that internal acts are also in some sense under the direction of civil laws is intended to express agreement with Pufendorf's critics, such as Leibniz in "The Judgment of an Anonymous Writer" §7, in Samuel Pufendorf, *The Whole Duty of Man, According to the Law of Nature,* ed. Ian Hunter and David Saunders (Indianapolis: Liberty Fund, 2003), pp. 267–305.

the design of it without proceeding to the execution, &c. all these are not subject to the severity of human punishment, even though it should happen that they are afterwards discovered.

XXIX. On this subject we must however make the following remarks. The first is, that if this kind of crimes be not subject to human punishment, it is because the weakness of man does not permit, even for the good of society, that he should be treated with the utmost rigour. We ought to have a just regard for humanity in things, which, though bad in themselves, do not greatly affect the public order and tranquillity. The second remark <192> is, that though acts, purely internal, are not subject to civil punishment, we must not for this reason conclude, that these acts are not under the direction of the civil laws. We have before established the contrary.* In a word, it is evident that the laws of nature expressly condemn such actions, and that they are punished by the Deity.

XXX. 2°. It would be too severe to punish every peccadillo; since human frailty, notwithstanding the greatest caution and attention, cannot avoid a multitude of slips and infirmities. This is a consequence of the toleration due to humanity.

XXXI. 3°. In a word, we must necessarily leave unpunished, those common vices which are the consequences of a general corruption; as for instance, ambition, avarice, inhumanity, ingratitude, hypocrisy, envy, pride, wrath, &c. for if a sovereign wanted to punish such dispositions with rigour, he would be reduced to the necessity of reigning in a desert. It is sufficient to punish those vices when they prompt men to enormous and overt acts.

XXXII. It is not even always necessary to punish crimes in themselves punishable, for there are cases in which the sovereign may pardon; and of this we must judge by the very end of punishment.[11] <193>

---

* Chap. i. § 22, &c. [in this third part of *PPL*.]
11. This is from DNG VIII.3 §15.

XXXIII. The public good is the ultimate end of all punishment. If therefore there are circumstances, in which, by pardoning, as much or more advantage is procured than by punishing, then there is no obligation to punish, and the sovereign even ought to shew clemency. Thus if the crime be concealed, or be only known to a few, it is not always necessary, nay it would sometimes be dangerous, to make it public by punishment; for many abstain from evil, rather from their ignorance of vice, than from a knowledge and love of virtue. Cicero observes, with regard to Solon's having no law against parricide, that this silence of the legislator has been looked upon as a great mark of prudence; forasmuch as he made no prohibition of a thing of which there had been yet no example, lest, by speaking of it, he should seem to give the people a notion of committing it, rather than deter them from it.

We may also consider the personal services which the criminal, or some of his family, have done to the state, and whether he can still be of great advantage to it, so that the impression made by the sight of his punishment be not likely to produce so much good as he himself is capable of doing. Thus at sea, when the pilot has committed a crime, and there is none on board capable of navigating the ship, it would be destroying all those in the vessel to punish him. This example may also be applied to the general of an army.

In a word,[12] the public advantage, which is the true measure of punishment, sometimes requires that the sovereign should pardon, because of the great number of criminals. The prudence of government demands <194> that the justice, established for the preservation of society, should not be exercised in such a manner as to subvert the state.

XXXIV. All crimes are not equal, and it is but equity there should be a due proportion between the crime and the punishment. We may judge of the greatness of a crime in general by its object, by the intention and malice of the criminal, and by the prejudice arising to society from it;

12. For "In a word," read: "Finally." The above is from DNG VIII.3 §16, except the example of the pilot, which is from §17 in fine, as is the rest of this paragraph. The following two paragraphs are based on §18.

and to this latter consequence, the two others must be ultimately referred.

XXXV. According to the dignity of the object,[13] the action is more or less criminal. We must place, in the first class, those crimes which interest society in general; the next are those which disturb the order of civil society; and last of all those which relate to individuals: the latter are more or less heinous, according to the value of the thing of which they deprive us. Thus he, who slays his father, commits a more horrid murder than if he had killed a stranger. He who insults a magistrate, is more to blame than if he had insulted his equal. A person who adds murder to robbery, is more guilty than he who only strips the traveller of his money.

XXXVI. The greater or lesser degree of malice also contributes very much to the enormity of the crime, and is to be deduced from several circumstances.

1°. From the motives which engage mankind to commit a crime, and which may be more or less easy to resist. Thus he, who robs or murders in cold <195> blood, is more culpable than he who yields to the violence of some furious passion.[14]

2°. From the particular character of the criminal, which, besides the general reasons, ought to retain him in his duty: "The higher a man's birth is," says Juvenal, "or the more exalted he is in dignity, the more enormous is the crime he commits."* "This takes place especially with respect to princes, and so much the more, because the consequences of their bad actions are fatal to the state, from the number of persons who

---

* Omne animi vitium tanto conspectius in se
  Crimen habet, quanto major qui peccat habetur.

———*More public scandal vice attends,*
As he is great and noble, who offends.

         J u v. Sat. viii. v. 140, 141.

13. The translator omits "that is, according to how considerable the offended persons are."

14. The first clause is from DNG VIII.3 §19, while clauses 2 and 3 are from §20. Clause 4 is from §22.

endeavour to imitate them." This is the judicious remark made by Cicero.* The same observation may also be applied to magistrates and clergymen.

3°. We must also consider the circumstances of time and place, in which the crime has been committed, the manner of committing it, the instruments used for that purpose, &c.

4°. Lastly, we are to consider whether the criminal has made a custom of committing such a crime, or, if he is but rarely guilty of it; whether he has <196> committed it of his own accord, or been seduced by others, &c.

XXXVII. We may easily perceive that the difference of these circumstances interests the happiness and tranquillity of society, and consequently either augments or diminishes the enormity of the crime.

XXXVIII. There are therefore crimes lesser or greater than others; and consequently they do not all deserve to be punished with equal severity; but the kind and precise degree of punishment depends on the prudence of the sovereign. The following are the principal rules by which he ought to be directed.[15]

1°. The degree of punishment ought ever to be proportioned to the end of inflicting it, that is, to repress the insolence and malignity of the wicked, and to procure the internal peace and safety of the state. It is upon this principle that we must augment or diminish the rigour of punishment. The punishment is too rigorous, if we can, by milder means obtain the end proposed; and, on the contrary, it is too moderate when it has not a force sufficient to produce these effects, and when the criminals themselves despise it.

---

* De Leg. lib. iii. cap. 14. *Nec enim tantum mali est peccare principes, quanquam est magnum hoc per seipsum malum; quantum illud, quod permulti imitatores principum existunt: quo perniciosius de republica merentur vitiosi principes, quod non solum vitia concipiunt ipsi, sed ea infundunt in civitatem. Neque solum obsunt, quod ipsi corrumpuntur, sed etiam quod corrumpunt; plusque exemplo, quam peccato, nocent.*

15. This paragraph is from DNG VIII.3 §§23–25 (including Barbeyrac's notes), except the passages in rule 7 concerning the waiving of formalities in pressing matters.

2°. According to this principle, every crime may be punished as the public good requires, without considering whether there be an equal or lesser punishment for another crime, which in itself appears more or less heinous: thus robbery, for instance, is of its own nature a less crime than murder; and yet highwaymen may, without injustice, be punished with death, as well as murderers. <197>

3°. The equality which the sovereign ought ever to observe in the exercise of justice, consists in punishing those alike who have trespassed alike; and in not pardoning a person, without very good reason, who has committed a crime for which others have been punished.

4°. It must be also observed, that we cannot multiply the kinds and degrees of punishment *in infinitum;* and as there is no greater punishment than death, it is necessary that certain crimes, though unequal in themselves, should be equally subject to capital punishment. All that can be said, is, that death may be more or less terrible, according as we employ[16] a milder or shorter method to deprive a person of life.

5°. We ought, as much as possible, to incline to the merciful side, when there are not strong reasons for the contrary. This is the second part of clemency. The first consists in a total exemption from punishment, when the good of the state permits it. This is also one of the rules of the Roman law.*

6°. On the contrary, it is sometimes necessary and convenient to heighten the punishment, and to set such an example as may intimidate the wicked, when the evil can be prevented only by violent remedies.†
<198>

7°. The same punishment does not make the same impression on all kinds of people, and consequently has not the same force to deter them from vice. We ought therefore to consider, both in the general penal

---

* *In poenalibus causis, benignus interpretandum est.* Lib. cv. § 2. ff. de Reg. Jur. Vid. sup. § 33.

† *Nonnunquam evenit, ut aliquorum maleficiorum supplicia exacerbantur, quoties nimirum, multis personis grassantibus, exemplo opus sit.* Lib. xvi. § 10. ff. de poenis.

16. Read: "according as we employ milder and shorter methods, or slow and cruel torments . . ."

sanction and in the application of it, the person of the criminal, and, in that, all those qualities of age, sex, state, riches, strength, and the like, which may either increase or diminish the sense of punishment. A particular fine, for instance, will distress a beggar, while it is nothing to a rich man: The same mark of ignominy will be very mortifying to a person of honour and quality, which would pass for a trifle with a vulgar fellow. Men have more strength to support punishments than women, and full-grown people more than those of tender years, &c. Let us also observe, that it belongs to the justice and prudence of government, always to follow the order of judgment and of the judiciary procedure in the infliction of punishments. This is necessary, not only that we may not commit injustice in an affair of such importance, but also that the sovereign may be secured against all suspicion of injustice and partiality. However, there are sometimes extraordinary and pressing circumstances, where the good of the state and the public safety do not permit us exactly to observe all the formalities of the criminal procedure; and provided, in those circumstances, the crime be duly proved, the sovereign may judge summarily, and without delay punish a criminal, whose punishment cannot be deferred without imminent danger to the state. Lastly, it is also a rule of prudence, that if we cannot chastise a criminal without exposing the state to great danger, the sovereign ought not <199> only to grant a pardon, but also to do it in such a manner as that it may appear rather to be the effect of *clemency* than of *necessity.*

XXXIX. What we have said relates to punishments inflicted for crimes of which a person is the sole and proper author. With respect to crimes committed by several, the following observations may serve as principles.

1°. It is certain that those, who are really accomplices in the crime, ought to be punished in proportion to the share they have in it, and according as they ought to be considered as principal causes, or subordinate and collateral instruments. In these cases, such persons suffer rather for their own crime than for that of another.

2°. As for crimes committed by a body or community, those only are really culpable who have given their actual consent to them; but they, who have been of a contrary opinion, are absolutely innocent. Thus

Alexander, having given orders to sell all the Thebans after the taking of their city, excepted those, who, in the public deliberations, had opposed the breaking of the alliance with the Macedonians.

3°. Hence it is,[17] that, with respect to crimes committed by a multitude, reasons of state and humanity direct, that we should principally punish those who are the ring-leaders, and pardon the rest. The severity of the sovereign to some will repress the audaciousness of the most resolute; and his clemency to others will gain him the hearts of the multitude.* <200>

4°. If the ring-leaders have sheltered themselves by flight, or otherwise, or if they have all an equal share in the crime, we must have recourse to a decimation, or other means, to punish some of them. By this method the terror reaches all, while but few fall under the punishment.

XL. Besides, it is a certain and inviolable rule, that no person can be lawfully punished for the crime of another, in which he has had no share. All merit and demerit is intirely personal and incommunicable; and we have no right to punish any but those who deserve it.[18]

XLI. It sometimes happens, however, that innocent persons suffer on account of the crimes of others; but we must make two remarks on this subject.

1°. Not every thing that occasions uneasiness, pain, or loss to a person, is properly a punishment; for example, when subjects suffer some grievances from the miscarriages and crimes of their prince, it is not, in respect to them, a punishment, but a misfortune.

The second remark is, that these kinds of evils, or indirect punishments, if we may call them so, are inseparable from the constitution of human affairs.

---

* Quintil. Declam. cap. vii. p. m. 237.

17. For "Hence it is, that . . ." read: "Furthermore, . . ." This paragraph is from DNG VIII.3 §28, with rule 4 being from note 1 to the same.

18. This paragraph and the beginning of the next are based on DNG VIII.3 §30.

XLII. Thus if we confiscate the effects of a person, his children suffer indeed for it; but it is not properly a punishment to them, since those effects ought to belong to them only on supposition their father had kept them till his death. In a word, we must either almost entirely abolish the use of punishments, or <201> acknowledge, that these inconveniencies, inseparable from the constitution of human affairs, and from the particular relations which men have to each other, have nothing in themselves unjust.[19]

XLIII. Lastly, it is to be observed, that there are crimes so enormous, so essentially affecting in regard to society, that the public good authorizes the sovereign to take the strongest precautions against them, and even, if necessary, to make part of the punishment fall on the persons most dear to the criminal. Thus the children of traitors, or state criminals, may be excluded from honours and preferments. The father is severely punished by this method, since he sees he is the cause why the persons dearest to him are reduced to live in obscurity. But this is not properly a punishment in regard to the children; for the sovereign, having a right to give public employments to whom he pleases, may, when the public good requires it, exclude even persons who have done nothing to render themselves unworthy of these preferments. I confess that this is a hardship, but necessity authorizes it, to the end that the tenderness of a parent for his offspring may render him more cautious to undertake nothing against the state. But equity ought always to direct those judgments, and to mitigate them according to circumstances.

XLIV. I am not of opinion that we can exceed these bounds, neither does the public good require it. It is therefore a real piece of injustice, established among several nations, namely, to banish or kill the <202> children of a tyrant or traitor, and sometimes all his relations, though

19. This paragraph is based on DNG VIII.3 §31; the next paragraphs are based on §32 and §33, respectively.

they were no accomplices in his crimes. This is sufficient to give us a right idea of the famous law of Arcadius* the Christian emperor.

CHAPTER V

Of the power of sovereigns over the Bona Reipublicae,[1] or the goods contained in the commonwealth.

I. The right of the sovereign over the goods contained in the commonwealth, relates either to the goods of the subject,[2] or to those which belong to the commonwealth itself as such.

II. The right of the prince over the goods of the subject may be established two different ways; for either it may be founded on the very nature of the sovereignty, or on the particular manner in which it was acquired.

III. If we suppose, that a chief ruler possesses, with a full right of property, all the goods contained in the commonwealth, and that he has collected, as it were, his own subjects, who originally hold their estates of him, then it is certain that the sovereign has as absolute a power over those estates, as every master of a family has over his own patrimony; and that the subjects cannot enjoy or dispose of those <203> goods or estates, but so far as the sovereign permits. In these circumstances, while the sovereign has remitted nothing of his right by irrevocable grants, his subjects possess their estates in a *precarious* manner, revocable at pleasure, whenever the prince thinks fit; they can only supply themselves with sustenance and other necessaries from them: In this case the sovereignty is accompanied with a right of absolute property.

---

* Cod. and L. Jul. Maj. lib. ix. tit. 8. leg. 5.
1. The Latin is added by the translator.
2. The translator throughout gives the singular "subject" for Burlamaqui's "subjects" ("sujets"). The first three paragraphs are from DNG VIII.5 §1.

IV. But, 1°. this manner of establishing the power of the sovereign over the goods of the subjects cannot be of great use; and if it has sometimes taken place, it has only been among the oriental nations, who easily submit to a despotic government.[3]

2°. Experience teaches us, that this absolute dominion of the sovereign over the goods of the subject does not tend to the advantage of the state. A modern traveller observes, that the countries, where this propriety of the prince prevails, however beautiful and fertile of themselves, become daily more desolate, poor, and barbarous; or that at least they are not so flourishing as most of the kingdoms of Europe, where the subjects possess their estates as their own property, exclusive of the prince.

3°. The supreme power does not of itself require, that the prince should have this absolute dominion over the estates of his subjects. The property of individuals is prior to the formation of states, and there is no reason which can induce us to suppose that those individuals entirely transferred to the sovereign the right they had over their own estates; <204> on the contrary, it is to secure a quiet and easy possession of their properties, that they have instituted government and sovereignty.

4°. Besides, if we should suppose an absolute sovereignty acquired by arms, yet this does not of itself give an arbitrary dominion over the property of the subject. The same is true even of a patrimonial sovereignty, which confers a right of alienating the crown; for this right of the sovereign does not hinder the subject from enjoying his respective properties.[4]

V. Let us therefore conclude, that, in general, the right of the prince over the goods of the subjects is not an absolute dominion over their properties, but a right founded on the nature and end of sovereignty, which

---

3. The first two remarks are from DHC II.15 §1 note 1; the third is based on DNG VIII.5 §2 and notes 1 and 2.

4. This fourth remark echoes Barbeyrac's criticism of how the distinction between usufructory versus patrimonial kingdoms was adopted by Pufendorf; see DGP I.3 §11, note 4.

invests him with the power of disposing of those estates in different manners, for the benefit of individuals as well as of the state, without depriving the subjects of their right to their properties, except in cases where it is absolutely necessary for the public good.

VI. This being premised, the prince, as sovereign, has a right over the estates of his subjects principally in three different manners.

The first consists in regulating, by wise laws, the use which every one ought to make of his goods and estate, for the advantage of the state and that of individuals.

The second, in raising subsidies and taxes. <205>

The third, in using the rights of sovereign or *transcendental* propriety.*

VII. To the first head we must reduce all *sumptuary laws,* by which bounds are set to unnecessary expences, which ruin families, and consequently impoverish the state. Nothing is more conducive to the happiness of a nation, or more worthy of the care of the sovereign, than to oblige the subjects to oeconomy, frugality, and labour.

When luxury has once prevailed in a nation, the evil becomes almost incurable. As too great authority spoils kings, so luxury poisons a whole people. The most superfluous things are looked upon as necessary, and new necessities are daily invented. Thus families are ruined, and individuals disabled from contributing to the expences necessary for the public good. An individual, for instance, who spends only three fifths of his income, and pays one fifth for the public service, will not hurt himself, since he lays up a fifth to increase his stock. But if he spends all his income, he either cannot pay the taxes, or he must break in upon his capital.

Another inconveniency is, that not only the estates of individuals are squandered away by luxury, but, what is still worse, they are generally carried abroad into foreign countries, in pursuit of those things which flatter luxury and vanity.

---

* Dominium eminens. [The translator gives "sovereign or transcendental propriety" for Burlamaqui's "domaine eminent," that is, "eminent domain."]

The impoverishing of individuals produces also another evil for the state, by hindering marriages. On the contrary, people are more inclined to mar-<206>riage, when a moderate expence is sufficient for the support of a family.

This the emperor Augustus was very sensible of; for when he wanted to reform the manners of the Romans, among the various edicts which he either made or renewed, he re-established both the sumptuary law, and that which obliged people to marry.

When luxury is once introduced, it soon becomes a general evil, and the contagion insensibly spreads from the first men of the state to the very dregs of the people. The king's relations want to imitate his magnificence; the nobility that of his relations; the gentry, or middle sort of people, endeavour to equal the nobility; and the poor would fain pass for gentry: Thus every one living beyond his income, the people are ruined, and all orders and distinctions confounded.

History informs us, that, in all ages, luxury has been one of the causes which has more or less[5] contributed to the ruin and decay even of the most powerful states, because it sensibly enervates courage, and destroys virtue. Suetonius observes, that Julius Caesar invaded the liberties of his country only in consequence of not knowing how to pay the debts he had contracted by his excessive prodigality, nor how to support his expensive way of living. Many sided with him, because they had not wherewith to supply that luxury to which they had been accustomed, and they were in hopes of getting by the civil wars enough to maintain their former extravagance.*

We must observe, in fine, that, to render the sumptuary laws more effectual, princes and magistrates <207> ought, by the example of their own moderation, to put those out of countenance who love extravagance, and to encourage the prudent, who would easily submit to follow the pattern of a good oeconomy and honest frugality.

* See Sall. ad Caesar. de Repub. ordinand.
5. Read: ". . . that has contributed most to the ruin . . ." This paragraph is almost entirely from Barbeyrac's first note to DNG VIII.5 §3, or more precisely from various thinkers that Barbeyrac quoted at length in that paragraph.

VIII. To this right of the sovereign of directing the subjects in the use of their estates and goods, we must also reduce the laws against gaming and prodigality, those which set bounds to grants, legacies, and testaments; and, in fine, those against idle and lazy people, and against persons that suffer their estates to run to ruin, purely by carelessness and neglect.[6]

IX. Above all, it is of great importance to use every endeavour to banish idleness, that fruitful source of disorders. The want of a useful and honest occupation is the foundation of an infinite number of mischiefs. The human mind cannot remain in a state of inaction, and if it be not employed on something good, it will inevitably apply itself to something bad, as the experience of all ages demonstrates. It were therefore to be wished, that there were laws against idleness, to prevent its pernicious effects, and that no person was permitted to live without some honest occupation either of the mind or body. Especially young people, who aspire after political, ecclesiastical, or military employments, ought not to be permitted to pass in shameful idleness, the time of their life most proper for the study of morality, politics, and religion. It is obvious that a wise <208> prince may, from these reflections, draw very important instructions for government.

X. The second manner, in which the prince can dispose of the goods or estates of his subjects, is, by demanding taxes or subsidies of them. That the sovereign has this right, will evidently appear, if we consider that taxes are no more than a contribution which individuals pay to the state for the preservation and defence of their lives and properties, a contribution absolutely necessary both for the ordinary and extraordinary expences of government, which the sovereign neither can nor ought to furnish out of his own fund: He must therefore, for that end and purpose, have a right to take away part of the goods of the subject by way of tax.[7]

---

6. This paragraph and the next are from DNG VIII.5 §3 and from Barbeyrac's sixth note to the same.
7. This and the two following paragraphs are from DNG VIII.5 §4.

XI. Tacitus relates a memorable story on this subject. "Nero," he says, "once thought to abolish all taxes, and to make this magnificent grant to the Roman people; but the senate moderated his ardour; and, after having commended the emperor for his generous design, they told him that the empire would inevitably fall, if its foundations were sapped; that most of the taxes had been established by the consuls and tribunes during the very height of liberty in the times of the republic, and that they were the only means of supplying the immense expences necessary for the support of so great an empire."

XII. Nothing is then generally more unjust and unreasonable than the complaints of the populace, <209> who frequently ascribe their misery to taxes, without reflecting that these are, on the contrary, the foundation of the tranquillity and safety of the state, and that they cannot refuse to pay them without prejudicing their own interests.

XIII. However, the end and prudence of civil government require not only that the people should not be overcharged in this respect, but also that the taxes should be raised in as gentle and imperceptible a manner as possible.[8]

XIV. And, 1°. the subjects must be equally charged, that they may have no just reason of complaint. A burden equally supported by all, is lighter to every individual; but if a considerable number release or excuse themselves, it becomes much more heavy and insupportable to the rest. As every subject equally enjoys the protection of the government, and the safety which it procures; it is just that they should all contribute to its support in a proper equality.

XV. 2°. It is to be observed however, that this equality does not consist in paying equal sums of money, but in equally bearing the burden im-

8. This is from DNG VIII.5 §5, while the defense of progressive taxation in the following four paragraphs is from §6, where Pufendorf presents and discusses Hobbes's views on the topic.

posed for the good of the state; that is, there must be a just proportion between the burden of the tax and the benefit of peace; for though all equally enjoy peace, yet the advantages, which all reap from it, are not equal. <210>

XVI. 3°. Every man ought therefore to be taxed in proportion to his income, both in ordinary and extraordinary exigencies.

XVII. 4°. Experience shews, that the best method of raising taxes, is to lay them on things daily consumed in life.

XVIII. 5°. As to merchandizes imported, it is to be observed, that if they are not necessary, but only subservient to luxury, very great duties may justly be laid on them.[9]

XIX. 6°. When foreign merchandizes consist of such things as may grow, or be manufactured at home, by the industry and application of our own people, the imposts ought to be raised higher upon those articles.

XX. 7°. With regard to the exportation of commodities of our own growth, if it be the interest of the state that they should not go out of the country, it may be right to raise the customs upon them; but on the contrary, if it is for the public advantage that they should be sent to foreign markets, then the duty of exportation ought to be diminished, or absolutely taken away. In some countries, by a wise piece of policy, rewards are given to the subjects, who export such commodities as are in too great plenty, and far surpassing the wants of the inhabitants.

XXI. 8°. In a word, in the application of all these maxims, the sovereign must attend to the good <211> of trade, and take all proper measures to make it flourish.

9. This and the next four paragraphs are mainly based on DNG VIII.5 §5.

XXII. It is unnecessary to observe, that the right of the sovereign, with respect to taxes, being founded on the wants of the state, he ought never to raise them but in proportion to those wants; neither should he employ them but with that view, nor apply them to his own private uses.

XXIII. He ought also to attend to the conduct of the officers who collect them, so as to hinder their importunity and oppression. Thus Tacitus commends a very wise edict of the emperor Nero, "who ordered that the magistrates of Rome and of the provinces should receive complaints against the publicans at all times, and regulate them upon the spot."

XXIV. The *sovereign* or *transcendental* property,* which, as we have said, constitutes the third part of the sovereign's power over the estates of his subjects, consists in the right of making use of every thing the subject possesses, in order to answer the necessities of the state.[10]

XXV. Thus, for example, if a town is to be fortified, he may take the gardens, lands, or houses of private subjects, situated in the place where the ramparts or ditches are to be raised. In sieges, he may beat down houses and trees belonging to private persons, to the end that the enemy may not be sheltered by them, or the garrison incommoded. <212>

XXVI. There are great disputes, among politicians, concerning this *transcendental property*. Some absolutely will not admit of it; but the dispute turns more upon the word than the thing. It is certain that the very nature of sovereignty authorizes a prince, in case of necessity, to make use of the goods and fortunes of his subjects; since in conferring the supreme authority upon him, they have at the same time given him the power of doing and exacting every thing necessary for the preservation and advantage of the state. Whether this be called *transcendental prop-*

---

* Dominium eminens. [This paragraph is based on DNG VIII.5 §3.]

10. The translator omits "in dire need" at the end here ("dans un bésoin pressant"). This paragraph and the five following are from DNG VIII.5 §7.

erty, or by some other name, is altogether indifferent, provided we are agreed about the right itself.

XXVII. To say something more particular concerning this *transcendental property,* we must observe it to be a maxim of natural equity, that when contributions are to be raised for the exigencies of the state, and for the preservation of some particular object, by persons who enjoy it in common, every man ought to pay his quota, and should not be forced to bear more of the burden than another.[11]

XXVIII. But since it may happen that the pressing wants of the state, and particular circumstances, will not permit this rule to be literally followed, there is a necessity that the sovereign should have a right to deviate from it, and to seize on the property of a private subject, the use of which, in the present circumstances, is become necessary to the public. Hence this right takes place only <213> in the case of a necessity of state, which ought not to have too great an extent, but should be tempered as much as possible with the rules of equity.

XXIX. It is therefore just in that case, that the proprietors should be indemnified, as near as possible, either by their fellow-subjects, or by the exchequer. But if the subjects have voluntarily exposed themselves, by building houses in a place where they are to be pulled down in time of war, then the state is not in rigour obliged to indemnify them, and they may be reasonably thought to have consented to this loss. This is sufficient for what relates to the right of the sovereign over the estates[12] of the subjects.

XXX. But, besides these rights, the prince has also originally a power of disposing of certain places called *public goods,* because they belong to

11. Read: ". . . every man ought to contribute in proportion to his interest in the thing" (". . . chacun doit y contribuer à proportion de l'intérêt qu'il y a").

12. The translation throughout translates Burlamaqui's "biens" with "estates." While this does seem to correspond to Burlamaqui's intentions in most cases, "biens" can also be taken in a broader sense to signify different kinds of property.

the state as such: but as these public goods are not all of the same kind, the right of the sovereign in this respect also varies.[13]

XXXI. There are goods intended for the support of the king and the royal family, and others to defray the expences of the government. The former are called the crown lands, or the patrimony of the prince; and the latter the public treasure, or the revenue of the state.

XXXII. With regard to the former, the sovereign has the full and entire profits, and may dispose of <214> the revenues arising from them as he absolutely pleases. So that what he lays up out of his income makes an accession to his own private patrimony, unless the laws of the land have determined otherwise. With regard to the other public goods, he has only the simple administration of them, in which he ought to propose only the advantage of the state, and to express as much care and fidelity as a guardian with respect to the estate of his pupil.

XXXIII. By these principles we may judge to whom the acquisitions belong, which a prince has made during his reign; for if these acquisitions arise from the goods intended to defray the public expences, they ought certainly to accrue to the public, and not to the prince's private patrimony. But if a king has undertaken and supported a war at his own expence, and without engaging or charging the state in the least, he may lawfully appropriate the acquisitions he has made in such an expedition.

XXXIV. From the principles here established it follows also, that the sovereign cannot, without the consent of the people or their representatives, alienate the least part either of the public patrimony, or of the crown lands, of which he has only the use. But we must distinguish between the goods themselves and the profits or produce of them. The king may dispose of the revenues or profits as he thinks proper, though he cannot alienate the principal.[14]

---

13. This paragraph and the three following are from DNG VIII.5 §8.
14. This paragraph and the two following are from DNG VIII.5 §11.

XXXV. A prince indeed, who has a right of laying taxes if he thinks meet and just, may, when <215> the necessities of the commonwealth require it, mortgage a part of the public patrimony: for it is the same thing to the people, whether they give money to prevent the mortgage, or it be levied upon them afterwards in order to redeem it.

XXXVI. This however is to be understood upon supposition, that things are not otherwise regulated by the fundamental laws of the state.

XXXVII. In respect to the alienation of the kingdom, or some part of it; from the principles hitherto established, we may easily form a judgment of the matter.

And, 1°. if there be any such thing as a[15] patrimonial kingdom, it is evident that the sovereign may alienate the whole, and still more so, that he may transfer a part of it.*

XXXVIII. 2°. But if the kingdom be not possessed as a patrimony, the king cannot, by his own authority, transfer or alienate any part of it; for then the consent of the people is necessary. Sovereignty of itself does not imply the right of alienation, and as the people cannot take the crown from the prince against his will, neither has the king a power of substituting another sovereign in his place without their consent.

XXXIX. 3°. But if only a part of the kingdom is to be alienated, besides the approbation of the king <216> and that of the people, it is necessary that the inhabitants of the part, which is to be alienated, should also consent; and the latter seems to be the most necessary. It is to no purpose that the other parts of the kingdom agree to the alienation of this prov-

---

* See Grotius, lib. ii. cap. vi.

15. The translator omits "truly" here. This paragraph and the seven following are from DNG VIII.5 §9, including the presentation of Grotius's view, where Burlamaqui adds a reference to DGP, as if that were his immediate source. In fact, most of the text here is taken from DNG.

ince, if the inhabitants themselves oppose it. The right of the plurality of suffrages does not extend so far, as to cut off from the body of the state those who have not once violated their engagements, nor the laws of society.

XL. And indeed it is evident, that the persons who first erected the commonwealth, and those who voluntarily came into it afterwards, bound themselves, by mutual compact, to form a permanent body or society, under one and the same government, so long at least as they inclined to remain in the territories of the same state; and it is with a view to the advantages which accrued to them in common from this reciprocal union, that they first erected the state. This is the foundation of their compacts in regard to government. Therefore they cannot, against their will, be deprived of the right they have acquired of being a part of a certain body politic, except by way of punishment. Besides, in this case, there is an *obligation* corresponding to the above *right*. The state, by virtue of the same compact, has acquired a right over each of its members, so that no subject can put himself under a foreign government, nor disclaim the authority of his natural sovereign.

XLI. 4°. It is however to be observed, that there are two general exceptions to the principles here <217> established, both of them founded on the right and privileges arising from necessity. The first is, that though the body of the state has not the right of alienating any of its parts, so as to oblige that part, against its will, to submit to a new master, the state however may be justified in abandoning one of its parts, when there is an evident danger of perishing if they continue united.

XLII. It is true that even under those circumstances, the sovereign cannot directly oblige one of his towns or provinces to submit to another government. He only has a power to withdraw his forces, or abandon the inhabitants; but they retain the right of defending themselves if they can: so that if they find they have strength sufficient to resist the enemy, there is no reason why they should not; and if they succeed, they may erect themselves into a distinct commonwealth. Hence the conqueror becomes the lawful sovereign of that particular country only by the consent of the inhabitants, or by their swearing allegiance to him.

XLIII. It may be said, that, properly speaking, the state or the sovereign do not alienate, in this case, such a part, but only renounce a society whose engagements are at an end by virtue of a tacit exception arising from necessity. After all, it would be in vain for the body to persist in defending such a part, since we suppose it unable to preserve or defend itself. It is therefore a mere misfortune which must be suffered by the abandoned part. <218>

XLIV. 5°. But if this be the right of the body with respect to the part, the part has also, in like circumstances, the same right with regard to the body. Thus we cannot condemn a town, which, after having made the best resistance it could, chuses rather to surrender to the enemy, than be pillaged and exposed to fire and sword.

XLV. In a word, every one has a natural right to take care of his own preservation by all possible means; and it is principally for the better attainment of this end, that men have entered into civil societies. If therefore the state can no longer defend and protect the subjects, they are disengaged from the ties they were under, and resume their original right of taking care of themselves, independently of the state, in the manner they think most proper. Thus things are equal on both sides; and the sentiment of Grotius, who refuses the body of the state, with respect to the part, the same right which he grants the part with respect to the body, cannot be maintained.[16]

XLVI. We shall conclude this chapter with two remarks. The first is, that the maxim which some politicians inculcate so strongly, namely, that the goods appropriated to the crown are absolutely unalienable, is not true, except on the terms, and agreeably to the principles here established.

16. For this paragraph, see Barbeyrac's Pufendorfian critique of Grotius in DGP II.6 §6 note 1.

What the same politicians add, that an alienation, succeeded by a peaceable possession for a long course of years, does not hinder a future right to what belonged to the crown, and the resumption of it by main force, on the first occasion, is altogether unreasonable.[17] <219>

The second observation is, that since it is not lawful for a king, independently of the will of the people or of their representatives, to alienate the whole or any part of his kingdom, it is not right for him to render it feudatory to another prince; for this is evidently a kind of alienation.

The End of the Third Part. <220>

17. This paragraph is from DNG VIII.5 §9 in fine, except for its ending, which is from §10.

In which are considered the different rights
of sovereignty with respect to foreign states;
the right of war, and every thing relating to it;
public treaties, and the right of ambassadors.

CHAPTER I

*Of war in general, and first of the right of the
sovereign, in this respect, over his subjects.*

I. Whatever has been hitherto said of the essential parts of sovereignty, properly and directly regards the internal administration of the state. But as the happiness and prosperity of a nation demands not only that order and peace should be maintained at home, but also that the state should be protected from the insults of enemies abroad, and obtain all the advan-<221>tages it can from other nations; we shall proceed to examine those parts of sovereignty which directly regard the safety and external advantages of the state, and discuss the most essential questions relating to this subject.

II. To trace things from their original, we must first observe, that mankind being divided into several societies called *states* or *nations,* and those political bodies forming a kind of society among themselves, are also subjected to those primitive and general laws, which God has given to all mankind, and consequently they are obliged to practise certain duties towards each other.

445

III. It is the system or assemblage of those laws that is properly called the law of *nations:* and these are no more than the laws of nature, which men, considered as members of society, in general, ought to practise towards each other;[1] or, in other words, the law of nations is no more than the general law of *sociability,* applied not to individuals composing a society, but to men, as forming different bodies called *states* or *nations.*

IV. The natural state of nations, with respect to each other, is certainly that of society and peace. Such is the natural and primitive state of one man with respect to another; and whatever alteration mankind may have made in regard to their original state, they cannot, without violating their duty, break in upon that state of peace and society, in which nature has placed them, and which, by her <222> *laws,* she has so strongly recommended to their observance.

V. Hence proceed several maxims of the law of nations; for example, that all states ought to look upon themselves as naturally equal and independent, and to treat each other as such on all occasions: likewise, that they ought to do no injury to any other, but, on the contrary, repair that which they may have committed. Hence also arises their right of endeavouring to provide for their safety and happiness, and of employing force and arms against those who declare themselves their enemies. Fidelity in treaties and alliances, and the respect due to ambassadors, are derived from the same principle. This is the idea we ought to form of the law of nations in general.

VI. We do not here propose to enter into all the political questions which may be started concerning the law of nations; we shall only examine two following articles, which, being the most considerable, include almost all the rest, I mean the *right of war,* that of *treaties and alliances,* and that of *ambassadors.*

---

1. Burlamaqui thus sides with Pufendorf and Barbeyrac against Grotius, arguing that there is no obligatory law of nations distinct from the laws of nature. See DGP I.1 §14 note 3.

VII. The subject of the right of war being finally important and extensive, merits to be treated with great exactness. We have already observed, that it is a fundamental maxim of the law of nature and nations, that individuals and states ought to live in a state of union and society, that they should not injure each other, but, on the con-<223>trary, they should mutually exercise the duties of humanity.

VIII. Whenever men practise these duties, they are said to be in a state of peace. This state is certainly the most agreeable to our nature, as well as the most capable of promoting happiness;[2] and indeed the law of nature was intended chiefly to establish and preserve it.

IX. The state opposite to that of union and peace, is what we call *war*, which, in the most general sense, is no more than the state of those who try to determine their differences by the ways of force. I say, this is the most general sense, for, in a more limited signification, common use has restrained the word *war* to that carried on between sovereign powers.*

X. Though a state of peace and mutual benevolence is certainly most natural to man, and most agreeable to the laws which ought to be his guide, war is nevertheless permitted in certain circumstances, and sometimes necessary both for individuals and nations. This we have sufficiently shewn in the second part of this work, by establishing the rights with which nature has invested mankind for their own preservation, and the means they may lawfully employ for attaining that end. The principles of this kind, which we have established with respect to particulars, equally, and even for stronger reasons, are applicable to nations. <224>

XI. The law of God no less enjoins a whole nation to take care of their preservation, than it does private men. It is therefore just that they should[3] employ force against those, who, declaring themselves their en-

---

* See lower down, chap. iii.

2. This paragraph, like paragraph 10 below, seems to be based on DNG VIII.6 §2.

3. The translator omits "be able to."

emies, violate the law of sociability towards them, refuse them their due, seek to deprive them of their advantages, and even to destroy them. It is therefore for the good of society, that people should be able to repress the malice and efforts of those who subvert the foundations of it; otherwise the human species would become the victims of robbery and licentiousness: for the right of making war is, properly speaking, the most powerful means of maintaining peace.[4]

XII. Hence it is certain that the sovereign, in whose hands the interest of the whole society is lodged, has a right to make war: but if it be so, we must of course allow him the right of employing the several means necessary for that end. In a word, we must grant him the power of levying troops, and obliging them to perform the most dangerous duties even at the peril of their lives. And this is one branch of the right of life and death which manifestly belongs to the sovereign.

XIII. But as the strength and valour of troops depend, in great measure, on their being well disciplined, the sovereign ought, even in times of peace, to train the subjects up to martial exercises, to the end that they may, when occasion requires, be more able to sustain the fatigues, and perform the different duties of war. <225>

XIV. The obligation, under which subjects are in this respect, is so rigorous and strong, that, strictly speaking, no man can be exempted from taking up arms when his country calls upon him for assistance; and his refusal would be a just reason not to tolerate such a person any longer in the society. If in most governments there are some subjects exempted from military exercises, this immunity is not a privilege that belongs to them by right; it is only a toleration that has no force, but when there are troops sufficient for the defence of the commonwealth, and the persons to whom it is granted follow some other useful and necessary em-

4. This striking formulation is not to be found among usual ones listed by Barbeyrac in DNG VIII.6 §2 note 4, except perhaps if it is meant as a rephrasing of Aristotle's dictum "we make war that we may live in peace."

ployment. Excepting this case, in time of need all the members of the state ought to take the field, and none can be lawfully exempted.[5]

XV. In consequence of these principles, military discipline should be very rigorous; the smallest neglect, or the least fault, is often of the last importance, and for that reason may be severely punished. Other judges make some allowance for the weakness of human nature, or the violence of passions; but in a council of war, there is not so much indulgence; death is often inflicted on a soldier, whom the dread of that very evil has induced to quit his post.

XVI. It is therefore the duty of those who are once enlisted, to maintain the post where the general has placed them, and to fight bravely, even though they run a risque of losing their lives. To conquer or die, is the law of such engagements; and it is certainly much better to lose one's life gloriously, by endeavouring to destroy that of the enemy, than to <226> die in a cowardly manner. Hence some judgment may be formed of what we ought to think of those captains of ships, who, by the orders of their superior, blow themselves up into the air, rather than fall into the hands of the enemy. Suppose the number of ships equal on both sides, if one of our vessels is taken, the enemy will have two more than we; whereas if one of ours is sunk, they will have but one more; and if the vessel, which wants to take ours, sinks with it, which often happens, the forces will remain equal.[6]

XVII. In regard to the question, whether subjects are obliged to take up arms, and serve in an unjust war, we must judge of it by the principles already established at the end of the first chapter of the third part, which treats of *the legislative power.*

XVIII. These are the obligations of subjects with respect to war and to the defence of government; but this part of the supreme power being

5. This paragraph and the following are from DNG VIII.2 §1.
6. This paragraph is based on DNG VIII.2 §4.

of great importance, the utmost precaution is required in the sovereign to exercise it in such a manner as may prove advantageous to the state. We shall here point out the principal maxims on this article of politics.

XIX. First then it is evident, that the force of a state, with respect to war, consists chiefly in the number of its inhabitants; sovereigns therefore ought to neglect nothing that can either support or augment the number of them.

XX. Among the other means, which may be < 227 > used for this purpose, there are three of great efficacy. The first is, easily to receive all strangers of a good character, who want to settle among us; to let them taste the sweets of government; and to make them share the advantages of civil liberty. Thus the state is filled with subjects, who bring with them the arts, commerce, and riches; and among whom we may, in time of need, find a considerable number of good soldiers.[7]

XXI. Another thing, conducive to the same end, is to favour and encourage marriages, which are the pledges of the state; and to make good laws for this purpose. The mildness of the government may, among other things, greatly contribute to incline the subjects to join together in wedlock. People loaded with taxes, who can hardly, by their labour, find wherewithal to supply the wants of life and the public charges, are not inclined to marry, lest their children should starve for hunger.[8]

XXII. Lastly, another means, very proper for maintaining and augmenting the number of inhabitants, is liberty of conscience. Religion is one of the greatest advantages of mankind, and all men view it in that light. Every thing tending to deprive them of this liberty, appears insupportable. They cannot easily accustom themselves to a government

7. Pufendorf makes a similar point in DNG III.3 §10.
8. Based on DNG VIII.5 §3 note 1. The expression "pépinières de l'état" or "the seedbeds of the state" (here confusingly translated as the "pledges" of the state) is from DNG VI.1 §1.

which tyrannizes over them in this article. France, Spain and Holland, present us with sensible proofs of the truth of these observations. Persecutions have deprived the first of a great part of her inhabitants; by which means she has been considerably weakened. The <228> second is almost unpeopled; and this depopulation is occasioned by the barbarous and tyrannical establishment called the *Inquisition,* an establishment equally affronting to God and pernicious to human society, and which has made a kind of desert of one of the finest countries in Europe. The third, in consequence of an entire liberty of conscience, which she offers to all the world, is considerably improved even amidst wars and disasters. She has raised herself, as it were, on the ruin of other nations, and by the number of her inhabitants, who have brought power, commerce and riches into her bosom, she enjoys a high degree of credit and prosperity.[9]

XXIII. The great number of inhabitants is therefore the principal strength of a country. But, for this end, the subjects must also be inured betimes to labour, and trained to virtue. Luxury, effeminacy, and pleasure, impair the body and enervate the mind. A prince therefore, who desires to put the military establishment on a proper footing, ought to take particular care of the education of youth, so as to procure his subjects the means of forming themselves, by a strict discipline, to bodily exercises, and to prevent luxury and pleasures from debauching their manners, or weakening their courage.

XXIV. Lastly, one of the most effectual means of having good troops, is to make them observe the military order and discipline with all possible care and exactness; to take particular care that the soldiers be punctually paid; to see that the sick be properly looked after, and to furnish them

9. Compared with Barbeyrac or Grotius, Burlamaqui seems reluctant to take a stand on the issue of religious toleration, the present passages constituting one of the chief exceptions to this rule. The remark that religious toleration has advantages in terms of population growth was popular among the defenders of freedom of conscience in the Netherlands; see, for example, Barbeyrac, *Traité de la morale des pères de l'église* (Amsterdam, 1728), §31.

with the assistance <229> they stand in need of; lastly, to preserve among them a knowledge of religion and of the duties it prescribes, by procuring them the means of instruction. These are the principal maxims which good policy suggests to sovereigns, by means of which they may reasonably hope always to find good troops among their subjects, such as shall be disposed to spill the last drop of their blood in defence of their country.

CHAPTER II

Of the causes of war.

I. If war be sometimes lawful, and even necessary, as we have already demonstrated; this is to be understood when it is undertaken only for just reasons, and on condition that the prince, who undertakes it, proposes, by that method, to obtain a solid and lasting peace. A war may therefore be either just or unjust, according to the cause which has produced it.

II. A war is just if undertaken for just reasons; and unjust if it be entered into without a cause, or at least without a just and sufficient motive.

III. To illustrate the matter, we may, with Grotius, distinguish between the justifying reasons, and the motives of the war. The former are those which render, or seem to render, the war just with respect to the enemy, so that in taking up arms against him we do not think we do him injustice. <230> The latter are the views of interest which determine a prince to come to an open rupture. Thus in the war of Alexander against Darius, the justifying reason of the former was, to revenge the injuries which the Greeks had received from the Persians. The motives were, the ambition, vanity, and avarice of that conqueror, who took up arms the more chearfully, as the expeditions of Xenophon and Agesilaus made him conceive great hopes of success. The justifying reason of the second *Punic* war was, a dispute about the city of Saguntum. The motive was, an old grudge entertained by the Carthaginians against the Romans for the hard terms they were obliged to submit to when reduced to a low condition, and the encouragement given them by the success of their arms in Spain.[1]

IV. In a war, perfectly just, the justifying reasons must not only be lawful, but also be blended with the motive; that is, we must never undertake a war but from the necessity of defending ourselves against an insult, of recovering our undoubted right, or of obtaining satisfaction for a manifest injury.

V. Thus a war may be vicious or unjust, with respect to the causes, four different ways.

  1°. When we undertake it without any just reason, or so much as an apparent motive of advantage, but only from a fierce and brutal fury, which delights in blood and slaughter. But it may be doubted, whether we can find an example of so barbarous a war.[2] <231>

VI. 2°. When we attack others only for our own interest, without their having done us any injury; that is, when we have no justifying causes: and these wars are, with respect to the aggressor, downright robberies.

VII. 3°. When we have some motives founded on justifying causes, but which have still only an apparent equity, and when well examined, are found at the bottom to be unlawful.

VIII. 4°. Lastly, we may say that a war is also unjust, when, though we have good justifying reasons, yet we undertake it from other motives, which have no relation to the injury received; as for instance, through vain glory, or the desire of extending our dominions, &c.

IX. Of these four sorts of war, the undertaking of which includes injustice, the third and last are very common, for there are few nations so

  1. This paragraph and the next draw on DGP II.1 §1 and DGP II.22 §2.
  2. The summary of Grotius's position presented in this and the four following paragraphs is taken from DNG VIII.6 §4 note 1.

barbarous as to take up arms without alledging some sort of justifying reasons. It is not difficult to discover the injustice of the third; as to the fourth, though perhaps very common, it is not so much unjust in itself, as with respect to the view and design of the person who undertakes it. But it is very difficult to convince him of it, the motives being generally impenetrable, or at least most princes taking great care to conceal them.*
<232>

X. From the principles here established we may conclude, that every just war must be made, either to defend ourselves and our property against those who endeavour to injure us by assaulting our persons, and by taking away or ruining our estates; or to constrain others to yield up to us what they ought to do, when we have a perfect right to require it of them; or lastly, to obtain satisfaction for the damages we have injuriously sustained, and to force those who did the injury to give security for their good behaviour.

XI. From hence we easily conceive what the causes of war may be. But to illustrate the subject still further, we shall give some examples of the principal unjust causes of war.

1°. Thus, for example, to have a just reason for war, it is not sufficient that we are afraid of the growing power of a neighbour. All we can do, in those circumstances, is innocently to try to obtain *real caution,* that he will attempt nothing against us; and to put ourselves in a posture of defence. But acts of hostility are not permitted, except when necessary, and they are never necessary so long as we are not morally certain that the neighbour we dread has not only the power, but also the inclination to attack us. We cannot, for instance, justly declare war against a neighbour, purely because he orders citadels or fortifications to be erected, which he may some time or other employ to our prejudice.[3]

---

* See the explication of these principles in Budeus's Jurisprud. hist. specim. § 28, &c.

3. Based on DGP II.22 §5.

XII. 2°. Neither does utility alone give the same right as necessity, nor is it sufficient to render <233> a war lawful. Thus, for example, we are not allowed to take up arms with a view to make ourselves masters of a place which lies conveniently for us, and is proper to cover our frontiers.[4]

XIII. 3°. We must say the same of the desire of changing our former settlements, and of removing from marshes and deserts to a more fertile soil.

4°. Nor is it less unjust to invade the rights and liberty of a people, under a pretext of their not being so polished in their manners, or of such quick understanding as ourselves. It was therefore unjust in the Greeks to treat those, whom they called *Barbarians,* as their natural enemies, on account of the diversity of their manners, and perhaps because they did not appear to be so ingenious as themselves.[5]

XIV. 5°. It would also be an unjust war to take up arms against a nation, in order to bring them under subjection, under pretence of its being their interest to be governed by us. Though a thing may be advantageous to a person, yet this does not give us a right to compel him to it. Whoever has the use of reason, ought to have the liberty of choosing what he thinks advantageous to himself.[6]

XV. We must also observe, that the duties which nations ought to practise towards each other, are not all equally obligatory, and that their deficiency in this respect does not always lay a foundation for a just war. Among nations, as well as individuals, there are duties attended with a rigorous and perfect obligation, the violation of which implies *an injury* <234> *properly so called;* and duties of an imperfect obligation, which give to another only an imperfect right. And as we cannot, in a dispute between individuals, have recourse to courts of law to recover what in

---

4. Based on DGP II.22 §6 note 1.
5. This paragraph draws on DGP II.22 §§8–10.
6. This is drawn from DGP II.22 §12, where Grotius also denies that there are men who are slaves by nature.

this second manner is our due; so neither can we, in contests between different powers, constrain them by force of arms.

XVI. We must however except from this rule, the cases of necessity in which the *imperfect* is *changed* into the *perfect right;* so that, in those cases, the refusal of him, who will not give us our due, furnishes us with a just reason for war. But every war, undertaken on account of the refusal of what a man is not obliged by the laws of humanity to grant, is unjust.[7]

XVII. To apply these principles, we shall give some examples. The right of passing over the lands of another is really founded on humanity, when we design to use that permission only on a lawful account; as when people, expelled their own country, want to settle elsewhere; or when, in the prosecution of a just war, it is necessary to pass through the territories of a neutral nation, &c. But this is only an office of humanity which is not due to another in virtue of a perfect and rigorous right, and the refusal of it does not authorise a nation to challenge it in a forcible manner.[8]

XVIII. Grotius however, examining this question, pretends, "that we are not only obliged to grant a passage over our lands to a small number of men < 235 > unarmed, and from whom we have consequently nothing to fear; but moreover that we cannot refuse it to a large army, notwithstanding the just apprehension we may have that this passage will do us a considerable injury, which is likely to arise either from that army itself, or from those against whom it marches: provided," continues he, "1°. that this passage is asked on a just account. 2°. That it is asked before an attempt is made to pass by force."

---

7. See DNG VIII.6 §3 note 2.

8. Grotius discussed granting passage in DGP II.2 §13, which Burlamaqui makes use of here. Burlamaqui uses Pufendorf's criticism of Grotius in DNG III.3 §5 and especially Barbeyrac's equally critical remarks in DGP II.2 §13 note 1 to work out his own account as it is laid out in this and the four following paragraphs.

XIX. This author then pretends, that, under those circumstances, the refusal authorises us to have recourse to arms, and that we may lawfully procure by force, what we could not obtain by favour, even though the passage may be had elsewhere by taking a larger circuit. He adds, "That the suspicion of danger from the passing of a great number of armed men, is not a sufficient reason to refuse it, because good precautions may be taken against it. Neither is the fear of provoking that prince, against whom the other marches his army, a sufficient reason for refusing him passage, if the latter has a just reason for undertaking the war."

XX. Grotius founds his opinion on this reason, that the establishment of property was originally made with the tacit reservation of the right of using the property of another in time of need, so far as it can be done without injuring the owner.

XXI. But I cannot embrace the opinion of this celebrated writer; for, 1°. whatever may be said, it <236> is certain that the right of passing through the territories of another is not a perfect right, the execution of which can be rigorously demanded. If a private person is not obliged to suffer another to pass through his ground, much less is a nation obliged to grant a passage to a foreign army, without any compact or concession intervening.

XXII. 2°. The great inconveniencies which may follow such a permission, authorise this refusal. By granting such a passage, we run a risque of making our own country the seat of war. Besides, if they, to whom we grant the passage, are repulsed and vanquished, let the reasons they had for making war be ever so just, yet will not the enemy revenge himself upon us who did not hinder those troops from invading him? But farther, suppose that we live in friendship with both the princes who are at war, we cannot favour one to the prejudice of the other, without giving this other a sufficient reason to look upon us as enemies, and as defective in that part of our duty which we owe to our neighbours. It would be in vain, on this occasion, to distinguish between a just and an unjust war, pretending that the latter gives a right of refusing the passage, but that the former obliges us to grant it. This distinction does not remove the difficulty; for, besides that it is not always easy to decide whether a war be just or unjust, it is a piece of rashness to thrust in our arbitration between two armed parties, and to intermeddle with their differences.[9]

XXIII. 3°. But is there nothing to fear from the <237> troops to whom the passage is granted? The abettors of the contrary opinion agree there is, for which reason they allow that many precautions ought to be observed. But whatever precautions we may take, none of them can secure us against all events; and some evils and losses are irreparable. Men that are always in arms are easily tempted to abuse them, and to commit outrages; especially if they be numerous, and find an opportunity of making a considerable booty. How often have we seen foreign armies ravage and appropriate to themselves the estates of a people who have called them to their assistance? Nor have the most solemn treaties and oaths been able to deter them from this black perfidiousness.* What then may we expect from those who are under no such strict engagement?

XXIV. 4°. Another observation we may make, which is of great use in politics, that almost all states have this in common, that the further we advance into the heart of a country, the weaker we find it. The Carthaginians, otherwise invincible, were vanquished near Carthage by Agathocles and Scipio. Hannibal affirmed, that the Romans could not be conquered except in Italy. It is therefore dangerous to lay open this secret to a multitude of foreigners, who, having arms at hand, may take advantage of our weakness, and make us repent our imprudence.

XXV. 5°. To this we must add, that in every state there are almost always mutinous and turbulent spirits, who are ready to stir up strangers either against their <238> fellow-citizens, their sovereign, or their neighbours. These reasons sufficiently prove, that all the precautions which can be taken cannot secure us from danger.

* See Just. lib. iv. cap. 4. & 8. and Liv. lib. vii. cap. 38.
9. This paragraph and the two following are drawn from DNG III.3 §5 note 7.

6°. Lastly, we may add the example of a great many nations, who have been very ill requited for letting foreign troops pass through their country.

XXVI. We shall finish the examination of this question by making two remarks. The first is, that it is evident from the whole of what has been said, that this is a matter of prudence; and that though we are not obliged to grant a passage to foreign troops, and the safest way is to refuse it, yet when we are not strong enough to resist those who want to pass at any rate, and by resisting we must involve ourselves in a troublesome war, we ought certainly to grant a passage; and the necessity to which we are reduced, is a sufficient justification to the prince whose territories those troops are going to invade.[10]

XXVII. My second remark is, that if we suppose, on one hand, that the war which the prince, who demands a passage through our country, makes, is just and necessary, and, on the other, that we have nothing to fear either from him that is to pass, or him against whom he marches; we are then indispensably obliged to grant a passage. For if the law of nature obliges every man to assist those whom he sees manifestly oppressed, when he can do it without danger and with hopes of success, much less ought he to be a hindrance to such as undertake their own defence. <239>

XXVIII. By following the principles here established, we may judge of the right of transporting merchandizes through the territories of another. This is also an imperfect right, and a duty of humanity, which obliges us to grant it to others; but the obligation is not rigorous, and the refusal cannot be a just reason for war.[11]

XXIX. Truly speaking, the laws of humanity indispensably oblige us to grant a passage to such foreign commodities as are absolutely necessary

---

10. Based on DNG III.3 §5.
11. This and the following paragraphs are based on DNG III.3 §6.

for life, which our neighbours cannot procure by themselves, and with which we are not able to furnish them. But, except in this case, we may have good reasons for hindering foreign commodities from passing through our country. Too great a resort of strangers is sometimes dangerous to a state; and besides, why should not a sovereign procure to his own subjects that profit, which would otherwise be made by foreigners, by means of the passage granted them?

XXX. It is not however contrary to humanity to require toll or custom for foreign commodities to which a passage is granted. This is a just reimbursement for the expences the sovereign is obliged to be at in repairing the high roads, bridges, harbours, &c.

XXXI. We must reason in the same manner in regard to commerce in general between different states. The same may be said of the right of being supplied with wives by our neighbours; a refusal on their side, though there be great plenty of women among them,[12] does not authorize us to declare war. <240>

XXXII. We shall here subjoin something concerning wars undertaken on account of religion. The law of nature, which permits a man to defend his life, his substance, and all the other advantages which he enjoys, against the attacks of an unjust aggressor, certainly grants him the liberty also of defending himself against those who would, as it were by force, deprive him of his religion, by hindering him to profess that which he thinks the best, or by constraining him to embrace that which he thinks to be false.[13]

XXXIII. In a word, religion is one of the greatest blessings man can enjoy, and includes his most essential interests. Whoever opposes him in this

12. The translator adds "though there be great plenty of women among them." This paragraph is from DNG III.3 §§13–14, while the preceding paragraph provided an abbreviated overview of DNG III.3 §7.
13. This paragraph elaborates on DNG VIII.6 §3 note 1.

respect, declares himself his enemy; and consequently he may justly use forcible methods to repel the injury, and to secure himself against the evil intended him. It is therefore lawful, and even just, to take up arms, when we are attacked for the cause of religion.[14]

XXXIV. But though we are allowed to defend ourselves in the cause of religion, we are not permitted to make war in order to propagate that which we profess, and to constrain those who have some principle or practice different from ours. The one is a necessary consequence of the other. It is not lawful to attack him who has a right to defend himself. If the defensive war is just, the offensive must needs be criminal. The very nature of religion does not permit that violent means should be used for its propagation; it consists in the internal persuasion. The right of mankind, in regard to the propagation of religion, is to inform and instruct those who are <241> in an error, and to use the soft and gentle methods of conviction. Men must be persuaded, and not compelled. To act otherwise, is to commit a robbery on them; a robbery so much the more criminal, as those who commit it endeavour to justify themselves by sacred authority. There is therefore no less folly, than impiety, in such a conduct.

XXXV. In particular, nothing is more contrary to the spirit of Christianity, than to employ the force of arms for the propagation of our holy religion. Christ, our divine master, instructed mankind, but never treated them with violence.[15] The apostles followed his example; and the enumerations which St. Paul makes of the arms he employed for the conversion of mankind, is an excellent lesson to Christians.*

---

* 2 Cor. chap. vi. v. 4, &c. and chap. x. v. 4.

14. This paragraph draws on DNG VII.8 §5 note 7, while the following summarizes Grotius's statements on wars of religion; Burlamaqui could be using Barbeyrac's summary in DNG VIII.6 §3 note 1. See also DNG VII.4 §11 note 2.

15. Grotius makes a similar statement in DGP II.20 §48, a statement that Barbeyrac summarizes in DNG VIII.6 §3 note 1, which seems to be Burlamaqui's main source here. Barbeyrac makes similar claims in *Traité de la morale des pères* §29, where he also adds the reference to the Pauline letters to the Romans that Burlamaqui uses here. The next paragraph repeats Barbeyrac's standpoint in DNG VIII.6 §3 note 1.

XXXVI. So far is a simple difference of opinion, in matters of religion, from being a just reason for pursuing, by force of arms, or disturbing in the least, those whom we think in an error; that, on the contrary, such as act in this manner, furnish others with a just reason of making war against them, and of defending those whom they unjustly oppress. Upon which occasion the following question occurs: *Whether protestant princes may not, with a good conscience, enter into a confederacy to destroy the Inquisition, and oblige the powers, who suffer it in their dominions, to disarm that cabal, under which Christianity has so long groaned, and which, under a false pretence to zeal and piety, exercises a tyranny most horrible in itself,* <242> *and most contrary to human nature?* Be that as it may, it is at least certain, that never would any hero have subdued monsters more furious and destructive to mankind, than he who could accomplish the design of purging the earth of these wicked men, who so impudently and cruelly abuse the specious shew of religion, only to procure wherewith to live in luxury and idleness, and to make both princes and subjects dependent on them.

XXXVII. These are the principal remarks which occur on the causes of war. To which let us add, that as we ought not to make war, which of itself is a very great evil, but to obtain a solid peace, it is absolutely necessary to consult the rules of prudence before we undertake it, however just it may otherwise appear. We must, above all things, exactly weigh the good or evil, which we may bring upon ourselves by it: For if in making war, there is reason to fear that we shall draw greater evils on ourselves, or those that belong to us, than the good we can propose from it; it is better to put up with the injury, than to expose ourselves to more considerable evils, than that for which we seek redress by arms.[16]

XXXVIII. In the circumstances here mentioned we may lawfully make war, not only for ourselves, but also for others; provided that he, in whose favour we engage, has just reason to take up arms, and that we are likewise

16. This forms a summary of DGP II.24.

under some particular tie or obligation to him, which authorises us to treat as enemies those who have done us no injury.[17] <243>

XXXIX. Now among those, whom we may and ought to defend, we must give the first place to such as depend on the defender, that is, to the subjects of the state; for it is principally with this view of protection that men, before independent, incorporated themselves into civil society. Thus the Gibeonites having submitted themselves to the government of the Israelites, the latter took up arms on their account, under the command of Joshua. The Romans also proceeded in the same manner. But sovereigns in these cases ought to observe the maxim we have established in sect. 37. They ought to beware in taking up arms for some of their subjects, not to bring a greater inconveniency on the body of the state. The duty of the sovereign regards first and principally the interest of the whole, rather than that of a part; and the greater the part is, the nearer it approaches to the whole.[18]

XL. 2°. Next to subjects come our allies, whom we are expressly engaged by treaty to assist in time of need; and this, whether they have put themselves entirely under our protection, and so depend upon it; or whether assistance be agreed upon for mutual security.

XLI. But the war must be justly undertaken by our ally; for we cannot innocently engage to help any one in a war, which is manifestly unjust. Let us add here, that we may, even without prejudice to the treaty, defend our own subjects preferably to our allies, when there is no possibility of assisting <244> them both at the same time; for the engagements of a government to its subjects always supersede those into which it enters with strangers.

17. Taken from DNG VIII.6 §14, a paragraph that summarizes DGP II.25, especially §4.

18. Based on DNG VIII.6 §14, except for the example which is from the passages in Grotius that the DNG paragraph summarizes, DGP II.25 §§1–2. The next two paragraphs are from the same paragraph in the DNG, or of DGP II.25 §4.

XLII. As to what Grotius says, that we are not obliged to assist an ally, when there is no hope of success; it is to be understood in this manner. If we see that our united forces are not sufficient to oppose the enemy, and that our ally, though able to treat with him on tolerable terms, is yet obstinately bent to expose himself to certain ruin; we are not obliged, by the treaty of alliance, to join with him in so extravagant and desperate an attempt. But then it is also to be considered, that alliances would become useless, if, in virtue of this union, we were not obliged to expose ourselves to some danger, or to sustain some loss in the defence of an ally.

XLIII. Here it may be enquired; when several of our allies want assistance, which ought to be helped first, and preferably to the rest? Grotius answers, that when two allies unjustly make war upon each other, we ought to succour neither of them; but if the cause of one ally be just, we must not only assist him against strangers, but also against another of our allies, unless there be some particular clause in a treaty, which does not permit us to defend the former against the latter, even though the latter has committed the injury. In fine, that if several of our allies enter into a league against a common foe, or make war separately against particular enemies, we must assist them all equally, <245> and according to treaty; but when there is no possibility of assisting them all at once, we must give the preference to the oldest confederate.[19]

XLIV. 3°. Friends, or those with whom we are united by particular ties of kindness and affection, hold the third rank. For though we have not promised them assistance, determined by a formal treaty; yet the nature of friendship itself implies a mutual engagement to help each other, so far as the stricter obligations the friends are under will permit; and the concern for each other's safety ought to be much stronger, than that which is demanded by the simple connection of humanity.[20]

19. This paragraph is from DNG VIII.9 §5 note 1.
20. This and the two following paragraphs are again from DNG VIII.6 §14, except that Burlamaqui is less critical of a right of interference than Pufendorf.

XLV. I say that we may take up arms for our friends, who are engaged in a just war; for we are not under a strict obligation to assist them: and this condition ought to be understood, if we can do it easily, and without any great inconveniency to ourselves.

XLVI. 4°. In fine, we may affirm that the single relation, in which all mankind stand to each other, in consequence of their common nature and society, and which forms the most extensive connection, is sufficient to authorise us in assisting those who are unjustly oppressed; at least if the injustice be considerable, and manifest, and the party injured call us to his assistance; so that we act rather in his name, than in our own. But even here we must make this remark, that we have a right to succour the distressed purely from humanity, but that <246> we are not under a strict obligation of doing it. It is a duty of imperfect obligation, which binds us only so far as we can practise it, without bringing a considerable inconveniency upon ourselves; for all circumstances being equal, we may, and even ought to prefer our own preservation to that of another.

XLVII. It is another question, whether we can undertake a war in defence of the subjects of a foreign prince, against his invasions and oppressions, merely from the principle of humanity? I answer, that this is permitted only in cases where the tyranny is risen to such a height, that the subjects themselves may lawfully take up arms, to shake off the yoke of the tyrant, according to the principles already established.[21]

XLVIII. It is true, that since the institution of civil societies, the sovereign has acquired a peculiar right over his subjects, in virtue of which he can punish them, and no other power has any business to interfere. But it is no less certain, that this right hath its bounds, and that it cannot be lawfully exercised, except when the subjects are really culpable, or at least when their innocence is dubious. Then the presumption ought to

21. This paragraph is taken either from DNG VIII.6 §14 or from DGP II.25 §8, but the next paragraph is clearly from the latter.

be in favour of the sovereign, and a foreign power has no right to in-termeddle with what passes in another state.

XLIX. But if the tyranny be arrived at its greatest height, if the oppres-sion be manifest, as when a <247> Busiris or Phalaris oppress their sub-jects in so cruel a manner, as must be condemned by every reasonable man living; we cannot refuse the subjects, thus oppressed, the protection of the laws of society. Every man, as such, has a right to claim the as-sistance of other men when he is really in necessity; and every one is obliged to give it him, when he can, by the laws of humanity. Now it is certain, that we neither do, nor can renounce those laws, by entering into society, which could never have been established to the prejudice of human nature: though we may be justly supposed to have engaged, not to implore a foreign aid for slight injuries, or even for great ones, which affect only a few persons.

But when all the subjects, or a considerable part of them, groan under the oppression of a tyrant, the subjects, on the one hand, re-enter into the several rights of natural liberty, which authorises them to seek assis-tance wherever they can find it; and, on the other hand, those who are in a condition of giving it them, without any considerable damage to themselves, not only may, but ought to do all they can to deliver the oppressed; for the single consideration of pity and humanity.[22]

L. It appears indeed, from ancient and modern history, that the desire of invading the states of others is often covered by those pretexts; but the bad use of a thing, does not hinder it from being just. Pirates navigate the seas, and robbers wear swords, as well as other people. <248>

___

22. Read: ". . . for the single reason that they are men and members of the human society that civil societies participate in." This paragraph is from DGP II.25 §8 note 1. The next paragraph is again from the main text of that paragraph.

CHAPTER III

Of the different kinds of war.

I. Besides the division above-mentioned of war into just and unjust, there are several others, which it is proper now to consider. And first, war is distinguished into *offensive* and *defensive*.

II. Defensive wars are those undertaken for the defence of our persons, or the preservation of our properties. Offensive wars are those which are made to constrain others to give us our due, in virtue of a perfect right we have to exact it of them; or to obtain satisfaction for a damage unjustly done us, and to force them to give caution for the future.[1]

III. 1°. We must therefore take care not to confound this with the former distinction; as if every defensive war were just, and, on the contrary, every offensive war unjust. It is the present custom to excuse the most unjust wars, by saying they are purely defensive. Some people think that all unjust wars ought to be called offensive, which is not true; for if some offensive wars be just, as there is no doubt of it, there are also defensive wars unjust; as when we defend ourselves against a prince who has had sufficient provocation to attack us.[2]

IV. 2°. Neither are we to believe, that he who first injures another, begins by that an offensive war, and that the other, who demands satisfaction for the <249> injury, is always upon the defensive. There are a great many unjust acts which may kindle a war, and yet are not the war; as the ill treatment of a prince's ambassador, the plundering of his subjects, &c. If therefore we take up arms to revenge such an unjust act, we commence an offensive, but a just war; while the prince who has done the injury,

1. This paragraph is based on DNG VIII.6 §3, while the next four are drawn from note 1 to the same.
2. The translator's "has had sufficient provocation" is not a good translation for the original "a raison." The French "avoir raison" can mean either "have reason" or "have just cause."

and will not give satisfaction, makes a defensive, but an unjust war. An offensive war is therefore unjust only, when it is undertaken without a lawful cause; and then the defensive war, which on other occasions might be unjust, becomes just.

V. We must therefore affirm, in general, that the first who takes up arms, whether justly or unjustly, commences an offensive war; and he who opposes him, whether with or without a reason, begins a defensive war. Those who look upon the word *offensive war* to be an odious term, as always implying something unjust; and who, on the contrary, consider a defensive war as inseparable from equity, confound ideas, and perplex a thing, which of itself seems to be sufficiently clear. It is with princes as with private persons. The plaintiff who commences a suit at law, is sometimes in the wrong, and sometimes in the right. It is the same with the defendant. It is wrong to refuse to pay a sum which is justly due; and it is right to forbear paying what we do not owe.

VI. In the third place, Grotius distinguishes war into *private, public,* and *mix'd.*[3] *Public war* he calls that which is made on both sides by the authority <250> of the civil power: *Private war,* that which is made between private persons, without any public authority: and, lastly, *mix'd war,* that which, on one side, is carried on by public authority, and, on the other, by private persons.

VII. We may observe concerning this division, that if we take the word *war* in the most general and extensive sense, and understand by it *all taking up arms with a view to decide a quarrel,* in contradistinction to the way of deciding a difference by recourse to a common judge, then this distinction may be admitted; but custom seems to explode it, and has restrained the signification of the word *war* to that carried on between sovereign powers. In civil society, private persons have not a right to make war; and as for the state of nature, we have already treated of the right which men have in that state to defend and preserve their persons

3. In DGP I.3 §1.

and properties; so that as we are here treating only of the right of sovereigns, with regard to each other, it is properly public, and not private war, that falls under our present consideration.

VIII. 4°. War is also distinguished into *solemn according to the laws of nations,* and *not solemn.* To render a war solemn, two things are requisite; the first, that it be made by the authority of the sovereign; the second, that it be accompanied with certain formalities, as a formal declaration, &c. but of this we shall treat more fully in its proper place. War not solemn, is that which is made either with-<251>out a formal declaration, or against mere private persons. We shall here only hint at this division, deferring a more particular examination of it, and an enquiry into its effects, till we come to treat of the formalities which usually precede war.[4]

IX. But a question is moved, relating to this subject, which is, whether a magistrate, properly so called, and as such, has a power of making war of his own accord? Grotius answers, that judging independently of the civil laws, every magistrate seems to have as much right, in case of resistance, to take up arms in order to exercise his jurisdiction, and to see his commands executed, as to defend the people intrusted to his care. Puffendorf, on the contrary, takes the negative, and passes censure on the opinion of Grotius.

X. But it is easy to reconcile these two authors, the dispute between them being merely about words. Grotius fixes a more vague and general idea to the term *war:** according to him, therefore, when a subordinate magistrate takes up arms to maintain his authority, and to reduce those to reason who refuse to submit to him, he is supposed to act with the approbation of the sovereign; who, by entrusting him with a share in the government of the state, has at the same time invested him with the power necessary to exercise it. And thus the question is only, whether

---

* See above, sect. vii. [i.e., §7 in this chapter.]

4. Based on DNG VIII.6 §9; the following paragraph is from §10 of the same chapter and on DGP I.3 §4.

every magistrate, as such, has need, on this occasion, of an express order
from the sovereign; so that the constitution of civil societies in general
re-<252>quire it, independently of the laws of each particular state.[5]

XI. Now if a magistrate can have recourse to arms for the reduction of
one person, of two, ten, or twenty, who either refuse to obey him, or
attempt to hinder the exercise of his jurisdiction, why may he not use
the same means against fifty, a hundred, a thousand? &c. The greater
the number of the disobedient, the more he will have occasion for force
to overcome their resistance. Now this is what Grotius includes under
the term *war.*

XII. Puffendorf agrees to this in the main; but he pretends that this
coercive power, which belongs to a magistrate over disobedient subjects,
is not a right of war; war seeming to be intirely between equals, or at
least such as pretend to equality. The idea of Puffendorf's is certainly
more regular, and agreeable to custom; but it is evident, that the difference between him and Grotius consists only in the greater or lesser extent
which each of them gives to the word *war.*

XIII. If it be objected, that it is dangerous to leave so much power to a
subordinate magistrate; this may be true: but then it proves only that
the prudence of legislators requires they should set bounds in this respect
to the power of magistrates, in order to prevent an inconveniency which
should otherwise arise from the institution of magistracy. <253>

XIV. But to judge of the power of the magistrates, or of generals and
leaders, in respect to war, properly so called, and which is carried on
against a foreign enemy, we need only to attend to their commissions;
for it is evident that they cannot lawfully undertake any act of hostility

---

5. This and the next paragraphs are taken from DGP I.3 §4 note 6. In paragraph
12 below, Burlamaqui expands on the issue before returning in paragraph 13 to his
repetition of Barbeyrac's footnote.

of their own head, and without a formal order of the sovereign, at least reasonably presumed, in consequence of particular circumstances.[6]

XV. Thus, for example, a general sent upon an expedition with an unlimited authority, may act against the enemy offensively, as well as defensively, and in such a manner as he shall judge most advantageous; but he can neither levy a new war, nor make peace of his own head. But if his power be limited, he ought never to pass the bounds prescribed, unless he is unavoidably reduced to it by the necessity of self-defence; for whatever he does in that case, is supposed to be with the consent and approbation of the sovereign. Thus, if an admiral has orders to be upon the defensive, he may, notwithstanding such a restraint, break in upon the enemy's fleet, and sink and burn as many of their ships as he can, if they come to attack him: all that he is forbidden, is to challenge the enemy first.

XVI. In general, the governors of provinces and cities, if they have troops under their command, may by their own authority defend themselves against an enemy who attacks them; but they ought not to carry the war into a foreign country, without an express order from their sovereign. <254>

XVII. It was in virtue of this privilege, arising from necessity, that Lucius Pinarius,* governor of Enna in Sicily for the Romans, upon certain information that the inhabitants designed to revolt to the Carthaginians, put them all to the sword, and thus preserved the place. But, except in the like case of necessity, the inhabitants of a town have no right to take up arms, in order to obtain satisfaction for those injuries which the prince neglects to revenge.

XVIII. A mere presumption of the will of the sovereign, would not even be sufficient to excuse a governor, or any other officer, who should un-

---

* Livy, lib. xxi. cap. xviii.
6. This and the three following paragraphs are from DNG VIII.6 §10.

dertake a war, except in case of necessity, without either a general or particular order. For it is not sufficient to know what part the sovereign would probably act, if he were consulted, in such a particular posture of affairs; but it should rather be considered in general, what it is probable a prince would desire should be done without consulting him, when the matter will bear some delay, and the affair is dubious. Now certainly sovereigns will never consent that their ministers should, whenever they think proper, undertake, without their order, a thing of such importance as an offensive war, which is the proper subject of the present inquiry.[7]

XIX. In these circumstances, whatever part the sovereign would have thought proper to act, if he had been consulted; and whatever success the war, undertaken without his orders, may have had; it is left to the sovereign whether he will ratify, or con-<255>demn the act of his minister. If he ratifies it, this approbation renders the war solemn, by reflecting back, as it were, an authority upon it, so that it obliges the whole commonwealth. But if the sovereign should condemn the act of the governor, the hostilities committed by the latter ought to pass for a sort of robbery, the fault of which by no means affects the state, provided the governor is delivered up, or punished according to the laws of the country, and proper satisfaction be made for the damages sustained.

XX. We may further observe, that in civil societies, when a particular member has done an injury to a stranger, the governor of the commonwealth is sometimes responsible for it, so that war may be declared against him on that account. But to ground this kind of imputation, we must necessarily suppose one of these two things, sufferance, or reception; viz. either that the sovereign has suffered this harm to be done to the stranger, or that he afforded a retreat to the criminal.[8]

7. This paragraph is from DNG VIII.6 §11. The following is again from §10 of the same chapter.
8. Read: "accused" rather than "responsible." This paragraph and the three following are from DNG VIII.6 §12.

XXI. In the former case it must be laid down as a maxim, that a sovereign, who knowing the crimes of his subjects, as for example, that they practise piracy on strangers; and being also able and obliged to hinder it, does not hinder it, renders himself criminal, because he has consented to the bad action, the commission of which he has permitted, and consequently furnished a just reason of war. <256>

XXII. The two conditions above-mentioned, I mean the knowledge and sufferance of the sovereign, are absolutely necessary, the one not being sufficient without the other, to communicate any share in the guilt. Now it is presumed, that a sovereign knows what his subjects openly and frequently commit; and as to his power of hindering the evil, this likewise is always presumed, unless the want of it be clearly proved.

XXIII. The other way, in which a sovereign renders himself guilty of the crime of another, is by allowing a retreat and admittance to the criminal, and skreening him from punishment. Puffendorf pretends, that if we are obliged to deliver up a criminal who takes shelter among us, it is rather in virtue of some treaty on this head, than in consequence of a common and indispensable obligation.

XXIV. But Puffendorf, I think, has, without sufficient reasons, abandoned the opinion of Grotius, which seems to be better founded. The principles of the latter, in regard to the present question, may be reduced to these following.

1°. Since the establishment of civil societies, the right of punishing public offences, which every person, if not chargeable himself with such a crime, had in the state of nature, has been transferred to the sovereign, so that the latter alone hath the privilege of punishing, as he thinks proper, those transgressions of his subjects, which properly interest the public.[9] <257>

9. Read: "which properly interest the body of which they are members." Pufendorf's position is also rejected by Barbeyrac, who refers to the relevant passages in Grotius in DNG VIII.6 §12 note 2. These passages are in DGP II.20 §§3–6 and are

XXV. But this right of punishing crimes is not so exclusively theirs, but that either public bodies, or their governors, have a right to procure the punishment of them in the same manner, as the laws of particular countries allow private people the prosecution of crimes before the civil tribunal.

XXVI. 3°. This right is still stronger with respect to crimes, by which they are directly injured, and which they have a perfect right of punishing, for the support of their honour and[10] safety. In such circumstances, the state, to which the criminal retires, ought not to obstruct the right that belongs to the other power.

XXVII. 4°. Now as one prince does not generally permit another to send armed men into his territories, upon the score of exacting punishment (for this would indeed be attended with terrible inconveniencies) it is reasonable[11] the sovereign, in whose dominions the offender lives, or has taken shelter, should either punish the criminal according to his demerits, or deliver him up, to be punished at the discretion of the injured sovereign. This is that delivering up, of which we have so many examples in history.

XXVIII. 5°. The principles here laid down, concerning the obligation of punishing or delivering up, regard not only the criminals who have always been subjects of the government they now live under, but also those who, after the commission of a crime, have taken shelter in the country. <258>

XXIX. 6°. In fine, we must observe that the right of demanding fugitive delinquents to punishment, has not for some ages last past been insisted

---

summarized by Barbeyrac in DNG VIII.3 §4 note 3, which also contains a presentation of Locke's similarly non-Pufendorfian approach. The main source for this and the next two paragraphs seems to be DGP II.21 §3.

    10. Read: "or." At the end of this paragraph, read "all other powers" ("toute autre puissance").

    11. Read: "necessary that." This paragraph is from DGP II.21 §4.

upon by sovereigns, in most parts of Europe, except in crimes against the state, or those of a very heinous nature. As to lesser crimes, they are connived at on both sides, unless it is otherwise agreed on by some particular treaty.

XXX. Besides the kinds of war, hitherto mentioned, we may also distinguish them into *perfect* and *imperfect*. A perfect war, is that which entirely interrupts the tranquillity of the state, and lays a foundation for all possible acts of hostility. An imperfect war, on the contrary, is that which does not intirely interrupt the peace, but only in certain particulars, the public tranquillity being in other respects undisturbed.

XXXI. This last species of war is generally called reprisals, of the nature of which we shall give here some account. By reprisals then we mean *that imperfect kind of war, or those acts of hostility which sovereigns exercise against each other, or, with their consent, their subjects, by seizing the persons or effects of the subjects of a foreign commonwealth, that refuseth to do us justice; with a view to obtain security, and to recover our right, and in case of refusal, to do justice to ourselves, without any other interruption of the public tranquillity.* [12]

XXXII. Grotius pretends, that reprisals are not founded on the law of nature and necessity, but <259> only on a kind of arbitrary law of nations, by which most of them have agreed, that the goods belonging to the subjects of a foreign state should be a pledge or security, as it were, for what that state, or the governor of it, might owe us, either directly, and in their own names, or by rendering themselves responsible for the actions of others, upon refusing to administer justice.

XXXIII. But this is far from being an arbitrary right, founded upon a pretended law of nations, whose existence we cannot prove, depending on the greater or less extent of custom no way binding in the nature of a law. The right we here speak of, is a consequence of the constitution

12. Based on DNG VIII.6 §13 and on note 1 to the same.

of civil societies, and an application of the maxims of the law of nature to that constitution.[13]

XXXIV. During the independence of the state of nature, and before the institution of civil government, if a person had been injured, he could come upon those only who had done the wrong, or upon their accomplices; because there was then no tie between men, in virtue of which a person might be deemed to have consented, in some manner, to what others did even without his participation.

XXXV. But since civil societies have been formed, that is to say, communities, whose members are all united together for their common defence, there has necessarily arisen from thence a conjunction of interests and wills; which is the reason, that as the <260> society, or the powers which govern it, engage to defend each other against every insult; so each individual may be deemed to have engaged to answer for the conduct of the society, of which he is a member, or of the powers which govern it.

XXXVI. No human establishment can supersede the obligation of that general and inviolable law of nature, *that the damage we have done to another should be repaired;* except those, who are thereby injured, have manifestly renounced their right of demanding reparation. And when such establishments hinder those who are injured, from obtaining satisfaction so easily as they might without them, this difficulty must be made up, by furnishing the persons interested with all the other possible methods of doing themselves justice.

XXXVII. Now it is certain that societies, or the powers which govern them, by being armed with the force of the whole body, are sometimes encouraged to laugh with impunity at strangers, who come to demand their due; and that every subject contributes, one way or other, to enable them to act in this manner; so that he may be supposed in some measure

13. This and the five following paragraphs are based on DGP III.2 §2 note 1.

to consent to it. But if he does not in reality consent, there is, after all, no other manner of facilitating, to injured strangers, the prosecution of their rights, which is rendered difficult by the united force of the whole body, than to authorise them to come upon all those who are members of it. <261>

XXXVIII. Let us therefore conclude, that by the constitution of civil societies, every subject, so long as he continues such, is responsible to strangers for the conduct of the society, or of him who governs it; with this clause, however, that he may demand indemnification, when there is any fault or injustice on the part of his superiors. But if it should be any man's misfortune to be disappointed of this indemnification, he must look upon it as one of those inconveniencies which, in a civil state, the constitution of human affairs renders almost inevitable. If to all these we add the reasons alledged by Grotius, we shall plainly see, that there is no necessity for supposing a tacit consent of the people to found the right of reprisals.

XXXIX. As reprisals are acts of hostility, and often the prelude or fore-runner of a compleat and perfect war, it is plain that none but the sovereign can lawfully use this right, and that the subjects can make no reprisals but by his order and authority.[14]

XL. Besides, it is proper that the wrong or injustice done us, and which occasions the reprisals, should be clear and evident, and that the thing in dispute be of great consequence. For if the injury be dubious, or of no importance, it would be equally unjust and dangerous to proceed to this extremity, and to expose ourselves to all the calamities of an open war. Neither ought we to come to reprisals, before we have tried, by the ordinary means, to obtain justice for the injury committed. For this purpose we must apply to the prince, whose subject <262> has done us the

14. This and the five following paragraphs are (again very nearly word for word) from DNG VIII.6 §13 note 1.

injustice; and if the prince takes no notice, or refuses satisfaction, we may then make reprisals, in order to obtain it.

XLI. In a word, we must not have recourse to reprisals, except when all the ordinary means of obtaining satisfaction have failed; so that, for instance, if a subordinate magistrate has refused us justice, we are not permitted to use reprisals before we apply to the sovereign himself, who will perhaps grant us satisfaction. In such circumstances, we may therefore either detain the subjects of a foreign state, if they with-hold ours; or we may seize their goods and effects. But whatever just reason we may have to make reprisals, we can never directly, and for that reason alone, put those to death whom we have seized upon, but only secure them, and not use them ill, till we have obtained satisfaction; so that, during all that time, they are to be considered as hostages.

XLII. In regard to the goods seized by the right of reprisals, we must take care of them till the time, in which satisfaction ought to be made, is expired; after which we may adjudge them to the creditor, or sell them for the payment of the debt; returning to him, from whom they were taken, the overplus, when all charges are deducted.

XLIII. We must also observe, that it is not permitted to use reprisals, except with regard to subjects, properly so called, and their effects; for as to strangers, who do but pass through a country, or <263> only come to make a short stay in it, they have not a sufficient connection with the state, of which they are only members but for a time, and in an imperfect manner; so that we cannot indemnify ourselves by them, for the loss we have sustained by any native of the country, and by the refusal of the sovereign to render us justice. We must farther except ambassadors, who are sacred persons, even in the height of war. But as to women, clergymen, men of letters, &c. the law of nature grants them no privilege in this case, if they have not otherwise acquired it by virtue of some treaty.

XLIV. Lastly, some political writers distinguish those wars which are carried on between two or more sovereigns, from those of the subjects against their governors. But it is plain, that when subjects take up arms against their prince, they either do it for just reasons, and according to the principles established in this work, or without a just and lawful cause. In the latter case, it is rather a revolt or insurrection, than a war, properly so called. But if the subjects have just reason to resist the sovereign, it is strictly a war; since, in such a crisis, there are neither sovereign nor subjects, all dependance and obligation having ceased. The two opposite parties are then in a state of nature and equality, trying to obtain justice by their own proper strength, which constitutes what we understand properly by the term *war.*[15] <264>

CHAPTER IV

Of those things which ought to precede war.

I. However just reason we may have to make war, yet as it inevitably brings along with it an incredible number of calamities, and oftentimes acts of injustice, it is certain that we ought not to proceed too easily to a dangerous extremity, which may perhaps prove fatal to the conqueror himself.

II. The following are the measures which prudence directs to be observed in these circumstances.

1°. Supposing the reason of the war is just in itself, yet the dispute ought to be about something of great consequence; since it is better even to relinquish part of our right, when the thing is not considerable, than to have recourse to arms to defend it.

2°. We ought to have, at least, a probable appearance of success; for it would be a criminal temerity, to expose ourselves to certain destruction, and to run into a greater, in order to avoid a lesser evil.

3°. Lastly, there should be a real necessity for taking up arms; that is, we ought not to have recourse to force, but when we can employ no

---

15. Compare this with DNG VII.8 §6 note 1.

milder method of recovering our right, or of defending ourselves from the evils with which we are menaced. <265>

III. These measures are agreeable not only to the principles of prudence, but also to the fundamental maxims of sociability, and the love of peace; maxims of no less force, with respect to nations, than individuals. By these a sovereign must therefore be necessarily directed; justice obliges him to it, in consequence of the very nature and end of government. For as he ought to take particular care of the state, and of his subjects, he should not expose them to the evils with which war is attended, except in the last extremity, and when there is no other expedient left but that of arms.

IV. It is not therefore sufficient that the war be just in itself, with respect to the enemy; it must also be so with respect to ourselves, and our subjects. Plutarch informs us, "that among the ancient Romans, when the Feciales had determined that a war might be justly undertaken, the senate afterwards examined whether it would be advantageous to engage in it."

V. Now among the methods of deciding differences between nations without a war, there are three most considerable. The first is an amicable conference between the contending parties; with respect to which Cicero judiciously observes, "that this method of terminating a difference by a discussion of reasons on both sides, is peculiarly agreeable to the nature of man; that force belongs to brutes, and that we never ought to have recourse to it, but when we cannot redress our grievances by any other method."[1] <266>

VI. The second way of terminating a difference between those who have not a common judge, is to put the matter to arbitration. The more potent indeed often neglect this method, but it ought certainly to be followed

---

1. This paragraph is from DGP II.23 §7.

by those who have any regard to justice and peace; and it is a way that has been taken by great princes and people.[2]

VII. The third method, in fine, which may be sometimes used with success, is that of casting lots. I say, we may sometimes use this way; for it is not always lawful to refer the issue of a difference, or of a war, to the decision of lots. This method cannot be taken, except when the dispute is about a thing, in which we have a full property,[3] and which we may renounce whenever we please. But in general, the obligation of the sovereign to defend the lives, the honour, and the religion[4] of his subjects, as also his obligation to maintain the dignity of the state, are of too strong a nature to suffer him to renounce the most natural and most probable means of his own security, as well as that of the public, and to refer his case to chance, which in its nature is entirely precarious.

VIII. But if upon due examination he, who has been unjustly attacked, finds himself so weak, that he has no probability of making any considerable resistance, he may reasonably decide the difference by the way of lot, in order to avoid a certain, by exposing himself to an uncertain danger; which, in this case, is the least of two inevitable evils. <267>

IX. There is also another method, which has some relation to lots. This consists in single combats, which have often been used to terminate such differences as were likely to produce a war between two nations. And indeed, to prevent a war, and its concomitant evils, I see no reason that can hinder us from referring matters to a combat between a certain number of men agreed upon by both parties. History furnishes us with several

2. This paragraph is from DGP II.23 §8 and from note 1 to the same.

3. For "we have a full property" read: "we have a full right" ("sur laquelle on a un plein droit").

4. This paragraph uses DGP II.23 §9. In note 1 to that paragraph, Barbeyrac refers the reader to DGP III.20 §42, which Burlamaqui has also used here and in the next paragraph. Burlamaqui adds to Grotius's account when he states that the sovereign has a duty to defend not only the honor and so on of the subjects but also their religion.

examples of this kind, as that of Turnus and Eneas, Menelaus and Paris, the Horatii and the Curiatii.[5]

X. It is a question of some importance, to know whether it be lawful[6] thus to expose the interest of a whole state to the fate of those combats. It appears on the one hand, that by such means we spare the effusion of human blood, and abridge the calamities of war; on the other hand, it promiseth fairer, and looks like a better venture, to stand the shock even of a bloody war, than by one blow to risque the liberty and safety of the state by a decisive combat; since, after the loss of one or two battles, the war may be set on foot again, and a third perhaps may prove successful.

XI. However, it may be said, that if otherwise there is no prospect of making a good end of a war, and if the liberty and safety of the state are at stake, there seems to be no reason against taking this step, as the least of two evils.

XII. Grotius, in examining this question, pretends that these combats are not reconcileable to in-<268>ternal justice, though they are approved by the external right of nations; and that private persons cannot innocently expose their lives, of their own accord, to the hazard of a single combat, though such a combat may be innocently permitted by the state or sovereign, to prevent greater mischiefs. But it has been justly observed, that the arguments used by this great man, either prove nothing at all, or prove, at the same time, that it is never lawful to venture one's life in any combat whatever.[7]

XIII. We may even affirm, that Grotius is not very consistent with himself, since he permits this kind of combats, when otherwise there is the

5. This paragraph is from DGP II.23 §10.
6. For "whether it be lawful" read: "whether one does well to." This and the following paragraph are from VIII.8 §5.
7. This paragraph is from DGP III.20. §43 and note 5 to the same. The next paragraph is from note 7.

greatest probability that he who prosecutes an unjust cause will be victorious, and thereby destroy a great number of innocent persons: For this exception evinces that the thing is not bad in itself, and that all the harm, which can be in this case, consists in exposing our own life, or that of others, without necessity, to the hazard of a single combat. The desire of terminating, or preventing a war, which has always terrible consequences, even to the victorious, is so commendable, that it may excuse, if not intirely justify those, who engage either themselves or others even imprudently in a combat of this kind. Be this as it may, it is certain that in such a case, those who combat by the order of the state, are entirely innocent; for they are no more obliged to examine whether the state acts prudently or not, than when they are sent upon an assault, or to fight a pitched battle. <269>

XIV. We must however observe, that it was a foolish superstition in those people who looked upon a set combat as a lawful method of determining all differences, even between individuals, from a persuasion that the Deity gave always the victory to the good cause; for which reason they called this kind of combat *the judgment of God.*[8]

XV. But if, after having used all our endeavours to terminate differences in an amicable manner, there remains no further hope, and we are absolutely constrained to undertake a war, we ought first to declare it in form.

XVI. This declaration of war considered in itself, and independently of the particular formalities of each people, does not simply belong to the law of nations, taking this word in the sense of Grotius, but to the law of nature itself. Indeed prudence, and natural equity, equally require, that before we take up arms against any state, we should try all amicable methods, to avoid coming to such an extremity. We ought then to summon him, who has injured us, to make a speedy satisfaction, that we may

---

8. This paragraph is from DGP III.20 §43.

see whether he will not have regard to himself, and not put us to the hard necessity of pursuing our right by the force of arms.[9]

XVII. From what has been said it follows, that this declaration takes place only in *offensive wars;* for when we are actually attacked, that alone gives us reason to believe that the enemy is resolved not to listen to an accommodation. <270>

XVIII. From thence it also follows, that we ought not to commit acts of hostility immediately upon declaring war, but should wait, so long at least as we can without doing ourselves a prejudice, until he who has done us the injury plainly refuses to give us satisfaction, and has put himself in a condition to receive us with bravery and resolution;[10] otherwise the declaration of war would be only a vain ceremony. For we ought to neglect no means to convince all the world, and even the enemy himself, that it is only absolute necessity that obliges us to take up arms, for the recovery or defence of our just rights; after having tried every other method, and given the enemy full time to consider.

XIX. Declarations of war are distinguished into *conditional* and *absolute.* The *conditional* is that which is joined with a solemn demand of restitution, and with this condition, that if the injury be not repaired, we shall do ourselves justice by arms. The *absolute* is that which includes no condition, and by which we absolutely renounce the friendship and society of him against whom we declare war. But every declaration of war, in whatever manner it be made, is of its own nature conditional;* for we ought always to be disposed to accept of a reasonable satisfaction, so soon as the enemy offers it; and on this account some writers reject this distinction of the declaration of war into conditional and absolute. But it may nevertheless be maintained, by supposing that he, against whom

* See above, numb. xviii.

9. This paragraph and the next two are from DNG VIII.6 §9 note 1.

10. The translator omits "and this is true even when there is but little hope that he would give us satisfaction."

war is declared purely and simply, has already shewn, that he had no design <271> to spare us the necessity of taking up arms against him. So far therefore the declaration may, at least as to the form of it, be pure and simple, without any prejudice to the disposition in which we ought always to be, if the enemy will hearken to reason: but this relates to the conclusion, rather than the commencement of a war; to the latter of which the distinction of conditional and absolute declarations properly belongs.[11]

XX. As soon as war has been declared against a sovereign, it is presumed to be declared at the same time not only against all his subjects, who, in conjunction with him, form one moral person; but also against all those who shall afterwards join him, and who, with respect to the principal enemy, are to be looked upon only as allies, or adherents.[12]

XXI. As to the formalities observed by different nations in declaring war, they are all arbitrary in themselves. It is therefore a matter of indifference, whether the declaration be made by envoys, heralds, or letters; whether to the sovereign in person, or to his subjects, provided the sovereign cannot plead ignorance of it.

XXII. With respect to the reasons why a solemn denunciation was required unto such a war, as by the law of nations is called just;[13] Grotius pretends it was, that the people might be assured that the war was not undertaken by private authority, but by the consent of one or other of the nations, or of their sovereigns. <272>

XXIII. But this reason of Grotius's seems to be insufficient; for are we more assured that the war is made by public authority, when a herald, for instance, comes to declare it with certain ceremonies, than we should

---

11. This paragraph is from DGP III.3 §7 and note 1 to the same.
12. This paragraph is from DGP III.3 §9.
13. For "is called just" read: "as can be called legitimate and solemn." This paragraph is from DGP III.3 §11.

be, when we see an army upon our frontiers, commanded by a principal person of the state, and ready to enter our country? Might it not more easily happen, that one, or a few persons, should assume the character of herald, than that a single man should, of his own authority, raise an army, and march at the head of it to the frontiers, without the sovereign's knowledge?[14]

XXIV. The truth is, the principal end of a declaration of war, or at least what has occasioned its institution, is to let all the world know that there was just reason to take up arms, and to signify to the enemy himself, that it had been, and still was, in his power to avoid it. The declarations of war, and the manifestos published by princes, are marks of the due respect they have for each other, and for society in general, to whom by such means they give an account of their conduct, in order to obtain the public approbation. This appears particularly by the manner in which the Romans made those denunciations. The person sent for this purpose took the gods to witness, that the nation, against whom they had declared war, had acted unjustly, by refusing to comply with what law and justice required.

XXV. Lastly, it is to be observed, that we ought not to confound the *declaration* with the *publication* <273> of war. This last is made in favour of the subjects of the prince who declares the war, and to inform them, that they are henceforth to look upon such a nation as their enemies, and to take their measures accordingly.

CHAPTER V

General rules to know what is allowable in war.

I. It is not enough that a war be undertaken with justice, or for a lawful reason, and that we observe the other conditions hitherto mentioned; but we ought also, in the prosecution of it, to be directed by the prin-

14. This paragraph and the next are from DGP III.3 §11 note 2.

ciples of justice and humanity, and not to carry the liberties of hostility beyond those bounds.

II. Grotius, in treating this subject, establishes three general rules, as so many principles, which serve to explain the extent of the rights of war.[1]

III. The *first* is, that every thing which has a connection morally necessary with the end of the war, is permitted, and no more. For it would be to no purpose to have a right to do a thing, if we could not make use of the necessary means to bring it about. But, at the same time, it would not be just, that, under a pretence of defending our right, we should think every thing lawful, and pro-<274>ceed, without any manner of necessity, to the last extremity.

IV. The *second rule.* The right we have against an enemy, and which we pursue by arms, ought not to be considered only with respect to the cause which gave rise to the war; but also with respect to the fresh causes which happen afterwards, during the prosecution of hostilities: Just as in courts of law, one of the parties often acquires some new right before the end of the suit. This is the foundation of the right we have to act against those who join our enemy, during the course of the war, whether they be his dependents or not.

V. The *third rule,* in fine, is, that there are a great many things, which, though otherwise unlawful, are yet permitted in war, because they are inevitable consequences of it, and happen contrary to our intention, otherwise there would never be any way of making war without injustice; and the most innocent actions would be looked upon as criminal, since there are but few, from which some evil may not accidentally arise, contrary to the intention of the agent.

VI. Thus, for example, in recovering our own, if just so much as is precisely our due cannot be had, we have a right to take more, but under

1. This paragraph and the three following are from DNG 1732 VIII.6 §7 note 1.

the obligation of returning the value of the overplus. Hence we may attack[2] a ship full of pirates, though there may be women, or children, or other innocent persons on board, who must needs be exposed to the danger of <275> being involved in the ruin of those whom we may justly destroy.

VII. This is the extent of the right we have against an enemy, in consequence of a state of war. By a state of war, that of society is abolished; so that whoever declares himself my enemy, gives me liberty to use violence against him *in infinitum*, or so far as I please; and that not only till I have repulsed the danger that threatened me, or till I have recovered, or forced from him, what he either unjustly deprived me of, or refused to pay me, but till I have further obliged him to give me good security for the future. It is not therefore always unjust to return a greater evil for a less.[3]

VIII. But it is also to be observed, that though these maxims are true, according to the strict right of war, yet the law of humanity fixes bounds to this right. That law directs us to consider, not only whether such or such acts of hostility may, without injury, be committed against an enemy; but also, whether they are worthy of a humane or generous conqueror. Thus, so far as our own defence and future security will permit, we must moderate the evils we inflict upon an enemy, by the principles of humanity.

IX. As to the manner of acting lawfully against an enemy, it is evident that violence and terror are the proper characteristics of war, and the method most commonly used. Yet it is also lawful to employ stratagem and artifice, pro-<276>vided it be without treachery, or breach of promise. Thus we may deceive an enemy by false news, and fictitious relations,

2. Read: "attack with cannons." This paragraph is from DGP III.1 §4.
3. This paragraph and the next are based on DNG VIII.6 §7.

but we ought never to violate our compacts or engagements with him, as we shall shew more particularly hereafter.[4]

X. By this we may judge of the right of stratagems; neither is it to be doubted but we may innocently use fraud and artifice, wherever it is lawful to have recourse to violence and force. The former means have even the advantage over the latter, in this, that they are attended with less mischief, and preserve the lives of a great many innocent people.

XI. It is true, some nations have rejected the use of stratagem and deceit in war; this, however, was not because they thought them unjust, but from a certain magnanimity, and often from a confidence in their own strength. The Romans, till very near the end of the second *Punic war,* thought it a point of honour to use no stratagem against their enemies.[5]

XII. These are the principles by which we may judge to what degree the laws of hostility may be carried. To which let us add, that most nations have fixed no bounds to the rights which the law of nature gives us to act against an enemy: and the truth is, it is very difficult to determine, precisely, how far it is proper to extend acts of hostility even in the most legitimate wars, in defence of our persons, or for the reparation of damages, or for obtaining caution for the future; especially as those, who engage in war, give each other, by a kind of tacit <277> agreement, an entire liberty to moderate or augment the violence of arms, and to exercise all acts of hostility, as each shall think proper.[6]

XIII. And here it is to be observed, that though generals usually punish their soldiers, who have carried acts of hostility beyond the orders prescribed; yet this is not because they suppose the enemy is injured, but because it is necessary the general's orders should be obeyed, and that military discipline should be strictly observed.

4. This paragraph is based on DGP III.1 §6.
5. This paragraph is from DGP III.1 §20.
6. This paragraph and the two following are from DNG VIII.6 §15.

XIV. It is also, in consequence of these principles, that those who, in a just and solemn war, have pushed slaughter and plunder beyond what the law of nature permits, are not generally looked upon as murderers or robbers, nor punished as such. The custom of nations is to leave this point to the conscience of the persons engaged in war, rather than involve themselves in troublesome broils, by taking upon them to condemn either party.

XV. It may be even said, that this custom of nations is founded on the principles of the law of nature. Let us suppose, that in the independance of the state of nature, thirty heads of families, inhabitants of the same country, should have entered into a league to attack or repulse a body, composed of other heads of families: I say, that neither during that war, nor after it is finished, those of the same country, or elsewhere, who had not joined the league of either side, ought, or could punish, <278> as murderers or robbers, any of the two parties who should happen to fall into their hands.[7]

XVI. They could not do it during the war; for that would be espousing the quarrel of one of the parties; and since they continued neuter in the beginning, they had clearly renounced the right of interfering with what should pass in the war: much less could they intermeddle after the war is over; because, as it could not be ended without some accommodation or treaty of peace, the parties concerned were reciprocally discharged from all the evils they had done to each other.

XVII. The good of society also requires that we should follow these maxims. For if those, who continued neuter, had still been authorised to take cognizance of the acts of hostility, exercised in a foreign war, and consequently to punish such as they believed to have committed any injustice, and to take up arms on that account; instead of one war, several might have arisen, and proved a source of broils and troubles. The more wars became frequent, the more necessary it was, for the tranquillity of

7. This paragraph and the three following are from DGP III.4 §4 and especially note I to the same.

mankind, not to espouse rashly other people's quarrels. The establishment of civil societies only rendered the practice of those rules more necessary; because acts of hostility then became, if not more frequent, at least more extensive, and attended with a greater number of evils.

XVIII. Lastly, it is to be observed, that all acts of <279> hostility, which can be lawfully committed against an enemy, may be exercised either in his territories, or ours, in places subject to no jurisdiction, or at sea.

XIX. This does not hold good in a neutral country; that is to say, whose sovereign has taken no share in the war. In such countries, we cannot lawfully exercise any acts of hostility; neither on the persons of the enemy, nor on their effects; not in virtue of any right of the enemy themselves, but from a just respect to the sovereign, who having taken neither side, lays us under a necessity of respecting his jurisdiction, and of forbearing to commit any acts of violence in his territories. To this we may add, that the sovereign, by continuing neuter, has tacitly engaged not to suffer either party to commit any hostilities within his dominions.

CHAPTER VI

Of the rights which war gives over the persons of the enemy, and of their extent and bounds.

I. We shall now enter into the particulars of the different rights which war gives over the enemy's person and goods; and to begin with the former.

1°. It is certain that we may lawfully kill an enemy; I say lawfully, not only according to the terms of external justice, which passes for such among all <280> nations, but also according to internal justice, and the laws of conscience. Indeed the end of war necessarily requires that we should have this power, otherwise it would be in vain to take up arms, and the law of nature would permit it to no purpose.[1]

---

1. This paragraph and the next are based on DNG 1732 VIII.6 §7 note 1 and on DGP III.4 §5.

II. If we consulted only the custom of countries, and what Grotius calls the *law of nations,* this liberty of killing an enemy would extend very far; we might say that it had no bounds, and might even be exercised on innocent persons. However, though it be certain that war is attended with numberless evils, which in themselves are acts of injustice, and real cruelty, but, under particular circumstances, ought rather to be considered as unavoidable misfortunes; it is nevertheless true, that the right which war gives over the person and life of an enemy has its bounds, and that there are measures to be observed, which cannot be innocently neglected.

III. In general, we ought always to be directed by the principles established in the preceding chapter, in judging of the degrees to which the liberties of war may be carried. The power we have of taking away the life of an enemy, is not therefore unlimited; for if we can attain the legitimate end of war, that is, if we can defend our lives and properties, assert our rights, and recover satisfaction for damages sustained, and good sureties for the future, without taking away the life of the enemy, it is certain that justice and humanity directs us to forbear it, and not to shed human blood unnecessarily. <281>

IV. It is true, in the application of these rules to particular cases, it is sometimes very difficult, not to say impossible, to fix precisely their proper extent and bounds; but it is certain, at least, that we ought to come as near to them as possible, without prejudicing our real interests. Let us apply these principles to particular cases.

V. 1°. It is often disputed, whether the right of killing an enemy regards only those who are actually in arms; or whether it extends indifferently to all those in the enemy's country, subjects or foreigners? My answer is, that with respect to those who are subjects, the point is incontestable. These are the principal enemies, and we may exercise all acts of hostility against them, by virtue of the state of war.[2]

2. This paragraph is based on DGP III.4 §6. The next is from §7 to the same chapter.

VI. As to strangers, those who settle in the enemy's country after a war is begun, of which they had previous notice, may justly be looked upon as enemies, and treated as such. But in regard to such as went thither before the war, justice and humanity require that we should give them a reasonable time to retire; and if they neglect that opportunity, they are accounted enemies.

VII. 2°. With regard to old men, women and children, it is certain that the right of war does not, of itself, require that we should push hostilities so far as to kill them; it is therefore a barbarous cruelty to do so. I say, that the end of war does not require this of itself; but if women, for instance, exercise <282> acts of hostility; if, forgetting the weakness of their sex, they usurp the offices of men, and take up arms against us, then we are certainly excused in availing ourselves of the rights of war against them. It may also be said, that when the heat of action hurries the soldiers, as it were in spite of themselves and against the order of their superiors, to commit those acts of inhumanity; for example, at the siege of a town, which, by an obstinate resistance, has irritated the troops; we ought to look upon those evils rather as misfortunes, and the unavoidable consequences of war, than as crimes that deserve to be punished.[3]

VIII. 3°. We must reason almost in the same manner, with respect to prisoners of war. We cannot, generally speaking, put them to death, without being guilty of cruelty. I say generally speaking; for there may be cases of necessity so pressing, that the care of our own preservation obliges us to proceed to extremities, which in any other circumstances would be absolutely criminal.[4]

IX. In general, even the laws of war require that we should abstain from slaughter as much as possible, and not shed human blood without necessity. We ought not, therefore, directly and deliberately to kill prisoners

---

3. This paragraph is based on DGP III.4 §9 and DGP III.11 §9; compare with DNG 1732 VIII.6 §7 note 1.

4. This paragraph is from DGP III §13.

of war, nor those who ask quarter, or surrender themselves, much less old men, women and children; in general, we should spare all those whose age and profession render them unfit to carry arms, and who have no other share in the war, than their being in the enemy's country. It is <283> easy also to conceive, that the rights of war do not extend so far, as to authorise the outrages committed upon the honour and chastity of women; for this contributes nothing either to our defence or safety, or to the support of our rights, but only serves to satisfy the brutality of the soldiers.*

X. Again, a question is here started, whether in cases, where it is lawful to kill the enemy, we may not, for that purpose, use all kinds of means indifferently? I answer, that to consider the thing in itself, and in an abstract manner, it is no matter which way we kill an enemy, whether by open force, or by fraud and stratagem; by the sword, or by poison.

XI. It is however certain that, according to the idea and custom of civilized nations, it is looked upon as a base act of cowardice, not only to cause any poisonous draught to be given to the enemy, but also to poison wells, fountains, springs, rivers, arrows, darts, bullets, or other weapons used against him. Now it is sufficient, that this custom of looking on the use of poison as criminal, is received among the nations at variance with us, to suppose we comply with it, when, in the beginning of the war, we do not declare that we are at liberty to act otherwise, and leave it to our enemy's option to do the same.[5]

XII. We may so much the more suppose this tacit agreement, as humanity, and the interest of <284> both parties equally require it; especially since wars are become so frequent, and are often undertaken on such slight occasions; and since the human mind, ingenious in inventing the means to hurt, has so greatly multiplied those which are authorised

---

* Grotius, lib. iii. cap. iv. § 19. [This paragraph is from DNG VIII.6 §7 note 1, where Barbeyrac presents Grotius's position in abbreviated form. The next paragraph is from the same note or from DGP III.4 §15.]

5. This paragraph and the next are from DGP III.4 §15 note 1.

by custom, and looked upon as honest. Besides, it is beyond all doubt, that when we can obtain the same end by milder and more humane measures, which preserve the lives of many, and particularly of those in whose preservation human society is interested, humanity directs that we should take this course.

XIII. These are therefore just precautions, which men ought to follow for their own advantage. It is for the common benefit of mankind, that dangers should not be augmented without end. In particular, the public is interested in the preservation of the lives of kings, generals of armies, and other persons of the first rank, on whose safety that of societies generally depends. For if the lives of these persons are in greater safety than those of others, when attacked only by arms; they are, on the other hand, more in danger of poison, &c. and they would be every day exposed to perish in this manner, if they were not protected by a regard to some sort of law, or established custom.

XIV. Let us add, in fine, that all nations that ever pretended to justice and generosity, have followed these maxims. The Roman consuls, in a letter they wrote to Pyrrhus, informing him that one of his people had offered to poison him, said, <285> that it was the interest of all nations not to set such examples.

XV. It is likewise disputed, whether we may lawfully send a person to assassinate an enemy? I answer, 1°. that he who for this purpose employs only some of his own people, may do it justly. When it is lawful to kill an enemy, it is no matter whether those employed are many or few in number. Six hundred Lacedaemonians, with Leonidas, entered the enemy's camp, and went directly to the Persian king (Xerxes's) pavilion; and a smaller number might certainly have done the same. The famous attempt of Mucius Scevola is commended by all antiquity; and Porsenna himself, whose life was aimed at, acknowledged this to be an act of great valour.[6]

6. This paragraph is from DGP III.4 §18.

XVI. 2°. But it is not so easy to determine whether we may for this purpose employ assassins, who by undertaking this task must be guilty of falshood and treason; such as subjects with regard to their sovereign, and soldiers to their general. In this respect there are, in my opinion, two points to be distinguished. First, whether we do any wrong, even to the enemy himself, against whom we employ traitors; and secondly, whether supposing we do him no wrong, we commit nevertheless a bad action.[7]

XVII. 3°. With regard to the first question, to consider the thing in itself, and according to the rigorous law of war, it seems, that, admitting the war to be just, no wrong is done to the enemy, <286> whether we take advantage of the opportunity of a traitor, who freely offers himself, or whether we seek for it, and bring it about ourselves.

XVIII. The state of war, into which the enemy has put himself, and which it was in his own power to prevent, permits of itself every method that can be used against him; so that he has no reason to complain, whatever we do. Besides, we are no more obliged, strictly speaking, to respect the right he has over his subjects, and the fidelity they owe him as such, than their lives and fortunes, of which we may certainly deprive them by the right of war.

XIX. 4°. And yet I believe that this is not sufficient to render an assassination, under such circumstances, entirely innocent. A sovereign, who has the least tenderness of conscience, and is convinced of the justice of his cause, will not endeavour to find out perfidious methods to subdue his enemy, nor be so ready to embrace those which may present themselves to him. The just confidence he has in the protection of heaven, the horror he conceives at the traitor's perfidy, the dread of becoming his accomplice, and of setting an example, which may fall again on himself and others, will make him despise and reject all the advantage he might propose to himself from such means.

---

7. This paragraph is partly drawn from DGP III.4 §18 note 11. The following seven paragraphs are from the same source.

XX. 5°. Let us also add, that such means cannot always be looked upon as entirely innocent, even with respect to the person who employs the assassin. The state of hostility, which supersedes <287> the intercourse of good offices, and authorises to hurt, does not therefore dissolve all ties of humanity, nor remove our obligation to avoid, as much as possible, the giving room for some bad actions of the enemy, or his people; especially those, who of themselves have had no part in the occasion of the war. Now every traitor certainly commits an action equally shameful and criminal.

XXI. 6°. We must therefore conclude with Grotius, that we can never in conscience seduce, or sollicit the subjects of an enemy to commit treason, because that is positively and directly inducing them to perpetrate a heinous crime, which otherwise would, in all probability, have been very remote from their thoughts.

XXII. 7°. It is quite another thing, when we only take advantage of the occasion and the dispositions we find in a person, who has had no need to be sollicited to commit treason. Here, I think, the infamy of the perfidy does not fall on him who finds it intirely formed in the heart of the traitor; especially if we consider, that, in this case between enemies, the thing, with respect to which we take advantage of the bad disposition of another, is of such a nature, that we may innocently and lawfully do it ourselves.

XXIII. 8°. Be that as it may, for the reasons above alledged, we ought not to take advantage of a treason which offered itself, except in an extraordinary case, and from a kind of necessity. And though the <288> custom of several nations has nothing obligatory in itself, yet as the people, with whom we are at variance, look upon the very acceptance of a certain kind of perfidy to be unlawful, as that of assassinating one's prince or general, we are reasonably supposed to comply with it by a tacit consent.

XXIV. 9°. Let us observe, however, that the law of nations allows some difference between a fair and legitimate enemy, and rebels, pirates, or highwaymen. The most religious princes make no difficulty to propose even rewards to those who will betray such persons; and the public odium of all, which men of this stamp lie under, is the cause that no body thinks the measure hard, or blames the conduct of the prince in using every method to destroy them.[8]

XXV. Lastly, it is permitted to kill an enemy wherever we find him, except in a neutral country; for violent means are not suffered in a civilised society, where we ought to implore the assistance of the magistrate. In the time of the second *Punic war*,* seven Carthaginian galleys rode in a harbour belonging to Syphax, who was then in peace both with the Romans and Carthaginians, and Scipio came that way with two galleys only. The Carthaginians immediately prepared to attack the Roman galleys, which they might easily have taken before they had entered the port; but being forced by a strong wind into the harbour, before the Carthaginians had time to weigh <289> anchor, they durst not attack them, because it was in a neutral prince's haven.[9]

XXVI. Here it may be proper to say something concerning prisoners of war. In former times, it was a custom almost universally established, that those who were made prisoners in a just and solemn war, whether they had surrendered themselves, or been taken by main force, became slaves, the moment they were conducted into some place dependent on the conqueror. And this right was exercised on all persons whatsoever, even on those who happened unfortunately to be in the enemy's country, at the time the war suddenly broke out.[10]

XXVII. Further, not only the prisoners themselves, but their posterity, were reduced to the same condition; that is to say, those born of a woman after she had been made a slave.[11]

* Livy, lib. xxviii. cap. xvii. numb. 12, & seq.
8. This paragraph is from DGP III.4 §18.
9. This paragraph is from DGP III.4 §8.
10. This paragraph is from DGP III.7 §1.
11. This paragraph is based on DGP III.7 §2. The following three paragraphs are based on DGP III.7 §3, §5, and §9, respectively.

XXVIII. The effects of such a slavery had no bounds; every thing was permitted to a master with respect to his slave, he had the power of life and death over him, and all that the slave possessed, or could afterwards acquire, belonged of right to the master.

XXIX. There is some probability, that the reason and end for which nations had established this custom of making slaves in war, was principally to induce the captors to abstain from slaughter, from a view of the advantages they reaped from their slaves. Thus historians observe, that civil wars were <290> more cruel than others, the general practice in that case being to put the prisoners to the sword, because they could not make slaves of them.

XXX. But Christian nations have generally agreed among themselves, to abolish the custom of making their prisoners yield perpetual service to the conqueror. At present it is thought sufficient to keep those that are taken in war, till their ransom is paid, the estimation of which depends on the will of the conqueror, unless there be a cartel, or agreement, by which it is fixed.

CHAPTER VII

Of the rights of war over the goods of an enemy.

I. As to the goods of an enemy, it is certain that the state of war permits us to carry them off, to ravage, to spoil, or even intirely to destroy them; for as Cicero very well observes, *It is not contrary to the law of nature, to plunder a person whom we may lawfully kill:* and all those mischiefs, which the law of nations allows us to do to the enemy, by ravaging and wasting his lands and goods, are called spoil or plunder.[1]

II. This right of spoil, or plunder, extends in general to all things belonging to the enemy; and the law of nations, properly so called, does

---

* Cic. de Off. lib. iii. cap. vi.

1. For the first two paragraphs, see DNG 1732 VIII.6 §7 note 1 and DGP III.5 §§1–2.

not exempt even sacred things; that is, things consecrated <291> either to the true God, or to false deities, and designed for the use of religion.

III. It is true, the practices and customs of nations do not agree in this respect; some having permitted the plunder of things sacred and religious, and others having looked upon it as a profanation. But whatever the customs of different people may be, they can never constitute the primitive rule of right. In order, therefore, to be assured of the right of war in regard to this article, we must have recourse to the law of nature and nations.

IV. I observe then, that things sacred are not in themselves different from those we call profane. The former differ from the latter, only by the religious use to which they were intended. But this application or use does not invest the things with the quality of holy and sacred, as an intrinsic and indelible character.[2]

V. The things thus consecrated still belong either to the state, or to the sovereign; and there is no reason why the prince, who has devoted them to religious purposes, may not afterwards apply them to the uses of life; for they, as well as all other public matters, are at his disposal.

VI. It is therefore a gross superstition to believe, that by the consecration, or destination of those things to the service of God, they change master, and belong no more to men, but are entirely with-<292>drawn from human commerce; and the property of them is transferred to God. This is a dangerous superstition, owing to the ambition of the clergy.

VII. We must therefore consider sacred things as public goods, which belong to the state or sovereign. All the liberty which the right of war gives over the goods belonging to the state, it also gives with respect to things called sacred. They may therefore be spoiled or wasted by the

2. For this paragraph and the three following, see DNG 1732 VIII.6 §7 note 1 and DGP III.5 §2.

enemy, at least so far as is necessary and conducive to the design of the war; a limitation not at all peculiar to the plunder of sacred or religious things.

VIII. For, in general, it certainly is not lawful to plunder[3] for plunder's sake, but it is just and innocent only, when it bears some relation to the design of the war; that is, when an advantage directly accrues from it to ourselves, by appropriating those goods, or at least, when by ravaging and destroying them, we in some measure weaken the enemy. It would be a madness, equally brutal and criminal, to do evil to another without a prospect of procuring some good, either directly or indirectly, to ourselves. It very seldom happens, for instance, that after the taking of towns, there is any necessity for ruining temples, statues, or other public or private structures: we should therefore generally spare all these, as well as the tombs and sepulchres.

IX. It may however be observed, with respect to things sacred, that they who believe they <293> contain something divine, and inviolable, are really in the wrong to meddle with them at all; but this is only, because they would then act against their conscience. And here, by the way, we may take notice of a reason given to clear the Pagans of the imputation of sacrilege, even when they pillaged the temples of the gods, whom they acknowledged as such; which is, they imagined that when a city was taken, the guardian deities of that place quitted, at the same time, their temples and altars, especially after those deities, with every thing else that was sacred, had been *invited out* with certain ceremonies. This is excellently described by Cocceius, in his dissertation *De Evocatione Sacrorum.*[4]

X. The learned Grotius furnishes us with wise reflections on this subject, to persuade generals to behave with moderation in regard to plunder,

3. The French expression is "faire du dégat," and it is not meant to include stealing but only destroying. This paragraph is taken from DNG 1732 VIII.6 §7 note 1. Grotius discusses the matter similarly in DGP III.12 §§1, 6.
4. The second half of this paragraph is taken from DGP III.5 §2 note 34.

from the advantages which may accrue to themselves from such a conduct. And first he says, "by these means we take from the enemy one of the most powerful weapons, despair. Besides, by sparing the enemy's country, we give room to believe that we are pretty confident of victory: and clemency is of itself proper to soften and engage the minds of men. All which may be proved by several illustrious examples."[5]

XI. Besides the power which war gives to spoil and destroy the goods of an enemy, it likewise confers a right of acquiring, appropriating, and justly retaining the goods we have taken from him, till the sum due to us is paid, including the expences <294> of the war, in which his refusal of payment engaged us; and whatever else we think necessary to secure to ourselves, by way of caution, from the enemy.

XII. By the law of nations, not only he that makes war for a just reason, but also every man, in a just war, acquires a property in what he takes from the enemy, and that without rule or measure, at least as to the external effects, with which the right of property is accompanied: that is to say, neutral nations ought to regard the two parties at war, as lawful proprietors of what they can take from each other by force of arms; the state of neutrality not permitting them to espouse either side, or to treat either of the contending powers as an usurper, pursuant to the principles already established.[6]

XIII. This is generally true, as well with respect to moveables as immoveables, so long as they are in the possession of him who has acquired them by the right of war. But if from the hands of the conqueror they have passed into the power of a third, there is no reason, if they are immoveables, why the ancient owner should not try to recover them from that third, who holds them of the enemy, by what title soever; for he has as good a right against the new possessor, as against the enemy himself.

5. This paragraph is from DGP III.12 §8.
6. This paragraph and the next two are from DGP III.6 §2 and note 1 to the same.

XIV. I said, *if they are immoveables;* for with respect to moveable effects, as they may easily be transferred by commerce into the hands of the subjects of a neutral state, often without their know-<295>ing that they were taken in war; the tranquillity of nations, the good of commerce, and even the state of neutrality, require that they should ever be reputed lawful prize, and the property of the person of whom we hold them. But the case is otherwise with respect to immoveables, they are such in their own nature; and those to whom a state, which has taken them from an enemy, would resign them, cannot be ignorant of the manner in which it possesses them.

XV. Here a question arises, when is it that things are said to be taken by the right of war, and justly deemed to belong to him who is in possession of them?[7] Grotius answers as a civilian, that a man is deemed to have taken moveable things by the right of war, so soon as they are secured from the pursuit of the enemy; or when he has made himself master of them in such a manner, that the first owner has lost all probable hopes of recovering them. Thus, says he, at sea, ships and other things are not said to be taken, till they are brought into some port or harbour belonging to us, or to some part of the sea where our fleet rides; for it is only then that the enemy begins to despair of recovering his property.

XVI. But, in my opinion, this manner of answering the question is altogether arbitrary. I see no reason why the prizes, taken from the enemy, should not become our property so soon as they are taken. For when two nations are at war, both of them have all the requisites for the acquisition <296> of property, at the very moment they take a prize. They have an intention to acquire a title of just property, namely, the right of war; and they are actually in possession of the thing. But if the principle, which Grotius supposes, were to be allowed, and the prizes taken from the enemy were not deemed a lawful acquisition, till they are transported to a place of safety, it would follow, that the booty which a small number

---

7. The question is discussed in DGP III.6 §3; in the next three paragraphs Burlamaqui also uses Barbeyrac's criticism in DGP III.6 §3 note 1.

of soldiers has taken in war, may be retaken from them by a stronger body of troops of the same party, as still belonging to the enemy, if this stronger body of troops has attacked the other before they had conveyed their booty to a place of safety.

XVII. The latter circumstance is therefore altogether indifferent, with respect to the present question. The greater or lesser difficulty the enemy may find, in recovering what has been taken from him, does not hinder the capture from actually belonging to the conqueror. Every enemy, as such, and so long as he continues such, retains the will to recover what the other has taken from him; and his present inability only reduces him to the necessity of waiting for a more favourable opportunity, which he still seeks and desires. Hence, with respect to him, the thing ought no more to be deemed taken, when in a place of safety, than when he is still in a condition of pursuing it. All that can be said, is, that in the latter case, the possession of the conqueror is not so secure as in the former. The truth is, this distinction has been invented only to establish the <297> rules of the right of postliminy, or the manner in which the subjects of the state, from whom something has been taken in war, re-enter upon their rights; rather than to determine the time of the acquisition of things taken by one enemy from another.

XVIII. This seems to be the determination of the law of nature in regard to this point. Grotius observes also, that by the customs established in his time,[8] it is sufficient that the prize has been twenty-four hours in the enemy's possession, to account it lost. Thuanus, in the year 1595, gives us an example, that this custom was observed also by land. The town of Liere in Brabant having been taken and retaken the same day, the plunder was returned to the inhabitants, because it had not been twenty-four hours in the hands of the enemy. But this rule was afterwards changed, with respect to the United Provinces; and in general we may observe, that every sovereign has a right to establish such rules, in regard to this point, as he thinks proper, and to make what agreement he pleases with

8. Add "among European countries."

other powers. There have been several made, at different times, between the Dutch and Spaniards, the Portugueze and the northern states.

XIX. Grotius applies these principles also to lands; they are not to be reputed lost so soon as they are seized on; but for this effect they are to be so secured with fortifications, that, without being forced, they cannot be repossessed by the first <298> owner. But to this case we may also apply the reflections already made. A territory belongs to an enemy as soon as he is master of it, and so long as he continues in possession of it. The greater, or lesser precautions to secure it, are nothing to the purpose.[9]

XX. But be this as it may, it is to be observed, that during the whole time of the war, the right we acquire over the things we have taken from the enemy, is of force only with respect to a third disinterested party; for the enemy himself may retake what he has lost, whenever he finds an opportunity, till by a treaty of peace he has renounced all his pretensions.

XXI. It is also certain, that in order to appropriate a thing by the right of war, it must belong to the enemy; for things belonging to people who are neither his subjects, nor animated with the same spirit as he against us, cannot be taken by the right of war, even though they are found in the enemy's country. But if neutral strangers furnish our enemy with any thing, and that with a design to put him into a condition of hurting us, they may be looked upon as taking part with our foe, and their effects may consequently be taken by the right of war.[10]

XXII. It is however to be observed, that in dubious cases it is always to be presumed, that what we find in the enemy's country, or in their ships, is deemed to belong to them; for besides that this <299> presumption is very natural, were the contrary maxim to take place, it would lay a

9. See DGP III.6 §4.
10. See DGP III.6 §5 and note 1 to the same.

foundation for an infinite number of frauds. But this presumption, however reasonable in itself, may be destroyed by contrary proofs.[11]

XXIII. Neither do the ships of friends become lawful prizes, though some of the enemy's effects are found in them, unless it is done by the consent of the owners; who by that step seem to violate the neutrality, or friendship, and give us a just right to treat them as an enemy.

XXIV. But in general we must observe, with respect to all these questions, that prudence and good policy require, that sovereigns should come to some agreement among themselves, in order to avoid the disputes which may arise from those different cases.

XXV. Let us also take notice of a consequence of the principles here established; which is, that when we have taken things from the enemy, of which he himself had stripped another by the right of war, the former possessor cannot claim them.[12]

XXVI. Another question is, whether things, taken in a public and solemn war, belong to the state, or to the individuals who are members of it, or to those who made the first seizure? I answer, that as the right of war is lodged in the sovereign alone, and undertaken by his authority, every thing taken is originally and pri-<300>marily acquired to him, whatever hands it first falls into.[13]

XXVII. However, as the war is burdensome to the subjects, both equity and humanity require that the sovereign should make them partake of the advantages which may accrue from it. This may be done, either by assigning to those who take the field a certain pay from the public, or by sharing the booty among them. As to foreign troops, the prince is

11. For this and the next paragraph, see DGP III.6 §6.
12. This paragraph is from DGP III.6 §7.
13. See DGP III.6 §8 and DNG VIII.6 §18.

obliged to give them no more than their pay; what he allows them above that, is pure liberality.[14]

XXVIII. Grotius, who examines this question at large, distinguishes between acts of hostility truly public, and private acts that are done upon the occasion of a public war. By the latter, according to him, private persons acquire to themselves principally, and directly, what they take from the enemy; whereas, by the former, every thing taken belongs to the whole body of the people, or to the sovereign. But this decision has been justly criticised. As all public war is made by the authority of the people, or of their chief, it is from this source we must originally derive whatever right individuals may have to things taken in war. In this case there must always be an express or tacit consent of the sovereign.

XXIX. It is also to be observed, that in treating this point Grotius has confounded different things. The question does not relate to the law of nations, <301> properly so called; for in whatever manner that law is understood, and whatever it be founded on, it ought to relate to the affairs in dispute between two different states. Now whether the booty belongs to the sovereign who makes war, or to the generals, or to the soldiers, or to other persons, that is nothing to the enemy, nor to other states. If what is taken be a good prize, it is of small consequence to the enemy in whose hands it remains. With regard to neutral people, it is sufficient that such of them as have purchased, or any other way acquired a moveable thing taken in war, cannot be molested, or prosecuted upon that account. The truth is, the regulations and customs, relating to this subject, are not of public right; and their conformity, in many countries, implies no more than a civil right, common to several nations separately.

XXX. As for what in particular relates to the acquisition of *incorporeal things* by the right of war, it is to be observed, that they do not become

14. This paragraph and the next two are based on DNG VIII.6 §18; see also DGP III.6 §10 note 1 and DGP III.6 §8 note 4. Note that Burlamaqui's footnote claims the regulations are "not of public right"—Barbeyrac's otherwise identical footnote stated the opposite.

our property, except we are in possession of the subject in which they inhere. Now the subjects they inhere in, are either things or persons. We often annex, for instance, to certain lands, rivers, ports and towns, particular rights, which always follow them, whatever possessors they come to; or rather, those who possess them, are thereby invested with certain rights over other things and persons.[15]

XXXI. The rights which belong directly and immediately to persons, regard either other persons, or only certain things. Those which are annexed to <302> persons over other persons, are not obtained but with the consent of the persons themselves; who are supposed not to have given a power over them to any man promiscuously, but to some certain person. Thus, for instance, though a king happens to be made prisoner of war, his enemies have not therefore acquired his kingdom with him.

XXXII. But with respect to personal rights over things, the bare seizure of the person of the enemy, is not a sufficient title to the property of all his effects, unless we really take possession of those effects at the same time. This may be illustrated by the example given by Grotius and Puffendorf: Alexander the Great having destroyed the city of Thebes, made a present to the Thessalians of an instrument, in which the latter acknowledged that they owed the Thebans a hundred talents.

XXXIII. These are the rights which war gives us over the effects of the enemy. But Grotius pretends, that the right by which we acquire things taken in war, is so proper and peculiar to a solemn war, declared in form, that it has no force in others, as in civil wars, &c. and that in the latter, in particular, there is no change of property, but in virtue of the sentence of a judge.[16]

---

15. This and the two following footnotes are from DNG VIII.6 §§19–20; see also DGP III.8 §4.
16. In DGP III.6 §27.

XXXIV. We may observe, however, upon this point, that in most civil wars no common judge is acknowledged. If the state is monarchical, the dispute turns either upon the succession to the crown, or upon a considerable part of the state's pretend-<303>ing that the king has abused his power, in a manner which authorises the subject to take up arms against him.[17]

XXXV. In the former case, the very nature of the cause, for which the war is undertaken, occasions the two parties of the state to form, as it were, two distinct bodies, till they come to agree upon a chief by some treaty. Hence, with respect to the two parties which were at war, it is on such a treaty that the right depends, which persons may have to that which has been taken on either side; and nothing hinders, but this right may be left on the same footing, and admitted to take place in the same manner, as in public wars between two states always distinct.

XXXVI. As to other nations, who were not concerned in the war, they have no more authority to examine the validity of the acquisitions, than they have to be judges of a war made between two different states.

XXXVII. The other case, I mean an insurrection of a considerable part of the state against the reigning prince, can rarely happen, except when that prince has given room for it, either by tyranny, or by the violation of the fundamental laws of the kingdom. Thus the government is then dissolved, and the state is actually divided into two distinct and independent bodies; so that we are to form here the same judgment as in the former case. <304>

XXXVIII. For much stronger reasons does this take place in the civil wars of a republican state; in which the war, immediately of itself, destroys the sovereignty, which subsists solely in the union of its members.

---

17. This paragraph and the six following are from DGP III.6 §27 note 2.

XXXIX. Grotius seems to have derived his ideas on this subject from the Roman laws; for these decreed, that prisoners taken in a civil war could not be reduced to slavery. This was, as Ulpian the civilian *remarks, because they looked upon a civil war not properly as a war, but as a *civil dissension;* for, adds he, a real war is made between those who are enemies, and animated with a hostile spirit, which prompts them to endeavour the ruin of each other's state. Whereas, in a civil war, however hurtful it often proves to the nation, the one party wants to save itself in one manner, and the other in another. Thus they are not enemies, and every person of the two parties remains always a citizen of the state so divided.

XL. But all this is a supposition, or *fiction of right,* which does not hinder what I have been saying from being true, and from taking place in general. And if, among the Romans, a person could not appropriate to himself the prisoners taken in a civil war, as real slaves, this was in virtue of a particular law received among them, and not on account of any defect of the conditions, or formalities, which, according to Grotius, are required by the law of nations, in a public or solemn war. <305>

XLI. Lastly, as to the wars of robbers and pirates, if they do not produce the effects above-mentioned, nor give to those pirates a right of appropriating what they have taken, it is because they are robbers, and enemies to mankind, and consequently persons whose acts of violence are manifestly unjust, which authorises all nations to treat them as enemies. Whereas, in other kinds of war, it is often difficult to judge on which side the right lies; so that the dispute continues, and ought to continue, undecided, with respect to those who are unconcerned in the war.[18]

---

* Lib. xxi. sect. 1. ff. de capt. & revers.
18. From DGP III.4 §4 note 1; see also DGP II.17 §19.

CHAPTER VIII

Of the right of sovereignty acquired over the conquered.

I. Besides the effects of war, hitherto mentioned, there remains one more, the most important of all, and which we shall here consider; I mean the right of sovereignty acquired over the conquered. We have already remarked, when explaining the different ways of obtaining the supreme power, that in general it may be acquired either in a violent manner, and by the right of conquest, &c.

II. We must however observe, that war or conquest, considered in itself, is not properly the cause of this acquisition; that is, it is not the immediate origin of sovereignty. For the supreme power is founded on the tacit or express consent of the peo-<306>ple, without which the state of war still subsists; for we cannot conceive how there can be an obligation to obey a person, to whom we have promised no subjection. War then is, properly speaking, no more than the occasion of obtaining the sovereignty; as the conquered chuse rather to submit to the victor, than to expose themselves to total destruction.[1]

III. Besides, the acquisition of sovereignty by the right of conquest cannot, strictly speaking, pass for lawful, unless the war be just in itself, and the end proposed authorises the conqueror to carry things to such extremity, as to acquire the supreme power over the vanquished: that is to say, either our enemy must have no other means of paying what he owes us, and of indemnifying us for the damages he has committed; or our own safety must absolutely oblige us to make him dependent on us. In such circumstances, it is certain that the resistance of a vanquished enemy, authorises us to push the acts of hostility against him so far, as to reduce him entirely under our power; and we may, without injustice,

---

1. This paragraph is based on DGP III.8 §1 note 1.

take advantage of the superiority of our arms, to extort from him the consent which he ought to give us of his own accord.[2]

IV. These are the true principles on which sovereignty, by the right of conquest, is grounded. Hence we may conclude, that if, upon this foundation, we were to judge of the different acquisitions of this nature, few of them would be found <307> well established; for it rarely happens, that the vanquished are reduced to such extremity, as not to be able to satisfy the just pretensions of the conqueror, otherwise than by submitting themselves to his dominion.

V. Let us however observe, that the interest and tranquillity of nations require, that we should moderate the rigour of the principles above established. If he who has constrained another, by the superiority of his arms, to submit to his dominion, had undertaken a war manifestly unjust, or if the pretext, on which it is founded, be visibly frivolous in the judgment of every reasonable person, I freely confess that a sovereignty, acquired in such circumstances, would be unjust; and I see no reason, why the vanquished people should be more obliged to keep such a treaty, than a man, who had fallen into the hands of robbers, would be under an obligation to pay, at their demand, the money he had promised them for the ransom of his life and liberty.[3]

VI. But if the conqueror had undertaken a war for some specious reason, though perhaps at the bottom not strictly just, the common interest of mankind requires, that we should observe the engagements we have entered into with him, though extorted by a terror in itself unjust; so long, at least, as no new reason supervenes, which may lawfully exempt us from keeping our promise. For as the law of nature directs that societies, as well as individuals, should labour for their preservation, it obliges us, <308> for this reason, not indeed to consider the acts of hostility committed by an unjust conqueror as properly just, but to look upon the engagement of an express, or tacit treaty, as nevertheless valid. So that

2. See DNG VII.7 §3. See also note 4 to the same.
3. Based on DNG VII.7 §4.

the vanquished cannot be released from observing it, under the pretext of its being caused by an unjust fear, as he might otherwise do, had he no regard to the advantages accruing from it to mankind.[4]

VII. These considerations will have still a greater weight, if we suppose that the conqueror, or his posterity, peaceably enjoy the sovereignty which he has acquired by right of conquest; and besides, that he govern the vanquished like a humane and generous prince. In such circumstances, a long possession, accompanied with an equitable government, may legitimate a conquest, in its beginning and principle the most unjust.[5]

VIII. There are modern civilians, who explain the thing somewhat differently. These maintain, that in a just war the victor acquires a full right of sovereignty over the vanquished, by the single title of conquest, independently of any convention; and even though the victor has otherwise obtained all the satisfaction, and indemnification, he could require.[6]

IX. The principal argument these writers make use of, is, that otherwise the conqueror could not be certain of the peaceable possession of what he has taken, or forced the conquered to give him, for his <309> just pretensions; since they might retake it from him, by the same right of war.

X. But this reason proves only that the conqueror, who has taken possession of the enemy's country, may command in it while he holds it, and not resign it, till he has good security that he shall obtain or possess, without hazard, what is necessary for the satisfaction and indemnity, which he has a right to exact by force. But the end of a just war does not always demand, that the conqueror should acquire an absolute and perpetual right of sovereignty over the conquered. It is only a favourable occasion of obtaining it; and for that purpose, there must always be an express or tacit consent of the vanquished. Otherwise, the state of war

4. Based on DGP III.19 §11 note 1. See also DNG VII.7 §3 note 4.
5. Based on DGP II.4 §8.
6. This and the four following paragraphs are from DGP III.8 §1 note 1.

still subsisting, the sovereignty of the conqueror has no other title than that of force, and lasts no longer than the vanquished are unable to throw off the yoke.

XI. All that can be said, is, that the neutral powers, purely because they are such, may, and ought to look upon the conqueror as the lawful possessor of the sovereignty, even though they should believe the war unjust on his side.

XII. The sovereignty thus acquired by the right of war, is generally of the absolute kind. But sometimes the vanquished enter into certain conditions with the conqueror, which limit, in some measure, the power he acquires over them. Be this as it may, it is certain that no conquest ever <310> authorises a prince to govern a people tyrannically; since, as we have before shewn, the most absolute sovereignty gives no right to oppress those who have surrendered; for even the very intention of government, and the laws of nature, equally conspire to lay the conqueror under an obligation, of governing those whom he has subdued, with moderation and equity.

XIII. There are, therefore, several precautions to be used in the exercise of the sovereignty acquired over the vanquished; such, for instance, was that prudent moderation of the ancient Romans, who confounded, in some measure, the vanquished with the victors, by hastening to incorporate them with themselves, and to make them sharers of their liberty and advantages. A piece of policy doubly salutary; which, at the same time that it rendered the condition of the vanquished more agreeable, considerably strengthened the power and empire of the Romans. "What would our empire now have been," says Seneca, "if the vanquished had not been intermixed with the victors, by the effect of a sound policy?" "Romulus, our founder," says Claudius in Tacitus, "was very wise with respect to most of the people he subdued, by making those, who were his enemies, the same day citizens."[7]

7. See DGP III.15 §3. For the following two paragraphs, see §4 and §5 to the same chapter respectively.

XIV. Another moderation in victory, consists in leaving to the conquered, either kings or people, the sovereignty which they enjoyed, and not to change the form of their government. No better method can be taken to secure a conquest: and of this we have several examples in <311> ancient history, especially in that of the Romans.

XV. But if the conqueror cannot, without danger to himself, grant all these advantages to the conquered; yet things may be so moderated, that some part of the sovereignty shall be left to them, or to their kings. Even when we strip the vanquished intirely of their independency, we may still leave them their own laws, customs, and magistrates, in regard to their private and public affairs, of small importance.

XVI. We must not, above all things, deprive the vanquished of the exercise of their religion, unless they happen to be convinced of the truth of that which the conqueror professes. This complaisance is not only of itself very agreeable to the vanquished, but the conqueror is absolutely obliged to it; and he cannot, without tyranny, oppress them in this article. Not that he ought not to try to bring the vanquished to the true religion; but he should only use such means, as are proportioned to the nature of the thing, and to the end he has in view; and such as have in themselves nothing violent, or contrary to humanity.[8]

XVII. Let us observe, lastly, that not only humanity, but prudence also, and even the interest of the victor, require that what we have been saying, with respect to a vanquished people, should be strictly practised. It is an important maxim in politics, that it is more difficult to keep, than to conquer pro-<312>vinces. Conquests demand no more than force, but justice must preserve them. These are the principal things to be observed, in respect to the different effects of war, and to the most essential questions relative to that subject. But as we have already had occasion to make

8. These arguments are from DGP III.15 §11 and note 3. Burlamaqui's statement is bolder than Grotius's: the latter merely claims noninterference in religious affairs is "by no means prejudicial to the conqueror." Burlamaqui could be following Barbeyrac, who repeatedly insists that religious toleration is a duty incumbent on every state; see, for example, DNG VII.4 §11 note 2.

mention of the article of neutrality, it will not be improper to say something more particular about it.

Of Neutrality.[9]

I. There is a *general,* and a *particular neutrality.* The general is, when
without being allied to either of the two enemies at war, we are disposed
to render to each the good offices which every nation is naturally obliged
to perform to other states.

II. The particular neutrality is, when we are particularly engaged to be
neuter by some compact, either tacit or express.

III. The latter species of neutrality is either full and intire, when we
behave alike towards both parties; or limited, as when we favour one side
more than the other.

IV. We cannot lawfully constrain any person to enter into a particular
neutrality; because every one is at liberty to make, or not make, particular
treaties, or alliances; or at least, they are not bound to do it but by virtue
of an imperfect obligation. But he, who has undertaken a just war, may
oblige <313> other nations to observe an exact and general neutrality;
that is to say, not to favour his enemy more than himself.

V. We shall give here an abstract, as it were, of the duties of neutral
nations. They are obliged equally to put in practice, towards both parties
at war, the laws of nature, as well absolute as conditional, whether these
impose a perfect, or only an imperfect obligation.

VI. If they do the one any office of humanity, they ought not to refuse
the like to the other, unless there be some manifest reason which engages
them to do something in favour of the one, which the other had otherwise no right to demand.

9. The whole discussion of neutrality is from Barbeyrac in DNG 1732 VIII.6 §7
note 2.

VII. But they are not obliged to do offices of humanity to one party, when they expose themselves to great danger, by refusing them to the other, who has as good a right to demand them.

VIII. They ought not to furnish either party with things which serve to exercise acts of hostility, unless they are authorised to do it by some particular engagement; and in regard to those which are of no use in war, if they supply one side with them, they must also the other.

IX. They ought to use all their endeavours to bring matters to an accommodation, that the injured party may obtain satisfaction, and the war be brought to a speedy conclusion. <314>

X. But if they be under any particular engagement, they should punctually fulfill it.

XI. On the other side, those who are at war must exactly observe, towards neutral nations, the laws of sociability, and not exercise any act of hostility against them, nor suffer their country to be plundered.

XII. They may however, in case of necessity, take possession of a place situated in a neutral country; provided, that as soon as the danger is over, they restore it to the right owner, and make him satisfaction for the damages he has received.

CHAPTER IX

Of public treaties in general.

I. The subject of public treaties constitutes a considerable part of the law of nations, and deserves to have its principles and rules explained with some exactness. By public treaties, we mean such agreements as can be made only by public authority, or those which sovereigns, considered as such, make with each other, concerning things which directly concern the welfare of the state. This is what distinguishes these agreements, not only from those which individuals make with each other, but also from the contracts of kings, in regard to their private affairs.[1] <315>

II. What we have before observed, concerning the necessity of introducing conventions betwixt private men, and the advantages arising from them, may be applied to nations and different states. Nations may, by means of treaties, unite themselves more particularly into a society, which shall reciprocally assure them of seasonable assistance, either for the necessaries and conveniencies of life, or to provide for their greater security upon the breaking out of a war.

III. As this is the case, sovereigns are no less obliged, than individuals, inviolably to keep their word, and be faithful to their engagements. The law of nations renders this an indispensable duty; for it is evident, that were it otherwise, not only public treaties would be useless to states, but moreover, that the violation of these would throw them into a state of dissidence and continual war; that is to say, into the most terrible situation. The obligation therefore of sovereigns, in this respect, is so much the stronger, as the violation of this duty has more dangerous consequences, which interest the public felicity.[2] The sanctity of an oath, which generally accompanies solemn treaties, is an additional motive to engage princes to observe them with the utmost fidelity; and certainly nothing is more shameful for sovereigns, who so rigorously punish such of their subjects as fail in their engagements, than to sport with treaties and public faith, and to look upon these only as the means of deceiving each other.

The royal word ought therefore to be inviolable, and sacred. But there is reason to apprehend, that if <316> princes are not more attentive to this point, this expression will soon degenerate into an opposite sense, in the same manner as formerly *Carthaginian faith** was taken for perfidy.

---

* Punica fides.
1. Based on DGP II.15 §1.
2. For "public felicity" read: "an infinity of particulars."

IV. We must likewise observe, that the several principles already established concerning the validity of conventions in general, agree to public treaties, as well as to the contracts of individuals. In both, therefore, there must be a serious consent, properly declared, and exempt from *error, fraud,* and *violence.*

V. If treaties, made in those circumstances, be obligatory between the respective states or sovereigns, they are also binding, with regard to the subjects of each prince in particular. They oblige, as compacts between the contracting powers; but they have the force of laws, with respect to the subjects considered as such; for it is evident that two sovereigns, who conclude a treaty, lay their subjects thereby under an obligation of doing nothing contrary to it.

VI. There are several distinctions of public treaties; and 1°. some turn simply on things, to which we were before obliged by the law of nature; and others superadd some particulars to the duties of natural law.[3]

VII. Under the former head we may rank all those treaties, by which we are purely and simply en-<317>gaged to do no injury to others, but, on the contrary, to perform all the duties of humanity towards them. Among civilised nations, who profess to follow the laws of nature, such treaties are not necessary. Duty alone is sufficient, without a formal engagement. But among the ancients, these treaties were thought expedient, the common opinion being, that they were obliged to observe the laws of humanity only to fellow-subjects, and that they might consider all strangers as foes, and treat them as such, unless they had entered into some engagement to the contrary: and of this we have many instances in history. The profession of free-booter, or pirate, was no way shameful among several nations; and the word *hostis,* which the Romans used to express an enemy, originally signified no more than a stranger.

---

3. For this and the next paragraph, see DGP II.15 §5; see also note 12 to the same.

VIII. Under the second kind I comprehend all those compacts, by which two nations enter into some new, or more particular obligation; as when they formally engage to things to which they were not bound, but in virtue of an imperfect obligation, or even to which they were no ways before obliged.

IX. 2°. Treaties, by which we engage to something more than what we were obliged to, in virtue of the law of nature, are also of two kinds; some *equal,* others *unequal.*[4]

   3°. Both are made either in time of war, or in full peace. <318>

X. Equal treaties, are those contracted with an entire equality on both sides; that is to say, when not only the engagements and promises are equal on both sides, either purely and simply, or in proportion to the strength of each contracting party; but also, when they engage on the same footing; so that neither of the parties is[5] in any respect inferior to the other.

XI. These treaties are made, either with a view to *commerce,* or to confederacy in war, or, in short, to any other matter. With respect to commerce, for example, by stipulating that the subjects, on either side, shall be free from all custom or toll, or that no more shall be demanded of them, than of the natives of the country, &c. Equal treaties, or leagues relating to war, are, when we stipulate, for example, that each shall furnish the other an equal number of troops, ships, and other things; and this in all kinds of war, defensive as well as offensive, or in defensive only, &c. Lastly, treaties of equality may also turn upon any other matter; as when it is agreed, that one shall have no forts on the other's frontiers; that one shall not grant protection to the other's subjects, in some criminal cases, but order them to be seized and sent back; that one shall not give the other's enemies passage through his country, and the like.[6]

   4. See DGP II.15 §6.
   5. For "is," read: "recognizes itself as."
   6. This paragraph is based on DGP II.15 §6, while the two following are based on §7 of the same paragraph.

XII. What we have been saying, sufficiently shews the meaning of unequal treaties. And these are, when the promises are either unequal, or such as lay harder conditions on one of the parties, than on the <319> other. The inequality of the things stipulated, is sometimes on the side of the most powerful confederate, as when he promises his assistance to the other, without requiring the like; and sometimes on the side of the inferior confederate, as when he engages to do more for the stronger, than the latter promises in return.

XIII. All the conditions of unequal treaties are not of the same nature; some there are, which though burdensome to the inferior ally, yet leave the sovereignty entire; others, on the contrary, include a diminution of the independance, and sovereignty of the inferior ally.

Thus, in the treaties between the Romans and the Carthaginians, at the end of the second *Punic war*, it was stipulated, that the Carthaginians should not begin any war, without the consent of the Roman people; an article which evidently diminished the sovereignty of Carthage, and made her dependent on Rome.

But the sovereignty of the inferior ally continues entire, though he engages, for example, to pay the other's army, to defray the expences of the war, to dismantle some towns, to give hostages, to look upon all those as friends or enemies, who are friends or enemies to the other, to have no forts, or strong holds in certain parts, to avoid sailing in particular seas, to acknowledge the pre-eminence of the other, and, upon occasion, to shew reverence and honour to his power and majesty, &c.

XIV. However, though these, and other similar <320> conditions, do not diminish the sovereignty, it is certain that such treaties of inequality are often of so delicate a nature, as to require the greatest circumspection; and that if the prince, who is superior to the other in dignity, surpasses him also considerably in strength and power, it is to be feared that the former will gradually acquire an absolute sovereignty over him, especially if the confederacy be perpetual.

XV. 4°. Public treaties are also divided into *real* and *personal.* The latter are those made with a prince, purely in regard to his person, and expire with him. The former are such, as are made rather with the whole body of the state, than with the king or government, and which consequently outlive those who made them, and oblige their successors.[7]

XVI. To know which of these two classes every treaty belongs to, the following rules may be laid down.

1°. We must first attend to the form and phrase of the treaty, to its clauses, and the views proposed by the contracting parties. *Utrum autem in rem, an in personam factum est, non minus ex verbis, quam ex mente convenientium aestimandum est.* Thus, if there be an express clause, mentioning that the treaty is perpetual, or for a certain number of years, or for the good of the state, or with the king for him and his successors, we may conclude that the treaty is real. <321>

2°. Every treaty made with a republic, is in its own nature real, because the subject, with whom we contract it, is a thing permanent.

3°. Though the government should happen to be changed from a republic into a monarchy, the treaty is still in force, because the body is still the same, and has only another chief.

4°. We must however make an exception here, which is, when it appears that the preservation of the republican government was the true cause of the treaty; as when two republics enter into an alliance, by which they agree to assist one another, against such as shall endeavour by force to alter their constitution, and deprive them of their liberties.

5°. In case of doubt, every public treaty made with a king ought to be deemed real, because, in dubious cases, the king is supposed to act as chief, and for the good of the state.

6°. Hence it follows, that as after the change of a democracy into a monarchy, the treaty is still in force, in regard to the new sovereign; so

---

* Leg. vii. § viii. ff. de Pactis. ["But whether a pact has been concluded in rem or in personam is to be gathered not less from the words than from the intention of the parties." Alan Watson, ed., *The Digest of Justinian,* rev. English language ed. (Philadelphia: University of Pennsylvania Press, 1998), 2.14.7.8.]

7. This and the following paragraphs are mainly from DNG VIII.9 §6 and note 4 to the same, and from §8 to the same chapter. See also DHC II.17 §7 and DGP II.16 §16, especially note 6.

if the government, from a monarchy, becomes a republic, the treaty made with the king does not expire, unless it was manifestly personal.

7°. Every treaty of peace is real in its own nature, and ought to be kept by the successor; for so soon as the conditions of the treaty have been punctually fulfilled, the peace effectually effaces the injuries which excited the war, and restores the nations to their natural situation.

8°. If one of the confederates has fulfilled what the treaty obliged him to, and the other should die before he performs the engagements on his part, the <322> successor of the deceased king is obliged either intirely to indemnify the other party for what he has performed, or to fulfill his predecessor's engagement.

9°. But if nothing is executed on either part, or the performances on both sides are equal, then if the treaty tends directly to the personal advantage of the king, or his family, it is evident, that so soon as he dies, or his family is extinct, the treaty must also expire.

10°. Lastly, we must observe that it is grown into a custom for successors to renew, at least in general terms, even the treaties manifestly acknowledged for real, that they may be the more strongly bound to observe them, and may not think themselves dispensed from that obligation, under a pretext that they have different ideas concerning the interests of the state, from those of their predecessors.

XVII. Concerning treaties, or alliances, it is often disputed, whether they may be lawfully made with those who do not profess the true religion? I answer, that by the law of nature there is no difficulty in this point. The right of making alliances is common to all men, and has nothing opposite to the principles of true religion; which is so far from condemning prudence and humanity, that it strongly recommends both.*

XVIII. To judge rightly of the causes which put <323> an end to public treaties, we must carefully attend to the rule of conventions in general.[8]

---

* See Grotius on war and peace, book ii. chap. xv. § 8, 9, 10, 11, 12.

8. These rules are drawn from DGP II.15 §§14–15 and from DNG VIII.9 §11.

1°. A treaty, concluded for a certain time, expires at the end of the term agreed on.

2°. When a treaty is once expired, it must not be supposed to be tacitly renewed; for a new obligation is not easily presumed.

3°. And therefore, if after the treaty expires, some acts are continued, which seem conformable to the terms of the preceding alliance, they ought rather to be looked upon as simple marks of friendship and benevolence, than as a tacit renovation of the treaty.

4°. We must however make this exception, unless such acts intervene, as can bear no other construction, than that of a tacit renovation of the preceding compact. Thus, for example, if one ally has engaged to pay another a certain sum annually, and after the expiration of the term of the alliance, the same sum be paid the following year, the alliance is tacitly renewed for that year.

5°. It is in the nature of all compacts in general, that when one of the parties violates the engagements into which he had entered by treaty, the other is freed, and may refuse to stand to the agreement; for generally each article of the treaty has the force of a condition, the want of which renders it void.

6°. This is generally the case, that is to say, when there is no agreement otherwise; for sometimes this clause is inserted, that the violation of any single article of the treaty shall not break it intirely, to the end that neither party should fly from their en-<324>gagements for every slight offence. But he who, by the action of another, suffers any damage, ought to be indemnified in some shape or another.

XIX. None but the sovereign can make alliances and treaties, either by himself, or by his ministers. Treaties concluded by ministers, oblige the sovereign and the state, only when the ministers have been duly authorised to make them, and have done nothing contrary to their orders and instructions. And here it may be observed, that among the Romans the word *foedus, a public compact,* or *solemn agreement,* signified a treaty made by order of the sovereign power, or that had been afterwards ratified; but when public persons, or ministers of state, had promised something relating to the sovereign power, without advice and command from it, this was called *sponsio,* or a simple promise and engagement.[9]

XX. In general it is certain, that when ministers, without the order of their sovereign, conclude a treaty concerning public affairs, the latter is not obliged to stand to it; and the minister, who has entered into the negotiation without instructions, may be punished according to the exigency of the case. However, there may be circumstances in which a prince is obliged, either by the rules of prudence, or even those of justice and equity, to ratify a treaty, though concluded without his orders.[10]

XXI. When a sovereign is informed of a treaty, made by one of his ministers without his orders, <325> his *silence* alone does not imply a *ratification,* unless it be accompanied with some act, or other circumstance, which cannot well bear another explication. And much more, if the agreement was made upon condition of its being ratified by the sovereign, it is of no force till he has ratified it in a formal manner.

CHAPTER X

Of compacts made with an enemy.

I. Among public compacts, those which suppose *a state of war,* and are made with an enemy, deserve particular attention. Of these there are two kinds; some which do not put an end to the war, but only moderate or suspend the acts of hostility; and others, which end the war intirely. But before we consider these compacts in particular, let us inquire into the validity of them in general.[1]

9. See DGP II.15 §3 and note 1.
10. See DGP II.15 §16 and DNG VIII.9 §12.
1. See DNG VIII.7 §1.

Whether we ought to keep our faith given to an enemy?

II. This question is certainly one of the most curious and important belonging to the law of nations. Grotius and Puffendorf are not agreed in this point. The former maintains, that all compacts made with an enemy ought to be kept with an inviolable fidelity. But Puffendorf is somewhat dubious with respect to those compacts, which leave us in a state of war, without a design to remove it. Let us therefore endeavour to establish some princi-<326>ples, by means of which we may determine with respect to these two opinions.

III. I observe, 1°. That though war of itself destroys the state of society between two nations, we must not thence conclude that it is subjected to no law, and that all right and obligation are absolutely at an end between enemies.

2°. On the contrary, every body grants that there is a right of war, obligatory of itself, between enemies, and which they cannot violate, without being defective in their duty. This is what we have proved before, by shewing that there are just and unjust wars; and that even in the justest, it is not allowable to push acts of hostility to the utmost extremity, but that we ought to keep within certain bounds; and consequently, that there are things *unjust* and *unlawful,* even with respect to an enemy. Since therefore war does not, of itself, subvert all the laws of society, we cannot from this alone conclude, that because two nations are at war with each other, they are dispensed from keeping their word, and from fulfilling the engagements they have made with each other, during the course of the war.

3°. As war is in itself a very great evil, it is the common interest of nations, not to deprive themselves voluntarily of the means which prudence suggests to moderate the rigour, and to suspend the effects of it. On the contrary, it is their duty to endeavour to procure such means, and to make use of them upon occasion; so far at least, as the attainment of the lawful end of war will permit. Now there is nothing but *public faith* that can procure, <327> to the parties engaged in war, the liberty to take breath; nothing but this can secure to towns, that have surrendered, the several rights which they have reserved by capitulation. What advantage would a nation gain, or rather, what is it they would not lose, if they were to have no regard to their faith given to an enemy, and if they looked upon compacts, made in such circumstances, only as the means of circumventing one another? Surely it is not to be supposed, that the law of nature approves of maxims so manifestly opposite to the common good of mankind. Besides, we ought never to wage war, merely for the sake of it, but only through necessity, in order to obtain a just and reasonable satisfaction, and a solid peace; from whence it evidently follows, that the right of war between enemies cannot extend so far, as to render hostilities perpetual, and to create an invincible obstacle to the re-establishment of the public tranquillity.

4°. And yet this would certainly be the consequence, if the law of nature did not lay us under an indispensable obligation of performing whatever agreement we have voluntarily made with the enemy during the war; whether these agreements tend only to suspend, or moderate acts of hostility, or whether they are designed to make them cease intirely, and to re-establish peace.

For, in short, there are only two ways of obtaining peace. The first is, the total and entire destruction of our enemy; and the second is, the entering into articles of treaty with him. If therefore treaties and compacts, made between enemies, were not in themselves sacred and inviolable, there would <328> be no other means of procuring a solid peace, than carrying on the war to the utmost extremity, and to the total ruin of our enemies. But who does not see that a principle, which tends to the destruction of mankind, is directly contrary to the law of nature and nations, whose principal end is the preservation and happiness of human society?

5°. There is no distinction, in this respect, between the different treaties that we may enter into with an enemy; for the obligation which the laws of nature lay upon us, to observe them inviolably, relates as well to those which do not put an end to the war, as to those which tend to re-establish peace. There is no medium, and we must lay it down as a general rule, that all compacts with an enemy are obligatory, or that none of them are really such.

And, indeed, if it were lawful, for instance, to break a solemn truce, and to detain, without any reason for it, people, to whom we had given passports, &c. what harm would there be in circumventing an enemy, under a pretext of treating of peace? When we enter into a negotiation of this kind, we are still enemies; and it is properly but a kind of truce, which we agree to, in order to see if there be any means of coming to an accommodation. If the negotiations prove unsuccessful, it is not then a new war which we begin, since the differences, that occasioned our taking up arms, are not yet adjusted; we only continue the acts of hostility which had been suspended for some time: so that we could no more rely on the enemy's sincerity, with respect to compacts which tend to re-establish peace, <329> than to those whose end is only to suspend, or moderate acts of hostility. Thus distrusts would be continual, wars eternal, and a solid peace unattainable.

6°. The more frequent unnecessary wars are become, through the avarice and ambition of sovereigns, the more a steady adherence to the principles, here established, is indispensably necessary for the interest of mankind. Cicero therefore justly affirms, that there is a right of war, which ought to be observed between the contending parties, and that the enemy retains certain rights, notwithstanding the war.*

Nor is it sufficient to say, as Puffendorf does,[2] that it is a custom which, among others, has obtained among civilized nations, out of particular respect to military bravery, that all compacts made with an enemy ought to be looked upon as valid. He should also have added, that this is an indispensable duty, that justice requires it, that it is not in the power of nations to establish things on another footing, and that they cannot justly deviate from the rules which the law of nature prescribes, in this case, for their common advantage.

---

* *Est etiam jus bellicum; fidesque jurisjurandi saepe cum hoste servanda.* Off. lib. iv. cap. 29.

2. This is in DNG VIII.7 §2. The criticism in the next paragraph is from note 1 to the same.

IV. It will not be difficult, by means of the principles here established, to answer the arguments by which Puffendorf pretends to shew, that all compacts made with an enemy, are not of themselves obligatory. We shall be content with observing, 1°. that those arguments prove nothing, because <330> they prove too much, &c. and 2°. all that can be concluded from them is, that we ought to act prudently, and take proper precautions before we pass our word, or enter into any engagement with an enemy; because mankind are apt to break their promises for their own interest, especially when they have to deal with people whom they hate, or by whom they are hated.

V. But it will be said, is it not a principle of the law of nature, that all conventions and treaties, extorted by injustice and violence, are void of themselves; and consequently, that he who has been forced to make them against his will, may lawfully break his word, if he thinks he can do it with safety?

Violence and force are the characteristics of war; and it is generally the conqueror that obliges the vanquished to treat with him, and by the superiority of his arms, constrains them to accept the conditions he proposes to them, whether the war he has undertaken be just or not. How then is it possible, that the law of nature and nations should declare treaties, made in those circumstances, to be sacred and inviolable?

I answer, that however true the principle on which this objection is founded, may be in itself, yet we cannot apply it, in all its extent, to the present question.[3]

The common interest of mankind requires, that we should make some difference between promises extorted by fear, among private persons, and those to which a sovereign prince or people is constrained, by the superiority of the arms of a conqueror, whose <331> pretensions were unjust. The law of nations then makes an exception here to the general rule of the law of nature, which disannuls conventions extorted by un-

---

3. Burlamaqui here sides with Grotius against Pufendorf, who presented a critical response to Grotius's view, which upheld the legitimacy of peace agreements made under threat of unjust violence. See DNG VIII.8 §1.

just fear; or, in other words, the law of nations holds for just on both sides, that dread or apprehension which induces enemies to treat with each other, during the course of a war; for otherwise, there would be no method, either of moderating its fury, or of putting a final period to it, as we have already demonstrated.

VI. But that nothing may be omitted, relating to this question, we shall add something for the further illustration of what we have been saying.

First then, it is necessary, I think, to distinguish here, whether he, who by the superiority of his arms has compelled his enemy to treat with him, had undertaken the war without reason; or whether he could alledge some specious pretext for it. If the conqueror had undertaken the war for some plausible reason, though perhaps unjust at bottom, then it is certainly the interest of mankind, that the law of nations should make us regard the treaties, concluded in such circumstances, as valid and obligatory; so that the conquered cannot refuse to observe them, under a pretext that they were extorted by an unjust fear.

But if we suppose that the war was undertaken without reason, or if the motive alledged be manifestly frivolous, or unjust, as Alexander's going to subdue remote nations, who had never heard of him, &c. As such a war is a downright robbery, I confess I do not think the vanquished more obliged to observe the treaty to which they were compelled, <332> than a man, fallen into the hands of thieves, is bound to pay a sum of money, which he had promised them, as a ransom for his life or liberty.[4]

VII. We must also add, as a very necessary remark, that even supposing the war was undertaken for some apparent and reasonable cause, if the treaty, which the conqueror imposes on the vanquished, includes some condition manifestly barbarous, and intirely contrary to humanity; we cannot, in those circumstances, deny the vanquished a right of receding from their engagement, and of beginning the war afresh, in order to free themselves, if they can, from the hard and inhuman conditions to which

4. Based on DGP III.19 §11 note 1.

they were subjected, by the abuse their enemy made of his victory, contrary to the laws of humanity. The justest war does not authorise the conqueror to keep no measures, or to use all liberties with respect to the vanquished; and he cannot reasonably complain of the breaking of a treaty, the conditions of which are both unjust in themselves, and full of barbarity and cruelty.

VIII. The Roman history furnishes us with an example to this purpose, which deserves our notice.

The Privernates had been several times subdued by the Romans, and as often revolted; but their city was at last retaken by the consul Plautius. In these distressed circumstances, they sent ambassadors to Rome to sue for peace. Upon a senator's asking them what punishment they thought they deserved; one of them answered, *That which is due to men who think themselves worthy of liberty.* Then the consul <333> asked them, whether there was any room to hope, that they would observe the peace, if their faults were pardoned? "The peace shall be perpetual between us," replied the ambassador, "and we shall faithfully observe it, if the conditions you lay upon us are just and reasonable; but if they are hard and dishonourable, the peace will not be of long continuance, and we shall very soon break it."

Though some of the senators were offended at this answer, yet most of them approved of it, and said that it was worthy of a man, and of a man who was born free: acknowledging therefore the rights of human nature, they cried out, that those alone deserved to be citizens of Rome, who esteemed nothing in comparison of liberty. Thus the very persons, who were at first threatened with punishment, were admitted to the privilege of citizens, and obtained the conditions they wanted; and the generous refusal of the Privernates to comply with the terms of a dishonourable treaty, gained them the honour of being incorporated into a state, which at that time could boast of the bravest, and most virtuous subjects in the universe.*

Let us therefore conclude, that a due medium is to be observed, that

* Livy, lib viii. cap. xx, xxi.

we ought inviolably to observe treaties made with an enemy, and that no exception of an unjust fear should authorise us to break our promise, unless the war was a downright robbery, or the conditions imposed on us were highly unjust, and full of barbarity and cruelty.

IX. There is still another case, in which we may <334> avoid the crime of perfidiousness, and yet not perform what we have promised to an enemy; which is, when a certain condition, supposed to be the basis of the engagement, is wanting. This is a consequence of the very nature of compacts; by this principle, the infidelity of one of the contracting parties sets the other at liberty: for according to the common rule, all the articles of the same agreement are included one in the other, in the manner of a condition, as if a person were expressly to say, *I will do such or such a thing, provided you do so or so.**

CHAPTER XI

Of compacts with an enemy, which do not put an end to the war.

I. Among those compacts which leave us in a state of war, one of the principal is a *truce.*

A truce is an agreement, by which we engage to forbear all acts of hostility for some time, the war still continuing.[1]

II. A truce is not therefore a peace, for the war continues. But if we agree, for instance, to certain contributions during the war, as these are granted only to prevent acts of hostility, they ought to cease during the truce; since, at that time, such acts are not lawful. And, on the contrary, if it be agreed <335> that any particular thing is to take place in time of peace, the time of truce is not included.

* See above.
1. See DNG VIII.7 §3.

III. As every truce leaves us in a state of war, it follows, that after the term is expired, there is no necessity that war should be declared again; because we do not commence a new war, but only continue that in which we were already engaged.

IV. This principle, that the war renewed after a truce is not a new war, may be applied to several other cases. In a treaty of peace, concluded between the bishop of Trent and the Venetians, it was agreed, *that each party should be put in possession of what they enjoyed before the last war.*

In the beginning of this war the bishop had taken a castle from the Venetians, which they afterwards retook. The bishop refused to give it up, under a pretext that it had been retaken after several truces, which had been made during the course of that war. The dispute was evidently to be decided in favour of the Venetians.

V. There are truces of several kinds.

1°. Sometimes, during the truce, the armies on both sides are in the field, and in motion; and these are generally limited to a few days. At other times the parties lay down their arms, and retire to their own countries; and in this case the truces are of longer duration.

2°. There is a *general truce* for all the territories and dominions of both parties; and a *particular truce* restrained to particular places; as for example, by sea, and not by land, &c. <336>

3°. Lastly, there is an absolute, indeterminate, and general truce, and a truce limited and determined to certain things; for example, to bury the dead, or if a besieged town has obtained a truce, only to be sheltered from certain attacks, or from particular acts of hostility, such as ravaging the country.[2]

VI. We must also observe, that, strictly speaking, a truce can be made only by express agreement; and that it is very difficult to establish a treaty of this kind on the footing of a tacit convention, unless the facts are such in themselves, and in their circumstances, that they can be referred to

2. See DNG VIII.7 §9 and DGP III.21 §10 and note 1 to the same.

no other principle, than to a sincere design of suspending acts of hostility for a time.

Thus, though for a time we abstain from acts of hostility, the enemy cannot from that alone conclude, that we have consented to a truce.[3]

VII. The nature of a truce sufficiently shews what the effects of it are.

1°. If the truce be general and absolute, all acts of hostility ought, generally speaking, to cease, both with respect to persons and things; but this should not hinder us, during the truce, to raise new troops, erect magazines, repair fortifications, &c. unless there be some formal convention to the contrary; for these are not in themselves acts of hostility, but defensive precautions, which may be taken in time of peace.

2°. It is a violation of the truce, to seize on any place possessed by the enemy, by corrupting the gar-<337>rison. It is also evident, that we cannot justly, during a truce, take possession of places deserted by the enemy, but really belonging to him, whether the garrison were withdrawn before or after the truce.

3°. In consequence hereof, we must restore those things belonging to the enemy, which during the truce have accidentally fallen into our hands, even though they had been formerly our property.

4°. During a truce, it is allowed to pass and repass from one place to another, but without any train or attendance that may give umbrage.[4]

VIII. And here it may be asked, whether they who, by any unexpected and inevitable accident, are found unfortunately in the enemy's country, at the expiration of a truce, can be detained prisoners, or ought to have the liberty of retiring? Grotius and Puffendorf maintain, that by the right of war we may detain them as prisoners; but Grotius adds, that it is certainly more humane and generous, not to insist on such a right. I am of opinion, that it is the consequence of a treaty of truce, that we should set such persons at liberty: for since, in virtue of that engagement,

3. See DNG VIII.7 §7.
4. This paragraph and the next are mainly based on DNG VIII.7 §§9–10 and on note 1 to §10.

we are obliged to grant them free egress and regress, during the time of the truce; we ought also to grant them the same permission after the truce is expired, if it appears manifestly that a superior force, or an un-expected accident, has hindered them from making use of it during the time agreed upon. Otherwise, as these accidents may happen every day, such a permission would often become a snare to make a great many <338> people fall into the hands of the enemy. Such are the principal effects of an absolute and general truce.

IX. With regard to a particular truce, determined to certain things, its effects are limited by the particular nature of the agreement.

1°. Thus if a truce be granted only for burying the dead, we ought not to undertake any thing new, which may alter our situation; for in-stance, we cannot, during that time, retire into a more secure post, nor intrench ourselves, &c. for he, who has granted a short truce for the interment of the dead, has granted it for that purpose only, and there is no reason to extend it beyond the case agreed on. Hence it follows, that if he, to whom such a truce has been allowed, should take advantage of it to intrench himself, for example, or for some other use, the other party would have a right to prevent him by force. The former could not com-plain; for it never could be reasonably pretended, that a truce, which was allowed for the interment of the dead, and restrained to that single act, gives a right to undertake, and carry on any other thing undisturbed. The only obligation it imposes on the person who has granted it, is, not forcibly to oppose the interment of the dead; though Puffendorf, indeed, is of a contrary opinion.*

2°. It is in consequence of the same principles, that if we suppose that by the truce persons only, and not things, are protected from acts of hostility; in this case, if in order to defend our goods we <339> wound any person, it is not a breach of the truce; for when the security of per-sons on both sides is agreed on, the right of defending against pillage is also reserved. And hence the security of persons is not general, but only

---

* See the Law of nature and nations, book viii. chap. vii. § 9.

for those who go and come without design to take any thing from the enemy, with whom such limited truce is made.[5]

X. Every truce obliges the contracting parties, from the moment the agreement is concluded. But the subjects on both sides are under no obligation in this respect, till the truce has been solemnly notified. Hence it follows, that if before this notification the subjects commit any acts of hostility, or do something contrary to the truce, they are liable to no punishment. The powers, however, who have concluded the truce, ought to indemnify those that have suffered, and to restore things, as much as possible, to their former state.[6]

XI. Lastly, if the truce should happen to be violated on one side, the other is certainly at liberty to proceed to acts of hostility, without any new declaration. Yet when it is agreed, that he who first breaks the truce shall pay a certain fine; if he pays the fine, or suffers the penalty, the other has not a right to begin acts of hostility, before the expiration of the term: but besides the penalty stipulated, the injured party has a right to demand an indemnification of what he has suffered by the violation of the truce. It is to be observed however, that the actions of private persons do not break a truce, unless the sovereign has some hand in them, either by order, or <340> by approbation; and he is supposed to approve what has been done, if he will neither punish, nor deliver up the offender, or if he refuses to restore the things taken during the cessation of arms.[7]

XII. Safe conducts are also compacts made between enemies, and deserve to be considered. By a safe conduct, we understand a privilege granted to some person of the enemy's party, without a cessation of arms; by which he has free passage and return, and is in no danger of being molested.[8]

---

5. The critique is from Barbeyrac in DGP III.21 §10 notes 1 and 2.
6. See DNG VIII.7 §8 note 1 and DGP III.21 §5.
7. See DNG VIII.7 §11 and DPG III.21 §§11–13.
8. This paragraph is based on DGP III.21 §14.

XIII. The several questions relating to safe conducts may be decided, either by the nature of the privilege granted, or by the general rules of right interpretation.[9]

1°. A safe conduct granted to soldiers, extends not only to inferior officers, but also to those who command in chief; because the natural and ordinary use of the word has determined it so.

2°. If leave be given to go to a certain part, it implies one also to return, otherwise the former permission would be often useless. There may, however, be cases, in which the one does not imply the other.

3°. He that has had leave to come, has not, generally speaking, liberty to send another in his place; and, on the contrary, he who has had a permission to send another person, cannot come himself; because these are two different things, and the permission ought to be naturally restrained to the person himself, to whom it was granted; for perhaps it would not have been given to another. <341>

4°. A father who has obtained a pass-port, cannot take his son with him, nor a husband his wife.

5°. As to servants, though not mentioned, it shall be presumed to be allowed to take one or two, or even more, according to the quality of the person.

6°. In a dubious case, and generally speaking, licence to pass freely, does not cease by the death of him who has granted it; the successor, however, may for good reasons revoke it: but in such a case the person, to whom the pass-port has been granted, ought to have notice given him, and the necessary time allowed him for betaking himself to a place of safety.

7°. A safe conduct, granted during pleasure, imports of itself a continuation of safe conduct, till expressly revoked; for otherwise, the will is supposed to subsist still the same, whatever time may be elapsed: but such a safe conduct expires, if the person who has given it, is no longer

---

9. The first two rules are from DGP III.21 §§15 and 16, respectively. The fourth is from §17 to the same paragraph. The sixth is from note 1 to §20, the seventh from note 1 to §21.

in the employment, in virtue of which he was impowered to grant such security.

XIV. The redemption of captives is also a compact often made, without putting an end to the war. The ancient Romans were very backward in the ransoming of prisoners. Their practice was to examine whether those, who were taken by the enemy, had observed the laws of military discipline, and consequently, whether they deserved to be ransomed. But the side of rigour generally prevailed, as most advantageous to the republic.[10]

XV. Yet in general, it is more agreeable, both to the good of the state, and to humanity, to ransom <342> prisoners; unless experience convinces us, that it is necessary to use that severity towards them, in order to prevent or redress greater evils, which would otherwise be unavoidable.

XVI. An agreement made for the ransom of a prisoner cannot be revoked, under a pretext that he is found to be much richer than we imagined: for this circumstance, of the prisoner's being more or less rich, has no relation to the engagement; so that if his ransom were to be settled by his worth, that condition should have been specified in the contract.[11]

XVII. As prisoners of war are not now made slaves, the captor has a right to nothing but what he actually takes: hence money, or other things, which a prisoner has found means to conceal, certainly remain his property, and he may consequently make use of them to pay his ransom. The enemy cannot take possession of what they know nothing of; and the prisoner lies under no obligation to make a discovery of all his effects.

XVIII. There is also another question, whether the heir of a prisoner of war is obliged to pay the ransom, which the deceased had agreed upon?

10. This paragraph is based on DGP III.21 §§23–24.
11. This and the three following paragraphs are based on DGP III.21 §§27, 28, 29, and 30, respectively.

The answer is easy, in my opinion. If the prisoner died in captivity, the heir owes nothing, for the promise of the deceased was made upon condition, that he should be set at liberty: but if he was set at liberty before he died, the heir is certainly chargeable with the ransom. <343>

XIX. One question more, is, whether a prisoner, who was released on condition of releasing another, is obliged to return to prison, if the other dies before he has obtained his releasement? I answer, that the released prisoner is not obliged to return into custody, for that was not stipulated in the agreement; neither is it just that he should enjoy his liberty for nothing. He must therefore give an indemnification, or pay the full value of what he could not perform.

CHAPTER XII

Of compacts made, during the war, by subordinate powers, as generals of armies, or other commanders.

I. All that has been hitherto said, concerning compacts between enemies, relates to those made by sovereign powers. But since princes do not always conclude such agreements themselves, we must now enquire into treaties made by generals, or other inferior commanders.

II. In order to know whether these engagements oblige the sovereign, the following principles will direct us.

1°. Since every person may enter into an engagement, either by himself or by another, it is plain that the sovereign is bound by the compacts made by his ministers or officers, in conse-<344>quence of the full powers and orders expressly given them.

2°. He that gives a man a certain power, is reasonably supposed to have given him whatever is a necessary consequence and appendage of that power, and without which it cannot be exercised. But he is not supposed to have granted him any thing further.

3°. If he, who has had a commission to treat, has kept within the bounds of the power annexed to his office, though he acts contrary to his private instructions, the sovereign is to abide by what he has done; otherwise we could never depend on engagements contracted by proxy.

4°. A prince is also obliged by the act of his ministers and officers, though done without his orders, if he has ratified the engagements they have made, either by an express consent, and then there is no difficulty, or in a tacit manner; that is to say, if being informed of what has passed, he yet permits things to be done, or does them himself, which cannot reasonably be referred to any other cause, than the intention of executing the engagements of his minister, though contracted without his participation.

5°. The sovereign may also be obliged to execute the engagements contracted by his ministers without his orders, by the law of nature, which forbids us to enrich ourselves at another's expence. Equity requires, that in such circumstances we should exactly observe the conditions of the contract, though concluded by ministers who had not full powers. <345>

6°. These are the general principles of natural equity, in virtue of which sovereigns may be more or less obliged to stand to the agreement of their ministers. But to what has been said, we must add this general exception: unless the laws and customs of the country have regulated it otherwise, and these be sufficiently known to the persons with whom the agreement is made.

7°. Lastly, if a public minister exceeds his commission, so that he cannot perform what he has promised, and his master is not obliged to it, he himself is certainly bound to indemnify the person with whom he has treated. But if there should be any deceit on his part, he may be punished for it, and his person, or his goods, or both, are liable to be seized, in order to make a recompence.[1]

III. Let us apply these general principles to particular examples.

1°. A commander in chief cannot enter into a treaty that regards the causes and consequences of the war; for the power of making war, in

---

1. This paragraph is loosely based on DNG VIII.9 §§12–13 and DGP III.22 §§2–4.

whatever extent it has been given, does not imply the power of finishing it.

2°. Neither does it belong to generals to grant truces for a considerable space of time; for 1°. that does not necessarily depend on their commission. 2°. The thing is of too great consequence to be left entirely to their discretion. 3°. And lastly, circumstances are not generally so pressing, as not to admit of time to consult the sovereign; which a general ought to do, both in duty and prudence, as much as possible, even with respect to things which he has a power to transact of himself. <346>

Much less, therefore, can generals conclude these kinds of truces, which withdraw all the appearance of war, and come very near a real peace.

3°. With respect to truces of a short duration, it is certainly in the power of a general to make them; for example, to bury the dead, &c.[2]

IV. Lieutenant-generals, or even inferior commanders, may also make particular truces, during the attack, for instance, of a body of the enemy intrenched, or in the siege of a town; for this being often very necessary, it is reasonably presumed, that such a power must needs be included in the extent of their commission.

V. But a question here arises, whether these particular truces oblige only the officers who granted them, and the troops under their command, or whether they bind the other officers, and even the commander in chief? Grotius declares for the first opinion, though the second appears to me the best founded; for 1°. since we suppose that it is in consequence of the tacit consent of the sovereign, that such a truce has been granted by an inferior commander, no other officer, whether equal or superior, can break the agreement, without indirectly wounding the authority of the sovereign.

2. See DGP III.22 §7. The last remark on short truces is in line with Pufendorf, DNG VIII.7 §13, against Grotius, DGP III.22 §8. Barbeyrac presents the Pufendorfian standpoint and elaborates on it in note 1 to the latter paragraph.

2°. Besides, this would lay a foundation for fraud and distrusts, which might tend to render the use of truces, so necessary on several occasions, useless and impracticable.[3]

VI. It does not belong to a general to release per-<347>sons taken in war, nor to dispose of conquered sovereignties and lands.[4]

VII. But it is certainly in the power of generals to grant, or leave things, which are not as yet actually possessed: because in war many cities, for example, and often men, surrender themselves, upon condition of preserving their lives and liberties, or sometimes their goods; concerning which the present circumstances do not commonly allow time sufficient to consult the sovereign. Inferior commanders ought also to have this right, concerning things within the extent of their commission.

VIII. In fine, by the principles here established, we may easily judge of the conduct of the Roman people, with respect to Bituitus king of the Arverni, and to the affair of the Caudine Forks.

CHAPTER XIII

Of compacts made with an enemy by private persons.

I. It sometimes happens in war, that private persons, whether soldiers or others, make compacts with an enemy. Cicero justly remarks, that if a private person, constrained by necessity, has promised any thing to the enemy, he ought religiously to keep his word.* <348>

II. And, indeed, all the principles hitherto established, manifestly prove the justice and necessity of this duty. Besides, unless this be allowed, frequent obstacles would be put to liberty, and an occasion given for massacres, &c.

---

* De Offic. lib. i. cap. xiii. [This first paragraph is from DGP III.23 §1.]
3. Based on DGP III.22 §8 note 2.
4. For this and the next paragraph, see DGP III.22 §9.

III. But though these compacts are valid in themselves, yet it is evident that no private person has a right to alienate public property; for this is not allowed even to generals of armies.[1]

IV. With respect to the actions and effects of each individual, though the covenants made with the enemy on these affairs may sometimes be prejudicial to the state, they are binding nevertheless. Whatever tends to avoid a greater evil, though detrimental in itself, ought to be considered as a public good; as for example, when we promise to pay certain contributions to prevent pillage, or the burning of places, &c. Even the laws of the state cannot, without injustice, deprive individuals of the right of providing for their own safety, by imposing too burdensome an obligation on the subjects, entirely repugnant to nature and reason.

V. It is in consequence of these principles that we think a captive bound to perform the promise he has made of returning to prison. Without this he would not be suffered to go home; and it is certainly better for him, and for the state, that he should have this permission for a time, than that he remain always in captivity. It was, therefore, to fulfill his duty, that Re-<349>gulus returned to Carthage, and surrendered himself into the hands of the enemy.*

VI. We must judge, in like manner, of the promise by which a prisoner engages *not to bear arms against the releaser.* In vain would it be objected, that such an engagement is contrary to the duty we owe to our country. It is no way contrary to the duty of a good citizen, to procure his liberty by promising to forbear a thing which it is in the enemy's power to hinder. His country loses nothing by that, but rather gains; since a prisoner, so long as he is not released, is as useless to it, as if he were really dead.

* Cicer. de Offic. lib. iii. cap. xxix. [This paragraph is based on DGP III.23 §6; the two following are from §7 and §8, respectively.]

1. This paragraph and the next are based on DGP III.23 §5 and note 1 to the same.

VII. If a prisoner has promised not to make his escape, he ought certainly to keep his word; even though he was in fetters when he made it. But if a person has given his word, on condition that he should not be confined in that manner, he may break it, if he be laid in irons.

VIII. But here some will ask, whether private men, upon refusing to perform what they have promised to the enemy, may be compelled to it by the sovereign? I answer, certainly: otherwise it would be to no purpose, that they were bound by a promise, if no one could compel them to perform it.[2] <350>

CHAPTER XIV

Of public compacts which put an end to war.

I. Compacts which put an end to war, are either *principals* or *accessories*. Principals are those which terminate the war, either by themselves, as a treaty of peace; or by a consequence of what has been agreed upon, as when the end of the war is referred to the decision of lot, to the success of a combat, or to the judgment of an arbitrator. Accessories are such, as are sometimes joined to the principal compacts, in order to confirm them, and to render the execution of them more certain. Such are hostages, pledges, and guarantees.[1]

II. We have already treated of single combats agreed on by both parties, and of arbitrators, considered as means of hindering or terminating a war: it now only remains that we speak of treaties of peace.

2. This paragraph is from DGP III.23 §10 note 1.
1. This paragraph is based on DGP III.20 §1.

III. The first question which presents itself on this subject is, whether compacts, which terminate a war, can be disannulled by the exception of an unjust fear which has extorted them?[2]

After the principles above established, to shew that we ought to keep our faith given to an enemy, it is not necessary to prove this point again. Of all public conventions, treaties of peace are those which a nation ought to look upon as most sacred and in-<351>violable, since nothing is of greater importance to the repose and tranquillity of mankind. As princes and nations have no common judge, to take cognizance of their differences, and to decide concerning the justice of a war, we could never depend on a treaty of peace, if the exception of an unjust fear was in this case to be generally admitted. I say *generally,* for when the injustice of the conditions of the peace is highly evident, and the unjust conqueror abuses his victory so far, as to impose the hardest, cruellest, and most intolerable conditions on the vanquished, the law of nations cannot authorise such treaties, nor lay an obligation on the vanquished tamely to submit to them. Let us also add, that though the law of nations ordains, that, except in the case here mentioned, treaties of peace are to be faithfully observed, and cannot be disannulled, under a pretext of an unjust constraint; it is nevertheless certain, that the conqueror cannot in conscience take the advantage of such a treaty, and that he is obliged, by internal justice, to restore all that he has taken in an unjust war.

IV. Another question is, to know whether a sovereign, or a state, is obliged to observe treaties of peace which they have made with their rebellious subjects? I answer, $1°$. that when a sovereign has reduced rebellious subjects by force of arms, he may deal with them as he sees best. $2°$. But if he has entered into any accommodation with them, he is thereby supposed to have pardoned them what is past; so that he cannot lawfully refuse to keep his word, under a pretext that he has given it to rebellious sub-<352>jects. This obligation is so much the more invio-

2. Pufendorf criticizes Grotius's view in DNG VIII.8 §1, but Burlamaqui sides with Grotius in DGP III.19 §11, as does Barbeyrac in note 1 to that paragraph. See also DGP III.19 §12.

lable, as princes are apt to give the name of rebellion to a resistance, by which the subject only maintains his just rights, and opposes the violation of the most essential engagements of sovereigns. History furnishes but too many examples of this kind.[3]

V. None but he who has the power of making war, has a right to terminate it by a treaty of peace. In a word, this is an essential part of sovereignty. But can a king, who is a prisoner, make a treaty of peace, which shall be valid, and binding to a nation? I think not, for there is no probability, that the people would have conferred the supreme power upon one, with a right to exercise it, even in matters of the greatest importance, at a time when he is not master of his own person. But with respect to contracts which a king, though a prisoner, has made concerning what belongs to him in private, they are certainly valid, according to the principles established in the preceding chapter. But what shall we say of a king who is in exile? If he has no dependance upon any person, it is undoubtedly in his power to make peace.[4]

VI. To know for certainty what things a king can dispose of by a treaty of peace, we need only consider the nature of the sovereignty, and the manner in which he possesses it.

1°. In patrimonial kingdoms, considered in themselves, nothing hinders but that the monarch may alienate the sovereignty, or a part of it.

2°. But princes, who hold the sovereignty only <353> in an usufructuary manner, cannot by any treaty alienate it, either in whole or in part. To render such alienations valid, the consent of the body of the people, or of the states of the kingdom, is necessary.

3°. With respect to the crown domains, or the goods of the kingdom, it is not generally in the power of the sovereign to alienate them.

4°. With regard to the effects of private subjects, the sovereign, as such, has a transcendental or supereminent right over the goods and

---

3. This issue is discussed by Pufendorf in DNG VIII.8 §2, to which Burlamaqui adds Barbeyrac's words from DGP III.19 §6 note 3.

4. This paragraph is from DGP III.20 §§2–3.

fortunes of private men; consequently he may give them up, as often as the public advantage or necessity requires it; but with this consideration, that the state ought to indemnify the subject for the loss he has sustained beyond his own proportion.[5]

VII. For the better interpretation of the articles of a treaty of peace, we need only attend to the general rules of interpretation, and the intention of the contracting parties.

1°. In all treaties of peace, if there be no clause to the contrary, it is presumed that the parties hold themselves reciprocally discharged from all damages occasioned by the war. Hence the clauses of general amnesty are only for the greater precaution.

2°. But the debts between individuals, contracted before the war, and the payment of which could not be exacted during the war, are not to be accounted forgiven by the treaty of peace.

3°. Unknown injuries, whether committed before, or during the war, are supposed to be com-<354>prehended in the general terms, by which we forgive the enemy the evil he has done us.

4°. Whatever has been taken since the conclusion of the peace, must certainly be restored.

5°. If the time be limited, in which the conditions of peace are to be performed, it must be interpreted in the strictest sense; so that when it is expired, the least delay is inexcusable, unless it proceeds from a superior force, or it manifestly appears that it is owing to no bad design.

6°. It is lastly to be observed, that every treaty of peace is of itself perpetual, and, as it were, eternal in its nature; that is to say, the parties are supposed to have agreed never to take up arms on account of the differences which occasioned the war, and for the future to look upon them as entirely at an end.[6]

5. This paragraph is from DGP III.20 §5 and from DNG VIII.8 §3.
6. The first rule is loosely based on DGP III.20 §15 note 1. The second and third rules are from §§16 and 17, respectively, while the fourth is from §20 in the same chapter. Rule 5 is from DNG VIII.8 §4, rule 6 from DNG VIII.7 §4.

VIII. It is also an important question to know, when a peace may be looked upon as broken.

1°. Some distinguish between *breaking a peace,* and *giving a new occasion of war.* To break a peace, is to violate an article of the treaty; but to give a new occasion of war, is to take up arms for a new reason not mentioned in the treaty.

2°. But when we give a new occasion of war in this manner, the treaty is by such means indirectly broken, if we refuse to make satisfaction for the offence: for then the offended having a right to take up arms, and to treat the offender as an enemy, against whom every thing is lawful, he must also certainly dispense with observing the conditions of the peace, though the treaty has not been formally broken with <355> respect to its tenor. Besides, this distinction cannot be much used at present; because treaties of peace are conceived in such a manner, as to include an engagement to live for the future in good friendship, in all respects. We must therefore conclude, that every new act of unjust hostility is an infringement of the peace.

3°. As to those who only repel force by force, they by no means break the peace.

4°. When a peace is concluded with several allies of him with whom the treaty has been made, the peace is not broken, if one of those allies takes up arms, unless it has been concluded on that footing. But this is what cannot be presumed, and certainly they who thus invade us without the assistance of others, shall be considered as the breakers of the peace.

5°. Acts of violence or hostility, which some subjects may commit of their own accord, cannot break the peace, except we suppose that the sovereign approves them; and this is presumed, if he knows the fact, has power to punish it, and neglects to do so.

6°. The peace is supposed to be broken, when, without a lawful reason, acts of hostility are committed, not only against the whole body of a state, but also against private persons; for the end of a treaty of peace is, that every subject should, for the future, live in perfect security.

7°. The peace is certainly broken by a contravention to the clear and express articles of the treaty. Some civilians, however, distinguish between the articles of *great importance,* and those of *small im-*<356>

portance. But this distinction is not only uncertain in itself, but also very difficult and delicate in its application. In general, all the articles of a treaty ought to be looked upon as important enough to be observed. We must, however, pay some regard to what is required by humanity, and rather pardon slight faults, than pursue the reparation of them by arms.

8°. If one of the parties is, by an absolute necessity, reduced to an impossibility of performing his engagements, we are not for that to look upon the peace as broken; but the other party ought either to wait some time for the performance of what has been promised, if there be still any hope of it, or he may demand a reasonable equivalent.

9°. Even when there is treachery on one side, it is certainly at the choice of the innocent party to let the peace subsist; and it would be ridiculous to pretend, that he who first infringes the peace can disengage himself from the obligation which he lay under, by acting contrary to that very obligation.[7]

IX. To treaties of peace, for the security of their execution, are sometimes joined hostages, pledges, and guarantees. Hostages are of several sorts; for they either give themselves voluntarily, or are given by order of the sovereign, or they are forcibly taken by the enemy. Nothing, for instance, is at present more common, than to carry off hostages for the security of contributions.[8]

X. The sovereign may, in virtue of his autho-<357>rity, oblige some of his subjects to put themselves into the hands of the enemy as hostages; for if he has a right, when necessity requires it, to expose them to the danger of their lives, much more may he engage their corporal liberty. But on the other hand, the state ought certainly to indemnify the hostages for the losses they may have sustained for the good of the society.

---

7. For this paragraph, see DGP III.20 §27. Rule 2 is from §27 note 1. Rules 3 to 5 are from §§28 through 30. Rule 6 is from §32; rule 7 from §§34 and 35. Rules 8 and 9 are from §§37 and 38.

8. This paragraph and the next are from DGP III.20 §52.

XI. Hostages are demanded, and given, for the security of the execution of some engagement; therefore it is necessary that they should be retained, in such manner as shall be judged proper, till the performance of what has been agreed on. Hence it follows that an hostage, who has made himself such voluntarily, or he who has been given by the sovereign, cannot make his escape. Grotius, however, grants this liberty to the latter; but his opinion does not seem to be well founded: for either it was the intention of the state, that the hostage should not remain in the hands of the enemy; or the state had not the power of obliging the hostage to remain. The former is manifestly false, for otherwise the hostage could be no security, and the convention would be illusive. Nor is the latter more true; for if the prince, in virtue of his transcendental property, can expose the lives of the citizens, why may he not engage their liberty? Thus Grotius himself agrees, that the Romans were obliged to return Clelia to Porsenna. But the case is not precisely the same, with respect to hostages taken by the enemy; for these have a right to make their escape, so long as they have not given their word to the contrary.[9]
<358>

XII. It is a question often controverted, whether he, to whom hostages are given, can put them to death, in case the enemy do not perform their engagement? I answer, that hostages themselves cannot give the enemy any power over their lives, of which they are not masters. As to the state, it has certainly the power of exposing the lives of the subjects, when the public good requires it. But in this case, all that the public good requires, is to engage the corporal liberty of the hostages; and they can no more be rendered responsible, at the peril of their lives, for the infidelity of the sovereign, than an innocent person can be treated as a criminal. Thus the state by no means engages the lives of hostages. He, to whom they are given, is supposed to receive them on these conditions; and though by the violation of the treaty they are at his mercy, it does not follow

9. This paragraph is based on DGP III.20 §54 note 1 and on DGP III.20 §51 note 2.

that he has a right to put them to death; he can only retain them as prisoners of war.[10]

XIII. Hostages, given for a certain purpose, are free so soon as that purpose is answered, and consequently cannot be detained upon any other account, for which no hostages were promised. But if we have broke our faith in any other case, or contracted a new debt, the hostages then may be detained, not as hostages, but in consequence of this rule of the law of nations, which authorises us to detain the persons of subjects for the deeds of their sovereigns.[11]

XIV. The query is, whether a hostage is at li-<359>berty by the death of the sovereign, who made the covenant? This depends on the nature of the treaty, for the security of which the hostage was given; that is to say, we must examine whether it be *personal,* or *real.*

But if the hostage becomes successor to the prince who gave him up, he is no longer obliged to be detained as an hostage, though the treaty be real; he ought only to put another in his place, whenever it is demanded. This case is supposed to be tacitly excepted; for it cannot be presumed that a prince, for example, who has given his own son and presumptive heir as an hostage, ever intended, that in case he should die, the state should be without its chief.[12]

XV. Sometimes pledges are also given for the security of a treaty of peace; and as we have said that hostages may be detained for other debts, this may also be applied to pledges.[13]

XVI. Another way, in fine, of securing peace, is, when princes or states, especially those who have been mediators of the peace, become guarantees, and engage their faith, that the articles shall be observed on both

---

10. For this paragraph, see DGP III.11 §18.
11. This paragraph is based on DGP III.20 §55.
12. This paragraph is based on DGP III.20 §55 and on DNG VIII.9 §6.
13. This paragraph is based on DGP III.20 §59.

sides; which engagement of theirs implies an obligation of interposing their good offices, to obtain a reasonable satisfaction to the party injured contrary to treaty, and even of assisting him against the injurious aggressor.[14] <360>

CHAPTER XV

Of the right of ambassadors.

I. It remains now for us to say something of ambassadors, and of the privileges which the law of nations grants them. The subject naturally leads us to it, since it is by means of these ministers that treaties are generally negotiated and concluded.

II. Nothing is more common than the maxim, which establishes that the persons of ambassadors are sacred and inviolable, and that they are under the protection of the law of nations. We cannot doubt but that it is of the utmost importance to mankind in general, and to nations in particular, not only to put an end to wars and disputes, but also to establish and maintain commerce and friendship with each other. Now as ambassadors are necessary to procure these advantages, it follows that God, who certainly commands every thing that contributes to the preservation and happiness of society, cannot but forbid the doing any injury to those persons; but, on the contrary, he orders we should grant them all the security and privileges, which the design and nature of their employment require.[1]

III. Before we enter into the application of the privileges which the law of nations grants to ambassadors, we must observe with Grotius, that they <361> belong only to ambassadors sent by sovereign powers to each other. For as to deputies sent by cities or provinces to their own sovereigns, it is not by the law of nations that we must judge of their privi-

---

14. This paragraph is based on DNG VIII.8 §7.
1. This paragraph is based on DNG VIII.9 §12 note 1.

leges, but by the civil law of the country. In a word, the privileges of ambassadors regard only foreigners; that is to say, such as have no dependance on us.

Nothing then hinders an inferior ally from having a right to send ambassadors to a superior ally; for in the case of an unequal alliance, the inferior does not cease to be independent.

It is a question, whether a king, vanquished in war and stript of his kingdom, has a right of sending ambassadors? But indeed this question is useless, with respect to the conqueror, who will not even so much as think whether he ought to receive ambassadors from a person whom he has deprived of his kingdom. With regard to other powers, if the conqueror has entered into the war for reasons manifestly unjust, they ought still to acknowledge that person for the true king, who really is so, so long as they can do it without some great inconveniency; consequently they cannot refuse to receive his ambassadors.

But in civil wars the case is extraordinary; for then necessity sometimes makes way for this right, so as to receive ambassadors on both sides. The same nation, in that case, is for a time accounted two distinct bodies of people. But pirates and robbers, that do not constitute a settled government, can have no right of nations belonging to them, nor consequently that of sending ambassadors,[2] un-<362>less they have obtained it by a treaty, which has sometimes happened.

IV. The ancients did not distinguish different sorts of persons sent by one power to another; the Romans called them all *legati,* or *oratores.* At present there are various titles given to these public ministers. But the employment is in the main the same; and the several distinctions are founded rather on the greater or lesser splendor with which they support their dignity, and on the greatness or smallness of their salary, than on any other reason derived from their character.[3]

2. Read: "cannot enjoy with respect to ambassadors the privileges of the law of nations." This paragraph is based on DGP II.18 §2 and on note 7 to the same.

3. This passage would seem to be drawn from Kornelius van Bynkershoek's *Traité du juge competent des ambassadeurs,* chapter 1 §1 (Barbeyrac's French translation of *De foro legatorum*).

V. The most common distinction of ambassadors, at present, is into *extraordinary* and *ordinary.* This difference was entirely unknown to the ancients. With them all ambassadors were extraordinary, that is to say, charged with only a particular negotiation; whereas the ordinary ambassadors are those who reside among foreign nations, to transact all kinds of political concerns, and even to observe what passes in the respective courts.

The situation of things in Europe, since the destruction of the Roman empire, the different sovereignties and republics that have been erected, together with the increase of trade, have rendered these ordinary ambassadors necessary. Hence several historians justly observe, that the Turks, who keep no ministers in foreign countries, act very impoliticly; for as they receive their news only by Jewish or Armenian merchants, they do not generally hear of things till very late, or their informa-<363>tions are bad, which often makes them take imprudent measures.[4]

VI. Grotius observes, that there are two principal maxims of the law of nations, concerning ambassadors. The first, *that we ought to admit them;* the second, *that their persons are sacred and inviolable.*[5]

VII. With regard to the first of these maxims, we must observe, that the obligation of admitting ambassadors, is founded in general on the principles of humanity: for as all nations form a kind of society among themselves, and consequently ought to assist each other by a mutual intercourse of good offices, the use of ambassadors becomes necessary between them for that very reason. It is therefore a rule of the law of nations, that we ought to admit ambassadors, and to reject none without a just cause.

VIII. But though we are obliged to admit ambassadors, it is only a bare duty of humanity, which produces but an imperfect obligation. So that a simple refusal cannot be regarded as an injurious act, sufficient to lay

4. Part of this paragraph seems to be from Bynkershoek 1 §§3–4.
5. For this and the three following paragraphs, see DGP II.18 §§3–4 with notes.

a just foundation for a war. Besides, the obligation to admit ambassadors regards as well those sent to us by an enemy, as those who come from an allied power. It is the duty of princes, who are at war, to seek the means of re-establishing a just and reasonable peace; and they cannot obtain it, unless they are disposed <364> to listen to the proposals that may be made on each side; which cannot be so well negotiated, as by employing ambassadors or ministers. The same duty of humanity also obliges neutral, or indifferent princes, to afford a passage through their territories to ambassadors sent by other powers.

IX. I mentioned that we ought not, without a just cause, refuse admittance to an ambassador; for it is possible that we may have very good reasons to reject him: for example, if his master has already imposed upon us under pretext of an embassy, and we have just reason to suspect the like fraud; if the prince, by whom the ambassador is sent, has been guilty of treachery, or of some other heinous crime against us; or, in fine, if we are sure that, under the pretext of negotiating, the ambassador is sent only as a spy, to pry into our affairs, and to sow the seeds of sedition.

Thus, in the retreat of the ten thousand, the history of which has been written by Xenophon, the generals resolved, that so long as they were in the enemy's country they would receive no heralds; and what moved them to this resolution, was their having found that the persons who had been sent among them, under the pretence of embassy, came really to spy into their affairs, and to corrupt the soldiers.

It may also be a just reason for refusing admittance to an ambassador, or envoy from an allied power, when by admitting him we are likely to give distrust to some other power, with whom it is proper we <365> should maintain a good understanding. Lastly, the person or character of the ambassador himself may furnish just reasons for our not admitting him. This is sufficient concerning the maxim relating to the admittance of ambassadors.

X. With regard to the other rule of the law of nations, which directs that the persons of ambassadors be looked upon as sacred and inviolable, it is a little more difficult to decide the several questions relating to it.

1°. When we say that the law of nations forbids any violence to ambassadors, either by word or action, we do not by this give any particular privilege to those ministers; for this is no more than what every man has a right to by the law of nature, a right that his life, his honour, and his property, be perfectly secure.[6]

2°. But when we add, that the persons of ambassadors are sacred and inviolable by the law of nations, we attribute some prerogatives and privileges to them, which are not due to private persons, &c.

3°. When we say that the person of an ambassador is sacred, this signifies no more than that we inflict a severer punishment on those who offer violence to an ambassador, than on such as commit an injury or insult to private persons; and the character of ambassadors, is the reason of our inflicting so different a punishment for the same kind of offence.

4°. Lastly, the reason why we call the persons of ambassadors sacred, is because they are not subject to the jurisdiction of the sovereign to whom <366> they are deputed, either in their persons, their retinue, or effects; so that we cannot proceed against them, according to the ordinary course of justice; and it is in this that their privileges chiefly consist.

XI. The foundation of these privileges, which the law of nations grants to ambassadors, is, that as an ambassador represents the person of his master, he ought of course to enjoy all the privileges and rights which his master himself, as a sovereign, would have, were he to come into the states of another prince, in order to transact his own affairs, to negotiate, for instance, or conclude a treaty, or an alliance, to regulate some branch of commerce, and other things of a similar nature, &c. Now when a sovereign goes into a foreign country, we cannot imagine that he loses his character and independance, and that he becomes subject to the prince whose territories he visits: on the contrary, he ought to continue as he was before, equal and independent of the jurisdiction of the prince, whose territories he enters; and the latter receives him on the same footing as he would choose to be received himself, if he went into the other's

6. See DGP II.18 §4 and note 2. See also Bynkershoek 5 §§3–4.

dominions.[7] Now we must grant the ambassador the same prerogative and immunities, in consequence of his representative character.

The very end and design of embassies render these privileges of ambassadors necessary; for it is certain, that if an ambassador can treat with the prince to whom he is sent, with a full independance, he will be much better qualified to perform his duty, and serve his master effectually, than if he were sub-<367>ject to a foreign jurisdiction, or if he and his retinue could be consigned over to justice, and his goods arrested and seized, &c. Hence it is, that all nations have, in favour of ambassadors, made a very just exception to the general custom, which requires, that people who reside in a foreign prince's dominions, shall be subject to that prince's laws.

XII. These principles being supposed, I affirm,

1°. That there is no difficulty with respect to ambassadors, who are deputed to a power with whom their master is at peace, and have injured no man. The most evident maxims of the law of nature require they should be perfectly secure. So that if we affront or insult such a minister, in any manner whatsoever, we give his master just reason for declaring war. Of this king David furnishes us with an example.*

2°. With regard to ambassadors who come from an enemy, and have done no harm before they are admitted, their safety depends entirely on the laws of humanity; for an enemy, as such, has a right to annoy his enemy. Thus, so long as there is no particular agreement upon this article, we are obliged to spare the ambassador of an enemy, only in virtue of the laws of humanity, which we ought always to respect, and which oblige us to have a regard for every thing tending to the preservation of order and tranquillity.

3°. But when we have promised to admit, or have actually admitted the ambassador of an ene-<368>my, we have thereby manifestly engaged to procure him entire security, so long as he behaves well. We must not

---

* 2 Sam. chap. x.
7. See DGP II.18 §4 and Bynkershoek 3 §§3–4.

even except heralds, who are sent to declare war, provided they do it in an inoffensive manner.

4°. With regard to ambassadors, who have rendered themselves culpable, either they have done the injury of their own head, or by their master's order.

If they have done it of their own head, they forfeit their right to security, and to the enjoyment of their privileges, when their crime is manifest and heinous: for no ambassador whatever can pretend to more privilege than his master would have in the same case; now such a crime would not be pardoned in the master.

By *heinous crimes,* we here mean such as tend to disturb the state, or to destroy the subjects of the prince to whom the ambassador is deputed, or to do them some considerable prejudice.

When the crime directly affects the state, whether the ambassador has actually used violence or not, that is to say, whether he has stirred up the subjects to sedition, or conspired himself against the government, or favoured the plot; or whether he has taken arms with the rebels or the enemy, or engaged his attendants so to do, &c. we may be revenged on him, even by killing him, not as a subject, but as an enemy; for his master himself would have no reason to expect better treatment. And the end of embassies, instituted no doubt for the general good of nations, does not require that we should grant to an ambassador, who first vio-<369>lates the law of nations, the privileges which that law allows to foreign ministers. If such an ambassador makes his escape, his master is obliged to deliver him up, when demanded.

But if the crime, however heinous or manifest, affects only a private person, the ambassador is not for that alone to be reputed an enemy to the prince or state. Suppose his master had committed a crime of the same nature, we ought to demand satisfaction of him, and not take up arms against him till he had refused it; so the same reason of equity directs, that the prince, at whose court the ambassador has committed such a crime, should send him back to his master, desiring him either to deliver him up, or to punish him: for to keep him in prison till his master shall recall him, in order to punish him, or declare that he has abandoned him, would be to testify some distrust of the justice of his master, and by that means affront him in some measure, because he is still represented by the ambassador.

5°. But if the crime be committed by the master's order, it would certainly be imprudence to send the ambassador back; since there is just reason to believe, that the prince who ordered the commission of the crime, will hardly surrender, or punish the criminal. We may, therefore, in this case, secure the person of the ambassador, till the master shall repair the injury done both by his ambassador and himself. In regard to those who do not represent the person of the prince, such as common messengers, trumpets, &c. we may kill them on the spot, if they come to insult a prince by order of their master. <370>

But nothing is more absurd than what some maintain, namely, that all the evil done by ambassadors, by order of their master, ought to be imputed intirely to the latter. Were it so, ambassadors would have more privilege in the territories of another prince, than their master himself, should he appear there: and, on the other hand, the sovereign of the country would have less power in his own dominions, than a master of a family has in his own house.[8]

In a word, the security of ambassadors ought to be understood in such a manner, as to imply nothing contrary to the security of the powers to whom they are sent, and who neither would, nor could receive them upon other terms. Now it is plain, that ambassadors will be less bold in undertaking any thing against the sovereign, or against the members of a foreign state, if they are apprehensive, that in case of treason, or some other heinous crimes, the government of that country can call them to an account for it, than if they had nothing to apprehend but correction from their master.

6°. When the ambassador himself has committed no crime, it is not lawful to use him ill, or to kill him by the law of *retaliation,* or *reprisals;*

---

8. The first five rules and half of the description of rule 5, that is, the portion of this paragraph that precedes this footnote, is from DGP II.18 §4 note 2. The passages immediately below are from DGP II.18 §4 note 5 in fine. The rest is based loosely on DGP II.18 §§6, 8, and 9.

for by admitting him under that character, we have renounced our right to any such revenge.

In vain would it be to object a great many instances of this kind of revenge, which are mentioned in history; for historians not only relate just and lawful actions, but also divers things done contrary to justice in the heat of anger, by the influence of some irregular and tumultuous passion. <371>

7°. What has been hitherto said of the rights of ambassadors, ought to be applied to their domestics, and all their retinue. If any of the ambassador's domestics has done an injury, we may desire his master to deliver him up. If he does not comply, he makes himself accessary to his crime, and in this case we have a right to proceed against him in the same manner, as if he had committed the fact himself.

An ambassador, however, cannot punish his own domestics; for as this is not conducive to the end of his employment, there is no reason to presume that his master has given it him.

8°. With respect to the effects of a foreign minister, we can neither seize them for payment, nor for security, in the way of justice; for this would suppose, that he was subject to the jurisdiction of the sovereign at whose court he resides. But if he refuses to pay his debts, we ought, after giving him notice, to apply to his master, and if the latter refuses to do us justice, we may seize the effects of the ambassador.

9°. Lastly, as to the right of asylums and protections, it is by no means a consequence of the nature and end of embassies. However, if it is once granted to the ambassadors of a certain power, nothing but the welfare of the state, authorises us to revoke it.

Neither ought we, without good reasons, to refuse ambassadors the other sorts of rights and privileges, which are established by the common consent of sovereigns; for this would be a kind of an affront to them.

The End of the Fourth and Last Part.

INDEX

subjects (*continued*)
sovereign's duty to understand
character of, 380; war against sovereign by, 479, 545–46; war in
defense of, 463; war, obligations
regarding, 448–49. *See also*
dependence
subordinate powers. *See* delegation of
powers
subsidies and taxes. *See* economy
succession: abdication of sovereignty
and, 361–62; cognate and agnate,
358–59; confederacies formed by,
336; sovereignty acquired by, 354–
60
sumptuary laws, 433–34

Tacitus, 372–73, 436, 438
taxation and subsidies. *See* economy
tax collectors, regulation of, 437
temperament and character traits,
moral imputability of, 215–16
Terence, 154n
Thuanus, 504
thumbs cut off to avoid military service, 214
toleration of religious difference,
advantages of encouraging, 450–51,
515
trade, proper encouragement of, 437
transcendental or sovereign property.
See sovereign or transcendental
property
translations of Burlamaqui's work, x,
xiii
treason, soliciting, 497–98
treaties, 517–25; defined, 517–18; equal
and unequal, 520–22; expiration
of, 523–24; means of securing,
549–52; ministers or governors
making, 524–25; obligation of sovereigns to keep word regarding,

518–19; peace treaties, 544–52; real
and personal, 522–23; sovereign
power of making, 524–25, 546;
types of, 519–23
treaties made with enemies, 525–32;
not putting an end to war, 532–39;
peace treaties, 544–52; by private
persons, 542–44; ransom or
redemption of prisoners, 538–39;
reasons for keeping, 526–32; safe
conducts, 536–38; by subordinate
powers, 539–42; truces, 532–36;
types of, 525
truces, 532–36
truth: liberty used in judgments of,
43–44; perfection of understanding in knowledge of, 37–38
Tully. *See* Cicero
Turks' lack of ambassadors, 554
Turnus, 482
tyranny: as disorder of monarchy,
336; as enemy of liberty, 340–41;
right to resist sovereign and, 371–
77; subjects quitting jurisdiction
due to, 367–68; war in defense of
oppressed, 465–66; weakness of,
385–86

Ulpian, 178n, 510
understanding, 34–38; ignorance and
error, 38–40; natural rightness of,
34–35; perfection in knowledge of
truth, 37–38
unequal treaties, 520–22
United Provinces, 451, 504, 505
United States, Burlamaqui's influence
in, x
universe: God not part of, 126; not
eternal, 128–29; not result of
chance, 128
unjust acts performed at command of
sovereign, 222–23, 400–401n, 401–3

This book is set in Adobe Garamond, a modern adaptation by
Robert Slimbach of the typeface originally cut around 1540 by the
French typographer and printer Claude Garamond. The Garamond
face, with its small lowercase height and restrained contrast between
thick and thin strokes, is a classic "old-style" face and has long been
one of the most influential and widely used typefaces.

Printed on paper that is acid-free and meets the requirements of
the American National Standard for Permanence of Paper for
Printed Library Materials, z39.48-1992. ∞

Book design by Louise OFarrell
Gainesville, Florida
Typography by Apex Publishing, LLC
Madison, Wisconsin
Printed and bound by Worzalla Publishing Company
Stevens Point, Wisconsin